Dead Men's Propaganda
Ideology and Utopia in Comparative Communications Studies

Terhi Rantanen

 Press

Published by
LSE Press
10 Portugal Street
London WC2A 2HD
press.lse.ac.uk

Text © Terhi Rantanen 2024

Images © listed individually in source captions

First published 2024

Cover design by Glen Wilkins

Print and digital versions typeset by Siliconchips Services Ltd.

ISBN (Paperback): 978-1-911712-18-3
ISBN (PDF): 978-1-911712-19-0
ISBN (EPUB): 978-1-911712-20-6
ISBN (Mobi): 978-1-911712-21-3

DOI: https://doi.org/10.31389/lsepress.wmf

The full text of this book has been peer-reviewed to ensure high academic standards. For our full publishing ethics policies, see https://press.lse.ac.uk

Suggested citation:
Rantanen, Terhi (2024) *Dead Men's Propaganda: Ideology and Utopia in Comparative Communications Studies*, London: LSE Press. https://doi.org/10.31389/lsepress.wmf. License: CC BY-NC 4.0

To read the free, open access version of this book online, visit https://doi.org/10.31389/lsepress.wmf or scan this QR code with your mobile device:

This book is dedicated to Outsiders, unwilling or willing

Preface

My working title for this book was 'Dead Men's Tales'. Unfortunately, it had to be rejected because it received too many hits in Google (104 million) – especially popular films, TV series, pirate books etc, which came first in an online search. Reluctantly I had to let it go, even though losing it lost the signifier: 'the dead keep their secrets'. This, I believe, perfectly summarised my core topic, which is to focus on men of the forefront generation who, between the 1920s and the 1950s, pioneered comparative communications research, who worked in the United States and who have now been almost forgotten. They took their secrets with them, and even extensive archival research reveals only fragments of their lived lives as a route to understanding their work. Later generations of scholars either forgot the forefront generation and their work or presented them in a less than complimentary light – perhaps only to show why the newcomers' work was superior to that of the pioneers.

The new title, 'Dead Men's Propaganda', also signals the obvious, but too seldom acknowledged, gender obliviousness of histories of intellectual achievements and the gender bias that, largely, excluded women from scholarly work. I did not intend to write a book almost exclusively about men but the further I progressed in my research, the clearer it became that women were largely absent from the comparative research of the period I was writing about. *Dead Men's Propaganda: Ideology and Utopia in Comparative Communications Studies* emphasises the gender wall I hit in my research, and it may, even if reluctantly, strengthen a version of history that canonises great men. But it does reflect what my book is about.

Analysing historical materials wearing conceptual lenses

As a social scientist I have learned to apply, if not a theoretical framework, theoretical concepts to empirical research, whether contemporary or historical. It took a long time for me to find the right conceptual heuristic to order and analyse the rich empirical materials on which I have drawn. The core concepts highlighted in the title, ideology and utopia, surprisingly did not come from far away but from a predecessor at my own university: from Karl Mannheim at the London School of Economics and Political Science (LSE) where I have worked for more than 20 years. Of course, I knew about Mannheim's work before starting on the long enquiry which has been crystallised in this book, especially his concept of a generation, but re-reading his work and learning about his life made me aware of how unfairly LSE treated him; how he has almost been written out of LSE's history and perhaps from the British history of sociology. The contribution of émigré scholars, notably from Central and Eastern Europe, to the growth of communications research is well known but Mannheim had the misfortune to be a doubly displaced émigré scholar (from Hungary and then from Germany) – as did others I consider in this work – notably Nathan Leites and Paul Kecskemeti. This is why I also needed Robert Merton's concepts of Insider/Outsider to undertake this work in the historical sociology of knowledge. Mannheim and Merton brought in two different intellectual traditions, the European and the American, which united, and divided, many of the figures about whom I write in this book. What unified the cases examined in my study? One central person was, of course, Harold Lasswell, whose wartime work brought together several of the émigré scholars whom I consider here, in their analysis of enemy propaganda.

The importance of propaganda research

I did not want to write here a history of a discipline, or a field, of communications studies, rather I wanted to show what potentially happens before research is 'disciplined' in the writing of a history of a field. I was, and am, interested in who is remembered as an Insider and who is forgotten as an Outsider by the generations that follow. To understand how ideologies and utopias operate I included scholars whose names we know, such as Lasswell, but also, émigré scholars from Europe such as Kecskemeti and Leites, and men of practice, non-academics, such as Kent Cooper of the Associated Press, who contributed to policy science as much as did many of the academics. I chose émigré scholars from what is coming to be known as 'the Other Frankfurt School', many frequently forgotten, as was the Outsider central to my conceptual scheme, Mannheim. This is why I focus on anti-communist émigré scholars, several of whom ended up doing policy science in the RAND Corporation in California rather than in universities, again disregarded by disciplinary histories. In my view, a historical sociology of knowledge needs to be understood in a larger societal context if we are to understand the opportunities and pressures academic and non-academic researchers face in different historical periods, if they are to survive and develop their work.

The pioneering comparative work I focus on centres on propaganda, a topic that again needs our attention in our increasingly turbulent contemporary world. There is simply so much valuable work, ignored for decades, that has again become relevant. However, it is important to remember that the men I consider did not only research propaganda, but they were also propagandists (how else to understand the architecture of the canonical work *Four Theories of the Press* by Fred S. Siebert, Theodore Peterson and Wilbur Schramm?). This is one of the dilemmas of policy science: how do researchers maintain their independence and critical thinking when their research is financed by inter-ested parties? Few would object to scholars working in the Allied war effort to hasten the defeat of the Axis powers – but Cold War warriors and those whose professional advancement depended on toeing funders' lines are more controversial. There are general and inescapable questions here: do research-ers set aside their own utopias and conform to dominant ideologies supported by accepted institutions? Should researchers put aside their own values, ide-ologies, and defer to others' utopias? How does independent research survive when ideologies are as strong as they were in the post-World War II world in the United States? Who provides a safer work environment for independent research: universities or research institutes?

Why a reader should read this book

I have intentionally written this book for readers outside my own field of media and communications studies. Most of my theoretical concepts come from outside my field, primarily from sociology and from its subfield, the sociology of knowledge. By applying theoretical concepts to historical mate-rials from numerous archives (listed at the end of this book), I am hoping to reach both those interested in social science and transatlantic history, and not only in the US, but beyond as well, even though most of the research featured took place in the US. The period I research, from the 1920s until the 1950s, largely pre-dates the establishment of the field of communications studies and included political scientists, sociologists, psychologists and non-academics who pioneered comparative communications research, but also émigré schol-ars who came from Europe to escape Nazi terror and contributed significantly to the discipline. By introducing names who were not included in the Frank-furt School, I am hoping to reach those interested in the role of European émigré scholars. And anybody who is interested in war propaganda research may discover how much important work has already been done by academics and non-academics.

Finally, I hope this book will help all of us realise how much our own fields, whether comparative studies in general or international communication in particular, have been influenced by work done almost a hundred years ago. It enables us to see that our research rests on ideologies and utopias alive at the time when our concepts were first created and used. All this calls for a Mannheimian historical sociology of knowledge, and I hope this is what I have contributed to in this book. Sometimes the dead do talk but only if we listen to them!

1. Why study ideology and utopia in early comparative communications?

> The fathers have eaten bitter fruit and the children's teeth are set on edge. It's all very well for the fathers, they know what they ate. The children don't know what was eaten. (Bateson 1966)

This is an unapologetically old-fashioned and unfashionable book, although highly relevant to the present. Both theoretically and empirically, I begin with the post-World War I period and ask why and how communications research took a comparative turn in the United States even before it became international communication, a subfield of communication studies. I analyse the developments of comparative communications across four decades between the 1920s and the 1950s in the US, including its origins in work undertaken primarily on propaganda in World Wars I and II. I present five historical studies of individuals or research groups to understand how, in comparative communications, knowledge was produced by a generation of scholars and men of practice who were influenced by two world wars. In this book, I call those largely forgotten individuals the *forefront* generation, marked by their shared experiences of the two world wars even if most of them did not fight on the front.

Returning to early propaganda research enables us to understand our contemporary world. Louis Wirth[1] (1897–1952) wrote nearly 100 years ago, in his preface to Karl Mannheim's (1893–1947) *Ideology and Utopia* (Mannheim 1929; 1936; 1960, p.xiii), that 'we are witnessing not only a general distrust of the validity of ideas but of the motives of those who assert them', and today this again rings true. We are now living in dangerous times and witnessing new global cold and hot wars after a relative long period of, if not peace, at least controlled military aggression. The scourge of war in Europe has escalated into a potential global conflict and has brought back ideological wars fought by propagandising news. Understanding how war propaganda research, latterly almost forgotten, was done before, between and after World Wars I and II, has much to teach us for in this work lies the

How to cite this book chapter:

Rantanen, Terhi (2024) *Dead Men's Propaganda: Ideology and Utopia in Comparative Communications Studies*, London: LSE Press, pp. 1–48.
https://doi.org/10.31389/lsepress.wmf.a. License: CC BY-NC 4.0

development of core scholarly methodologies, notably content analysis. In the present age of misinformation, of propaganda and of increasing ignorance about science, I argue that we need to go back to Mannheim's idea of *Wissenssoziologie*, which aimed to analyse the 'crisis in our thought' (Mannheim 1960, p.84).

Contemporary populism has made science one of its main targets. Mede et al. (2022, p.1) suggest that populism proposes 'a virtuous ordinary people, and not allegedly corrupt academic elites, should determine the production of truth'. Populism often celebrates 'common sense' over expertise; it offers 'counter knowledge, proposing politically charged alternative knowledge authorities instead of established ones' (Ylä-Anttila 2018, p.356). When populism questions scientific knowledge it challenges those who produce it, labelling them as an elite. However, elites themselves rarely critically study their own work, and this is why the sociology of knowledge becomes one of the ways to understand how knowledge is produced. To learn from previous research, we need to study the conditions in which research was done to understand how researchers developed their conceptual frameworks and methodologies, but also study the beliefs which animated them, their utopias and ideologies. By doing so I also challenge the field of international communication that neglects/does not recognise its own origins, utopias and ideologies.

All this draws us to Mannheim's *Wissenssoziologie*, now often called the sociology of knowledge or the history and theory of knowledge production (Gurukkal 2019). Gabel (1991, p.33) writes, 'Mannheim is the philosopher *par excellence* of times of crisis: misunderstood in peaceful periods, he is likely to be censored in periods of unrest'. Mannheim's work lives on in his *Wissenssoziologie*, which was transformed by Robert Merton (1910–2003) into an American sociology of knowledge, and also in his own liberalism (Hvidsten 2019), which he defended throughout periods of extreme polarisation of ideologies and politics (see also Bessner 2018; Speier 1989), such as we are now seeing again. Mannheim's *Wissenssoziologie*, once defined as an 'elucidation of the relations between existence and thought' (Eisenstadt 1987, p.77), could be seen as an area within the larger field known as the 'sociology of culture', defined as a theory of the relationships between culture and society (Remmling 1961, p.25). In this study I use Mannheim's *Wissenssoziologie* approach, complemented by Merton's *sociology of knowledge* (1937; 1968), together with Mannheim's concept of a *generation* (1927; 1928; 2000) and Merton's (1972) concepts of *Insiders/Outsiders*.

In this opening chapter, I discuss, first, what I mean by comparative communications and caution that this is not a history of communication research. Second, I introduce Mannheim and Merton as academics behind their work. Third, I review their key concepts of *Wissenssoziologie*, sociology of knowledge, ideology, utopia, generation, and Insider/Outsider. Finally, I return back to present times before short introductions to each of the succeeding chapters.

1.1 Previous research and its value

I use the term comparative communications, referring to an emerging set of interdisciplinary research as carried out by academics and non-academics in the period mainly before the field of communication studies was institutionalised in universities from the 1950s onwards. I define early comparative communications in the US as that where researchers or research teams with diverse cultural, practical or academic skills, and in different locations, developed specific theories, concepts and/or methods to analyse materials or data concerning communications, often from more than one source or (geographical) location simultaneously.

Therefore, this book is *not* a history of a field, or a discipline of communication studies already conducted by others. The first histories of communication studies were written by those who played a key role in establishing it and were often partly or wholly autobiographical (see, for example, Berelson 1959; Chaffee 1974; Lang 1979; Schramm 1957, 1959, 1963, 1980, 1985; Schramm, Chaffee and Rogers 1997). The pioneering academic work on the history of US communication studies started to appear from the 1970s (see, for example, Dennis and Wartella 1996; Glander 2000; Hardt 1979; 1992; Park and Pooley 2008; Peters 1986; Pooley 2017; Rogers 1994; Simonson 2010; Simonson et al 2012; Simpson 1994; Sproule 1997; 2008). Increasingly, non-US academics, together with US scholars or independently, have published on the history of US communication studies (see, for example, Klaus and Seethaler 2016; Löblich and Scheu 2011; Simonson et al. 2019; Simonson and Park 2016; Wahl-Jorgensen 2004). Previous research has helped me to concentrate on academic and non-academic comparative communications that has not been fully covered before. This is also why I have left, for example, Paul Lazarsfeld's[2] (1901–1976) life and work aside in the context of comparative communications, since it has been researched before (see, for example, Coser 1984; Morrison 1988; 2008; 2022; Sills 1987; Simonson and Weimann 2003).

I argue that we cannot understand comparative communications without taking into consideration work carried out not only in other academic disciplines – primarily in political science, sociology and psychology – but also by researchers of different nationalities and by non-academics. Martin Jay's (1973/1996) outstanding work, *The Dialectical Imagination: A History of the Frankfurt School and the Institute of Social Research 1923–1950*, laid the groundwork for the study of European scholars who found refuge in the US when fleeing from European dictatorships. Like Jay, I study émigré scholars, but unlike him I concentrate on those who were not members of the Frankfurt School and who have been so far written out of the narrative of their generation. Here, in contrast, I will establish claims to our continued attention of contemporaries of those who were non-Marxist, and in some cases actively anti-communist, but who had vital roles in shaping comparative communications. Those 'hidden from history' who merit our attention include Nathan Leites (1912–1987), Paul Kecskemeti (1901–1980) and Karl Mannheim (who found refuge in the UK rather than the US), as well as native-born US citizens whose work once enjoyed celebrity but has latterly faded from our collective horizon, most notably Harold Lasswell (1902–1979).

I also consider the important roles of native-born US citizens working outside the academy in (1) research groups and institutions funded by private foundations and/or the US government; (2) the Associated Press news agency; (3) committees and working groups, such as the Hutchins Commission; and (4) international organisations such as UNESCO. Often the work of non-academics is ignored, especially if they are not 'intellectuals' in accordance with a narrow definition of the term. The chapters in this book feature both academics and other specialists such as news agency directors (most notably Kent Cooper, 1880–1965) and consultants. These non-academics worked, often but not always, with academics, in policy science, the term used when researchers are providing policymakers with pragmatic, problem-solving recommendations (Lasswell 1951a, p.4). Many individuals and institutional sites have been marginalised through the establishment of a dominant narrative concentrating on the Frankfurt School and native-born US academics working in universities. Similarly marginalised have been the methodologies developed by them, notably quantitative and qualitative content analysis, as well as the study of propaganda. This is, obviously, not to say that it was *only* in the US, as Lang (1979) has shown, where significant work in developing comparative communications took place, only that the US conjuncture was of key significance and has, I contend, been misunderstood. Researching these individuals highlights not only their roles but also how often these specialists shared the ideologies and utopias of academics in the same period.

I draw theoretically on the work of Mannheim, in particular his 1929 *Ideologie und Utopie*, which is the focus of this opening chapter (Section 1.4) and to which I return in Chapter 7. I draw extensively on Mannheim's work in mapping early comparative communications by the individuals and these institutional sites, notably by drawing on Mannheim's concepts of ideology, utopia and generation, together with the concepts introduced by Merton of Insider and Outsider. By revisiting Mannheim's work, I do so in full awareness of what is seen as a wide-ranging critique of his 'weaknesses'. Perhaps the most famous of Mannheim's critics is Karl Popper (1902–1994), who is said to have had a 'lasting rhetorical victory' (1957/2002) over Mannheim (Fuller 2006, p.19). Theodor Adorno's (1903–1969) critique (Adorno 1955) of Mannheim is also well-known, as is Friedrich Hayek's (1899–1992) 'ridicule' of Mannheim (Hammersley 2021; Howie 1961, p.55; Lassman 1992, p.223) and Clifford Geertz's (1926–2006) critique, which he framed as Mannheim's dilemma (1973). Other critics of Mannheim's alleged weaknesses include Merton (1937; 1949/1968) with his 'disposal' of *Wissenssoziologie* (Sica 2010, p.180) and Edward Shils' (1910–1995) (1974; 1975, pp.xvii–xviii) 'turn against' him (Pooley 2007).

In contrast to these critiques of Mannheim's work, and especially their rejection of Mannheim's alleged historicism, I see value in his historical approach, in what he saw as the 'deeply rooted connection between episte-mology in its concrete historical varieties and the corresponding "existential situation"' (Mannheim 1960, p.261). Mannheim's emphasis on situated and changing conjunctures gives the lie to allegations, as made by Popper in his *Poverty of Historicism* (1957), that Mannheim was postulating 'inexorable laws of historical destiny' (Popper 2002, p.vi) and presented 'vulgar Marx-ism' (Woldring 1986, p.180). Mannheim did not argue for historical destiny. Mannheim wrote (1960) that:

> the changes in relationships between events and ideas are not the result of wilful and arbitrary design, but that these relationships, both in their simultaneousness and in their historical sequence, must be regarded as following a certain necessary regularity, which, although not superficially evident, does nevertheless exist and can be understood. (p.81)

I am aware of how much work (see, for example, Bourdieu 1986; 1988; 1993; Kögler 1997; Kuhn 1962; Purhonen 2016) has been done since Mannheim. As Kögler (1997, p.142) argues, both Mannheim's concept of *Weltanschauung* and Bourdieu's concept of *habitus* have contributed to the balance of 'sym-bolic thought and social structures'. However, I still argue that we need to go back to the work of Mannheim and Merton to learn what was achieved in times even more tumultuous than our own, and to focus on the importance of communications in modern societies. In this situation, in today's new atmos-phere of fear, it is timely to return to studies conducted in circumstances that were not entirely different from the current ones. I argue that in our time of polarised politics it is crucial to understand how comparative communi-cations, and especially its content, were shaped not only by academics but also by men of practice institutionally located outside the academy and how knowledge was produced in a world that, like ours, was falling apart.

1.2 Karl Mannheim: a brief biography

Karl (né Károly) Mannheim's career developed in three countries: Hungary, Germany and the UK (Manheim 1947). His life exemplifies that of a cosmopol-itan academic in very turbulent times. He was the son of a Hungarian Jewish textile merchant Gustav (né Gusztáv) Gerzon Man(n)heim (born in 1875 in Ada, Serbia, death year unknown) and a German Jewish mother, Rosa (Roza) Eylenburg (1867–1944), and was born in Budapest in 1893 (Whitty 2004). Mannheim learned German from an early age and studied at the University of Berlin from 1913 to 1915, where he was a student of Georg Simmel (1858–1918), and then at the University of Budapest (Woldring 1986, p.6). In Buda-pest, known for its unique cosmopolitan culture, he joined the Sunday Circle (*Vasárnapi Kör, Sonntagskreis*) (Barboza 2020, p.26; Gabel 1991, p.4), which

Figure 1.1: The Sunday Circle in Budapest

Source: Petőfi Literary Museum, reproduced with permission. Date unknown.

met between 1915 and 1918 to discuss various philosophical and artistic problems that happened to interest its members at a given moment (Congdon 1991, p.45; Gluck 1985, pp.9–11; Kadarkay 1991, p.176). Its members, pictured in Figure 1.1, influenced Mannheim's concept of a generation (Perivolaropoulou 1992) and included intellectuals such as Georg Lukács (1885–1971), Károly (Karl) Polányi (1886–1964) and Mihály (Michael) Polányi (1891–1976) and artists such as Béla Bartók (1881–1945) (Karádi 1985, p.9). Dr Julia Mannheim-Láng (née Károlyné Júlia (Juliska) Láng (1893–1955)), a psychoanalyst, was also a member and became Mannheim's lifelong companion, adviser and spouse (Borgos 2021; Wolff 1971/1993, p.1). They are pictured together in Figure 1.2. Mannheim-Láng's influence is clearly seen on Mannheim's work, but she barely gets a mention in biographies of Mannheim, although *Ideology and Utopia* (1936; 1960) is dedicated to her, and she is said to have put aside her own writing to work on Mannheim's legacy (Borgos 2021).

Mannheim's doctoral thesis was published in 1922 as *Strukturanalyse der Erkenntnistheorie* (*The Structural Analysis of Knowledge*) (Mannheim 1922), eventually leading to his conceptualisation of *Wissenssoziologie* in his *Ideologie und Utopie* (*Ideology and Utopia: An Introduction to the Sociology of Knowledge*) (1929; 1936) (Kettler Meja and Stehr 1984). After the overthrow of the short-lived Hungarian Soviet Republic, in which Mannheim accepted university positions for which he was later criticised (Congdon 1991, p.266), in 1919 he helped Lukacs and other communist friends to escape from Hungary in a period when over 100,000 people were forced to flee the country (Weidlinger 2019, p.27). Gabel (1991) writes that these 'tragic series of aborted revolutions helped Mannheim together with other members of the Hungarian

Figure 1.2: Karl Mannheim and Julia Mannheim-Láng

Source: Archiv für die Geschichte der Soziologie in Österreich (AGSÖ), reproduced with permission. Date unknown.

intelligentsia sensitivise to the concept of utopia' (p.6). Mannheim followed his friends, fleeing first to Vienna and then in 1922 to Heidelberg, where he received a lectureship in sociology of the press at the Heidelberg Institut für Zeitungswesen (Institute for Newspaper Research) between 1929 and 1930 (Averbeck 1999; Averbeck 2001, pp.456, 464; Mannheim 1980). From 1930 to 1933 Mannheim served as a professor of sociology and political economy at the Johann Wolfgang Goethe University in Frankfurt am Main. This was a remarkable achievement since Jewish and socialist scholars rarely secured chairs in German universities. Fewer than 8 per cent of the professoriate at Frankfurt were Jewish, and most of those were in medicine (Rutkoff and Scott 1986, p.87).

When Mannheim's *Ideology and Utopia* was first published in German in 1929 (and in English in 1936), the idea behind it, that social structures and human behaviour would have an influence on the production of knowledge, was at that time found radical, and perhaps still is. Not surprisingly, Mannheim's book soon became a target of criticism from contemporaries on both the political left (see, for example, Jay 1973/1996; 1974/1994) and the right (see, for example, Pooley 2007). This continued throughout his career and after his early death in 1947. While still living in Germany, Mannheim was criticised by conservatives and Nazis for being influenced by Karl Marx

(1818–1883), and by radicals for being insufficiently influenced by Marx. His academic critics included Adorno, Max Horkheimer (1895–1973), Herbert Marcuse (1898–1979) and Hannah Arendt (1906–1975) (Adorno 1955; Congdon 1991, pp.297–99; Fischer 2009; Jay 1973/1996; 1974; 1994; Meja and Stehr 1990; Speier 1989, p.36). To quote Fischer (2009, p.339),

> the Frankfurt School's dispute with Mannheim and the sociology of knowledge was what Louis Althusser (1918–1990) … once called a *Kampfplatz*, a site of struggle, where nothing less than the legacy of Marx's historical materialism was at stake.

Mannheim thus became an academic Outsider, the concept discussed later in this chapter, despite being a member of the Institut für Sozialforschung – best known as the academic home of Horkheimer, Adorno and those celebrated Insiders at the Frankfurt School. As Merton (1972, p.15) writes, the Outsider, 'no matter how careful and talented, is excluded in principle from gaining access to the social and cultural truth'. Mannheim was left alone with very few colleagues to defend him.

Mannheim had to flee again when Hitler came to power in Germany in 1933. He was among the first 14[3] to be stripped of his university professorship and was forced into exile by the Nazis because, although he was a German citizen, he was also seen as a foreigner, a Jew, and a friend of the Nazis' enemies (Karácsony 2008, p.99). Mannheim considered several options, among them emigrating to Czechoslovakia and the US (Gábor 1996, p.59). He and Juliska Láng first fled to Amsterdam,[4] and then to London. He was invited to join the London School of Economics and Political Science (LSE) by Harold Laski (1893–1950) and benefitted from the organised efforts of the Academic Assistance Council set up to rescue eminent scholars persecuted by the Nazis (Cox 2021; Kettler and Meja, 1995, p.3; Pooley 2007, pp.372, 375). He was hired as a lecturer at LSE in 1933 and paid first an annual salary of £500 (around £46,000 in 2023 terms) and then £600 annually jointly by the Rockefeller Foundation.[5] Mannheim became a British citizen in in 1940 (Whitty 2004). Even though already in the UK, Mannheim was on the Gestapo's secret *Sonderfahnungsliste* (Black Book), compiled by the Gestapo and its informants between 1936 and 1940, as an enemy of Germany, to be arrested after Germany's invasion of the UK (Oldfield 2022, pp.3, 8, 269).

According to Karácsony (2008, p.100), this second emigration was harder for Mannheim, not only because he had to learn English and learn his way around British academic life in general and sociology in particular (a problem he did not have to face when emigrating to Germany) but also because it was particularly hard to get a position at a university as one among so many emigrant intellectuals. Mannheim himself wrote that 'This is the second time that I have experienced something like this, but I always have the strength to begin anew, unbroken' (Congdon 1991, p.303). But this may have been too optimistic as it turned out that in his English years he would be bombarded with criticism, much of it harsh (Pooley 2007, p.375). Shils refers to this emigration as an 'unmitigated catastrophe for Mannheim' (Shils 1995, p.234). This view was shared by sociologists in the UK (Albrow 1989, p.200; Bulmer 1985, p.21).

When in London, Mannheim wrote several letters on behalf of his colleagues still in danger in Europe (among them Hans Gerth (1908–1978) and Norbert Elias (1897–1990)) so that they could emigrate to the UK (Gábor 1996, pp.68–89, 121–23, 126). Mannheim held an appointment as lecturer at LSE from 1933 to 1943, teaching for example a course on 'Woman and Her Place in Society'.[6] He never obtained a chair at LSE, but the University of London appointed him as chair in the Institute of Education in 1945. According to Pooley, at LSE Mannheim became a 'kind of intellectual punching bag' and 'many of his colleagues were hellbent on ridding him from the School' (2007, pp.371–72). Mannheim was very close to needing to leave the UK for the US when LSE warned him in 1939 that his services were not needed. US colleagues tried to rescue him by offering him a lecture tour, which he could not accept because of the UK's immigration restrictions.[7] Lyon (2011) writes that after Mannheim's early supporters had left LSE, including William Beveridge (1879–1963), Laski and Bronislaw Malinowski (1884–1942), he lacked support under the subsequent directorship, which had become increasingly anxious to shed its reputation for being too political. He also lost the support of his head of the department, Morris Ginsberg (1889–1970), who may have felt that he stood in Mannheim's shadow[8] (Woldring 1986, p.53).

During World War II, when LSE was in exile in Cambridge, Mannheim became an active member of the Moot group (1938–1947), consisting mainly of Christian intellectuals who met regularly to discuss educational and social reconstruction. According to Grimley (2007), Mannheim had a 'strong conviction of the importance of the Christian basis of European society and enjoyed conferring with Christian intellectuals' and became the central figure in the group. He was also elected as a member of the prestigious Athenaeum Club for 'men with intellectual interests' in 1944, proposed in 1942 by the Archbishop of Canterbury and seconded by J.H. Oldman (1874–1969), who established the Moot group.[9] Whitty (2004) writes that, although Mannheim had shown some interest in education as early as the 1920s, it became the main focus of Mannheim's work only towards the end of his life. Just before Mannheim's death (he suffered from heart problems) in London in 1947, he was offered a position as the first head of UNESCO's European office (Kettler 2012; Kettler and Loader 2013, pp.23–24; Manheim 1947; Whitty 2004). He was just about to become an Insider, defined by Merton (1972, p.21) as 'a member of specified groups and collectivities or occupants of specified social statuses' (Merton 1972, p.21).

Hammersley (2022, p.179) argues that Mannheim poses two key questions in his work, and both of these are useful for this book: 'What is the relationship between science and politics?' and 'What is the meaning and value of science?' Hammersley goes on to write that 'Mannheim believes that in this way sociology can play a crucial role in the political education of future leaders and of citizens generally' (p.181). This is an important point, with further consequences for what Harold Lasswell called policy science (see Section 1.4).

1.3 Robert K. Merton and his critique of Mannheim's *Wissenssoziologie*

Robert K. Merton (1910–2003; pictured, Figure 1.3), 17 years Mannheim's junior, was born as Meyer Robert Schkolnick in Philadelphia into a Yiddish-speaking Jewish family who had immigrated to the US in 1904. His mother was Ida Rasovskaya (circa 1882–year of death unknown), a socialist and self-taught philosopher born in Kiev, and his father Harry (Aaron) Schkolnickoff (circa 1875–year of death unknown) (Bush 2021). At the age of 19 Robert changed his last name to Merton (Merton 1994). Unlike Mannheim, Merton did not come from a privileged family. His father worked as a carpenter's assistant after losing his dairy farm. Merton studied for his first degree at Temple University but received his PhD in 1936 from Harvard. His thesis was entitled *Science, Technology and Society in Seventeenth Century England* (Merton 1938). At Harvard he took a course taught by Talcott Parsons (1902–1979) and became well-read in European sociological theory (Merton 1994), but he came from different epistemological premises than Mannheim (Izzo 1998, p.213).

Figure 1.3: Robert K. Merton, *c.* 1950

Source: Photo by Pictorial Parade/Copyright Getty Images, *c.* 1950. Also in Robert K. Merton Papers, Rare Book & Manuscript Library, Columbia University in the City of New York.

In 1941 Merton moved to Columbia University, where he would collaborate at its Bureau of Applied Social Research with Lazarsfeld (Berelson 1959; Calhoun 2003; 2010). With Lazarsfeld and other colleagues, Merton carried out studies of propaganda and communication during World War II, primarily concentrating on psychological warfare research to understand the influence of effective propaganda (Pooley and Katz 2008, p.771). Merton is considered one of the innovators of modern sociology, especially the sociology of knowledge, but his early work in communication (see, for example, Lazarsfeld and Merton 1943; 1948/1964; Merton, Fiske and Curtis 1946; Merton and Lazarsfeld 1950) has received less attention (Calhoun 2003; 2010; Deflem 2018; Simonson 2010).

Where did these two academics – Mannheim, a European, and Merton, an American – meet? It seems they did not, but certainly their ideas did. According to Kaiser (1998, p.69), only a few months after the English edition of *Ideology and Utopia* was published in 1936, the 26-year-old Merton produced his first critique of Mannheim's *Wissenssoziologie*. Merton's work was to provide a 'general survey of the subject', but more than two-thirds of it concentrated specifically on Mannheim's *Ideology and Utopia* (Merton 1937). This was followed by a longer essay in 1941 entitled 'Karl Mannheim and the Sociology of Knowledge' (Merton 1941; 1957). In Merton's (1949; 1968) critique of Mannheim, he compared 'the European and American variants of the sociological study of communications', using the criteria: (1) characteristic subject matter and definitions; (2) concepts of data; (3) utilisation of research techniques; and (4) social organisation of their research activities (p.494).

Merton (1949; 1968) drew on early mass communication research in the US to critique Mannheim's *Wissenssoziologie* and to point out the differences between what he called the 'European species' (*Wissenssoziologie*) and the 'American species' (the sociology of mass communications) (p.493). Merton himself, unsurprisingly, preferred the American species to the European. Sica (2010) now considers unjustified Merton's criticism of Mannheim, which drew on mass communication research. But at the same time Merton indirectly provided parameters that can still be applied when using the sociology of knowledge in analysing comparative research in communications in this book.

When criticising Mannheim's *Wissenssoziologie*, Merton writes that 'the sociology of knowledge is most directly concerned with the intellectual products of *experts*, whether in science or philosophy, in economic or political thought' (1949; 1968, p.495, my emphasis), but argued that it involved 'little research on the *audiences* for various intellectual and cultural products, [where] the American variant (mass communication research) has done a great deal' (p.506, my emphasis). However, unlike Merton, I am not interested in audiences per se, although in several chapters I write about generations as audiences, but rather in how knowledge is produced in comparative communications, and how academics and experts of that same generation of researchers influenced one another and in how they invited other researchers into or pushed them out of comparative communications, constituting them in Mertonian terms as Insiders and Outsiders when it became international communication.

But why does the debate between Mannheim and Merton matter? Although Merton was critical of Mannheim, he transformed Mannheim's *Wissenssoziologie* into an American version of the sociology of knowledge. In this process he left out some of Mannheim's original ideas, notably any traces of Marxism, but also added new elements such as his own concepts of Insiders and Outsiders. Both scholars, despite the differences in their thinking, argued for analysis of the production of knowledge. This highlights the importance of communication studies but also casts doubt on Merton's objectivity since he was himself an 'Insider'. Consequently, we need to question critically how comparative communications fits into the picture Merton painted of communication research as a whole. This debate thus brings to the surface the tensions between European and US research and calls for comparative study of the two.

1.4 *Ideology and Utopia*

Central to Mannheim's work were the twin concepts of ideology and utopia. It is difficult to find clear definitions in Mannheim's work of these two concepts because of the 'essayistic and discursive character of his writings, along with the complexity of the issues he was addressing' (Hammersley 2022, p.177) despite the two concepts forming the title of the work for which Mannheim is best known. Mannheim (1936, p.176) himself was the first to acknowledge that 'to determine in any given case, what is ideological and what is utopian is extremely difficult' (Vogt 2016, p.373). As Vogt (2016, p.367) writes,

> According to Mannheim, when an idea 'departs from the real' it is either a utopia, or an ideology (Mannheim, 1936: 173). Utopias describe a situation which is not the present situation, but one which could be hoped for, or presumed to follow, sometime in the future. In contrast, ideologies depart from the real by providing inaccurate descriptions of present conditions. An ideology is thus a description which serves to idealize and highlight certain features of the present and to overlook or obscure others.

The inseparability of the two concepts is clear and Mannheim's (1935) contribution to the *Encyclopaedia of the Social Sciences* provides perhaps his clearest accounts of the concepts. As Geoghegan (2004, p.124) argues, in Mannheim's work, ideology cannot be understood without an appreciation of the fundamental role of utopia. Mannheim (1935, p.201) writes:

> The term utopian … may be applied to any process of thought that receives its impetus not from the direct force of social reality but from the concepts, such as symbols, fantasies and dreams, ideas and the like, which in the most comprehensive sense of that term are

non-existent. Viewed from the standpoint of sociology, such mental constructs may in general assume two forms: they are 'ideological' if they serve the purpose of glossing power or stabilizing the existing social reality; 'utopian' if they inspire collective activity which aims to change such reality to conform with their goals, which transcend reality.

Mannheim, by introducing the concept of utopia and not concentrating only on the concept of ideology as many of his contemporary Marxist scholars did, opened up a new way of thinking about social change. Sargent (2008, p.267) writes that, 'for Mannheim, while both ideologies and utopias pose problems, utopias must be kept alive because they include the seeds of needed social change'. In his concept of ideology, Mannheim's departure from many mainstream Marxist theorists (see, for example, Anderson 1980; Eagleton 2007) has particular value through four different arguments, all of which are important for the purposes of this book. These are: (1) loosening the relationship between class and ideology, especially in relation to intellectuals; (2) recognising that ideology is sometimes hidden, especially from those living through it; (3) widening the definition of ideology beyond traditional politics; and (4) arguing that ideologies and utopias are so interwoven that one cannot exist without the other.

(1) The relationship between class and ideology

Ideology, one of Mannheim's key concepts, is indeed often associated with those Marxist writers, who generally agree that 'there is a powerful, effective and dominant ideology in contemporary capitalist societies and that this dominant ideology creates an acceptance of capitalism in the working class' (Abercrombie, Hill and Turner 1980, p.1). Since I am not a Marxist but a researcher carrying out research into the individuals who started comparative communications in the US, I must ask how useful Mannheim's concept of ideology is for my analysis.

Mannheim's work appeals to me because it emphasises the role and analysis of historical knowledge production. With his concept of ideology, he made a departure from many Marxist writers while acknowledging his debt to them (see, for example, Adair-Toteff 2019, pp.3–4). Mannheim criticises mainstream Marxists for treating economic class as the only significant factor, as in the notions of base and superstructure, and proposes additional categories such as those of generation and gender (Abercrombie, Hill and Turner 1980, p.35; Eisenstadt 1987, p.78; Kettler and Meja 1993). He is also critical of the concepts of false consciousness and its unmasking (Adair-Toteff 2019, p.5), although the concept of false consciousness could be used when elaborating Mannheim's concept of ideology and utopia (Gabel 1976, p.182).

One of the most famous and most often criticised of Mannheim's concepts is that of free-floating intellectuals (*freischwebende Intelligenz*). The difference between intellectuals and the intelligentsia is not always clear, at least when the terms are translated into English, but the difference has been discussed by others (see, for example, Gouldner 1979; Hannerz 1992). Hannerz (1992, p.143) observes that neither intellectuals nor intelligentsia necessarily make their home in academia, and the individuals whose work is central to my argument bear out his proposition. The concept of free-floating intellectuals was originally used by Alfred Weber (1868–1958), under whom Mannheim habilitated in Heidelberg (Loader 1997, p.229), but it acquired celebrity only after Mannheim used it (Karácsony 2008). Karácsony writes that:

> Mannheim considered that the special position of the intellectuals has, unlike any other group of society, two kinds of boundaries. On the one hand, due to birth, wealth and profession they belong to a class of society, while on the other they share, and care for, a common culture. According to Mannheim the latter is of greater importance: having risen to the world of culture the intellectuals were freed from the values and other boundaries of society, and that is why they are 'free-floating'. (p.109)

Loader (1997, p.228) argues that Mannheim's concept of free-floating intellectuals is actually more radical than Weber's. He writes that intellectuals, in Mannheim's thinking, are not a homogenous group but a group 'that is characterized by conflict, the struggle for cultural hegemony, in which intellectuals played the more restrained role of advisors'. Loader concludes that:

> Although Mannheim's intelligentsia could clarify temporary constellations within the competition, although they provided a medium for communication between the competing groups, they could not grant a privileged position to any of those groups. In short, they could not become spiritual leaders. (p.229)

Mannheim argues on the one hand that intellectuals have more freedom than other classes (if they can be defined as a class) but on the other hand that they face internal competition from their peers and Mannheim's troubled personal experience of LSE bears out his proposition. Simultaneously, they aspire to reach society at large but usually fail to do so. One of the grounds on which the close relationship between intellectuals and society is justified is indeed that their research serves wider social goals, not only academic purposes, and this dual role is signified in Lasswell's term policy science. According to Lasswell (1951a, p.4), who introduced the term, policy science includes: (1) the methods by which the policy process is investigated; (2) the results of the study of policy; and (3) the findings of disciplines making the most important contributions to the intelligence needs of the time. As he (1951a, p.13) further writes,

social scientists are not the only contributors in the policy sciences
… There is some recognition of the fact that men of experience in
active policymaking can make greater contributions to basic analysis than the academic experts have admitted.

Often the work of non-academics is ignored, especially if they are not 'intellectuals' in accordance with a narrow definition of the term. The chapters in
this book feature both academics and other specialists traditionally seen as
important contributions to policy science, such as news agency directors and
consultants. Researching these figures highlights something that has hitherto
been neglected: not only their roles in shaping the study of comparative communications but also how often these specialists shared the ideologies and
utopias of contemporary academics.

Mannheim's critics often asked whether intellectuals *can* ever remain free
from ideological bias. Sagarin and Kelly (1969, p.300) point out these critics have asked a wrong question and instead should have asked whether
intellectuals *will* remain free-floating. This is also my question: to what extent,
if any, do intellectuals remain free from ideology and utopias when doing
policy science? Mannheim argues for the importance of communication in
shaping intellectual outlooks between separate groups (Heeren 1971, p.33).
According to him, 'innovations arise either from shift in a collective situation
or from a changing relationship between groups or between individuals and
their group' (quoted by Heeren 1971, p.33). Intellectuals thus include not
only academics but men of practice, and communication inside and between
their groups is both a central focus of the account which follows, and an
instance of a nexus thus far largely neglected in scholarly accounts of comparative communications.

(2) Recognising that ideology is sometimes hidden

According to Mannheim (1960), ideology appears when the thinking of ruling groups becomes so intensively interest-bound to a specific situation that
they are simply no longer able to see facts that would undermine their sense
of domination (p.36). In this situation,

knowledge is distorted and ideological when it fails to take account
of the new realities applying to a situation, and when it attempts to
conceal them by thinking of them in categories which are inappro-
priate. (p.86)

In my reading of Mannheim, one of the key insights is that ideology is something not necessarily recognised by those who produce it (such as academics)
or by those who experience it. Ideology can be like the air that we breathe: we
take for granted that it is there but do not necessarily pay any attention to its

quality. However, those who produce knowledge have a special responsibility to critically review the role of ideology in their knowledge production. This is why *Wissenssoziologie* is so important.

It is also important to understand that Mannheim's historicism does not equate with a historical destiny, predetermined condition or a historical law that determines the future. It acknowledges that the criteria for what is seen as the 'truth' differ in different historical periods and have been influenced by society at large, and that society differs from one historical period to the next. As Shils (1974, p.84) writes, 'Mannheim believed that every society and epoch had its own intellectual culture, of which every single work produced in it was a part'. 'Truth' is always bound to time, and as new political periods emerge so do new tasks for research. Kaiser (1998, p.53) writes that, 'as the clouds of fascism gathered, Mannheim believed that he and his fellow sociologists had a moral obligation to understand the failings of Germany's liberal democracy'. In a similar way, now, as we face a new period when what is seen as 'truth' is again challenged, and even if we are unable yet to conduct research on this current period, we can at least return to a previous historical time and consider whether there is something there that will help us to analyse the present.

Mannheim (1934, p.118) wrote as early as 1934 about the importance of studying elites, and about intellectuals being one category of these elites, not only from the standpoint of their formation but because 'the relation of these elites to the totality of society presents new problems which, in their turn, may suggest important clues to the explanation and understanding of the present situation'. According to Mannheim, intellectuals are one of four types of elites: 'the political, the organizing, the scholastic, and the artistically religious elites that produce different pattern of culture in the various spheres of social life' (Mannheim 1934, p.108), but he also notes that in a mass society the number of elites increases (Mannheim 1934, p.110). My interpretation of Mannheim, at its simplest, supports the argument that studying the relationship between society and elites in a historical context helps us understand the present situation. An elite is either close to other elites – as intellectuals (including academics), for example, may be to political or military circles – or distant from or even opposed to them. This relationship always changes, and how it is seen by later generations is subject to constant change. Sometimes, especially during a crisis, the close relationship between intellectuals and society is seen as acceptable, and even promoted, while in other times it is critically reviewed and morally judged. This applies to many of the men discussed in this book, whereby any evaluation or re-evaluation of them depends on the generation doing it. Many of the subjects of later chapters were seen in the 1960s and 1970s as old-fashioned and reactionary (see, for example, Bessner 2018), and some of them continue to be ignored or are further criticised. But the present period of propaganda calls for consideration of those who have conducted earlier propaganda research, who, I propose, have been unjustly and wastefully neglected.

(3) Widening the definition of ideology beyond traditional politics

The concept of ideology is often understood as a set of beliefs about politics or culture. In my view, and for the purposes of this book, a wide-ranging definition is important, since I am analysing not only structures but also individual life stories. The concept of ideology encompasses not only beliefs about politics but also beliefs about the role of women, race, sexual orientation and much else in societies. Sexism, racism and homophobia have an important role in political ideologies and their analysis helps us understand the under-representation of underprivileged groups in the comparative communications of the period under study. Apart from this 'invisibility', one needs to be careful about making an argument about the totalitarian nature of the concept of ideology. Mannheim (1960) writes:

> The individual members of the working class, for instance, do not experience *all* the elements of an outlook which could be called the proletarian *Weltanschauung*. Every individual participates only in fragments of this thought-system, the totality of which is not in the least a mere sum of these fragmentary individual experiences. As a totality the thought-system is integrated systematically and is no mere causal jumble of fragmentary experiences of discrete members of the group. (quoted by Kögler 1997, p.147)

Thus, the concept of ideology is not homogenous or permanent but, according to Mannheim, open and flexible. He saw his project as:

> justifying a dynamic theory of the relation of knowledge to reality as against static theories of philosophy that treat the historical, developmental and sociological as contingent to that which is durable and unchanging. (Breiner 2013, p.40)

Unlike many Marxist theorists of ideology, Mannheim was also more interested in change than in the status quo, even if ideologies are often seen as all-powerful and long-lasting, especially by those living through them.

(4) Ideologies and utopias are interwoven

The concept of utopia is as difficult to define as the concept of ideology. Wirth argues that ideologies attempt to maintain the status quo while utopias seek to change the prevailing order (quoted in Adair-Toteff 2019, p.6). Gabel (1991, p.85) wryly observes that 'utopians are not rarely in insane asylums' and that utopia is traditionally defined as an unattainable project, characterised by its ambiguity having its positive and negative role (p.85). For me, Mannheim's most important contribution is not only in linking both concepts but insisting that they are equally important, as the title of his book suggests. Again, Mannheim is often acknowledged as one of the key original authors on utopia, together with Thomas More (1478–1535) and Friedrich Engels (1820–1895) (Wallerstein 1986, p.1295). For Mannheim, the concept of utopia balances the concept of ideology by offering an alternative to – a different vision from – the power of ideology. Mannheim observes that 'the representatives of a given order will label as utopian all conceptions of existence which from their point of view can in principle never be realized' (Mannheim 1960, pp.176–77). This is why the concept of utopia is so important: it potentially provides an escape, even if sometimes only an imaginary escape, from the hardships of coercive and often taken-for-granted ideologies. Here there are obvious similarities between Mannheim's concepts and those of the Frankfurt School. However, Mannheim was not a believer in revolution, and diagnosed the Russian and Hungarian revolutions as 'utopist' distortions of reality (Kadarkay 1991, p.294).

While much theoretical work has been dedicated to the concept of ideology, the concept of utopia has received much less attention, to the extent that it was labelled in the 1970s as unfashionable (Levitas 2013, p.94). There are academics who have taken Mannheim's concept forward. The concept of utopia is often understood in close connection with related concepts such as: identity (Ricoeur 1986); the end of utopia (Marcuse 1970; Marcuse and Sherover 1979); the decline of utopian ideas (Berlin 2013); retrotopia (Bauman 2017); hope (Bloch 1959/1986); or social change (Levitas 1979). However, one has to be cautious not to romanticise the concept of utopia. It is tempting to think that one of the two concepts of ideology or of utopia might be somehow less distorted, but in fact it is important to remember that both are distorted. As Wallerstein (1986, p.1307) puts it, 'utopias are always ideological'. Or, as Geoghegan (2004, p.126) writes, 'the claim that ideology and utopia are incongruent with reality entails the epistemological claim that these two modes of experience are "distortions" of reality'.

Levitas (2000, p.26) gives three different reasons why we should take the concept of utopia seriously: (1) it is the expression of what is missing in societies; (2) it is the sense of a counterfactual model of all or part of a social or political system; and (3) it attempts to articulate the features of a good society. However, as Levitas (2013, p.6) herself observes, the concept of utopia operates on two levels: (1) the level of the subjective (individuals) and (2) the level of the objective, external condition of the world. This distinction between the two levels is very useful for the purposes of this book, since in the context of comparative communications utopias reflect both.

Mannheim's key question, according to Wallerstein, is: 'which social standpoint vis-a-vis history offers the best chance for reaching an optimum of truth?' (Wallerstein 1986, p.1299). As applied to the subject of this book, this question could become: which concept, that of ideology or of utopia, has been dominant in shaping comparative communications? But, again, only by studying individuals can we understand how their ideologies and utopias change during their lifetimes, and how they themselves, as active agents, contributed to these changes. By comparing and contrasting the concepts of ideology and utopia in comparative communications research, *Wissenssoziologie* becomes possible. Mannheim writes that,

> in unmasking ideologies, we seek to bring to light an unconscious process, not in order to annihilate the moral existence of persons making certain statements, but in order to destroy the social effi-cacy of it. (quoted by Sargent 2008, p.265)

Mannheim's definitions of the concepts of ideology and utopia have often been simplified, with ideology presented as something that is inherited from the past, while utopia is perceived as about the future (Geoghegan 2004, p.124). I find this problematic and show through my analysis that the rela-tionship between the past, the present and the future is complicated and more challenging. My argument is that comparative communications, in the US, has shifted between ideology and utopia, with the two often contradicting and/or replacing each other, but never completely liberating itself from either. In subsequent chapters, I analyse different studies of comparative commu-nications carried out between the 1920s and the 1950s, mainly in the US, by individual researchers and by groups consisting of specialists of different nationalities. These studies reflect the dominant ideologies of their funders, but also the utopias of the researchers, *mutatis mutandis*. In order to do this, I need another concept: that of a generation, as defined by Mannheim.

1.5 The concept of a generation

Like Mannheim's other concepts, his concept of a generation (Mannheim 1927; 1928) has been heavily criticised but also much used. Pilcher (1994, p.492) argues that Mannheim's seminal work represents the strongest soci-ological account of generations but that it is only a theoretical treatment of the problem and does not contain an empirical model or give any guidelines for how to carry out research using the concept. There have also been many attempts to summarise Mannheim's concept of a generation. Purhonen (2016, p.95), for example, writes that for Mannheim:

> generations emerge only under special historical circumstances and are thus something 'more' than simply age cohorts; they are a group of people of similar age bonded by a shared experience that can eventually result in a distinct self-consciousness, a worldview and, ultimately, political action.

For me, the concept of a generation is yet another attempt by Mannheim to break down categories of ideology and utopia by not reducing these to a class, in a similar way to what he did with his notion of a free-floating intelligentsia. Much of Mannheim's work, even when he writes about generations, is about intellectuals, whom he saw as having more autonomy than the working class and also as having some agency in terms of societal change.

There has been previous research, especially in the field of international relations but also in communication and journalism studies in Germany, where Mannheim's concept of generations has been applied to understanding paradigmatic changes in academic research (see, for example, Meyen 2015; Roskin 1974; Steele and Acuff 2012). For the purpose of this book, I focus on three specific propositions of Mannheim's concept: (1) generations are socially constructed either by their own members or by other generations; (2) generations are both national and transnational; and (3) belonging to the same generation does not necessarily result in a shared ideology or utopia but also includes intra- and intergenerational conflicts.

(1) Social construction of generations

For Mannheim, a generation is not biological, based on age, but socially constructed (Schuman and Scott 1989, p.359). His radical notion helps us to understand the concept of a generation in two different ways, both based on generations as 'discursive constructs that arise from narratives' (Timonen and Conlon 2015, p.2). This could be understood first as how members of a generation define themselves, or what Ben-Ze'ev and Lomsky-Feder describe as a 'story told by a generation' and second as how other generations define previous generations, or what Ben-Ze'ev and Lomsky-Feder call a 'story about a generation' (Ben-Ze'ev and Lomsky-Feder 2009, p.1048). The distinction is important since generations sometimes define themselves but at other times are defined by others. Both notions are problematic in their possible exclusivity, and this is why Merton's concepts of Insiders and Outsiders are needed, as discussed later in this chapter. I analyse here the 'story told by a generation' by telling a 'story about a generation' created through shared experiences of two world wars that shook its world.

I investigate one particular generation, the 'forefront generation', active between the 1920s and the 1950s, of academics, intellectuals and men of action. Members of this generation had often not themselves fought in either world war – being in many cases too old – but had provided intelligence support and been deeply influenced by both wars in terms of how they interpreted the world, and as a result shifted in their work between utopias and ideology. Mannheim wrote of a 'generation for whom the war was the defining *experience* and post-war issues were decisive for their *attitude*' (Neun Kunze and Mannheim 2018, p.8, my emphasis). I use his concept not only to understand and track ideological and utopian change but also to shift away from analysing ideology solely in terms of structures towards studying individual histories.

However, when writing a 'story about the generation', one has to be wary of falling into the story of a generation as founding fathers, the *Gründerväter* of a discipline or a field, often told either by contemporaries or by following generations (see, for example, Berelson 1959; Meyen 2015). Meyen (2015, p.22) writes that 'the succession of generations of professors can in any case only be adequately described through the metaphor of "parents", "children" and "grandchildren"', but I find this problematic because it takes us back not only to biological generations but also to their uneven status in most societies. There is also another aspect to this. Horowitz (1996, p.357) writes, quoting Solzhenitsyn (1973) in *The Gulag Archipelago*, that 'certain events and peoples are remembered and others are forgotten by virtue of the monopoly role of intellectuals who write the past'. Who is remembered and who is forgotten is thus a matter of choice when writing about the history of comparative communications. I am also very much influenced by those contemporary writers who have chosen the 'canonical' texts (Katz et al. 2002), while also deliberately choosing to leave aside some of these texts and to include authors not seen as part of the canon. Why have I chosen these men? I chose them because I am myself an Outsider, a female academic migrant, albeit in a different country from the US, and I wanted to use my own 'outsideness' as a starting point, to show what is easily forgotten when national 'canonical' texts are chosen only by Insiders. Histories of communication studies have primarily been written by those who are Insiders in terms of their nationality, namely US scholars writing about the history of US communication studies (a notable exception to the rule is the work of Simonson and Park 2016; Simonson et al. 2019) or who have themselves been key players in the field in the US. However, I am still left with the same dilemma: by picking up on just a few, am I strengthening again the myth of 'canonical' texts? If so, I am at least challenging the established canon that has ignored many members when writing a story about a generation.

For Mannheim, the concept of ideology plays a key role with the concept of utopia in his *Wissenssoziologie* when he is analysing how knowledge was produced. Many academics only remember the so-called 'Mannheim's paradox', a concept invented by Geertz (1973), who argues that if all knowledge is ideological no analysis rises above ideology, and thus that it is almost impossible to be fully analytical (Jehlen 1986, p.12). According to Breiner (2013, p.39), Mannheim's paradox can be seen:

> when we try to understand *contending ideologies* that constitute a political field at any one historical moment both as they inform and criticise one another, and when we seek to test the possibilities for their realisation in light of the historical developmental tendencies and political tensions in their sociological context, our constructions of this context is itself informed by these ideologies. (my emphasis)

Mannheim (1960) writes that all historical knowledge is relational knowledge and is 'always bound up with existing life-situation of the thinker' (p.71). He further says that:

every time we uncover an opponent's political ideas and world-view as ideology, we achieve this only from *the vantage point of another ideology*, and so there is no vantage point outside of ideology to understand and criticise ideology. (quoted by Breiner 2013, p.39, my emphasis)

To try to simplify this: a researcher, when trying to critically analyse a historical period, cannot do so wholly objectively because he/she is also influenced by the very same or other ideologies. This is also a dilemma for this book. When I try to critically analyse the period under research, how much am I influenced by the ideologies of that time as well as by ideologies of my own?

In my view, Geertz's response to Mannheim's dilemma, in his sociology of meaning (Jehlen 1986, p.12), is no more a solution to the dilemma than is Mannheim's *Wissenssoziologie*. We are still influenced by ideologies, but Mannheim's observation that we understand ideology as a kind of knowledge that arises from 'our experience in actual life situations' (Breiner 2013, p.6) has been important for my analysis. As Breiner writes,

Moreover, it also requires we understand each ideology as a (Mannheim 1936/1960, p.43) particular perspective on social reality. It furthermore requires we construct an account of the ways each of these points of view *interact with each other* in *conflictual or complementary* ways as we move from one perspective to the other. And lastly it requires that we understand that the way ideologies in a particular period interact with each other *horizontally* is at the same time a vertical response to a historical sociological reality, at once 'temporal, spatial, and situational.' (Breiner 2013, p.6, my emphasis)

Still, by shedding light on individuals, some already forgotten, even when I concentrate on the *Salon des Refusés*, I involuntarily contribute to a history of 'great men' (Rakow 2008, pp.115–16). As Knobloch-Westerwick and Glynn (2011) write, in research, 'women's contributions are systematically undervalued in patterns of citation, social contribution, and incorporation into disciplinary literatures, including communication' (cited by Ashcraft and Simonson 2016, p.49). In the course of my research, I have seen over and over again how women's contributions have been systematically undervalued, to the extent that they remain nameless and unacknowledged in written documents, often being referred to as 'girls' in their professional roles as secretaries ('secretary to') and research assistants (acknowledged in footnotes) or as partners ('my wife', sometimes thanked in acknowledgements). This is especially poignant when one is aware that many of those women had had their own careers in Europe and lost these when they emigrated to the US or elsewhere with the men they were married to. Although their lives were saved, their working lives came to an end.

At the same time, the exclusion of women yet again highlights the importance of Mannheim's *Wissenssoziologie* for exploring the relationships between culture and society. It was taken for granted that research was conducted by white men and that women were excluded from equal professional roles. As Hammersley (2022, p.185) writes, for Mannheim the main function of sociology seemed to be to:

> examine prevalent political worldviews and their social contexts,
> in order to understand them and to identify what is true and false
> within them, in order to develop a more objective perspective.

This is yet another example of how ideology works in each period and how we need to add the issue of gender and race to critiques of the sociology of knowledge (Thompson 1991; Philips 2001). I also argue that, by conducting research on the men discussed in this book, we can use them to understand why women were, and largely continue to be, absent from comparative communications. When I apply the concepts of Insider and Outsider, it is necessary to remember that the Outsiders were also those left out of written archival materials dominated by white men.[10]

(2) Generations are both national and transnational

A generation has most often been defined in the context of a single nation, although Mannheim himself did not indicate this. Mannheim writes:

> Members of a generation are 'similarly located', first of all, in so far
> as they all are exposed to the same phase of the collective process.
> This, however, is a merely mechanical and external criterion of the
> phenomenon of 'similar location'. For a deeper understanding, we
> must turn to the phenomenon of the 'stratification' of experience
> (*Erlebnisschichtung*), just as before we turned to 'memory'. (Mann
> heim 2000, p.297)

'Similar location', in my view, does not mean to Mannheim a geographical location. However, when the concept of a generation has been used in historical studies of a field, they have mostly been labelled by nationality, as in the cases, for example, of German or US communication studies. While I acknowledge that academia is most often defined nationally, similar location cannot be the only criterion when defining generations. Edmunds and Turner (2005, p.573) write of generations 'by reference to historical and cultural traumas, the experience of which *transcends* class and *nationality*' (my emphasis). According to these authors, 'while generations and generational change have traditionally been understood in national terms, there are reasons to suppose that globally experienced traumatic events may facilitate the development of global generations' (p.564). For Edmunds and Turner, the 1960s generation was the first example of a global generation, but I argue that there were earlier global or, as I would call them, transnational generations such as the forefront generation in the US. As Beck (2011, p.1350) writes, 'the mediation of world crises creates an awareness that strangers in distant places are following the same events with the same fears and worries as oneself. Strangers become neighbours!' In the context of this book, strangers became neighbours when European émigré scholars fled to the US and started working next to their American colleagues. I thus extend Mannheim's concept of a generation beyond the national level and ask whether a generation can cosmopolitanise not only itself but also others, to develop and maintain 'openness towards peoples, places and experiences from different cultures, especially those from different "nations"' (Tomlinson 1999, p.469).

I thus suggest that a transnational perspective is also needed to analyse, using Mannheim's concept of a generation, relationships between individuals and between research groups with differing ideologies and utopias. According to Shils (1974, p.83), Mannheim had a 'profound distaste for individualism'. In this book I provide a micro-sociological perspective that includes individual and generational life histories. My interest in the micro-sociological aspect derived from my own methodology, called mediagraphy (Rantanen 2004), which I developed in order to study individuals and globalisation using such concepts as generation, class and ideology. In this book I present five historical studies of individuals or research groups. Many of them were émigré[11] scholars from Europe, and all were caught up in the destructive events of the first half of the 20th century. Still, despite the differences in their life stories, there were multiple connections with long-term consequences that have not been identified before. However, a generation, while possibly united by the same transitional ideologies or utopias, is also pregnant with conflicts when its members encounter each other in the same location, as émigré scholars did when they arrived in the US from Europe. These conflicts included jobs, funding, promotion and material rewards.

(3) Not always a shared ideology or utopia

There is a potential pitfall in making an unfounded generalisation when we analyse both 'a story told by a generation' and 'a story about a generation' as supposedly homogenous units that share the same ideologies and utopias. As Mannheim (2000, p.306) observes,

> Within this community of people with a common destiny there can then arise particular generation-units. These are characterized by the fact that they do not merely involve a loose participation by a number of individuals in a pattern of events shared by all alike though interpreted by the different individuals differently, but an

identity of responses, a certain affinity in the way in which all move with and are formed by their common experiences.

Although Mannheim writes about 'an identity of responses', not about similar ideologies and utopias, one has to be mindful of not seeing differences within a generation. Mannheim (quoted by Kögler 1997, p.146) writes that,

> from a sociological point of view, both 'nations' and 'epochs' are much too undifferentiated to serve as a basis of reference in describing the historical process. The historian knows that a certain epoch will appear as dominated by just one intellectual current only when we have a bird's eye view of it. Penetrating deeper into the historical detail, we shall see every epoch as divided among several currents.

The diversity of responses calls for two other concepts, those of intra- and intergenerational conflicts. While Mannheim himself does not use these concepts, they have become closely associated with his work. As Connolly (2019, p.154) argues, it was Norbert Elias who worked with Mannheim for over two decades (Kilminster 1993) and whose work, rather than Mannheim's, emphasised generational conflicts. International relations theorists have used these concepts in analysing conflicts as inherent in generational change. Most notably, Roskin (1974) applied Kuhn's framework of paradigms and scientific revolutionary change to the making of foreign policy (Steele 2012, p.28), while different generations of feminism, often cast as 'mother daughter conflicts' (Lucas and Sisco 2012, p.165), have been analysed by using Mannheim's concept. Meyen (2015) combines Kuhn's (1962) concept of a paradigm with the concept of a generation when conducting research on German communication scholars, arguing that it was the institutionalisation of the field that defined the generations of communication scholars in Germany. What I take from Mannheim and these others is the presence of intra- and intergenerational conflicts in relation to the concept of a generation. Of the two notions, that of intergenerational conflicts has probably caught more attention, at least in the fields of sociology and of international relations, while intragenerational conflicts have received less attention (Xu 2019, p.135) or have been analysed using the concept of a paradigm change.

Following Mannheim's idea critically, the forefront generation analysed in this book, although its members experienced two world wars, did not necessarily share the same ideologies and utopias. There are so many other factors, including gender. As Sargent (2008, p.272) writes, 'Mannheim is known to have been a supporter of and advocate for women in German academia', and 'he had written on the sociology of women at a time that such work was extremely rare'. According to Kettler and Meja 1993, p.5), in Mannheim's work, 'despite vital differences in their social genealogies, women and intellectuals both exemplify groups constitutive of social structure without fitting in the Marxist scheme of social classes'. In the forefront generation I write about, women remain almost invisible and voiceless, and thus make it impossible to analyse conflicts in which they were involved.

Some of the men whose life stories I analyse in this book were also different from each other because of their race, nationality, class, location, or even academic training and background. Unlike much earlier work on émigré scholars (see, for example, Jay 1973/1996 on the Frankfurt School), my work here focuses on non-Marxist scholars and communications experts who have to a large extent been ignored. I argue that they should receive attention simply because if we ignore them we miss an important part of the story about the generation and even fail to understand how ideologies and utopias work. Having taken inspiration from Mannheim and others in relation to generational conflicts, it is time to introduce the concepts of Insiders and Outsiders.

1.6 Insiders and Outsiders

When Merton introduced his concepts of Insiders and Outsiders, his starting point was again Mannheim. By going back to Mannheim's (1960, pp.137–38) concept of the 'classless position' of 'socially unattached intellectuals' (*freischwebende Intelligenz*), and his argument that these intellectuals were able to 'comprehend the conflicting tendencies of the time since, among other things, they are "recruited from constantly varying social strata and life-situations"', Merton then argues that Mannheim was in effect claiming that there is a category of socially free-floating intellectuals who are both Insiders and Outsiders, benefitting from their collectively diverse social origins and transcending group allegiances. This, in turn, would make it possible for them to 'observe the social universe with special insight and a synthesizing eye' (Merton 1972, p.29).

Merton emphasises the uneven power relationships between Insiders and Outsiders. At the same time, he writes that 'there is nothing fixed about the boundaries separating Insiders from Outsiders' (p.28) and concludes his article provocatively channelling Marx: 'Insiders and Outsiders in the domain of knowledge, unite. You have nothing to lose but your claims. You have a world of understanding to win' (p.44). Here Merton himself should go back to *Wissenssoziologie* to acknowledge that those who work in institutions that produce knowledge are both collaborative and competitive. Even further, his categories of Insiders and Outsiders take for granted that Insiders are all white men. Merton writes that,

> Although Insider doctrines have been intermittently set forth by white elitists through the centuries, white male Insiderism in American sociology during the past generations has largely been of the tacit or de facto rather than doctrinal or principled variety. (1972, pp.12–13)

Here Merton is ignoring the power of ideology but recognises racism and gender. Merton (1972, pp.11–12) argues that certain groups of Insiders, at every moment of history, have monopolistic and/or privileged access to particular kinds of knowledge, while Outsiders are excluded. In the context of this book, I am studying male individuals and research groups who produced studies in comparative communications, and I am linking them with the ideologies and utopias of their time. In looking for guidance on doing this, the concepts of Insiders and Outsiders help me to explore not only the *power relationships* of individuals and research groups vis-à-vis society but also those between themselves.

Many émigré scholars, including the most successful such as Lazarsfeld, never felt fully accepted in US academia (see, for example, Coser 1984, pp.119–20; Kettler 2002; Lazarsfeld 1969). This, of course, was also true in the UK as Mannheim's less-than-happy experience of LSE testifies. Merton (1972, p.18) writes that:

> under the stress of war, scientists have been known to violate the values of and norms of universalism in which they were socialized, allowing their status as nationals to dominate over their status as social scientists.

Since this book is about the forefront generation following two wars, Merton's categories become highly pertinent. What did émigré scholars do to become the Insiders of a generation? Academics and experts shared an interest in comparative communications, and especially in news and propaganda, but they have also been separated by their respective 'insideness' or 'outsideness'. Who was an Insider and who an Outsider in this generation? Who had the power to define their own ideology, after they were brought together by their utopian preoccupations? And when a generation of comparative communications researchers coming from different backgrounds and countries is brought together can they cosmopolitanise themselves 'across bounds' in order to 'overcome space- and time-bound limitations on the generalizability of ... theories, assumptions, and propositions' (Blumler, McLeod and Rosengren 1992, pp.2, 7–8; Meng and Rantanen 2015, p.12)?

Merton's (1972, pp.11–12) concepts of Insiders and Outsiders can help to explain how particular groups of Insiders, at every moment of history, have had monopolistic and/or privileged access to particular kinds of knowledge, while Outsiders have been excluded from these. Applying this to the early development of comparative communications, I argue that we also need to explore who became the Insiders and the Outsiders, and whether an individual researcher's position could change. This is especially important when conducting research on histories of communication research, which have often been written by those who were involved themselves – or by their country*men*. Merton writes:

The Insider argues that the authentic understanding of group life can be achieved only by those who are directly engaged as members in the life of the group ... If direct engagement in the life of a group is essential to understanding it, then the only authentic history is contemporary history, written in fragments by those most fully involved in making inevitably limited portions of it. Rather than constituting only the raw materials of history, the documents prepared by engaged Insiders become all there is to history. But once the historian elects to write the history of a time other than his own, even the most dedicated Insider, of the national, sex, age, racial, ethnic, or religious variety, becomes the Outsider, condemned to error and misunderstanding. (1972, p.31)

However, being or becoming an Insider is not only a matter of having access. Merton also writes that, once the basic principle is adopted,

the list of Insider claims to a monopoly of knowledge becomes indefinitely expansible to all manner of social formations based on ascribed (and, by extension, on some achieved) *statuses*. According to the doctrine of the Insider, the Outsider, no matter how careful and talented, is excluded in principle from gaining access to the social and cultural truth. (1972, p.13)

Merton also discusses nationalism as a form of exclusion, quoting Albert Einstein (1879–1955):

If my theory of relativity is proven successful, Germany will claim me as a German and France will declare that I am a citizen of the world. Should my theory prove untrue, France will say that I am a German and Germany will declare that I am a Jew. (Merton 1972, p.28)

As my analysis shows, becoming an academic Insider turned out to be much more difficult for émigré scholars than for those who were born and raised in the US.

Although in Merton's (1949/1968) evaluation of *Wissenssoziologie* it is his American version that 'wins on almost every count' (Sica 2010, pp.172–73), he does briefly state that 'those distinctive emphases are bound up with the environing social structures in which they developed' (Merton 1949/1968, p.494), thus acknowledging the value of Mannheim's work and the influence of environment or even of ideology. In Sica's view, Merton was himself 'aiming toward that happy combination of the two which possesses the scientific virtues of both and the superfluous vices of neither' (Merton 1949/1968, p.494), although 'it's very clear that European style irritates him' (Sica 2010, p.173). I argue here that we need both *Wissenssoziologie* and a sociology of knowledge in order to be able to understand how comparative communications came into being, even if there is no happy reconciliation to be achieved between the two.

1.7 Why does this matter now?

While, as noted, this is an unapologetically old-fashioned book, there are several current trends that make me think that Mannheim's 'crisis in our thought' (Mannheim 1960, p.96) is still relevant today. As Merton (1972, p.9) writes,

> As the society becomes polarized, so do the contending claims to truth. At the extreme, an active and reciprocal distrust between groups finds expression in intellectual perspectives that are no longer located within the same universe of discourse. The more deep-seated the mutual distrust, the more does the argument of the other appear so palpably implausible or absurd that one no longer inquires into its substance or logical structure to assess its truth claims. Instead, one confronts the other's argument with an entirely different sort of question: how does it happen to be advanced at all?

Ideologies and utopias have changed, but Mannheim realised the impact that they had and would continue to have in the future (Adair-Toteff 2019, p.2). We need only to consider populism in the politics of many countries today. According to Norris and Inglehart (2019, p.4), 'populism questions pluralist beliefs about the rightful location of power and authority in any state, including the role of elected representatives in democratic regimes'. They write that:

> [populism's] favorite targets include the mainstream media ('fake news'), elections ('fraudulent'), politicians ('drain the swamp'), political parties ('dysfunctional'), public-sector bureaucrats ('the deep state'), judges ('enemies of the people'), protests ('paid rent-a-mob'), the intelligence services ('liars and leakers'), lobbyists ('corrupt'), intellectuals ('arrogant liberals') and scientists ('who needs experts?'), interest groups ('get-rich-quick lobbyists'), the constitution ('a rigged system'), international organizations like the European Union ('Brussels bureaucrats') and the UN ('a talking club'). (p.4)

In 2022, when Russia invaded Ukraine, the issue of the concept of 'truth' again became pertinent. The difference between war propaganda and news often disappeared. What was seen as news in Russia was seen as propaganda in the West, and what was seen as news in the West was seen as propaganda in Russia. Many of the actors discussed in this book devoted much of their research to studying war propaganda before, during and after World War II, often inspired by *Wissenssoziologie* and psychoanalysis, which both aimed to reveal the 'truth' below the surface. While I focus here on a period long gone, this raises the continuing importance of Mannheim's call for a *Wissenssoziologie*. It seeks to show how difficult it often is for contemporaries to analyse their own and one another's research, and how only a historical account can reveal the blind spots of a particular period. One of the reasons why Mannheim was so heavily criticised may have been that he touched the Achilles heel of his fellow academics at that time by asking them to look critically at their own research. What many of them did was instead to look critically at Mannheim's work.

Academics and experts may now face a new political situation where academic institutions are struggling with decreasing financial support, where external funding may also be under threat; when international organisations are also targets for populist parties, and where governments may fund research if this suits their own purposes. In an atmosphere of growing international political tensions that has already escalated into new wars and a new Cold War, propaganda research in comparative communications will again be in demand, but – once again – who sets the terms? Academics and experts – understood here as an inclusive term covering all kinds of researchers, not only academics and intellectuals – have now become a target of populist criticism. They may find themselves today in circumstances not entirely different from those of the period under study.

Finally, although academia today has become increasingly transnational and, although many of the issues faced by early comparative communications projects are again present, the ultimate power relationships are still those within national research teams. To use Merton's concepts, who is now the Insider and who is now the Outsider?

1.8 Plan of the book and details of sources

This introduction has set out the key concepts behind the book. It is followed by five chapters focusing on: an academic (Harold D. Lasswell); a man of experience (Kent Cooper); a wartime project involving academics (both US and émigré scholars such as Nathan Leites and Paul Kecskemeti) and non-academics; post-war academics and researchers working primarily at RAND (Research and Development) Corporation in Santa Monica, California, and lastly a post-war project of three academics representing different fields (Fred S. Siebert, Theodore Peterson and Wilbur Schramm). Empirically, I use materials located in a plurality of archives, as well as books, newspapers and magazines from the period under investigation, and previously published research. All of them are listed in Archival Sources at the end of the book.

The men studied did not all belong to the same age cohort, as their birth years ranged from 1880 to 1918, but they were all influenced by World War I and World War II. In each of my case-study chapters, I try to show how they all struggled between utopias and ideologies and how they shared ideas as members of a generation. Their positions as Insiders or Outsiders also changed over time and their generational unity gave way to some division.

Harold D. Lasswell's work developed from his early study of World War I propaganda to his Cold War studies of the 1950s. In Chapter 2, I review his conceptual and methodological movement from a study of symbols to the quantitative content analysis for which he is best known, as well as his transformation from a young utopian academic to a father figure who saw himself as a policy scholar and who aimed to be a good citizen and cultivate good citizenship in others. Lasswell's influence, primarily through his policy science studies and his personal networks, shaped his own and succeeding generations, although, as many father figures experience, he suffered an Oedipal fate at the hands of successor generations. I argue that Lasswell was an intergenerational figure who deserves resurrection. This chapter is based primarily on my research in the Manuscripts and Archives of Yale University Library, and in the Hanna Holborn Gray Special Collections Research Center of the University of Chicago Library.

Kent Cooper was a professional news agency man and a manager. He borrowed academic concepts when advocating cooperative ownership of news and the free flow of news without government interference. Cooper became general manager of the Associated Press (AP), the most important US-based news agency and one of the four biggest Western news agencies during the period 1925–1943. He wrote two books, *Barriers Down: The Story of the News Agency Epoch* (1942) and *The Right to Know* (1956), both of which have influenced many generations of communication industry managers, policymakers and academics. The arguments for free flow of information, for example, clearly resonated with those academics, diplomats and journalists, who debated the merits and demerits of a New World Information and Communication Order (NWICO) in UNESCO and in the UN in the 1970s and 1980s (MacBride 1980). Cooper's career exemplifies how ideologies are promoted by news organisations in order to advance their own interests. In Chapter 3 I argue that Cooper, using the AP's and his own status, was more influential than were any academics in shaping social, corporate and policy outcomes. This chapter is based on primary research in the AP archive in New York, Reuters' archive in London, the Lilly Library, and the Media School Archive, University of Indiana in Bloomington.

Chapter 4 investigates a period when the US government recruited academics such as Lasswell to carry out research as part of the World War II war effort. Research teams combined men, and some women, of professional experience and academic competence, of both US and foreign origins, to develop new methods of analysis of enemy propaganda. European intellectuals such as Nathan Leites and Paul Kecskemeti were of particular importance but their contribution has been ignored in the dominant scholarly tradition. I argue that war comparative communications made its participants into a unified generation where Insiders and Outsiders temporarily came together, united by the same ideology but separated by their individual status. In terms of intellectual history, these neglected scholars have an unacknowledged importance, for example as relays for Mannheim's work into the Anglosphere (Kecskemeti translated Mannheim's work; Mannheim 1953). This chapter is based on my primary research in the Manuscripts and Archives of Yale University Library in New Haven, the Hanna Holborn Gray Special Collections Research Center at the University of Chicago Library, the New School archives in the M.E. Grenander Department of Special Collections & Archives at the State University of New York in Albany, the Robert D. Farber University Archives and Special Collections at Brandeis University, the RAND Corporation Archives in Santa Monica, California, and the Truman Presidential Library in Independence, Missouri.

Chapter 5 addresses the question of why comparative communications did not emerge as a field of its own, like comparative politics, but as a subfield of international communication, and later of political communication, within communication studies. I identify the environment – both academic and societal, national and international – in which research was carried out, concurrently with communication studies becoming institutionalised in universities. I analyse the role of UNESCO and other organisations as major funders of international communications studies, and international news flows are studied by using content analysis. I explore the post-World War II careers of scholars who had worked together as well as separately during the war, and the clashes between nationalism and cosmopolitanism which their history exemplified. In this chapter I argue that a hitherto unified generation became divided, not only following the ideological clashes of the time, marked by the Cold War and McCarthyism, but also by the new discipline of communication research. I note that émigré scholars such as Kecskemeti and Leites rarely became full professors in academia. This chapter is mainly based on my research in the University of Chicago Library, Illinois, the Rockefeller Archive Center Archives in Sleepy Hollow, New York, as well as in the New School archives in New York, the Robert D. Farber University Archives & Special Collections Department in Waltham, Massachusetts, the RAND Corporation Archives in Santa Monica and the M.E. Grenander Department of Special Collections & Archives at the State University of New York in Albany.

In Chapter 6 I argue, through an analysis of the individuals, research traditions, ideas, institutions and relationships behind the seminal publication *Four Theories of the Press* (1956), by Fred S. Siebert (1901–1982), Theodore Peterson (1918–1997) and Wilbur Schramm (1907–1987), together with George D. Stoddard (1897–1981), president of the University of Illinois from 1946 to 1953, who hired Schramm. I argue that this 'canonical' book was a compromise between the diverse interests of its authors, their backgrounds, ideas, and national and international politics. It lies at an intersection of contradictory but also overlapping elements and gave rise to new concepts of a press system and of press theory in an international context. I also argue that *Four Theories* united, albeit temporarily, three generations of men with different backgrounds and values. At the same time, because of the changes in the international and domestic political climate, academics who participated in international networks came under the suspicion of the US government.

In order to rescue themselves, they may have felt they needed to show their loyalty to their domestic government and funders, especially in relation to communism. The book exemplifies all these tensions between ideologies and utopias of the period, but following generations have all been looking at it from their own periods. This chapter draws on my primary research in the University of Illinois Archives in Urbana, Illinois, the home university and publisher of *Four Theories*. It is an expanded and revised version of an article published in *The International Journal of Communication* (2017).

The last chapter, coming after these personified histories, returns to the concepts of *Wissenssoziologie*, of the sociology of knowledge, of ideology and utopia, of a generation of Insiders/Outsiders, and to Merton's criteria, in order to analyse how and why comparative research in communications was done, and what kinds of influence this foundational shaping has had on the generations that followed the forefront generation. The legacy of comparative communications continues to influence what is now known as international communication studies. We can see the influence of the forefront generation in at least three aspects: (1) its interdisciplinary character; (2) its policy research orientation; and (3) its transposition of ideology and utopia. Unlike in political science, where comparative politics was accepted as a field of its own, in media and communication studies there is no distinct subfield of comparative communications that became international communication, a subfield that still exists as a field of battle between ideologies and utopias, often mixed together.

Notes

1 Louis Wirth (1897–1952) was born in Gemünden in Germany to Jewish parents, Joseph (1866–1936) and Rosalie (née Lorig, 1868–1948), and moved to live with his uncle in Omaha, Nebraska, at the age of 14. After studying at the University of Chicago he worked as a social worker from 1919 to 1922, then received his MA and PhD from the University of Chicago, where he was in the Department of Sociology continuously from 1926, becoming full professor in 1940. Between 1932 and 1937 he helped every member of his family out of Germany, most of them migrating to the US. At that time he also started translating Mannheim's *Ideology and Utopia* and wrote a preface to it (Wirth 1936). The archival records at the University of Chicago Library show his attempts to help Mannheim come to the US. His daughter Elizabeth Wirth Marvick (1905–2005) edited a book on Nathan Leites's work (Wirth Marvick 1977) ('Guide to the Louis Wirth papers, 1918–1952' 2008; Salerno 1987; Smith 1988, p.148).

2 Paul Lazarsfeld (1901–1976) was born in Vienna to Sophie or Sofie Lazarsfeld (née Munk, 1881–1976), a therapist, and Robert Lazarsfeld (1872–circa 1939), a lawyer, both Jewish. He was awarded a PhD in

mathematics at the University of Vienna. Lazarsfeld received a scholarship from the Rockefeller Foundation to visit US universities in 1933–1935 and decided to stay in the US. By leaving Vienna behind, he also left Marxism behind and called himself 'A Marxist on leave'. As Lazarsfeld put it himself: 'A fighting revolution requires economics (Marx); a victorious revolution requires engineers (Russia), a defeated revolution calls for psychology (Vienna)' (Coser 1984, pp.112, 119). He founded Columbia University's Bureau of Applied Social Research and is widely considered to be one of the founders of communication studies (Morrison 1988; 2008; 2022).

[3] Ramstad, E.K. (1947) 'Karl Mannheim. An Appreciation'. *T&T*, p.142. Paul Kecskemeti Papers. The Robert D. Farber University Archives & Special Collections Department at Brandeis University.

[4] O. Jassi to L. Wirth on 6 May 1933; K. Mannheim to L. Wirth on 13 October 1933. Louis Wirth Papers. Hanna Holborn Gray Special Collections Research Center, University of Chicago Library.

[5] Salary. Professor Karl Mannheim. Part-time lecturer, no date. Karl Mannheim File. The London School of Economics and Political Science (LSE) Archive.

[6] Timetable for Professor Mannheim on 26 May 1934. Karl Mannheim File. LSE Archive.

[7] K. Mannheim to L. Wirth on 17 September 1939; L. Wirth to B. Malinowski on 31 October 1939; K. Mannheim to L. Wirth on 4 March 1940. Louis Wirth Papers. Hanna Holborn Gray Special Collections Research Center, University of Chicago Library.

[8] Letter from Julia Mannheim from London to Ernest Manheim (1900–2002), Karl Mannheim's cousin, in Kansas City, MO, on 21 February 1947. Transliteration by Karin Eisner. Archiv für die Geschichte der Soziologie in Österreich (AGSÖ). https://agso.uni-graz.at/archive/manheim/en/4_gb/index.htm

[9] Professor Karl Mannheim. Candidate for election on 1 September 1942. The Athenaeum Club Archive.

[10] It has been difficult to find information about women in their roles as mothers and spouses in academic research. I am grateful to Dr Laura Killick, who showed me how valuable genealogy sites are when trying to find more not only about women but about migrant families in general where birth certificates have been lost and names have been changed. She helped me in my attempts to find missing years of birth and death but there were times when I have not been able to find the missing information or it is not accurate.

[11] I am using the term 'émigré' rather than 'refugee' or 'migrant' as an umbrella term covering all of these.

References

Abercrombie, Nicholas; Hill, Stephen; and Turner, Bryan S. (1980) *The Dominant Ideology Thesis*, UK: Allen & Unwin.

Adair-Toteff, Christopher (2019) 'Mannheim, Shils, and Aron and the "End of Ideology" Debate', *Politics, Religion & Ideology*, vol. 20, no. 1, pp.1–20. https://www.doi.org/10.1080/21567689.2018.1554481

Adorno, Theodor W. (1955) 'Das Bewußtsein der Wissenssoziologie', in Ders, Prismen (ed.) *Kulturkritik und Gesellschaft*, Germany: Suhrkamp, pp.32–50.

Albrow, Martin (1989) 'Sociology in the United Kingdom after the Second World War', in Genov, Nikolaï (ed.) *National Traditions in Sociology*, UK: Sage, pp.194–219.

Anderson, Perry (1980) *Arguments within English Marxism*, UK: NLB.

Ashcraft, Karen L. and Simonson, Peter (2016) 'Gender, Work, and the History of Communication Research: Figures, Formations, and Flows', in Simonson, Peter and Park, David W. (eds) *The International History of Communication Study*, USA: Routledge, pp.47–68.

Averbeck, Stefanie (1999) *Kommunikation als Prozeß. Soziologische Perspektiven in der Zeitungswissenschaft 1927-1934*, Germany: LIT Verlag.

Averbeck, Stefanie (2001) 'The Post-1933 Emigration of Communication Researchers from Germany: The Lost Works of the Weimar Generation', *European Journal of Communication*, vol. 16, no. 4, pp.451–475. https://doi.org/10.1177/0267323101016004002

Barboza, Amalia (2020) *Karl Mannheim*, Germany: Herbert von Halem Verlag.

Bateson, Gregory (1966) *From Versailles to Cybernetics*. https://www.krabarchive.com/ralphmag/batesonP.html

Bauman, Zygmunt (2017) *Retrotopia*, UK: Polity Press.

Beck, Ulrich (2011) 'Cosmopolitanism as Imagined Communities of Global Risk', *American Behavioral Scientist*, vol. 55, no. 10, pp.1346–61. https://www.doi.org/10.1177/0002764211409739

Ben-Ze'ev, Efrat and Lomsky-Feder, Edna (2009) 'The Canonical Generation: Trapped between Personal and National Memories', *Sociology*, vol. 43, no. 6, pp.1047–65. https://doi.org/10.1177/0038038509345698

Berelson, Bernard (1959) 'The State of Communication Research', *Public Opinion Quarterly*, vol. 23, no. 1, pp.14–17. https://doi.org/10.1086/266840

Berlin, Isaiah (2013) *The Crooked Timber of Humanity: Chapters in the History of Ideas* (2nd ed.), USA: Princeton University Press.

Bessner, Daniel (2018) *Democracy in Exile: Hans Speier and the Rise of the Defense Intellectual*, USA: Cornell University Press.

Bloch, Ernst (1959/1986) *The Principle of Hope*, UK: Basil Blackwell.

Blumler, Jay G.; McLeod, Jack M.; and Rosengren, Karl E. (1992) 'An Introduction to Comparative Communication Research', in Blumler, Jay G.; McLeod, Jack M.; and Rosengren, Karl E. (eds) *Comparatively Speaking: Communication and Culture Across Space and Time*, USA: Sage, pp.3–18.

Borgos, Anna (2021) *Women in the Budapest School of Psychoanalysis: Girls of Tomorrow*, UK: Routledge.

Bourdieu, Pierre (1979/1984) *Distinction: A Social Critique of the Judgement of Taste*, UK: Routledge.

Bourdieu, Pierre (1986) 'The Forms of Capital', in Richardson, John G. (ed.) *Handbook of Theory and Research for the Sociology of Education*, USA: Greenwood, pp.241–58.

Bourdieu, Pierre (1988) *Homo Academicus*, USA: Stanford University Press.

Bourdieu, Pierre (1993) *The Field of Cultural Production*, USA: Columbia University Press.

Breiner, Peter (2013) 'Karl Mannheim and Political Ideology', in Freedman, Michael; Sargent, Lyman T.; and Stear, Marc (eds) *The Oxford Handbook of Political Ideologies*, UK: Oxford University Press, pp.38–55.

Bulmer, Martin (1985) 'The Development of Sociology and of Empirical Social Research in Britain', in Bulmer, Martin (ed.) *Essays on the History of British Sociological Research*, UK: Cambridge University Press, pp.3–38.

Bush, Michael (2021) 'Robert K. Merton'. *Oxford Bibliographies in Criminology*. https://www.doi.org/10.1093/OBO/9780195396607-0299

Calhoun, Craig (2003) *Robert Merton Remembered. Footnotes*, vol. 31, no. 3, pp.3–8. https://www.asanet.org/wp-content/uploads/fn_2003_03_march.pdf

Calhoun, Craig (2010) 'Introduction: On Merton's Legacy and Contemporary Sociology', in Calhoun, Craig (ed.) *Robert K. Merton: Sociology of Science and Sociology as Science*, USA: Columbia University Press, pp.1–31.

Chaffee, Steven H. (1974) 'The Pathways of Proteus', *Journalism Monographs*, vol. 36, pp.1–8.

Congdon, Lee (1991) *Exile and Social Thought: Hungarian Intellectuals in Germany and Austria, 1919–1933*, USA: Princeton University Press.

Connolly, John (2019) 'Generational Conflict and the Sociology of Generations: Mannheim and Elias Reconsidered', *Theory, Culture & Society*, vol. 36, no. 7–8, pp.153–72. https://doi.org/10.1177/0263276419827085

Coser, Lewis A (1984) *Refugee Scholars in America. Their Impact and Their Experiences*, USA: Yale University Press.

Cox, Michael (2021) '"His Finest Hour": William Beveridge and the Academic Assistance Council'. https://blogs.lse.ac.uk/lsehistory/2021/04/28/his-finest-hour-william-beveridge-and-academic-assistance-council

Deflem, Mathieu (2018) 'Merton, Robert K', in Turner, Bryan S. (ed.) *The Wiley Blackwell Encyclopaedia of Social Theory*, USA: Wiley-Blackwell, pp.1–3. https://drive.google.com/file/d/1ccnjy6CpqGsQfML2XUr1oj61DJ7QFIWi/view?pli=1

Dennis, Everette E. and Wartella, Ellen (1996) *American Communication Research. The Remembered History*, USA: Lawrence Erlbaum Associates.

Eagleton, Terry (2007) *Ideology: An Introduction*, UK: Verso.

Edmunds, June and Turner, Bryan S. (2005) 'Global Generations: Social Change in the Twentieth Century', *The British Journal of Sociology*, vol. 56, no. 4, pp.559–77. https://doi.org/10.1111/j.1468-4446.2005.00083.x

Eisenstadt, Shmuel N. (1987) 'The Classical Sociology of Knowledge and Beyond', *Minerva*, vol. 25, no. 1/2, pp.77–91. https://doi.org/10.1007/BF01096857

Fischer, Ariane (2009) 'Settling Accounts with the Sociology of Knowledge: The Frankfurt School, Mannheim, and the Marxian Critique of Ideology Qua Mental Labor', *The South Atlantic Quarterly*, vol. 108, no. 2, pp.331–63. https://doi.org/10.1215/003828762008036

Fuller, Steve (2006) *The Philosophy of Science and Technology Studies*, UK: Routledge.

Gabel, Joseph (1976) 'Utopian Consciousness and False Consciousness', *Telos*, vol. 29, Fall, pp.181–86. https://doi.org/10.3817/0976029181

Gabel, Joseph (1991) *Mannheim and Hungarian Marxism*, USA: Transaction.

Gábor, Éva (1996) *Mannheim Károly levelezése 1911–1946*, Hungary: Argumentum Kiadó M T A Lukács Archívum. http://real-eod.mtak.hu/650/1/ArchivumiFuzetek_1996_12.pdf

Geertz, Clifford (1973) *The Interpretation of Cultures*, USA: Harper and Row.

Geoghegan, Vincent (2004) 'Ideology and Utopia', *Journal of Political Ideologies*, vol. 9, no. 2, pp.123–38. https://doi.org/10.1080/13569310410001691172

Glander, Timothy (2000) *Origins of Mass Communications Research during the American Cold War: Educational Effects and Contemporary Implications*, UK: Routledge.

Gluck, Mary (1985) *Georg Lukács and His Generation, 1900–1918*, USA: Harvard University Press.

Gouldner, Alwin W. (1979) *The Future of Intellectuals and the Rise of the New Class: A Frame of Reference, Theses, Conjectures, Arguments, and an Historical Perspective on the Role of Intellectuals and Intelligentsia in the International Class Contest of the Modern Era*, UK: Macmillan.

Grimley, Matthew (2007) Moot (Act. 1938–1947). *Oxford Dictionary of National Biography*. https://www.oxforddnb.com/view/10.1093/ref:odnb/9780198614128.001.0001/odnb-9780198614128-e-67745

'Guide to the Louis Wirth papers, 1918–1952' (2008) University of Chicago Library. https://www.lib.uchicago.edu/e/scrc/findingaids/view.php?eadid=ICU.SPCL.WIRTH

Gurukkal, Rajan (2019) *History and Theory of Knowledge Production: An Introductory Outline*, UK: Oxford University Press. https://doi.org/10.1093/oso/9780199490363.001.0001

Hammersley Martyn (2021) 'Planning versus the Market: The Dispute between Hayek and Mannheim and Its Contemporary Relevance', *British Journal of Sociology*, vol. 72, no. 5, pp.1464–78. https://doi.org/10.1111/1468-4446.12893

Hammersley, Martyn (2022) 'Karl Mannheim's Ideology and Utopia and the Public Role of Sociology', *Journal of Classical Sociology*, vol. 22, no. 2, pp.176–98. https://doi.org/10.1177/1468795X20986382

Hannerz, Ulf (1992) *Cultural Complexity: Studies in the Social Organization of Meaning*, USA: Columbia University Press.

Hardt, Hanno (1979) *Social Theories of the Press: Early German and American Perspectives*, USA: Sage Publications.

Hardt, Hanno (1992) *Critical Communication Studies: Communication, History, and Theory in America*, UK: Routledge.

Heeren, John (1971) 'Karl Mannheim and the Intellectual Elite', *The British Journal of Sociology*, vol. 22, no. 1, pp.1–15. https://doi.org/10.2307/588721

Horowitz, Irving L. (1996) 'Culture, Politics and McCarthyism: A Retrospective from the Trenches', *The Independent Review*, vol. 1, no. 1, pp.101–10. https://www.independent.org/pdf/tir/tir_01_1_07_horowitz.pdf

Howie, Marguerite R. (1961) 'Karl Mannheim and the Sociology of Knowledge', *The Journal of Education*, vol. 143, no. 4, pp.55–71. https://doi.org/10.1177/002205746114 30040

Hvidsten, Andreas H. (2019) 'Karl Mannheim and the Liberal Telos of Realism', *International Relations*, vol. 33, no. 3, pp.475–93. https://doi.org/10.1177/0047117819846544

Izzo, Alberto (1998) 'Conditioning or Conditionings? Revisiting an Old Criticism on Mannheim by Merton', in Merton, Robert K.; Mongardini,

Carlo; and Tabboni, Simonetta (eds) *Robert K. Merton and Contemporary Sociology*, USA: Transaction, pp.213–20.

Jay, Martin (1973/1996) *The Dialectical Imagination: A History of the Frankfurt School and the Institute of Social Research, 1923–1950*, USA: University of California Press.

Jay, Martin (1974/1994) 'The Frankfurt School's Critique of Karl Mannheim and the Sociology of Knowledge', in Bernstein, Jay M. (ed.) *The Frankfurt School: Critical Assessments*, UK: Routledge, pp.175–90.

Jehlen, Myra (1986) 'Introduction: Beyond Transcendence', in Bercovitch, Sacvan and Jehlen, Myra (eds) *Ideology and Classic American Literature*, UK: Cambridge University Press, pp.1–20.

Julia Mannheim (née Láng) (1893–1995) *Psychoanalytikerinnen. Biografisches Lexikon*. https://www.psychoanalytikerinnen.de/greatbritain _biographies.html#Mannheim

Karádi, Éva (1985) 'Einleitung', in Karádi, Éva and Vezér, Erzsébet (eds) *Georg Lukács, Karl Mannheim und der Sonntagskreis*, Germany: Sendler, pp.7–27.

Kadarkay, Arpad (1991) *Georg Lukacs: Life, Thought and Politics*, UK: Basil Blackwell.

Kaiser, David (1998) 'A Mannheim for All Seasons: Bloor, Merton, and the Roots of the Sociology of Scientific Knowledge', *Science in Context*, vol. 11, no. 1, pp.51–87. https://doi.org/10.1017/S026988970000291X

Karácsony, András (2008) 'Soul–Life–Knowledge: The Young Mannheim's Way to Sociology', *Studies in East European Thought*, vol. 60, no. 1/2, pp.97–111. https://doi.org/10.1007/s11212-008-9040-4

Katz, Elihu; Peters, John Durham; Liebes, Tamar; and Orloff, Avril (2002) (eds) *Canonic Texts in Media Research: Are There Any? Should There Be? How About These?* UK: Polity.

Kecskemeti, Paul (1952) 'Introduction', in Mannheim, Karl *Essays on the Sociology of Knowledge*, UK: Routledge and Kegan Paul, pp.1–32.

Kettler, David (2002) *Contested Legacies: The German-Speaking Intellectual and Cultural Emigration to the US and UK, 1933–1945*, Germany: Galda & Wilch.

Kettler, David (2012) *The Liquidation of Exile: Studies in the Intellectual Emigration of the 1930s*, UK: Cambridge University Press.

Kettler, David and Loader, Colin (2013) 'Weimar Sociology', in Gordon, Peter E. and McCormick, John P. (eds) *Weimar Thought: A Contested Legacy*, USA: Princeton University Press, pp.15–34.

Kettler, David and Meja, Volker (1993) 'Their "Own Peculiar Way": Karl Mannheim and the Rise of Women', *International Sociology*, vol. 8, no. 1, pp.5–55. https://doi.org/10.1177/026858093008001001

Kettler, David; Meja, Volker; and Stehr, Nico (1984) *Karl Mannheim*, UK: Tavistock.

Kilminster, Richard (1993) 'Norbert Elias and Karl Mannheim: Closeness and Distance', *Theory, Culture & Society*, vol. 10, no. 3, pp.81–114. https://doi.org/10.1177/026327693010003005

Klaus, Elisabeth and Seethaler, Josef (2016) *What Do We Really Know about Herta Herzog? Exploring the Life and Work of a Pioneer of Communication Research*, USA: Peter Lang.

Knobloch-Westerwick, Silvia and Glynn, Carroll J. (2011) 'The Matilda Effect—Role Congruity Effects on Scholarly Communication: A Citation Analysis of Communication Research and Journal of Communication Articles', *Communication Research*, vol. 40, no. 1, pp.3–26. https://doi.org/10.1177/0093650211418339

Kögler, Hans H. (1997) 'Alienation as Epistemological Source: Reflexivity and Social Background after Mannheim and Bourdieu', *Social Epistemology*, vol. 11, no. 2, pp.141–64.

Kuhn, Thomas (1962) *The Structure of Scientific Revolutions*, USA: University of Chicago Press.

Lang, Kurt (1979) 'The Critical Functions of Empirical Communication Research: Observations on German-American Influences', *Media, Culture & Society*, vol. 1, no. 1, pp.83–96. https://doi.org/10.1177/016344377900100107

Lassman, Peter (1992) 'Responses to Fascism in Britain, 1930–1945. The Emergence of the Concept of Totalitarianism', in Turner, Stephen P. and Käsler, Dirk (eds) *Sociology Responds to Fascism*, UK: Routledge, pp.214–40.

Lasswell, Harold D. (1951a) 'The Policy Orientation', in Lasswell, Harold D. and Lerner, Daniel (eds) *The Policy Sciences: Recent Developments in Scope and Method*, USA: Stanford University Press, pp.3–15.

Lazarsfeld, Paul F. (1969) 'An Episode in the History of Social Research. Memoirs', in Fleming, Donald and Bailyn, Bernard (eds) *The Intellectual Migration. Europe and America, 1930–1960*, USA: Harvard University Press, pp.270–337.

Lazarsfeld, Paul F. and Merton, Robert K. (1943) 'Studies in Radio and Film Propaganda', *Transactions of the New York Academy of Sciences*, vol. 6, no. 2, pp.58–74. https://doi.org/10.1111/j.2164-0947.1943.tb00897.x

Lazarsfeld, Paul F. and Merton, Robert K. (1948/1964) 'Mass Communication, Popular Taste and Organized Social Action', in Bryson, Lyman (ed.) *The Communication of Ideas*, USA: Institute for Religious and Social Studies, pp.95–118.

Levitas, Ruth (1979) 'Sociology and Utopia', *Sociology*, vol. 13, no. 1, pp.19–33. https://doi.org/10.1177/003803857901300102

Levitas, Ruth (2000) 'For Utopia: The (Limits of the) Utopian Function in Late Capitalist Society', *Critical Review of International Social and Political Philosophy*, vol. 3, no. 2–3, pp.25–43. https://doi.org/10.1080/13698230008403311

Levitas, Ruth (2013) *Utopia as Method: The Imaginary Reconstitution of Society*, UK: Palgrave.

Loader, Colin (1997) 'Free Floating: The Intelligentsia in the Work of Alfred Weber and Karl Mannheim', *German Studies Review*, vol. 20, no. 2, pp.217–34. https://doi.org/10.2307/1431946

Löblich, Maria and Scheu, Andreas M. (2011) 'Writing the History of Communication Studies: A Sociology of Science Approach', *Communication Theory*, vol. 21, no. 1, pp.1–22. https://doi.org/10.1111/j.1468-2885.2010.01373.x

Lucas, Jennifer C. and Sisco, Tauna S. (2012) 'Generations and Gender in the 2008 US Democratic Primaries', in Steele, Brent J. and Acuff, Jonathan M. (eds) *Theory and Application of the 'Generation' in International Relations and Politics*, USA: Palgrave Macmillan, pp.147–76.

Lyon, E. Stina (2011) 'Karl Mannheim and Viola Klein: Refugee Sociologists in Search of Social Democratic Practice', in Marks, Shula; Weindling, Paul; and Wintour, Laura (eds) *In Defence of Learning: The Plight, Persecution, and Placement of Academic Refugees, 1933–1980s*. Proceedings of the British Academy. British Academy Scholarship Online, pp.177–90. https://doi.org/10.5871/bacad/9780197264812.003.0012

MacBride, Sean (1980) *Many Voices, One World: Communication and Society Today and Tomorrow: Towards a New More Just and More Efficient World Information and Communication Order*, UK: Kogan Page.

Manheim, Ernest (1947) 'Karl Mannheim, 1893–1947', *American Journal of Sociology*, vol. 52, no. 6, pp.471–74. https://doi.org/10.1086/220067

Mannheim, Karl (1922) *Die Strukturanalyse der Erkenntnistheorie*. Kant-Studien, no. 57, Germany: Reuther & Reichard.

Mannheim, Karl (1927) 'Das Problem der Generationen', *Kölner Zeitschrift für Soziologie und Sozialpsychologie*, vol. 7, no. 2, pp.157–85.

Mannheim, Karl (1928) 'Das Problem der Generationen', *Kölner Zeitschrift für Soziologie und Sozialpsychologie*, vol. 8, no. 3, pp.309–30.

Mannheim, Karl (1929) *Ideologie und Utopie*, Germany: F. Cohen.

Mannheim, Karl (1932/1993) 'The Sociology of Intellectuals', *Theory, Culture & Society*, vol. 10, no. 3, pp.69–80. https://doi.org/10.1177/026327693010003004

Mannheim, Karl (1934) 'The Crisis of Culture in the Era of Mass-Democracies and Autarchies', *The Sociological Review*, vol. 26, no. 2, pp.105–29. https://doi.org/10.1111/j.1467-954X.1934.tb01902.x

Mannheim, Karl (1935) 'Utopia', in Seligman, Edwin R.A. (ed.) *Encyclopaedia of the Social Sciences*, USA: Macmillan, pp.200–03.

Mannheim, Karl (1936) *Ideology and Utopia: An Introduction to the Sociology of Knowledge*. Translated by Louis Wirth and Edward Shils. UK: Routledge & Kegan Paul, Trench, Trubner & C0; USA: Harcourt, Brace & Co.

Mannheim, Karl (1953) *Essays on Sociology and Social Psychology*. Edited by Paul Kecskemeti, UK: Routledge & Kegan Paul.

Mannheim, Karl (1960) *Ideology and Utopia. An Introduction to the Sociology of Knowledge*. Translated by Louis Wirth and Edward Shils. UK: Routledge & Kegan Paul.

Mannheim, Karl (1980) 'Eine soziologische Theorie der Kultur und ihrer Erkennbarkeit (Konjuktives und kommunikatives Denken)', in Kettler, David; Meja, Volker; and Stehr, Nico (eds) *Karl Mannheim. Strukturen des Denkens*, Germany: Suhrkamp Verlag, pp.155–322.

Mannheim, Karl (2000) 'The Problem of Generations', in Paul Kecskemeti (ed.) *Essays on the Sociology of Knowledge. Collected Works* (Vol. 5), UK: Routledge, pp.276–322.

Mannheim, Karl and Gábor, Éva (2003) *Selected Correspondence (1911–1946) of Karl Mannheim, Scientist, Philosopher, and Sociologist*, USA: Edwin Mellen Press.

Marcuse, Herbert (1970) *Five Lectures: Psychoanalysis, Politics, and Utopia*, UK: Allen Lane.

Marcuse, Herbert and Sherover-Marcuse, Erica (1979) *The Aesthetic Dimension: Toward a Critique of Marxist Aesthetics*, USA: Beacon Press.

Mede, Niels G.; Schäfer, Mike S.; Metag, Julia; and Klinger, Kira (2022) 'Who Supports Science-Related Populism? A Nationally Representative Survey on the Prevalence and Explanatory Factors of Populist Attitudes toward Science in Switzerland.' *PloS One*, vol. 17, no. 8, pp.1–20. https://doi.org/10.1371/journal.pone.0271204.t002

Meja, Volker and Stehr, Nico (1990) *Knowledge and Politics: The Sociology of Knowledge Dispute*, UK: Routledge.

Meng, Bingchun and Rantanen, Terhi (2015) 'A Change of Lens: A Call to Compare the Media in China and Russia', *Critical Studies in Media Communication*, vol. 32, no. 1, pp.1–15.
https://doi.org/10.1080/15295036.204.997831

Merton, Robert K. (1937) 'The Sociology of Knowledge', *Isis*, vol. 27, no. 3, pp.493–503. http://dx.doi.org/10.1086/347276

Merton, Robert K. (1938) 'Science, Technology and Society in Seventeenth Century England', in Sarton, George (ed.) *Osiris: Studies on the History and Philosophy of Science, and on the History of Learning and Culture*, Belgium: St. Catherine Press, pp.362–632.

Merton, Robert K. (1941) 'Karl Mannheim and the Sociology of Knowledge', *Journal of Liberal Religion*, vol. 2, pp.125–47.

Merton, Robert K. (1949) *Social Theory and Social Structure*, USA: Free Press.

Merton, Robert K. (1957) 'Karl Mannheim and the Sociology of Knowledge', in Merton, Robert K. (ed.) *Social Theory and Social Structure*, USA: Free Press, pp.489–508.

Merton, Robert K. (1968) *Social Theory and Social Structure* (1968 enlarged ed.) USA: Free Press.

Merton, Robert K. (1972) 'Insiders and Outsiders: A Chapter in the Sociology of Knowledge', *American Journal of Sociology*, vol. 78, no. 1, pp.9–47. https://doi.org/10.1086/225294

Merton, Robert K. (1973) *The Sociology of Science: Theoretical and Empirical Investigations*, USA: University of Chicago Press.

Merton, Robert K. (1994) *A Life of Learning (1994 Charles Homer Haskins Lecture)* USA: American Council of Learned Societies.

Merton, Robert K.; Fiske, Marjorie; and Curtis, Alberta (1946) *Mass Persuasion; The Social Psychology of a War Bond Drive*, USA: Harper & Brothers.

Merton, Robert K. and Lazarsfeld, Paul F. (1950) *Continuities in Social Research: Studies in the Scope and Method of 'The American Soldier'*, USA: Free Press.

Meyen, Michael (2015) *Fachgeschichte als Generationsgeschichte*. http://blexkom.halemverlag.de/fachgeschichte-als-generationsgeschichte

Morrison, David (1988) 'The Transference of Experience and the Impact of Ideas: Paul Lazarsfeld and Mass Communication Research', *Encyclopaedia of Communication*, vol. 10, pp.185–209.

Morrison, David E. (2008) 'Opportunity Structures and the Creation of Knowledge: Paul Lazarsfeld and the Politics of Research', in Park, David W. and Pooley, Jefferson (eds) *The History of Media and Communication Research*, USA: Peter Lang, pp.179–204.

Morrison, David (2022) 'Lazarsfeld's Legacy| Paul Lazarsfeld: Living in Circles and Talking Around Tables', *International Journal of Communication*, vol. 16, pp.616–25. https://ijoc.org/index.php/ijoc/article/view/18891/3664

Neun, Oliver; Kunze, Jan-Peter; and Mannheim, Karl (2018) *Karl Mannheim Schriften Zur Soziologie*, Germany: Springer Fachmedien Wiesbaden, pp.15–32. https://doi.org/10.1007/978-3-658-22120-1

Norris, Pippa and Inglehart, Ronald (2019) *Cultural Backlash: Trump, Brexit, and Authoritarian Populism*, UK: Cambridge University Press.

Oldfield, Sybil (2022) *The Black Book: The Britons on the Nazi Hit List*, UK: Profile Books.

Park, David W. and Pooley, Jefferson (2008) *The History of Media and Communications Research: Contested Memories*, USA: Peter Lang.

Perivolaropoulou, Nia (1992) 'Karl Mannheim et sa génération'. *Mil neuf cent. Revue d'histoire intellectuelle (Cahiers Georges Sorel)*, vol. 10, no. 1, pp.165–86.

Peters, John D. (1986) *Reconstructing Mass Communication Theory*, USA: Stanford University.

Philips, Susan U. (2001) 'Gender Ideology: Cross-cultural Aspects', in Smelser, Neil J. and Baltes, Paul B. (eds.) *International Encyclopedia of the Social & Behavioral Sciences*, UK: Pergamon, pp. 6016–20. https://doi.org/10.1016/B0-08-043076-7/03962-0

Pilcher, Jane (1994) 'Mannheim's Sociology of Generations: An Undervalued Legacy', *The British Journal of Sociology*, vol. 45, no. 3, pp.481–95.

Pooley, Jefferson (2007) 'Edward Shils' Turn against Karl Mannheim: The Central European Connection', *The American Sociologist*, vol. 38, no. 4, pp.364–82. https://doi.org/10.1007/s12108-007-9027-5

Pooley, Jefferson (2017) 'Wilbur Schramm and the "Four Founders" History of U.S. Communication Research', *Коммуникации. Медиа. Дизайн*, vol. 2, no. 4, pp.5–16. http://dx.doi.org/10.17613/M6Q859

Pooley, Jefferson and Katz, Elihu (2008) 'Further Notes on Why American Sociology Abandoned Mass Communication Research', *Journal of Communication*, vol. 58, no. 4, pp.767–86. https://doi.org/10.1111/j.1460-2466.2008.00413.x

Popper, Karl (1957/2002) *The Poverty of Historicism* (2nd ed.), UK: Taylor & Francis Group.

Purhonen, Semi (2016) 'Generations on Paper: Bourdieu and the Critique of "Generationalism"', *Social Science Information*, vol. 55, no. 1, pp.94–114. https://doi.org/10.1177/0539018415608967

Rakow, Lana F. (2008) 'Feminist Historiography and the Field: Writing New Histories', in Park, David W. and Pooley, Jefferson (eds) *The History of Media and Communication Research: Contested Memories*, USA: Peter Lang, pp.113–39.

Rantanen, Terhi (2004) *The Media and Globalisation*, UK: Sage.

Remmling, Gunter W. (1961) 'Karl Mannheim: Revision of an Intellectual Portrait', *Social Forces*, vol. 40, no. 1, pp.23–30. https://doi.org/10.2307/2573467

Ricoeur, Paul (1986) *Lectures on Ideology and Utopia*, USA: Columbia University Press.

Rogers, Everett (1994) *A History of Communication Study: A Biographical Approach*, USA: Free Press.

Roskin, Michael (1974) 'From Pearl Harbor to Vietnam: Shifting Generational Paradigms and Foreign Policy'. *Political Science Quarterly*, vol. 89, no. 3, pp.563–88. https://doi.org/10.2307/2148454

Rutkoff, Peter M. and Scott, William B. (1986) *New School: A History of the New School for Social Research*, USA: Free Press.

Sagarin, Edward and Kelly, Robert J. (1969) 'Karl Mannheim and the Sociology of Knowledge', *Salmagundi*, no. 10/11, pp.292–302.

Salerno, Roger A. (1987) *Louis Wirth: A Bio-bibliography*, USA: Greenwood.

Sargent, Lyman T. (2008) 'Ideology and Utopia: Karl Mannheim and Paul Ricoeur', *Journal of Political Ideologies*, vol. 13, no. 3, pp.263–73. https://doi.org/10.1080/13569310802374479

Schramm, Wilbur (1957) 'Twenty Years of Journalism Research', *Public Opinion Quarterly*, vol. 21, no. 1, pp.91–107. https://doi.org/10.1086/266689

Schramm, Wilbur (1959) 'Comments on "The State of Communication Research"', *The Public Opinion Quarterly*, vol. 23, no. 1, pp.6–9. https://doi.org/10.1086/266841

Schramm, Wilbur (1963) 'Communication Research in the United States', in Schramm, Wilbur (ed.) *The Science of Human Communication*, USA: Basic Books, pp.1–16.

Schramm, Wilbur (1980) 'The Beginnings of Communication Study in the United States', *Annals of the International Communication Association*, vol. 4, no. 1, pp.73–82. https://doi.org/10.1080/23808985.1980.11923795

Schramm, Wilbur; Chaffee, Steven H.; and Rogers, Everett M. (1997) *The Beginnings of Communication Study in America: A Personal Memoir*, USA: Sage.

Schuman, Howard and Scott, Jacqueline (1989) 'Generations and Collective Memories', *American Sociological Review*, vol. 54, no. 3, pp.359–81. https://doi.org/10.2307/2095611

Shils, Edward (1974) '"Ideology and Utopia" by Karl Mannheim', *Daedalus*, vol. 103, no. 1, pp.83–89. http://www.jstor.org/stable/20024190

Shils, Edward (1975) *Center and Periphery: Essays in Macrosociology*, USA: University of Chicago Press.

Shils, Edward (1985) 'On the Eve: A Prospect in Retrospect', in Bulmer, Martin (ed.) *Essays on the History of British Sociological Research*, UK: Cambridge University Press, pp.165–78.

Shils, Edward (1995) 'Karl Mannheim', *The American Scholar*, vol. 64, no. 2, pp.221–35. http://www.jstor.org/stable/41212318

Sica, Alan (2010) 'Merton, Mannheim, and the Sociology of Knowledge', in Calhoun, Craig (ed.) *Robert K. Merton: Sociology of Science and Sociology as Science*, USA: Columbia University Press, pp.164–80.

Sills, David L. (1987) *Paul Lazarsfeld 1901–1976. A Biographical Memoir. National Academy of Sciences*. http://www.nasonline.org/publications /biographical-memoirs/memoir-pdfs/lazarsfeld-paul-f.pdf

Simonson, Peter (2010) *Refiguring Mass Communication: A History*, USA: University of Illinois Press.

Simonson, Peter; Morooka, Junya; Xiong, Bingjuan; and Bedsole, Nathan (2019) 'The Beginnings of Mass Communication: A Transnational History', *Journal of Communication*, vol. 69, no. 5, pp.513–38. https://doi.org/10.1093/joc/jqz027

Simonson, Peter and Park, David W. (2016) *The International History of Communication Study*, USA: Routledge.

Simonson, Peter; Peck, Janice.; Craig, Robert T.; and Jackson, John (2012) (eds) *The Handbook of Communication History*, UK: Taylor & Francis Group.

Simonson, Peter and Weimann, Gabriel (2003) 'Critical Research at Columbia', in Katz, Elihu; Peters, John Durham; Liebes, Tamar; and Orloff, Avril (eds) *Canonic Texts in Media Research*, UK: Polity, pp.12–38.

Simpson, Christopher (1994) *Science of Coercion: Communication Research and Psychological Warfare, 1945–1960*, USA: Oxford University Press.

Smith, Dennis (1988) *The Chicago School: A Liberal Critique of Capitalism*, UK: Macmillan Education.

Solzhenitsyn, Alexandr (1973) *The Gulag Archipelago*, USA: Harper & Row.

Speier, Hans (1989) *The Truth in Hell and Other Essays on Politics and Culture, 1935–1987*, USA: Oxford University Press.

Sproule, J. Michael (1997) *Propaganda and Democracy: The American Experience of Media and Mass Persuasion*, UK: Cambridge University Press.

Sproule, J. Michael (2008) '"Communication": From Concept to Field to Discipline', in Park, David W. and Pooley, Jefferson (eds) *The History of Media and Communication Research: Contested Memories*, USA: Peter Lang, pp.163–78.

Steele, Brent J. (2012) 'Never Trust Anyone Who Remembers Jerry Rubin: The Promise of Generational Conflict', in Steele, Brent J. and Acuff, Jonathan M. (eds) *Theory and Application of the 'Generation' in International Relations and Politics*, USA: Palgrave Macmillan, pp.25–46.

Steele, Brent J. and Acuff, Jonathan M. (2012) *Theory and Application of the 'Generation' in International Relations and Politics*, USA: Palgrave Macmillan.

Thompson, John B. (1991) *Ideology and Modern Culture: Critical Social Theory in the Era of Mass Communication*, Polity Press.

Timonen, Virpi and Conlon, Catherine (2015) 'Beyond Mannheim: Conceptualising How People "Talk" and "Do" Generations in Contemporary Society', *Advances in Life Course Research*, vol. 24, June, pp.1–9.

Tomlinson, John (1999) *Globalization and Culture*, USA: University of Chicago Press.

Vogt, Kristoffer C. (2016) 'The Post-industrial Society: From Utopia to Ideology', *Work, Employment & Society*, vol. 30, no. 2, pp.366–76. https://www.jstor.org/stable/26655576

Wahl-Jorgensen, Karin (2004) 'How Not to Found a Field: New Evidence on the Origins of Mass Communication Research', *Journal of Communication*, vol. 54, no. 3, pp.547–64. https://doi.org/10.1111/j.1460-2466.2004.tb02644.x

Wallerstein, Immanuel (1986) 'Marxisms as Utopias: Evolving Ideologies', *American Journal of Sociology*, vol. 91, no. 6, pp.1295–308. https://doi.org/10.1086/228422

Weidlinger, Tom (2019) *The Restless Hungarian: Modernism, Madness, and The American Dream*, USA: SparksPress.

Whitty, Geoff (2004) 'Mannheim, Karl [Károly] (1893–1947)'. *Oxford Dictionary of National Biography*. https://doi.org/10.1093/ref:odnb/53147.

Wirth, Louis (1936) 'Preface', in Mannheim, Karl *Ideology and Utopia. An Introduction to the Sociology of Knowledge.* Translated by Louis Wirth and Edward Shils, UK: Routledge & Kegan Paul, pp.xi–xii.

Wirth Marvick, Elizabeth (1979) *Psychopolitical Analysis. Selected Writings of Nathan Leites*, USA: SAGE.

Woldring, Henk E.S. (1986) *Karl Mannheim. The development of his thought: Philosophy, sociology and social ethics, With a detailed biography,* New York: St Martin's Press.

Wolff, Kurt H. (1971/1993) *From Karl Mannheim*, USA: Transaction.

Xu, Bin (2019) 'Intragenerational Variations in Autobiographical Memory: China's "Sent-Down Youth" Generation', *Social Psychology Quarterly*, vol. 82, no. 2, pp.134–57. https://doi.org/10.1177/0190272519840641

Ylä-Anttila, Tuukka (2018) 'Populist Knowledge: "Post-truth" Repertoires of Contesting Epistemic Authorities', *European Journal of Cultural and Political Sociology*, vol. 5, no. 4, pp.356–88. https://doi.org/10.1080/2325423.2017.1414620

2. Harold D. Lasswell: propaganda research from the 1920s to the 1950s

Safe Colleague
Amiable,
Respectful:
And
No
Intellectual.

Lasswell's poem (no date)[1]

Harold D. Lasswell (1902–1979) was a world-renowned political scientist and a founder of comparative communications. Too young to fight in World War I and too old in World War II, nevertheless Lasswell showed in his consultancy roles, during and after World War II, the importance of studying war propaganda and later other types of propaganda and then communication in general. As he evolved from a young idealist to an ideologist, he saw no tension in being both an independent academic and a loyal servant of his country and its government. His life story offers interesting material for analysis of an academic career, but also of the usefulness of Mannheim's concepts of ideology and utopia, of generation and of Merton's Insider/Outsider position. I argue that Lasswell was an intergenerational figure whose work sheds light on relationships between generations and on conflict, and the avoidance of conflict, between them. He shifted his focus from utopias to ideologies, from political science to policy science, but never faltered in his belief that communism was the enemy. He started as an Outsider, but eventually became an Insider in academia and in policymaking. Lasswell's devotion and dedication were tested in the early 1950s, the McCarthy period, when he had to provide evidence that he was not a communist himself, because his studies of communism had aroused suspicion.

It is important to remember that white, American-born men with elite educations or with elite jobs (such as Lasswell) were not the most obvious Outsiders in the way, for example, women or people of colour were. But we

How to cite this book chapter:

Rantanen, Terhi (2024) *Dead Men's Propaganda: Ideology and Utopia in Comparative Communications Studies*, London: LSE Press, pp. 49–83.
https://doi.org/10.31389/lsepress.wmf.b. License: CC BY-NC 4.0

should also remember that Lasswell may have carried a secret during the time when the American Psychiatric Association, in 1952, diagnosed homosexuality as a sociopathic personality disturbance. A year later President Eisenhower signed an executive order banning homosexuals, as a potential security risk, from working for the federal government (Gross 1993; Johnson 2004). My research into Lasswell's life encountered no conclusive evidence, only persistent contemporary rumours, of his sexuality. But if Lasswell was homosexual, and if this had become known, it would have made him an Outsider not only in academia but also in US society as a whole. However, as Kirchick (2022, p.16) argues, sexual orientation is a secret history, *ad usum Delphini*, that requires 'reading between the lines' of any documents found. The documents I have studied reveal, even without reading between lines, close friendships between men and a range of relationships with them, some of which may have been sexual. Letters that often went through secretaries unsurprisingly made no reference to sexual orientation. However, as Nardi wrote, 'middle-class men only become heterosexuals when they define themselves and organized their affective and physical relations to exclude any sentiments or behavior that might be marked as homosexual' (1999, p.31).

This chapter is divided into two parts, in accordance with the interplay of utopias and ideologies in each of the two most distinctive intellectual periods of Lasswell's life, which I define as (1) the academic period of progressive internationalism (1918–1938) and (2) the policy science period of pragmatism and promotion of US interests (1939–early 1970s). Lasswell spent the first period mainly in Chicago and in Europe, while during the second he was based mainly in Washington, New York and New Haven. The first period ended with a time of uncertainty, when Lasswell was in danger of losing his academic career. During both periods he was influenced by and contributed to different ideologies and utopias. The more of an Insider Lasswell became, the less we see him to be preoccupied with utopias.

Although earlier work has examined Lasswell's career (see, for example, Almond 1987; Dunn 2019; Gary 1999; Rogers 1994; Rogow 1969; Rosten 1971; Torgerson 2019a), very little has considered his importance as a pioneer in comparative communications studies. This chapter thus concentrates particularly on his comparative communications studies, which I define as 'those where researchers or research teams with diverse cultural, practical and academic skills, and possibly in different locations, use specifically defined theories, concepts and/or methods to analyse materials/data concerning communications' (see Chapter 1). Lasswell fitted into all those categories, although his theorising of comparative communications primarily involved the concept of propaganda.

2.1 The academic period of progressive internationalism

Analysis of Lasswell's early development shows a sharp difference between how he was raised and how his university studies changed his thinking. He was born in 1902 in Donnellson, a town of 300 people in Illinois, the son of a Presbyterian minister, Linden D. Lasswell (1868–1943), and a teacher, Anna Prather Lasswell (1868–1943) (Almond 1987, p.249), both well educated (Perry 1982, p.280). Lasswell was a 'psychological only child', using his own expression, because his older brother had died when he was five years old. Lasswell felt a loner and an Outsider at school because he was poor at sports and smaller and younger than most of his classmates (Perry 1982, p.280). The family lived in a number of small towns in Illinois.[2] His highly religious and teetotal parents had very little money and he supported them financially throughout his working career. Lasswell, who never married, cared for his parents for the rest of their lives, but he left behind their religion and their ideology, as he did their lifestyle.

Lasswell came to be known for his 'essential demand of privacy and abstinence of deep emotional entanglements in their customary forms, particularly marriage and family' (Caldwell 1979, p.47), and as a 'kind of secretive', a 'very private' but 'very elegant man'. He owned 'an elegant apartment, with Persian rugs on the floor and original oil paintings on the walls and Louis XVI chairs' at One University Place in New York, to which he rarely invited friends. Lasswell was also known for his love of dining in style and of good whiskies 'he imbibed exceptionally well' (Eulau 1979, pp.88–89; see also Rosten 1991, p.279). The only known influences on Lasswell's childhood other than that of his parents were those of another relative and of his schooling. During the summers of 1916 and 1917 he visited his uncle, a medical doctor, in Indiana and learned among other things about the work of Sigmund Freud (1856–1939) (Freedman 1981, p.104). By the time Lasswell went to college, he already knew some of Freud's work in German (Perry 1982, p.280; Rosten 1971, p.79). He is also known to have become familiar with Karl Marx's (1818–1883) writing when he was still at high school (Almond 1987, p.250).

So, how does a young Outsider become an Insider? If one is lucky, having an influential mentor opens many doors. At the very early age of 16, in 1918, Lasswell, after graduating from high school as an outstanding student and receiving a scholarship, started his studies at the University of Chicago (Perry 1982, p.280). (Figure 2.1 was taken while he was in Chicago.) In 1922 he became a graduate student under the tutelage of Charles E. Merriam (1874–1953, pictured in Figure 2.2), who chaired the Department of Political Science from 1923 to 1940 (Heaney and Hansen 2006, p.589). Lasswell was one of several young recruits in the department, but was clearly Merriam's particular *protégé* (Sproule 1997, pp.69–70) and favourite (Perry 1982, p.280). It has even been argued that Merriam built his kind of political science for people like Lasswell (Seidelman and Harpham 1985, p.133).

As a student Lasswell worked as a teaching and research assistant for Merriam, who became not only his mentor but also his friend. The correspondence between Merriam and Lasswell was intense and lasted for several decades. They called each other in their correspondence 'Dear Chief' (Merriam) and 'My dear Doctor' or 'Judge' (Lasswell)[3] and saw each other regularly during those years, both in their professional roles and privately. Their

Figure 2.1: Harold D. Lasswell, 1935

Source: University of Chicago Photographic Archive, apf1-03681, Hanna Holborn Gray
Special Collections Research Center, University of Chicago Library.
http://photoarchive.lib.uchicago.edu/db.xqy?one=apf1-03681.xml
Notes: The photo was taken in 1935 when Lasswell was assistant professor of political
science at the University of Chicago (1922–1938).

Figure 2.2: Charles E. Merriam

Source: University of Chicago Photographic Archive, apf1-04419, Hanna Holborn Gray
Special Collections Research Center, University of Chicago Library.
http://photoarchive.lib.uchicago.edu/db.xqy?one=apf1-04419.xml
Notes: Photo undated, photographer J.E. Waters. Merriam was the Morton D. Hull distin-
guished service professor of political science and chairman of the Department of Political
Science at the University of Chicago. During World War I, Merriam was a captain in the
US Army Signal Corp, and served as commissioner for public information in Rome, Italy.

correspondence started with the young Lasswell's detailed letters from Europe to his supervisor in the 1920s and ended with an equal relationship between two professionals who also clearly enjoyed each other's company outside work. Merriam opened many doors to the young Lasswell by writing letters of introduction and recommendation and by recommending him for different jobs.

Lasswell's first book chapter was co-authored with Merriam and came out in 1924 (Merriam and Lasswell 1924) and they went on to work together on many occasions throughout the 1920s and 1930s in the US, Europe and Russia.[4] Merriam was a very well-connected man with networks inside and outside academia. In addition to his many academic roles, Merriam was a policy scientist *par excellence*, serving on various committees from the Hoover to the Roosevelt administrations and was a central figure in US political science (Berndtson 1987, pp.91–92; Seidelman and Harpham 1985, p.101). Merriam's (1919) own experience of working in 1917–1918 in Rome as a propagandist for the American High Commissioner for Public Information contributed to Lasswell's interest in propaganda research (Smith 1969, pp.53–55) and Merriam offered Lasswell a job as an instructor in his academic department in 1924.[5]

Lasswell, according to his own account, was influenced during his college years by Merriam, George Herbert Mead (1863–1931) and John Dewey (1859–1952) and later at LSE by Graham Wallas (1858–1932).[6] During his studies he became interested in symbolic interactionism, and especially in the role of symbols as a binding factor in societies, which later led into studying communication (Littlejohn 1978, p.55). The Chicago School of Political Science in the 1920s and 1930s was known for advancing a new, empirical 'science of politics' that inspired Lasswell's trust in the social sciences' capacity to 'produce precise and useful knowledge' (Torgerson 2019a, p.122). Later Lasswell was remembered to have continuously cited Mannheim,[7] with whom Lasswell shared an interest in elites (Chapter 5). Politically, Lasswell was a lifelong Democrat (Farr, Hacker and Kazee 2008, p.28).

In this way, the son of a preacher man and a teacher turned into a promising young academic thanks to an influential mentor whose connections were able to open many doors. It all looked very good for the young Lasswell, but he was still dependent on the relationship with Merriam. It was time to leave Chicago to complete his education abroad.

Propaganda studies

Even as late as the 1930s, the Chicago School (including political science and sociology) was much influenced by German academics. Edward Shils[8] (1910–1995), for example, recalled (1995, pp.223–34) attending a class on several mornings each week given by Wirth (1897–1952), the translator of Mannheim's *Ideologie und Utopie*, on the history of German sociology. Shils (1995, p.225) also met Hans Speier[9] (1905–1990), who had emigrated from Germany to the US in 1933 and would become one of Lasswell's future collaborators, as discussed in Chapters 4 and 5.

Many US social scientists, among them some of Lasswell's teachers at the University of Chicago including Merriam (Karl 1974, pp.37–38), had traditionally gone to Germany to study. Merriam had encouraged Lasswell to go to Europe to collect materials for his PhD, personally guaranteeing a loan to finance his travel.[10] Lasswell not only went to Germany; in the 1920s he also visited Geneva, Vienna, Paris and London, as well as Berlin – some of these cities several times. He first went to Geneva in 1923, where he observed sessions at the League of Nations. In a letter to Merriam, he analysed its weaknesses and concluded that (referring to the Treaty of Versailles):

> the isolationism of the U.S. is humiliating to an American ... unless he admits that America would have made an ass of herself and supported the unqualified French thesis on its reparations.[11]

Lasswell's letters from this period in Geneva reveal his increasing criticism of the internationalism of the period. His time in London at LSE in 1923 had a more positive influence on him, especially in his policy science orientation, which had already been set at the University of Chicago. Little has hitherto been known about Lasswell's visit to London, mainly because when he left Chicago in 1938 and moved to Washington, DC, the vans carrying his effects were involved in an accident, destroying his professional and personal files. Some of his lost files created a small sensation when they were found after the crash, as reported by the *Chicago Daily Tribune* ('Solve Red Angle in Crash Death' 1938), since they included books by Marx and pamphlets about communism (Muth 1990, p.14).

The Yale University archival collection holds the letters Lasswell sent during his time in Europe to his parents, who kept them, and the University of Chicago Library collection has some of his letters to Merriam. He wrote to Merriam:

> I am having the most glorious time [in] England [that] I ever imagined to exist ... And the most impressive thing about the whole business is the extreme opinionation of the scholars. Take Laski, for instance. He has a formula to solve every international or national problem past present or prospective: or look at Wallas, who is outfitted with an armor quite as complete, though not quite as obvious.[12]

He was a frequent writer, often sending three letters in a week to his parents, with detailed and vivid descriptions of his life as a 21-year-old PhD student experiencing London. Lasswell was clearly impressed by the Fabians and their policy research. He was excited about meeting Sidney (1859–1947) and Beatrice Webb (1858–1943) in October 1923 and wrote to his parents:

> I have had the pleasure of meeting the Webbs ... Sidney Webb has for thirty years been turning out books on public administration,

the history of trade unionism, socialism; organized the Fabian Society for the study of social questions, exercised a powerful initiative in the organization of the London School of Economics and Political Science; accepted the responsibility for the political tactics of Labour and had the cooperation of a wife who is in every respect his equal. Most of their books are joint productions. And they have cooperated on any number of government reports … blue books. I think it was H. G. Wells (1866–1946) who remarked that theirs was a very fruitful marriage in blue books.[13]

While at LSE, Lasswell attended a lecture by Bertrand Russell (1872–1970), which made him conclude that 'science must be captured by men of good will', spent an evening at the 'Nursery, of younger elements of the Fabian Society', met with Laski, and attended lectures given by George Bernard Shaw (1856–1950) and Graham Wallas (1858–1932).[14] He was also much impressed by his fellow students, describing them as:

definitely in training for some branch of the public service, Consuls, diplomats, M.P.s [Members of Parliament] and the like are on exhibit and in transit in various stages of embryological evolution.[15]

He was equally impressed by the number of foreign students at the School. Lasswell spent only one term at LSE and regretted that he could not stay longer[16] (Rantanen 2020). He was clearly influenced by LSE thinking, whereby social science was there to help societies flourish and understand the causes of things (LSE's motto is 'rerum cognoscere causas') for the betterment of society.

In London, Lasswell learned about the power of the international mass media and about the European news agency cartel (more in Chapter 3) – curiously from a Foreign Office civil servant. This was new to him. He wrote to his parents, warning about the confidentiality of his information.[17] (Here is one of the early connections with Kent Cooper's career, much of which was devoted to trying to improve the AP's position within the cartel, discussed in Chapter 3.)

You may have noticed that since the war the great news collecting associations have by contract divided the world into zones, and have arranged to interchange news from zone to zone. Thus the great English agency is Reuters, the French is Havas, the German is Wolff, and the largest American is Associated Press … The wireless is now being used unceasingly as an agent of information and obfuscation.

Lasswell considered the limitations affecting the news, including issues of accuracy, unconscious bias, and how all the relevant facts about a situation were never known. The information he acquired about European news found its way into his PhD thesis, where he specifically referred to Reuters (see Lasswell 1927, pp.3, 80). After leaving LSE, Lasswell continued his research in

Paris, where he collected most of the materials for his PhD. At the age of 24, in 1926, he was awarded his PhD by the University of Chicago (Freedman 1981, p.104). His dissertation was published in 1927 as *Propaganda Technique in the World War* (Lasswell 1927), and he rapidly became a leading expert in the US on war propaganda, which then led him to develop the research methodology of content analysis. The times he spent at Chicago and in Europe were Lasswell's formative years of preparation for his professional future. His interest in propaganda and communication and in policy science all originated from the time at Chicago and from his travels in Europe. However, one element is still missing: psychoanalysis.

The combination of symbols and propaganda

Lasswell had found his topic, propaganda, but had not yet found *how* to study it. Sigmund Freud was to become a major influence for him and he later called these years his *Wanderjahre* in Europe, highly praising Wallas at LSE and the thinkers around Henri Bergson (1859–1941), as well as Freud (Lerner 1968, p.406). In 1928, in Vienna, he met Anna Freud (1895–1982), Sigmund Freud's daughter.[18] Lasswell had been granted a postdoctoral fellowship by the Social Science Research Council (SSRC)[19] for 1927–1928 and spent most of that year in Berlin, where he was briefly psychoanalysed by Theodor Reik (1888–1969), a student of Freud, and became interested in psychoanalysis as a method of studying politics (Rosten 1991, p.281).[20] In Berlin, in 1929 he also spent time with Harry Stack Sullivan (1892–1949), a psychiatrist and psychoanalyst, who struggled with prejudice against homosexuals both in his professional and private life (Wake 2008, p.151). Lasswell had known Sullivan since 1926, when he had suggested a meeting between himself, Merriam and Edward Sapir (1884–1939), a notable anthropologist and linguist (Perry 1982, p.280).

Lasswell's interest in psychoanalysis was pioneering in his field, and was later shared by, for example, Adorno and Horkheimer. The first publication of the authoritarian personality research of the Frankfurt School, *Studien über Autorität und Familie* (*Studies on Authority and the Family*), came out in 1936 (Institut für Sozialforschung 1936), while *The Authoritarian Personality* (1950) by Adorno, Else Frenkel-Brunswik (1908–1958), Daniel Levinson (1920–1994) and Nevitt Sanford (1909–1995) appeared only in 1950 (Almond 1987, p.254). According to Dorzweiler (2015, pp.356–57), Horkheimer, Franz Neumann (1900–1954) and Lasswell all considered culture to be the body of symbols and practices employed by elites to maintain their social and political authority. The members of the Frankfurt School did not openly criticise Lasswell, despite their theoretical and methodological differences, and even published an article from him (Lasswell 1935a) in their *Zeitschrift* in 1935 (Dorzweiler 2015, pp.353, 363). As Dorzweiler (2015, p.371) concluded, 'throughout the 1930s and early 1940s Lasswell, Horkheimer and Neumann not only supported each other's work but also shared areas of interest, most notably the politics of culture'.

In 1928, at the age of 26, Lasswell was invited to speak before the Vienna Psychoanalytic Society, in which Freud and his colleagues participated. He delivered a paper entitled: 'Can We Distinguish Different Types among Our Politicians and Is Their Taking Up Politics Conditioned by Certain Definite Factors in Themselves?' (Freedman 1981, p.104). In 1930, after his return from Europe, he published his book *Psychopathology and Politics* (Lasswell 1930). It is a remarkable book in which Lasswell analysed life stories of politicians, including their sexuality, and divided them into different types. It remains a pioneering work in its methodology and materials, even if one does not agree with its conclusions. As Lasswell (1938, p.37) himself puts it, 'the many disasters of World War I had led the political scientist to the door of the psychiatrists' (quoted by Herman 1995, p.24). According to Gabriel Almond[21] (1911–2002) (1987, p.254), the book was 'the first relatively systematic, empirical study of the psychological aspects of political behavior'. Gary wrote that 'Lasswell's students (Almond was one of them) and contemporaries contend that Lasswell fundamentally challenged conventional political science with his distinctive uses of behavioralism and Freudian theory' (1999, pp.67, 69).

Lasswell's interest in psychoanalysis was also reflected in his study of symbols. In his early work on propaganda, he was interested in hidden, 'latent' meaning in the same way that Freudian psychoanalysts are interested in hidden meanings in speech. He defined propaganda as a 'technique', a 'manipulation of collective attitudes by the use of significant symbols (words, pictures, tunes) rather than violence, bribery or boycott' (Lasswell 1935b, p.189). His goal was to reveal both facts and the hidden aspects of propaganda through the study of symbols. He was inquiring into not only what was being said but also what was *not* said when symbols were used. Lasswell was influenced by the Freudian concept of a symbol, famously defined in Freud's (Freud and Strachey 1899/1954) analysis of dreams, originally published in 1899, as revealing its true meaning to the extent that 'the compared term will disappear' (Jones no date). In this way, Lasswell became interested in the relationship between the symbols used in propaganda, for example in relation to communism (Lasswell and Blumenstock 1938; 1939) and to fascism (Lasswell 1933). Lasswell's co-author of studies of communist propaganda published in the late 1930s, Dorothy Blumenstock Jones (1911–1980), was his student at the University of Chicago and during World War II became the chief of the Motion Picture Analysis Division of the Office of War Information (OWI). Blumenstock is one of the forgotten women in communication research (Varão 2021).

Thus Lasswell's early work leans on European research traditions and had not yet been influenced by the rising popularity, notably in the 1950s, of behaviourism (Berndtson 1997). His approach to studying propaganda was very different from the well-known Lasswellian slogan 'who says what in which channel, to whom, with what effect?' (Lasswell 1948, p.37) for which Lasswell is best known in communication studies. This model of communication, published after World War II implies a one-way flow of influence with no feedback and no room for recipient interpretation that concentrates on manifest, rather than latent, content. The European influence on Lasswell's early work was significant and it was inspirational when he started developing content analysis. Lasswell also showed an early interest in qualitative and later in quantitative (for more on which, see Chapter 4) research. His article, entitled 'Prussian Schoolbook and International Amity', was an early example of content analysis, where he sought 'in every case to indicate by some quantitative measurement the importance of the item to which reference is made' (Lasswell 1925a, p.718). He also published in 1925 'The Status of Research on International Propaganda and Opinion' (Lasswell 1925b). Both articles reflect his interest in what would become established as communication research. He chose here a new topic, propaganda, which would later lead him to become interested in studying communication more generally. Lasswell was not alone in his interest in studying propaganda. As Torgerson (2019b, p.232) observes:

> the advent of propaganda and its dramatic rise during WW1 caused a disillusionment among post-war progressives in the 1920s with the notion of 'the public', as seen in Lippmann's *Public Opinion* (1922) and *The Phantom Public* (1925). Citing Lippmann among others, Lasswell framed his *Propaganda Technique in the World War* (1927) explicitly in terms of this disillusionment, writing that: 'The whole discussion about the ways and means of controlling public opinion testifies to the collapse of a traditional species of democratic romanticism and to the rise of a dictatorial habit of mind'. (Lasswell 1927, p.4)

Lasswell, like many of his contemporaries, had lost his optimistic, utopian belief that the public was able to resist propaganda. In his doctoral thesis of 1927, he notes his almost exclusive reliance on American, British, French and German experience. He writes that:

> this study is a preliminary and highly provisional analysis of the group of propaganda problems connected with the control of international antipathies and attractions in wartime. How may hate be mobilized against an enemy? How may the enemy be demoralized by astute manipulation? How is it possible to cement the friendship of neutral and allied peoples? (Lasswell 1927, p.12)

He also paid attention to the role of the press and of news, which again connects him with Cooper's work (see Chapter 3). Lasswell (1927, p.80) wrote:

> the Germans were aghast at the efficiency of Allied propaganda and they undertook to steel their people against it by protesting

loudly against the official French and British Press and Press services. Rudolf Rotheit (1919) declared that one of the conditions of peace must be the emancipation of the World Press from the clutches of enemy telegraphic agencies. Even the schools had such copying exercises as 'Reuter's Agency, the fabricator of War lies' ... The Germans took Northcliffe as the symbol of the British Press and poured vials of abuse on his head.[22]

Lasswell pioneered the empirical study of the concept of propaganda. He was among the first not only to collect empirical materials but also to analyse them – in the beginning entirely qualitatively: there was no methodology or theory in the largely descriptive thesis. He noticed that:

> actual propaganda, wherever studied, has a large element of the fake in it. This varies from putting a false date line on a despatch, through the printing of unverified rumours, the printing of denials in order to convey an insinuation, to the 'staging of events'. (1927, p.206)

He also emphasised the totality of propaganda – how it appeals to all sectors of society:

> Effective propaganda is catholic in its appeal. It ignores no loyalty inside a nation. Protestants, Catholics, Jews, workers, financiers, farmers, merchants, city dwellers, and rural elites, sportsmen and philosophers, men of affairs and academicians, women and men, old and young; every possible line of cleavage in the nation is appealed to by some direct or indirect device. (Lasswell 1927, p.201)

He wrote about the role of the press in propaganda, how everybody becomes involved, how difficult propaganda is to resist, and how all are drawn into it whatever their educational background or status.

> A literate world, a reading world, a schooled world prefers to thrive on argument and news. It is sophisticated to the extent of using print; and he that takes to print shall live or perish by the Press. All the apparatus of diffused erudition popularizes the symbols and forms of pseudo-rational appeal; the wolf of propaganda does not hesitate to masquerade in the sheepskin. All the voluble men of the day – writers, reporters, editors, preachers, lecturers, teachers, politicians – are drawn into the service of propaganda to amplify a master voice. All is conducted with the decorum and the trapper of intelligence, for this is a rational epoch, and demands its raw meat cooked and garnished by adroit and skilful chefs. (Lasswell 1927, p.221)

Lasswell later criticised his own thesis, calling it 'an essay in technique', where:

> we are not informed whether the author actually read or glanced
> through all the copies of the principal mass-circulation newspapers,
> periodicals, books and pamphlets of Germany and other countries;
> or whether he read British, French and American materials as fully
> as German. (1949, p.42)

Despite this self-criticism, Lasswell rapidly became a leading expert on propaganda. His course on public opinion and propaganda at the University of Chicago in 1926–1927[23] was probably the first ever taught on this topic (Rogers 1994, p.215). In Lasswell's (1933, p.521) view, propaganda in its broadest sense is the technique of influencing human action by the manipulation of representations. He later writes that:

> every government on the globe, whether despotism or democracy,
> whether at war or at peace, relies upon propaganda—more or less
> efficiently harmonized with strategy, diplomacy, and economics—
> to accomplish its ends. (Lasswell, Smith and Casey 1946, p.1)

Ascher and Hirschfelder-Ascher (2003, p.62) note that for Lasswell propaganda was neither intrinsically good or bad but an instrument of persuasion that could be used for positive or negative causes. They emphasise the importance of the concept of symbol and its power in Lasswell's thinking not only as an instrument but also as a marker of continuity with changing meanings and associations (Ascher and Hirschfelder-Ascher 2003, p.61). Lasswell's definition of propaganda was broad enough to pave the way for the conceptualising and study of what came to be known as mass communication, but there was still a strong link to political science because of the role of governments in disseminating propaganda.

The period of early propaganda studies witnessed a radical change in relation to the previous period: the concepts of propaganda and, indirectly, of communication (as news influencing public opinion) were introduced. What had earlier been seen only as foreign, in both meanings of the word, came increasingly to be viewed as different, suspicious and even dangerous. But the concept of propaganda was defined and seen in relation to earlier concepts such as those of public opinion and of news. All this together fertilised further research and indirectly, and often subconsciously, emphasised the importance of the study of communication.

The 1930s was a particularly interesting and exciting period at Chicago, when class and class conflict were the dominating issues. Almond, one of Lasswell's doctoral students, recalls:

> hearing the class-struggle analysis of Communists, Trotskyites and
> socialists on the University of Chicago campus, in the Reynolds

Club, on open-air demonstrations and in graduate seminars led by
Merriam, Lasswell, Harold Gosnell [1896–1997], Frederick Schuman [1904–1981] and others, where students were exposed to the
ideas of Marx, Freud, Max Weber [1864–1920], Vilfredo Pareto
[1848–1923], Gaetano Mosca [1858–1941], and Roberto Michels
[1876–1936]. (Almond 1998, pp.xx–xxi)

But Almond emphasises that 'ideas were brought down to earth in *American* accents and tested against *American* experience' (Almond 1998, pp.xx–
xxi, emphasis added). Gary adds Mannheim to the list of academics who
had influence on Lasswell's thinking, but also emphasises the importance of
Pareto in relation to 'political symbolism, ideology, power, myth and the sociology and psychology of the ruling classes' (Gary 1999, p.70).

Lasswell fitted well in this environment and began to gain celebrity as an
instructor and assistant professor. Leo Rosten (1908–1997) wrote about his
memories of Lasswell as a teacher, later as his mentor and friend (Rosten
1971, p.284), in 1927:

I thought him a bit of a freak: pedantic, verbose, and quite ill at ease.
He wore his hair in a short, stiff, Prussian cut, and his knowledge
in a high, stiff, abrasive manner. He was only twenty-five, and he
lectured us desperately, with a glazed stare into space, unaware of
whether we understood him and unconcerned what we might be
thinking. (Rosten 1971, p.274)

Through his studies in the US and in Europe, as well as through his mentors
and teachers, he was deeply influenced by European academic thinking. A
former student of Lasswell described him in the following way:

He was an assistant professor, not much more than a graduate student himself, and he had many young men and women around the
University who were attracted by his brilliance; by his willingness to
listen to them; and by the boldness of his imagination.[24]

Lasswell's departure from the University of Chicago

In the 1930s Lasswell continued to combine psychoanalysis with the study
of politics (see, for example, Lasswell 1930; 1931; 1935c), while also further
developing ways to study the content of propaganda. In 1938 he left the University of Chicago for reasons Almond (1987, p.260) describes as 'push and
pull' and Rogers (1994, p.216) as 'Lasswell's midlife crisis'. It is difficult to find
archival evidence of the reasons why Lasswell left Chicago. Rosten (1991,
p.284) writes that Robert Hutchins (1899–1977), president of the University of
Chicago, 'let it be known' that neither Lasswell nor Gosnell, another protégé
of Merriam, could hope for promotion. Schramm, Chaffee and Rogers (1997,

p.29) write that the main reason may have been that Lasswell had been denied promotion to full professor, what was known as the Chicago School having come to an end as a cross-disciplinary experiment in 1931 (Dunn 2019, p.17) but Rogers (1994, p.217) argues that Lasswell had been treated well at Chicago, earning $4,500 a year, and was tenured. Another reason possibly was that Lasswell wanted to pursue his interest in psychiatry at the Washington School of Psychiatry, co-founded by Sullivan in 1936, to collaborate with him and Sapir; however, he failed to do so (Gary 1999, p.82; Muth 1990, p.14; Rogers 1994, p.217) 'for a variety of reasons' including Sapir's death, or falling out with Sullivan, and financial support being cancelled (Perry 1982, p.356; Rogers 1994, p.218). Yet another plausible reason concerned a possible decline in support for his own career and projects, with Merriam's approaching retirement in 1940 and the university's decreasing interest in empirical research.

A fourth possible reason may have been that the university had come under attack by Charles R. Walgreen (1873–1939), head of a national chain of drugstores, who caused his niece to withdraw as a student at the University of Chicago and in 1934 wrote a letter criticising the institution for its 'communistic' influence ('C.R. Walgreen Takes Niece From College' 1935). In 1935 a committee of the Illinois State Legislature investigated alleged communism at the University of Chicago (Bell 1949). The result was that the University of Chicago was cleared, even by Walgreen. Lasswell was not mentioned in the course of investigation, but the formal investigation was preceded by a pamphlet, 'How Red Is the University of Chicago', that included his name several times, referred to his lectures at the Workers School and to him being 'one of the red aiding and associating professors' (Hewitt 1935, pp.12, 88).

Although Lasswell was not personally criticised, the Walgreen incident signalled a change in how the university was seen in public discourse outside academia. His departure from Chicago marks a period in his life when he stopped publishing in political science. Lasswell's own obituary stated that 'from 1937 to 1950, not a single article of his was published in a political science journal because of resistance to his ideas' (Ennis 1978). However, Lasswell had many articles published in psychiatric journals, 'introducing psychiatrists to the interrelationship of psychiatry and the social science' (Ennis 1978). Lasswell's re-entry into political science took place in 1955, when he was elected president of the American Political Science Association (Ennis 1978). After a long time as an Outsider, his peers thus made him the ultimate Insider in his own field.

2.2 The policy science period of pragmatism to promote mainly US interests

Lasswell's new career started in Washington, working for the government in various consultancy roles and conducting research funded by private foundations. He became a policy scientist (Peters 1986, p.535), the term he himself later established, and his first known use of the term 'policy sciences' dates from 1943 in then unpublished personal memoranda (Lasswell 1943/2003; Torgerson 2019a, p.128). Lasswell's work during World War II at the Wartime Communications Research Unit at the Library of Congress and later with the Commission on Freedom of the Press was to change his career. In both roles, he deepened his knowledge about communication and became a policy scientist in that area. In this period he established connections with men who shared his ideas about propaganda, democracy and threats to democracy.

Lasswell became, from 1940 to 1943, director of the Experimental Division for the Study of Wartime Communications at the Library of Congress, funded, like many other wartime research projects, by the Rockefeller Foundation (see, for example, Gary 1999; Levyatan 2009; Nietzel 2016; Pooley 2019; Simpson 1994). As Gary (1999, p.89) has argued, wartime communications research is an example of collaboration among the academy, private foundations and the state. The Rockefeller Foundation coordinated several projects including Lasswell's. During the war, he directed an office that used content analysis to analyse propaganda. Almond writes:

> the Department of Justice set up a special war policies unit to help administer the Foreign Agents Registration Act and the Sedition Act. Both of these tasks involved content analysis of the media of communication: on the world scale, as the propaganda war heated up in 1939 and 1940, and on the domestic organizational scale, as Nazis and fascists infiltrated foreign language groups and media in the United States. Lasswell gave expert testimony in a number of trials under this legislation; he was also instrumental in the effort to have quantitative content analysis admitted as evidence in the federal courts. (Almond 1987, p.262)

For the first time, the content of war propaganda became a systematic object of study, analysed daily by a team of researchers. The need to know more in order to 'anticipate the enemy' (Lasswell 1949, p.48) fostered this research. It gave Lasswell an opportunity to experiment with and attempt to prove the usefulness of content analysis, which came to be seen not only as the method for analysing content but also as something that could predict the future (Lasswell 1949, pp.49–51). What was called public opinion analysis amounted in fact to analysing US newspaper coverage of certain topics, and then producing a quick internal analysis for decision-makers and analysts. Content analysis was used by trained staff who worked to a tight schedule, producing reports on a daily basis.[25]

This was not individual work but was carried out by a team consisting of men (and women in assisting roles) who later became leading academics in the field of political science or researchers working for the government, or both, often on Lasswell's recommendation (as detailed in more depth in

Chapters 4 and 5). Many of these had either known one another before, often from their time at the University of Chicago, or were émigrés with a European background whose names have been almost forgotten and whose role I analyse in these later chapters. They became lifelong friends and 'comrades in arms', united by their wartime experience, later calling themselves 'the old gang'.[26] Farr, Hacker and Kazee (2006, p.581, years added) included some of these, but not all, in their all-male list:

> The war-time chiefdom, most important, allowed Lasswell to draw around him a brilliant group of young policy-scientists-in-the-making, including [Daniel] Lerner [1917–1980], Abraham Kaplan [1918–1993], Bruce Lannes Smith [1909–1987], Heinz Eulau [1915–2004], Gabriel Almond, David Truman [1913–2003], Ithiel de Sola Pool [1917–1984], Nathan Leites, Edward Shils, Morris Janowitz [1919–1988], Irving Janis [1918–1990], and Sebastian de Grazia [1917–2000]. He and they collaborated with other intelligence specialists on duty in Washington, like Samuel Stouffer [1900–1960], Paul Lazarsfeld, Kurt Lewin [1890–1947], Bernard Berelson [1912–1979], Wilbur Schramm [1907–1987], Hans Speier [1905–1990], Carl Hovland [1912–1961], Hadley Cantril [1906–1969], and Ralph Casey [1890–1977]. As brought together by war, they defended democracy, advised decision-makers, analyzed policy, devised research, invented methods like content analysis, wrote quickly and at length under deadline, and created an interdisciplinary 'corps of scholars seasoned by responsibility' (Lasswell 1951b, p.133), who would invent communications research as a field and foment a behavioral revolution in the social sciences.

It is important to remember that the academics were not in charge – the military and civil servants were. This was not always a happy relationship, and there were also tensions between different departments.[27] Lasswell probably enjoyed some autonomy because his funding came from the Rockefeller Foundation, but his position in the organisation as a whole was not the most central. Many different governmental departments conducted research on different aspects of communication. The most important criterion was that the research should serve the interests of the US government in its goal of winning the war. His own ideology unsurprisingly now matched completely the US government's ideology.

The Commission on Freedom of the Press

Lasswell served between 1944 and 1947 as a member of the Commission on Freedom of the Press, also called the Hutchins Commission after its chair, Robert Hutchins (pictured with committee members in Figure 2.3), president

Figure 2.3: Robert Maynard Hutchins chairing a meeting of the Commission on Freedom of the Press ('The Hutchins Commission')

Source: University of Chicago Photographic Archive, apf1-13545, Hanna Holborn Gray Special Collections Research Center, University of Chicago Library. http://photoarchive.lib.uchicago.edu/db.xqy?one=apf1-13545.xml
Notes: Photo undated. Robert Maynard Hutchins (head of table, left), University of Chicago president (1929–1945) and chancellor (1945–1951), commission chairman. Commission members (from left): Arthur M. Schlesinger, professor of History at Harvard; Ruth A. Inglis, commission staff member; Robert Redfield, dean of the Division of Social Sciences; William E. Hocking, professor of philosophy emeritus at Harvard; Robert D. Leigh, commission director; Llewellyn White, commission assistant director; Zechariah Chafee, Jr., professor of law at Harvard and commission vice-chairman; Kurt Riezler, professor of philosophy at the New School for Social Research; Beardsley Ruml, chairman of the board of R.H. Macy and Company, Incorporated; Charles E. Merriam, professor of political science emeritus; George N. Shuster, president of Hunter College; Archibald MacLeish, former assistant secretary of state for public affairs.

of the University of Chicago, who formed the commission and invited Lasswell and Merriam to join it (see, for example, Blanchard 1977; McIntyre 1987). This membership gave Lasswell and Merriam another opportunity to work together, which they clearly enjoyed, also exchanging notes about the future agenda. Merriam was very clear about his goals, based, as he put it, on:

> my own personal experiences beginning as a printer's devil and through my observations and experiences in the area of metropolitan government, the politics and administration of Washington, and my observation of the relation of the social sciences to the techniques of communications.[28]

This highly educated group of men met 17 times and interviewed 58 witnesses. Their staff spoke to 225 others, while commission members and staff prepared 176 documents for review (Commission on Freedom of the Press 1947, pp.v–viii). The membership of this committee was again significant for Lasswell's career: as one member put it, it was 'the best club he had ever belonged to'.[29] This was although he was quite junior compared to its other members. It gave Lasswell an opportunity to define what he thought were the principles of a free press: (1) accuracy of observations and quotation; (2) disclosure of source: reporting facts enabling the audience to evaluate the competence and bias of the direct and quoted source; and (3) separation of fact and opinion.[30] Obviously, these principles were not invented by Lasswell, but they show his understanding of journalism.

The report concerned perceived threats to the freedom of the press and produced a new policy of accountability that was then reworked by Theodore (Ted) Peterson (1918–1997) into the US social responsibility theory (McIntyre 1987, p.137) as set out in *Four Theories of the Press* (Siebert, Peterson and Schramm 1956; see Chapter 6), while also having a link with Cooper's campaign on the freedom of news. Interestingly, the committee also had foreign advisers. It is difficult to separate the foreign from the domestic when the report (Commission on Freedom of the Press 1947) stated that 'the world seems to be on the brink of suicide' (p.99), and that an irresponsible press could bring about 'universal catastrophe' (p.4) and even the end 'of democracy and perhaps of civilization' (p.106) (quoted in Bates 2018, p.4791).

There was, again, an embedded comparative aspect to the report, because the commission also published a separate report on international communication, *Peoples Speaking to Peoples* by Llewellyn White (1899–1959) and Robert Devore Leigh (1890–1961) (White and Leigh 1946). A considerable amount of research for this report was done by interviewing officials in the mass-communications industries and in government. The research team also talked with hundreds of experts in the field of international communication, including heads of state, members of parliament, officials, and top executives of major news agencies, newspapers, and other media companies, both in the US and abroad (White and Leigh 1946, p.115), including Kent Cooper (see Chapter 3). The report recommended, in relation to the role of the US and its citizens in international communication, that:

> (1) The government and the people of the U.S. should recognize the importance of a mutual understanding, as between peoples, of each other's true character and purposes and should be prepared not only to communicate to others as truthful and comprehensive account of our national life and purposes but to receive and to circulate in the same spirit reciprocal communication with regard to other nations and people. (White and Leigh 1946, p.vi)

The commission made a number of recommendations, including the creation of an autonomous unit in the US Economic and Social Council, and coordinated closely with UNESCO and with the Commission on Human Rights to 'promote the free flow of true information and the removal of artificial barriers restricting such free flow' (White and Leigh 1946, p.109), thus emphasising the role of international and intergovernmental organisations.

Thus, during the war years, Lasswell himself became a policy scientist in communications, both domestic and international. This was the time when he really expanded his networks through his collaboration with US and émigré academics, with policymakers, the army and the government. Lasswell, the Chicagoan and Europeanised American, was now in Washington to serve his government and his country.

Lasswell as a defence intellectual

After World War II Lasswell was appointed in 1946 as professor of Law at Yale University (pictured in his office there in Figure 2.4), where he had been a visiting lecturer (though when his appointment was under consideration there were accusations made against him that he was a 'commie').[31] Later, in 1947, he became one of the four members (of 22) of the faculty of the Yale Law School who did not sign the letter protesting the government's loyalty programme to the president, the secretary of state and the speaker of the House of Representatives (Emerson and Helfeld 1948, p.2). He also continued to work for the US government in different roles. His most long-standing role, however, was as a consultant for RAND (Research and Development Corporation), founded in 1948 and originally funded by the US government and the Douglas Aircraft Company in Santa Monica, California. He continued

Figure 2.4: Harold D. Lasswell in his office at Yale

Source: Photographer unknown. Harold Dwight Lasswell Papers (MS 1043), Manuscripts and Archives, Yale University Library.
https://findit.library.yale.edu/catalog/digcoll:4346702
Notes: Lasswell was professor of law at Yale from 1946 to 1952; professor of law and political science, 1952–1961; Edward J. Phelps professor of law and political science, 1961–1967; Ford Foundation professor of law and the social sciences, 1967–1970; emeritus, 1970–18 December 1978.

in this last role until the early 1970s and RAND paid him from $40,000 to $60,000 annually.[32] This was a substantial sum of money additional to his salary as a university professor at Yale, which was $20,000 in 1966.[33] Before he was appointed to this role, Lasswell had to prove that he was not a communist, following allegations that he had been 'a Communist Party member, associated closely and sympathetically with Communist Party members and openly and actively expressed sympathy with many communist doctrines and ideologies.'[34] He had to report in detail his professional life since starting as a student at the University of Chicago, his travels, the people he had met and the research he had done. He also had to compile a list of over 100 people who had known him and could testify on his behalf, including colleagues and students from the University of Chicago, Merriam and Almond, and many of his wartime collaborators, including Speier and Joseph M. Goldsen (1916–1998; see Chapter 4), his colleague from the Library of Congress period.[35]

Lasswell passed the security check and started working with many other academics to produce classified research for RAND Corporation. This work was to play a significant role in setting up new research programmes, including the Research Program in International Communication at the Massachusetts Institute of Technology's (MIT) Center for International Studies (CIS) (Bessner 2018, p.3; see Chapter 5). According to Bessner (2018, p.179), together with Lazarsfeld's Bureau of Applied Social Research at Columbia and Hovland's Communication and Attitude Change Program at Yale, the CIS was one of the early Cold War's most academically and politically influential programmes dedicated to communication studies.

In one of Lasswell's first meetings at RAND Corporation, the group discussed what would happen if the next world war broke out and if the US used the atom bomb to defeat the new enemy, the Soviet Union.[36] Later, with RAND Corporation's support, an evaluation of wartime content analysis was carried out by the very same people who had used it during the World War II (see Chapter 5).[37] Many of the academics who had first collaborated during the war and at RAND also participated in Project RADIR (Revolution and the Development of National Relations) at Stanford University's Hoover Institute in the years following World War II, as discussed further in Chapter 5. The Hoover research consisted of three series: elite, symbolic and institutional studies. These were based partly on confidential work at the Library of Congress by Lasswell's Experimental Division for the Study of Wartime Communications, and by the Organizations and Propaganda Analysis Section that Lasswell had set up in the Special War Policies Unit of the Department of Justice (Eulau 1966, p.392; Lasswell and Lerner 1965; Lerner, de Sola Pool and Schueller 1951).

A selected list of unclassified publications[38] shows that many articles published in academic journals came from RAND Corporation supported studies, many of these on the Soviet Union and communism (Sherburne 1953). Together with the research based on wartime studies by 'defense intellectuals' – as Bessner (2018, p.3) called them – RAND produced a major proportion of the studies in what came to be known as communication studies. Through his collaboration with RAND Corporation, Lasswell became one of the most prominent defence intellectuals of his time.

2.3 Conclusion

Lasswell is most often remembered as one of the world's leading political scientists and one of the inventors of content analysis, but what he should also be remembered for is his contribution to early comparative communications. He was in many ways a remarkable academic, a man who effortlessly crossed existing disciplinary boundaries but also opened up new and previously unknown avenues of research. The young Lasswell, in his interest in propaganda and psychoanalysis, was a loner, a pathbreaker, but he also had an influential supporter in Merriam, who provided mentorship, friendship, research collaboration and jobs for him. Lasswell learned well from Merriam, about not only how to do research but also how to network. He learned how to build networks between academics, policymakers, experts, politicians and men with power in general. He was known as a 'prodigious team-worker; whose associates in published work could be counted by hundreds' (Caldwell 1979, p.47). His letters revealed how he supported the men he had worked with during World War II in their subsequent careers and how these very same men became influential in their respective fields, as Chapter 5 will show. Lasswell defined the research topics to receive funding, including propaganda research and content analysis. His career shows how it is possible to become an Insider despite a rather modest background. It required high intelligence, hard work and ambition but also powerful mentors, eminent and loyal students and colleagues both in the academic and in the non-academic worlds. And perhaps most of all it required sharing the values of the dominant US ideology of the period, including militarism and anti-communism.

In this chapter Lasswell's career is divided into two different periods, although these are partly overlapping (for example, Lasswell's dislike of communism). This is why he can be described as an intergenerational figure. As a young man he was much influenced by the University of Chicago and by LSE in their approaches to applied research. He was an interesting mixture of European, international and US national pragmatist thinking, both new and progressive. The older Lasswell saw no difference between his goals and those of the US government. For him, policy science now meant research that was applied and thus useful beyond academia, and the good political scientist was *inter alia* a good citizen.[39] This idea can be traced back not only to his mentor, Merriam, and to the spirit of the Chicago School, but also to Sidney and Beatrice Webb and their applied critical work and thus to LSE. Easton (1950, p.451) argued that in the first half of his career Lasswell followed the Weberian tradition, which 'refused to prioritize values, indicate preferences in terms of goals, or privilege a particular theoretical perspective'. However, later in his career he sought to 'say something about our ultimate social objectives' and considered that the social sciences could offer a normative perspective by 'knowing what these goals ought to be' (quoted by Zittoun 2019, p.211).

The change from a young utopian idealist inspired by continental European ideas into a defence intellectual for whom US governmental interests were close to his heart was not a unique development in that period. On a very general level it can be seen as reflecting fluctuations in the dominant US ideologies of the time between isolationism and internationalism. Clearly, Lasswell was influenced by these dominant ideologies, and even contributed to them in his research. At the same time, throughout his entire career he supported the émigré scholars from Europe with whom he had collaborated during World War II. Personally, he may have felt that his two early passions, psychoanalysis and the study of symbols, never achieved the acceptance he had hoped for, but meanwhile he was materially well rewarded by his university and by RAND Corporation and could afford the lifestyle he wanted. At RAND Corporation he may, ironically, have experienced a freedom that was not possible elsewhere: to meet and talk with his European colleagues about past times, while developing tools to fight the Cold War against communism. He changed from a young man who wanted to prevent wars into an old man who wanted to win them.

By becoming a policy scientist, Lasswell changed from an Outsider into an Insider. He first wanted to be an Insider at the University of Chicago but was not granted a full professorship. By leaving the university and starting a new career mainly as a policy scientist, before getting his chair at Yale, he secured access to materials he would not have been able to access as an Outsider, even as an academic. This is one of the key factors in defining 'Insiderness', according to Merton (1972, pp.11–12), who explains how particular groups of Insiders have enjoyed monopolistic and/or privileged access to particular kinds of knowledge while Outsiders have been excluded from these. In the course of all this, Lasswell also achieved access to other elites, especially the military.

However, there are also other types of Outsideness, perhaps its most 'felt' forms. Partly this has to do with structures, partly with private life. If Lasswell was homosexual, he had to keep his sexual orientation the most well-guarded of secrets, especially during the McCarthy period, when communists and homosexuals, the 'Commie-queer bogeyman' (Gross 1993, p.12), were targets of the witch hunts, especially in the federal government (Johnson 2004). His working life at RAND Corporation was also partly secret since much of the research could not be made public. If Lasswell was homosexual, his access to RAND Corporation, the inner sanctum of military research, was an achievement during a time when the dominant ideology was not only anti-communist but also anti-homosexual. As Chauncey, Duberman and Vicinus (1991, p.13) write, the history of homosexuality goes well beyond filling in missing gaps in our knowledge of the past. It has already demonstrated that personal sexual behaviour is never a simply private matter, but always shaped by and shapes the wider social and political milieux.

What made Lasswell a pioneer in early comparative communications? His contribution started with his PhD thesis on war propaganda and continued with the work that followed over some decades. He defined propaganda as a concept and developed a method of studying it. Later, his contribution was largely a methodological one in developing comparative content analysis, particularly of different types of propaganda. As a method, content analysis became popular across the whole field of communication studies, not only in early comparative communications studies. News flow studies of the 1950s (International Press Institute 1953; Kayser 1953) used mainly quantitative content analysis to compare news flows from different countries, as they did in the 1960s (Galtung and Ruge 1965), in the 1970s (Hester 1971) and in the 1980s (Sreberny-Mohammadi et al. 1985) (see Chapter 5). This tradition is still alive and regularly produces new work every year.

But, for Lasswell, content analysis may have been his biggest personal disappointment. As Janowitz (1969, p.156) observes, it is striking that in Lasswell's (1963) book on the future of political science there is not a single reference to content analysis. So much effort and resources went into developing this, as shown in Chapters 4 and 5, but at the same time it never quite achieved his aim of discerning the latent meaning of messages in order to 'anticipate the enemy' (Lasswell 1949, p.48). Janowitz wrote:

> for Lasswell himself, as well as for interested social scientists and sympathetic critics, quantitative content analysis failed to achieve its expected potentialities, although political science, sociology, and social psychology have been enriched by particular penetrating monographs and specific research studies. (1968, p.652)

Lasswell's personal journey from a young idealist to a propaganda specialist working for the US government was not an unusual one for men of his generation. In the end he was not lonely but part of a crowd supported by others who shared the dominant ideologies of the time, of heterosexuality, the exclusion of women from public life, patriotism and anti-communism. Only by studying other members of the forefront generation, both academics and non-academics, is it possible to understand how similar their paths were. This is why my next chapter is about Kent Cooper, general manager of the AP. Cooper met Lasswell only a couple of times, but despite this, and despite their different careers, their life stories are characterised by remarkably similar utopias and ideologies.

Notes

[1] H.D. Lasswell's poem, no date. Harold Dwight Lasswell Papers, Bio-
graphical/Memorabilia Files 1043, Series V, Box 5, Folder 3. Manuscripts
and Archives, Yale University Library.

[2] Ershkowitz, M. The roots of a genius, manuscript, 1995. Harold Dwight
Lasswell Papers, Biographical/Memorabilia Files 1043, Series V, Box 4,
Folder 15. Manuscripts and Archives, Yale University Library.

[3] Letters between C.E. Merriam and H.D. Lasswell. Charles E. Merriam
Papers, Box 34 Folder 4; Box 35, Folder 3; Box 51, Folder 1, Box 65,
Folders 1–4. Hanna Holborn Gray Special Collections Research Center,
University of Chicago Library; Harold Dwight Lasswell Papers, General
Files, 1920–1978, 1043, Series I, Box 64, Folder 859. Manuscripts and
Archives, Yale University Library.

[4] Lasswell, H.D. Summary of activities, dictated on 19 October 1951. Harold Dwight Lasswell Papers, Biographical/Memorabilia Files 1043, Series
V, Box 213, Folder 15. Manuscripts and Archives, Yale University Library.

[5] H.D. Lasswell to his parents on 16 March 1924 from Paris. In his letter he
calls Merriam 'Friend Merriam' and talks about his career interests including studying public opinion and whether he is going to fit in the department. Harold Dwight Lasswell Papers, General Files 1043, Series I, Box 56,
Folder 779. Manuscripts and Archives, Yale University Library.

[6] Lasswell, H.D. Summary of activities. Dictated on 19 October 1951. Harold Dwight Lasswell Papers, Biographical/Memorabilia Files 1043, Series
V, Box 213, Folder 15. Manuscripts and Archives, Yale University Library.

[7] Myres S. McDougal (1906–1998) remembers Lasswell continuously
citing Mannheim as someone he should study. M.S. McDougal to W.
Ascher on 13 September 1982. Harold Dwight Lasswell Papers, Bio-
graphical/Memorabilia Files 1043, Series V, Box 4, Files, Folder 13.
Manuscripts and Archives, Yale University Library.

[8] Edward Albert (Abraham) Shils (1910–1995) was born in Springfield,
MA, to Ukrainian and Belorussian Jewish immigrant parents but grew
up in Philadelphia, where as a high school student he became interested
in Max Weber's work and learned German. He studied at the University
of Pennsylvania and later at Cambridge University, where he received
an MA in 1961. He worked as a research assistant for Louis Wirth at the
University of Chicago when Wirth was translating Mannheim's *Ideology
and Utopia*. During the war Shils served at the Office of War Information (OWI) and afterwards had a joint appointment as a lecturer at LSE
1946–1950 and as an associate professor at the University of Chicago,
where he was appointed distinguished service professor in 1971 (Bulmer
1996; Epstein 1996).

⁹ Hans Heinrich Speier (1905–1990) was born in Berlin to Adolf and Anna (née Person) Speier, a white-collar worker and housewife, both conservative Lutherans (Bessner 2018, pp.17–18). He studied economics, modern history and sociology at the Universities of Berlin and Heidelberg and received a DPhil from the University of Heidelberg, where he was Mannheim's first doctoral student and an assistant to professor Emil Lederer. Speier was a lecturer in political sociology and economics before emigrating to the US in 1933 with his Jewish spouse, Lisa (Louise) Griesbach (1903–1965). Speier was one of 10 intellectuals who formed the University in Exile and recruited other refugees to form its faculty at the New School. He served as a professor of sociology at the New School in 1933–1942 and 1947–1948. He joined RAND Corporation in 1949 and worked there for 15 years (Bessner 2018; 'Hans Speier Papers, 1922–1989' (no date)).

¹⁰ Affidavit for Army-Navy-Air Force Personnel Security Board, 1951. Harold Dwight Lasswell Papers, Biographical/Memorabilia Files 1043, Series V, Box 213, Folder 15. Manuscripts and Archives, Yale University Library.

¹¹ H.D. Lasswell to C.E. Merriam on 8 October 1923 from Geneva. Charles E. Merriam Papers, Box 34, Folder 4. Hanna Holborn Gray Special Collections Research Center, University of Chicago Library.

¹² H.D. Lasswell to C.E. Merriam on 8 October 1923 from London. Charles E. Merriam Papers, Box 34, Folder 4. Hanna Holborn Gray Special Collections Research Center, University of Chicago Library.

¹³ H.D. Lasswell to his parents on 15 October 1923 from London. Harold Dwight Lasswell Papers, General Files 1043, Series I, Box 56, Folder 775. Manuscripts and Archives, Yale University Library.

¹⁴ H.D. Lasswell to his parents on 4 November 1923 from London. Harold Dwight Lasswell Papers, General Files 1043, Series I, Box 56, Folder 775. Manuscripts and Archives, Yale University Library; H.D. Lasswell to C.E. Merriam on 8 October 1923 from London. Charles E. Merriam Papers, Box 34, Folder 4. Hanna Holborn Gray Special Collections Research Center, University of Chicago Library.

¹⁵ H.D. Lasswell to his parents on 9 November 1923 from London. Harold Dwight Lasswell Papers, General Files 1043, Series I, Box 56, Folder 775. Manuscripts and Archives, Yale University Library.

¹⁶ H.D. Lasswell to his parents on 2 December 1923 from London. Harold Dwight Lasswell Papers, General Files 1043, Series I, Box 56, Folder 775. Manuscripts and Archives, Yale University Library.

¹⁷ H.D. Lasswell to his parents on 16 October 1923 from London. Harold Dwight Lasswell Papers, General Files 1043, Series I, Box 56, Folder 775. Manuscripts and Archives, Yale University Library.

18 H.D. Lasswell to his parents on 12 August 1928 from Vienna. Harold
    Dwight Lasswell Papers, General Files 1043, Series I, Box 56, Folder 775.
    Manuscripts and Archives, Yale University Library.

19 The Social Science Research Council (SSRC) was born in 1923 from
    the foundations of the Laura Spelman Rockefeller Memorial Fund, the
    Carnegie Corporation, the Julius Rosenwald Fund and the Russell Sage
    Foundation. The major political scientist behind the SSRC's birth was
    Merriam (Seidelman and Harpham 1985, p.106).

20 H.D. Lasswell to his parents on 2 December 1928 from Berlin. Harold
    Dwight Lasswell Papers, General Files 1043, Series I, Box 56, Folder 775.
    Manuscripts and Archives, Yale University Library.

21 Gabriel Abraham Almond (1911–2002) was born in Rock Island, Illinois,
    to Russian rabbi David Moshe Almond (né Pruzhinski) (1872–1956),
    a migrant from Russia, and to Lisa (Lizzie, Elizabeth) Leah Almond
    (née Tulsky Eslon) (1882–1953), a migrant from Ukraine, both Jewish.
    He did his undergraduate and postgraduate studies at the University of
    Chicago. He was married to Anna Dorothea Almond (née Kaufmann)
    (1914–2000), who was born in Düsseldorf, Germany. In 1942 he joined
    the Office of War Information to study propaganda and subsequently
    went to Germany to study the effect of strategic bombing on attitudes
    and behaviour. Almond became a member of the Institute of Interna-
    tional Studies at Yale University in 1946 and later taught at Princeton and
    Stanford, from where he retired from in 1976 but continued writing until
    his death in 2002 (Verba, Pye and Eulau 2005).

22 Lord Northcliffe, born Alfred Harmsworth (1865–1922) founded the
    Daily Mail newspaper and headed the British war propaganda operation
    of World War I. He was seen by Germans as the embodiment of Allied
    propaganda (Tworek 2019, p.1980).

23 Courses given by Prof. Harold D. Lasswell at the University of Chicago.
    Charles E. Merriam Papers, Box 64, Folder 22. Hanna Holborn Gray
    Special Collections Research Center, University of Chicago Library.

24 Transcript of Oral History Interview with Philleo Nash. Interview by
    Jerry N. Hess on 24 June 1966, p.24, Harry S. Truman Library,
    https://www.trumanlibrary.gov/library/oral-histories/nash

25 H.D. Lasswell to J.M. Goldsen on 16 February 1942. Memorandum
    regarding research programme on coding method. Experimental
    Division for the Study of War Time Division. Harold Dwight Lasswell
    Papers, General Files 1043, Series I, Box 38, Folder 516. Manuscripts and
    Archives, Yale University Library.

26 H.D. Lasswell to B. Berelson on 31 October 1946. Harold Dwight Lass-
    well Papers, General Files 1043, Series I, Box 18, Folder 229. Manuscripts
    and Archives, Yale University Library.

[27] R.K. Kane Memorandum to the members of the staff. Bureau of Intelligence on 18 March 1942. Harold Dwight Lasswell Papers, General Files 1043, Series I, Box 52, Folder 727–29. Manuscripts and Archives, Yale University Library.

[28] C.E. Merriam to H.D. Lasswell on 18 June 1944. Charles E. Merriam Papers, Box 65, Folder 3. Hanna Holborn Gray Special Collections Research Center, University of Chicago Library.

[29] C.E. Merriam to H.D. Lasswell on 30 November 1946. Charles E. Merriam Papers, Box 65, Folder 2. Hanna Holborn Gray Special Collections Research Center, University of Chicago Library.

[30] Lasswell, Harold D. Memorandum: Standards for Mass Communication. Document No 70, no date. The Commission on Freedom of the Press Records, Box 3, Folder 6. Hanna Holborn Gray Special Collections Research Center, University of Chicago Library.

[31] Lasswell, H.D. Summary of activities. Dictated on 19 October 1951. Harold Dwight Lasswell Papers, Biographical/Memorabilia Files 1043, Series V, Box 213, Folder 15. Manuscripts and Archives, Yale University Library.

[32] Agreements between H.D. Lasswell and RAND. Harold Dwight Lasswell Papers, General Files 1043, Series I, Box 79, Folder 998. Manuscripts and Archives, Yale University Library.

[33] Salary note, 1966. Harold Dwight Lasswell Papers, Bibliographical/Memorabilia Files 1043, Series V, Box 4, Folder 16. Manuscripts and Archives, Yale University Library.

[34] M.J. Fitzgerald (Army-Navy-Air Force Security Board) to Lasswell on 29 August 1951. Harold Dwight Lasswell Papers, Bibliographical/Memorabilia Files 1043, Series V, Box 213, Folder 15. Manuscripts and Archives, Yale University Library.

[35] Lasswell, H.D. Summary of activities. Dictated on 19 October 1951. Harold Dwight Lasswell Papers, Bibliographical/Memorabilia Files 1043, Series V, Box 213, Folder 16. Manuscripts and Archives, Yale University Library.

[36] Conference on methods for studying the psychological effects of unconventional methods. RAND, Social Science Division, 3 February 1949. Harold Dwight Lasswell Papers, General Files 1043, Series I, Box 89, Folder 1095. Manuscripts and Archives, Yale University Library.

[37] See, for example, George, A. The intelligence value of content analysis, no date; Hans Speier to Lasswell on 8 April 1949. Harold Dwight Lasswell Papers, General Files 1043, Series I, Box 89, Folder 1095. Manuscripts and Archives, Yale University Library.

[38] A selected list of unclassified publications, no date. Harold Dwight Lasswell Papers, General Files 1043, Series I, Box 80, Folder 1004. Manuscripts and Archives, Yale University Library.

[39] Kirkpatrick, J. Harold D. Lasswell and the great tradition, 1980. Harold Dwight Lasswell Papers, Biographical/Memorabilia Files, 1043, Series V, Box 52, Folder 14. Manuscripts and Archives, Yale University Library.

References

Adorno, Theodor W.; Frenkel-Brunswik, Else; Levinson, Daniel J.; and Sanford, R. Nevitt (1950) *The Authoritarian Personality*, USA: Harper & Brothers.

Almond, Gabriel A. (1987) *Harold Dwight Lasswell, 1902–1978: A Biographical Memoir*, USA: National Academy of Sciences. http://www.nasonline.org/publications/biographical-memoirs/memoir-pdfs/lasswell-harold.pdf

Almond, Gabriel A. (1998) *Plutocracy and Politics in New York City*, USA: Westview Press.

Ascher, William and Hirschfelder-Ascher, Barbara (2003) *Revitalizing Political Psychology. The Legacy of Harold D. Lasswell*, USA: Lawrence Erlbaum.

Bates, Stephen (2018) 'Media Censures: The Hutchins Commission on the Press, the New York Intellectuals on Mass Culture', *International Journal of Communication*, vol. 12, pp.4784–801. https://ijoc.org/index.php/ijoc/article/view/8223

Bell, Laird (1949) 'Are We Afraid of Freedom?' *Bulletin of the American Association of University Professors (1915–1955)*, vol. 35, no. 2, pp.301–12. https://doi.org/10.2307/40220354

Berndtson, Erkki (1987) 'The Rise and Fall of American Political Science: Personalities, Quotations, Speculations', *International Political Science Review/Revue Internationale de Science Politique*, vol. 8, no. 1, pp.85–100. http://www.jstor.org/stable/1600723

Berndtson, Erkki (1997) 'Behavioralism: Origins of the Concept'. Prepared for Presentation at the XVIIth World Congress of the International Political Science Association 17–21 August, Seoul, South Korea. https://web.archive.org/web/20090514010256/http:/www.valt.helsinki.fi/vol/tutkimus/julkaisut/verkko/behavior.htm

Bessner, Daniel (2018) *Democracy in Exile: Hans Speier and the Rise of the Defense Intellectual*, USA: Cornell University Press.

Blanchard, Margaret A. (1977) 'The Hutchins Commission, the Press and the Responsibility Concept', *Journalism Monographs*, vol. 49, May, pp.1–59. http://www.aejmc.org/home/wp-content/uploads/2012/09/Margaret-A.-Blanchard.The-Hutchins-Commission.May-1977.pdf

Bulmer, Martin (1996) 'Edward Shils as a Sociologist', *Minerva*, vol. 34, no. 1, pp.7–21. https://www.jstor.org/stable/41821007

Caldwell, Mary E. (1979) 'Statement Made at or Prepared for Memorial Service in New Haven, at the Yale Law School Auditorium, on April 7, 1979', in *Harold Dwight Lasswell, 1902–1978: Ford Foundation Professor Emeritus of Law and the Social Sciences, Yale University: In Commemoration and Continuing Commitment*, USA: Yale Law School, Policy Sciences Center, Ogden Foundation, pp.44–49.

Chauncey, George; Duberman, Martin B.; and Vicinus, Martha (1991) 'Introduction', in Duberman, Martin; Vicinus, Martha; Chauncey, George (eds) *Hidden From History: Reclaiming the Gay and Lesbian Past*, UK: Penguin, pp.1–13.

Commission on Freedom of the Press (1947) *A Free and Responsible Press. A General Report on Mass Communication: Newspapers, Radio, Motion Pictures, Magazines, and Books*, USA: University of Chicago Press.

'C.R. Walgreen Takes Niece from College; Drug Chain Head Attacks 'Red Teaching' at the University of Chicago' (1935) *The New York Times*, 12 April. https://www.nytimes.com/1935/04/12/archives/cr-walgreen-takes-niece-from-college-drug-chain-head-attacks-red.html

Dorzweiler, Nick (2015) 'Frankfurt Meets Chicago: Collaborations between the Institute for Social Research and Harold Lasswell, 1933–1941', *Polity*, vol. 47, no. 3, pp.352–75. https://doi.org/10.1057/pol.2015.10

Dunn, William N. (2019) *Pragmatism and the Origins of the Policy Sciences Rediscovering Lasswell and the Chicago School*, UK: Cambridge University Press.

Easton, David (1950) 'Harold Lasswell; Policy Scientist for a Democratic Society', *The Journal of Politics*, vol. 12, no. 3, pp.450–77. https://doi.org/10.2307/2126297

Emerson, Thomas I. and Helfeld, David M. (1948) 'Loyalty among Government Employees', *The Yale Law Journal*, vol. 58, no. 1, pp.1–143. https://doi.org/10.2307/793350

Ennis, Thomas W. (1978) 'Harold D. Lasswell Dead at 76; Was Top US Political Scientist', *The New York Times*, 20 December. https://www.nytimes.com/1978/12/20/archives/harold-d-lasswell-dead-at-76-was-top-us-political-scientist.html

Epstein, Joseph (1996) 'My Friend Edward', *Minerva*, vol. 34, no. 1, pp.103–23. https://www.jstor.org/stable/41821015

Eulau, Heinz (1966) *Political Behavior in America: New Directions*, USA: Random House.

Eulau, Heinz (1979) 'Statement Made at Service in New York City, at the New York Academy of Sciences, on December 21, 1978 and Other Memorial Items', in *Harold Dwight Lasswell, 1902–1978: Ford Foundation Professor Emeritus of Law and the Social Sciences, Yale University: In Commemoration and Continuing Commitment*, USA: Yale Law School, Policy Sciences Center, Ogden Foundation, pp.87–97.

Farr, James; Hacker, Jacob S.; and Kazee, Nicole (2006) 'The Policy Scientist of Democracy: The Discipline of Harold D. Lasswell'. *American Political Science Review*, vol. 100, no. 4, pp.579–87. https://doi.org/10.1017/S0003055406062459

Farr, James; Hacker, Jacob S.; and Kazee, Nicole (2008) 'Revisiting Lasswell', *Policy Sciences*, vol. 41, no. 1, pp.21–32. https://doi.org/10.1007/s11077-007-9052-9

Freedman, Lawrence Z. (1981) 'Harold Dwight Lasswell (1902–1978): In Memoriam', *Political Communication*, vol. 1, no. 2, pp.103–06. https://doi.org/10.1080/10584609.1981.9962720

Freud, Sigmund and Strachey, James (1899/1954) *The Interpretation of Dreams* (new ed.), UK: Allen and Unwin.

Galtung, Johan and Ruge, Mari Holmboe (1965) 'The Structure of Foreign News', *Journal of Peace Research*, vol. 2, no. 1, pp.64–91. https://doi.org/10.1177/002234336500200104

Gary, Brett J. (1999) *The Nervous Liberals: Propaganda Anxieties from World War I to the Cold War*, USA: Columbia University Press.

Gross, Larry P. (1993) *Contested Closets: The Politics and Ethics of Outing*, USA: University of Minnesota.

'Hans Speier Papers, 1922–1989' (no date) M.E. Grenander Department of Special Collections and Archives, University Libraries, University at Albany, State University of New York. https://archives.albany.edu/description/catalog/ger084

Heaney, Michael T. and Hansen, John M. (2006) 'Building the Chicago School', *American Political Science Review*, vol. 100, no. 4, pp.589–96. https://doi.org/10.1017/S0003055406062460

Herman, Ellen (1995) *The Romance of American Psychology: Political Culture in the Age of Experts*, USA: University of California Press.

Hester, Al (1971) 'An Analysis of News Flow from Developed and Developing Nations', *Gazette*, vol. 17, no. 1–2, pp.29–43. https://doi.org/10.1177/0016549271017001

Hewitt, Nelson E. (1935) *How Red Is the University of Chicago?* USA: Advisory Associates.

Institut für Sozialforschung (1936) *Studien über Autorität und Familie: Forschungsberichte aus dem Institut für Sozialforschung*, Bd. 5, France: F. Alcan.

International Press Institute (1953) *The Flow of News: A Study*, Switzerland: International Press Institute.

Janowitz, Morris (1968) 'Harold D. Lasswell's Contribution to Content Analysis'. *The Public Opinion Quarterly*, vol. 32, no. 4, pp.646–53. https://doi.org/10.1086/267652

Janowitz, Morris (1969) 'Content Analysis and the Study of the "Symbolic Environment"', in Rogow, Arnold A. (ed.) *Politics, Personality, and Social Science in the Twentieth Century: Essays in Honor of Harold D. Lasswell*, USA: University of Chicago Press, pp.155–70.

Johnson, David K. (2004) *The Lavender Scare: The Cold War Persecution of Gays and Lesbians in the Federal Government*, USA: University of Chicago Press.

Jones, J. (no date) *The Meaning of Symbols in Psychoanalysis*. http://www.freudfile.org/psychoanalysis/symbols.html

Karl, Barry D. (1974) *Charles E. Merriam and The Study of Politics*, USA: University of Chicago Press.

Kayser, Jacques (1953) *One Week's News: Comparative Study of 17 Major Dailies for a Seven-Day Period*, France: UNESCO. https://unesdoc.unesco.org/ark:/48223/pf0000062870

Kirchick, James (2022) *Secret City: The Hidden History of Gay Washington*, USA: Henry Holt and Company.

Lasswell, Harold D. (1925a) 'Prussian Schoolbooks and International Amity', *Journal of Social Forces*, vol. 3, no. 4, pp.718–22. https://doi.org/10.2307/3005082

Lasswell, Harold D. (1925b) 'The Status of Research on International Propaganda and Opinion', *Papers and Proceedings of the American Sociological Society*, vol. 20, pp.198–209.

Lasswell, Harold D. (1927) *Propaganda Technique in the World War*, USA: A.A. Knopf.

Lasswell, Harold D. (1930) *Psychopathology and Politics*, USA: University of Chicago Press.

Lasswell, Harold D. (1931) 'The Measurement of Public Opinion', *American Political Science Review*, vol. 25, no. 2, pp.311–26. https://doi.org/10.2307/1947659

Lasswell, Harold D. (1933) 'The Psychology of Hitlerism', *Political Quarterly*, vol. 4, no. 3, pp.373–84. https://doi.org/10.1111/j.1467-923X.1933.tb02291.x

Lasswell, Harold D. (1935a) 'Collective Autism as a Consequence of Culture Contact: Notes on Religious Training and the Peyote Cult at Taos', *Zeitschrift für Sozialforschung*, vol. 4, no. 2, pp.232–47. https://doi.org/10.5840/zfs19354260

Lasswell, Harold D. (1935b) 'The Person: Subject and Object of Propaganda', *The Annals of the American Academy of Political and Social Science*, vol. 179, no. 1, pp.187–93. https://doi.org/10.1177/000271623517900124

Lasswell, Harold D. (1935c) *World Politics and Personal Insecurity*, USA: McGraw-Hill.

Lasswell, Harold D. (1938b) 'What Psychiatrists and Political Scientists Can Learn from One Another', *Psychiatry*, vol. 1, no. 1, pp.33–39. https://doi.org/10.1080/00332747.1938.11022172

Lasswell, Harold D. (1948) 'The Structure and Function of Communication in Society', in Bryson, Lyman (ed.) *The Communication of Ideas*, USA: Institute for Religious and Social Studies, pp.37–51.

Lasswell, Harold D. (1949) 'Why Be Quantitative', in Lasswell, Harold D. and Leites, Nathan (eds) *Language of Politics: Studies in Quantitative Semantics*, USA: G.W. Stewart, pp.40–52.

Lasswell, Harold D. (1951b) 'The Immediate Future of Research Policy and Method in Political Science', *American Political Science Review*, vol. 45, no. 1, pp.133–142. https://doi.org/10.2307/1950887

Lasswell, Harold D. (1963) *The Future of Political Science*, USA: Atherton Press.

Lasswell, Harold D. (1943/2003) 'On the Policy Sciences in 1943', *Policy Sciences*, vol. 36, no. 1, pp.71–98. https://doi.org/10.1023/A:1022999931810

Lasswell, Harold D. and Blumenstock, Dorothy (1938) 'The Technique of Slogans in Communist Propaganda', *Psychiatry*, vol. 1, no. 4, pp.505–20. https://doi.org/10.1080/00332747.1938.11022212

Lasswell, Harold D. and Blumenstock, Dorothy (1939) 'The Volume of Communist Propaganda in Chicago', *The Public Opinion Quarterly*, vol. 3, no. 1, pp.63–78. https://doi.org/10.1086/265260

Lasswell, Harold D. and Lerner, Daniel (1965) *World Revolutionary Elites: Studies in Coercive Ideological Movements*, USA: Massachusetts Institute of Technology Press.

Lasswell, Harold D.; Smith, Bruce Lannes; and Casey, Ralph D. (1946) *Propaganda, Communication, and Public Opinion: A Comprehensive Reference Guide*, USA: Princeton University Press.

Lerner, Daniel (1968) 'Lasswell, Harold D.', in Sills, David L. (ed.) *International Encyclopaedia of the Social Sciences*, USA: Free Press, pp.405–10.

Lerner, Daniel; de Sola Pool, Ithiel; and Schueller, George K. (1951) *The Nazi Elite*, USA: Stanford University Press.

Levyatan, Yaniv (2009) 'Harold D. Lasswell's Analysis of Hitler's Speeches', *Media History*, vol. 15, no. 1, pp.55–69. https://doi.org/10.1080/13688800802583299

Lippmann, Walter (1922) *Public Opinion*, USA: Harcourt, Brace and Company.

Lippmann, Walter (1925) *The Phantom Public*, USA: Harcourt, Brace and Company.

Littlejohn, Stephen W. (1978) *Theories of Human Communication*, USA: Merrill.

McIntyre, Jerilyn S. (1987) 'Repositioning a Landmark: The Hutchins Commission and Freedom of the Press', *Critical Studies in Media Communication*, vol. 4, no. 2, pp.136–60. https://doi.org/10.1080/15295038709360122

Merriam, Charles E. (1919) 'American Publicity in Italy', *The American Political Science Review*, vol. 13, no. 4, pp.541–55. https://doi.org/10.2307/1944209

Merriam, Charles E. and Lasswell, Harold D. (1924) 'Current Public Opinion and the Public Service Commissions', in Cooke, Morris Llewellyn (ed.) *Public Utility Regulation*, USA: Ronald Press, pp.276–95.

Merton, Robert K. (1972) 'Insiders and Outsiders: A Chapter in the Sociology of Knowledge', *American Journal of Sociology*, vol. 78, no. 1, pp.9–47. https://doi.org/10.1086/225294

Muth, Rodney (1990) 'Harold Dwight Lasswell: A Biographical Profile', in Muth, Rodney; Finley, Mary M; and Muth, Marcia F. (eds) *Harold D. Lasswell: An Annotated Bibliography*, USA: New Haven Press, pp.1–48.

Nardi, Peter M. (1999) *Gay Men's Friendships: Invincible Communities*, USA: University of Chicago Press.

Nietzel, Benno (2016) 'Propaganda, Psychological Warfare and Communication Research in the USA and the Soviet Union during the Cold War', *History of the Human Sciences*, vol. 29, no. 4–5, pp.59–76. https://doi.org/10.1177/0952695116667881

Perry, Helen S. (1982) *Psychiatrist of America: The Life of Harry Stack Sullivan*, USA: Belknap Press of Harvard University Press.

Peters, John D. (1986) 'Institutional Sources of Intellectual Poverty in Communication Research', *Communication Research*, vol. 13, no. 4, pp.527–59. https://doi.org/10.1177/009365086013004002

Pooley, Jefferson (2019) *The Remobilization of the Propaganda and Morale Network, 1947–1953*. https://doi.org/10.33767/osf.io/g9rp4

Rantanen, Terhi (2020) 'An American in London – Harold D Lasswell at LSE in 1923', *LSE History blog*. https://blogs.lse.ac.uk/lsehistory/2020/01/14/an-american-in-london-harold-d-lasswell-at-lse-in-1923/

Rogers, Everett M. (1994) *A History of Communication Study: A Biographical Approach*, USA: Free Press.

Rogow, Arnold A. (ed.) (1969) *Politics, Personality, and Social Science in the Twentieth Century: Essays in Honor of Harold D. Lasswell*, USA: University of Chicago Press.

Rosten, Leo (1971) *People I Have Loved, Known or Admired*, UK: W.H. Allen.

Rosten, Leo (1991) 'Harold D. Lasswell', in Shils, Edward (ed.) *Remembering the University of Chicago. Teachers, Scientists, and Scholars*, USA: University of Chicago Press, pp.276–86.

Rotheit, Rudolf (1919) *Die Friedensbedingungen der deutschen Presse — Los von Reuter und Havas!* Germany: Puttkammer & Mühlbrecht.

Schramm, Wilbur; Chaffee, Steven H.; and Rogers, Everett M. (1997) *The Beginnings of Communication Study in America: A Personal Memoir*, USA: Sage.

Seidelman, Raymond and Harpham, Edward J. (1985) *Disenchanted Realists: Political Science and the American Crisis*, USA: State University of New York Press.

Sherburne, Edward G. (1953) 'International Communications Research', *Public Opinion Quarterly*, vol. 16, no. 1, pp.481–701. https://doi.org/10.1007/BF02713258

Shils, Edward (1995) 'Karl Mannheim', *The American Scholar*, vol. 64, no. 2, pp.221–35. https://www.jstor.org/stable/41212318

Siebert, Fred S.; Peterson, Theodore; and Schramm, Wilbur (1956) *Four Theories of the Press: The Authoritarian, Libertarian, Social Responsibility, and Soviet Communist Concepts of What the Press Should Be and Do*, USA: University of Illinois Press.

Simpson, Christopher (1994) *Science of Coercion: Communication Research and Psychological Warfare, 1945–1960*, USA: Oxford University Press.

Smith, Bruce L. (1969) 'The Mystifying Intellectual History of Harold D. Lasswell', in Rogow, Arnold A. (ed.) *Politics, Personality, and Social Science in the Twentieth Century: Essays in Honor of Harold D. Lasswell*, USA: University of Chicago Press, pp.41–106.

Smith, Dennis (1988) *The Chicago School: A Liberal Critique of Capitalism*, UK: Macmillan Education.

'Solve Red Angle in Crash Death; Papers Traced' (1938) *Chicago Daily Tribune*, 24 October.

Sproule, J. Michael (1997) *Propaganda and Democracy: The American Experience of Media and Mass Persuasion*, USA: Cambridge University Press.

Sreberny-Mohammadi, Annabelle; Nordenstreng, Kaarle; Stevenson, Robert; and Ugboajah, Frank O. (1985) *Foreign News in the Media: International Reporting in 29 Countries*, No 93, France: UNESCO. https://unesdoc.unesco.org/ark:/48223/pf0000065257

Torgerson, Douglas (2019a) 'Lasswell in the Looking Glass: A "Mirror" for Critical Policy Studies', *Critical Policy Studies*, vol. 13, no. 1, pp.122–30. https://doi.org/10.1080/19460171.2018.1512877

Torgerson, Douglas (2019b) 'Lasswell in the Looking Glass: Another Look', *Critical Policy Studies*, vol. 13, no. 2, pp.230–35. https://doi.org/10.1080/1460171.2019.1618355

Tworek, Heidi (2019) *News from Germany. The Competition to Control World Communications, 1900–1945*, USA: Harvard University Press.

Varão, Rafiza (2021) 'A First Glance at the Work of Dorothy Blumenstock Jones', *Revista Mediterránea de Comunicación/Mediterranean Journal of Communication*, vol. 12, no. 2, pp.17–34. https://www.doi.org/10.14198/MEDCOM.19325

Verba, Sidney; Pye, Lucian; and Eulau, Hans (2005) *Gabriel A. Almond January 12, 1911–December 25, 2002. Biographical Memoirs*, Vol. 87, USA: National Academies Press. https://www.nasonline.org/publications/biographical-memoirs/memoir -pdfs/almond-gabriel-a.pdf

Wake, Naoko (2008) 'On Our Memory of Gay Sullivan: A Hidden Trajectory', *Journal of Homosexuality*, vol. 55, no. 1, pp.150–65. https://www.tandfonline.com/doi/abs/10.1080/00918360802129444

White, Llewellyn and Leigh, Robert D. (1946) *Peoples Speaking to Peoples: A Report on International Mass Communication from the Commission on Freedom of the Press*, USA: University of Chicago Press.

Zittoun, Philippe (2019) 'The Two Lasswells: Implications for Critical Policy Studies', *Critical Policy Studies*, vol. 13, no. 2, pp.211–15. https://doi.org/10.1080/19460171.2019.1620622

3. Kent Cooper, *Barriers Down* and *The Right to Know*

> True and Unbiased News—the highest original moral concept ever developed in America and given the world. (Cooper 1942, p.v)

To understand comparative communications as the exclusive property and practice of the academy is to overlook contributions made in non-academic institutional contexts and the impact of such research beyond and on the academy. Kent Cooper (1880–1965) was from 1925 until 1943 general manager of the Associated Press (AP), one of the world's largest news agencies (press associations), the largest in the US, and had a worldwide impact on communication policies. It is crucially important to study the work of non-academics because they have influenced as much, or sometimes even more, than academics themselves how comparative communications has been practised and understood by politicians, policymakers, journalists and general audiences. I argue that Cooper's writings, especially his books *Barriers Down* (Cooper 1942) and *The Right to Know* (Cooper 1956), show how boundaries between academic and non-academic writings were not fixed and how comparative communications, from its very start, in its policy science orientation, became influenced by the writings of non-academics.

Cooper was not an academic; he was a man of practice. His writing was atheoretical, he did not present a methodology or list his sources, but he did write about international news and propaganda comparatively and with a view to promoting international structural change. In Chapter 1 I defined early comparative communications in the US as that where researchers or research teams with diverse cultural, practical or academic skills, and in different locations, developed specific theories, concepts and/or methods to analyse materials or data concerning communications often from more than one source or (geographical) location simultaneously. Cooper's 'research' is based on his practical skills and his experience, his use of concepts, his access to materials and his comparison of locations, but it is not academic research. His writings could hardly be called research even when using Lasswell's policy science

How to cite this book chapter:

Rantanen, Terhi (2024) *Dead Men's Propaganda: Ideology and Utopia in Comparative Communications Studies*, London: LSE Press, pp. 85–124.
https://doi.org/10.31389/lsepress.wmf.c. License: CC BY-NC 4.0

criteria, but he did provide 'policymakers with pragmatic, problem-solving recommendations' (Lasswell 1951a, p.4) and presented results that made 'the most important contributions to the intelligence needs of the time' (Lasswell 1951a, p.13). Cooper used concepts, mostly borrowed and undefined, including propaganda, news flows, freedom of news, monopoly and the right to know, that became widely used in policy science dealing with news for several decades. The titles of his two books have been borrowed even by academics (Lemberg 2019; Schudson 2015). Cooper emphasised the independence of news from propaganda and saw governments as enemies of free flows of information. He used the institution he worked for to promote policy science and succeeded in making major impact on US communication policy during and after World War II. Cooper's writings were both utopian and ideological and consequently influenced future research in international communication even decades later.

Cooper was a member of an organisational elite, and studying his work helps us to understand the relationships between different elites and how they contribute to society at large (Mannheim 1934, p.108). If we only study academic institutions, we easily fail to understand the influence of non-academic elites who are often more powerful than intellectual elites because of the institutional power their organisations such as the AP held and practised. Cooper's work shows how and why men of action were able to influence the development of comparative communications and how difficult it is to separate academic research from political actions. Similarly, Cooper's life story can be analysed through the concepts of ideology and utopia, of generational conflicts, and of Insideness/Outsideness. Because his professional life was so closely connected with one organisation, this chapter also highlights the role of institutions, not only individuals, in the production and mobilisation of knowledge. Cooper's writings are an early example of work that politicised news agencies as the most powerful actors in international news flows after World War II, and would become an object of criticism in the 1970s (Carlsson 2003, p.35).

Cooper was born in Columbus, Indiana, a town of 4,000, to a lawyer and Democratic congressman, George W. Cooper (1851–1899), and a teacher, Sina (née Green) (1849–1904), who, unlike most women of her time, had attended university (Cooper 1959, p.5). This was a family of the political elite and the young Cooper spent two winters in Washington, DC, (Cooper 1959, p.311), but later, as a result of his father's early illness and death, had to leave his studies at Indiana University in 1898 after only one year to become a newspaper reporter. After working for three years as a reporter, bureau manager and travelling representative for the United Press Associations (UP) founded in 1907, the AP's new competitor, he joined the AP in 1910, working first as a travelling traffic inspector before slowly climbing to become general manager in 1925 (Cooper 1959; Schwarzlose 1989a). Faithful to this same organisation almost all his working life, Cooper was a company man and what Lasswell

(1951a, p.13) called a man of action. He devoted his life to the AP, which he described as 'the greatest co-operative effort' and as dedicated to 'cooperative, non-profit-making news collection and dissemination, honestly collected, and truthfully written' ('A.P. Called Greatest Cooperative Effort' 1926). For Cooper, the AP itself was his ideology. His belief in the superiority of its cooperative ownership model, and then in its expansion outside the US, could sound almost religious.

Since Cooper's career is so bound up with the organisation he worked for, it is important to look first at the AP itself. After introducing the AP and Cooper's key 'concepts', the chapter is divided into three further parts, following the stages of Cooper's career. The first of these stages I call 'Cooper as a liberal internationalist, 1914–1925', the second 'Cooper as a pragmatic policymaker, 1925–1936' and the third 'Cooper as an ideologist, 1942–1956'. In each of these periods, Cooper played a different role on the Insider/Outsider spectrum either in relation to his organisation or to other organisations and individuals whose work has been analysed in this book. Of the three, the third period was the most public as a result of several campaigns run by the AP, of Cooper's subsequent publications (1942; 1956) and of the attention he received. Cooper as a liberal internationalist (1914–1925) partly coincided with Lasswell's academic period of progressive internationalism and as an ideologist brings together all characters in this book to support the US during the Cold War.

3.1 The AP as a national and international news agency

As one of the world's oldest news agencies, the Associated Press (AP) of New York dates from 1846, when five New York City newspapers funded a pony express route through Alabama to bring north news of the Mexican War faster than the US Post Office could deliver it (Komor 2021; Schwarzlose 1989a). The AP was organised as a cooperative, a non-profit agency where members shared their news with each other but with nobody outside the organisation. Its early history was marked by rivalries from both inside (there were several regional Associated Presses) and outside the organisation (Knights 1967). It gradually became the largest news agency in the US and, then known as the AP of Illinois, achieved a practical monopoly in 1893 (Rantanen 2012; Schwarzlose 1989c).

After a monopoly suit against it, the AP of Illinois was reorganised in 1900 under a new charter of the State of New York as the immediate successor of a former Illinois corporation carrying the same name and as a 'mutual and co-operative organization for the interchange and collection of news' (*Inter-Ocean Publishing Co. v. Associated Press* 1900). Its members were required to exchange news between themselves but also received news from the AP correspondents in return for membership fees. Its charter prohibited it from seeking profit or declaring dividends.[1] The most radical change made in the new by-laws, compared with the Illinois by-laws, was the introduction of an unqualified veto power of certain members over the admission of an applicant that competed with existing members of the AP ('AP Enjoined from Observing Membership Provision By-laws' 1944).

The AP's leading position in the US domestic market had long been secured thanks to its contract with the European news cartel consisting of Reuters in the UK, Havas in France and Wolff in Germany, which since 1870 had divided the world's news market between themselves by signing mutual agreements with one national agency in each country (Rantanen 1990; Rantanen 2006). The AP's membership of the cartel, although subordinate to Reuters, Havas and Wolff, had secured its monopoly over the cartel's foreign news in the US market, and had often played a key role in its competition with other domestic agencies, as in 1893 when Melville E. Stone (1848–1929), Cooper's predecessor, travelled to London to ask for an agreement with Reuters ('Directors and Members of the AP' 1918) for the then newly founded AP of Illinois. The AP made an agreement with Reuters that granted exclusive rights to the cartel's news for AP members inside the US, but at the same time prevented AP members from operating outside their home country or receiving foreign news from any agencies outside the cartel (Rantanen 2012). The agreement was a final blow to AP's main competitor of that time, the United Press (UP), which went bankrupt in 1893 (Gramling 1940/1969; Rantanen 2012; Rosewater 1930; Schwarzlose 1989c).

The AP's monopoly on the domestic market did not last long. Two new private news agencies, the United Press Associations (later confusingly also UP) and the International News Service (INS), were founded in 1907 and 1909, respectively (Rosewater 1930, p.346), and became the AP's new private competitors. Unlike the AP, whose foreign operations were restricted by the cartel agreement, the new UP and INS were free to operate anywhere in the world and especially encouraged by the US government, as early as 1916, to work in South America (Rantanen 1992, p.15; Renaud 1985, p.11). The UP could potentially have replaced the AP in the cartel, and archival documents show evidence of many meetings between the UP and Reuters over 20 years.[2] Several times Reuters toyed with the idea of substituting the UP for the AP, but it never happened. Instead, the UP started establishing its own correspondent networks round the world. Roy W. Howard (1883–1964), president of the UP in 1912–1920, remained critical of the cartel, writing that:

> The reason for my deciding against the alliance was that I knew it would put the UP as much at the mercy of the moribund and venal agencies, as the AP was. (Rantanen 1992, p.13)

The AP continued to dominate the domestic market. By the early 1940s, 81 per cent of US morning newspapers and 59 per cent of evening newspapers were

AP members. Their aggregate circulation represented 96 per cent of the total circulation of morning newspapers, and 77 per cent of that of evening newspapers ('Text of Federal Court's Decision' 1943). In 1942, 1,703 of the 1,747 English-language daily papers in the US received the services of one or more of three major press associations: the AP, the UP or INS. In the same year almost 1,200 papers were receiving AP services, 817 subscribed to UP and 261 to INS. This became a problem because the AP's membership was restricted and existing members could block the entry of new members, with voting power centralised in the hands of its largest and most influential members.[3]

In 1942, the AP faced an antitrust lawsuit based on the Sherman Act of 1890 and the Clayton Act of 1914. The lawsuit, brought by the US Department of Justice, claimed that AP membership restrictions violated the basic principle of non-profit consumer cooperatives, which was that membership should be open, on equal terms ('Supreme Court Rules against AP' 1945). This was a major blow to the AP, which immediately organised a public campaign, using its own members as a forum to fight against the lawsuit. Cooper's book *Barriers Down* (1942) was written at the request of the AP Board when the agency faced this lawsuit. It was during this period that Cooper was also asked to be interviewed by the Hutchins Commission, which reviewed the AP's ownership in critical terms, although the commission's final report did not address the AP specifically.

3.2 Cooper and his key 'concepts'

There are many connections between Cooper, and the other men, both academics and men of practice, studied in this book. After World II there were several research projects that studied international news coming from news agencies, and news flow studies have continued their popularity to-date (Chapters 4 and 5). The work of Peterson, Siebert and Schramm (Chapter 6) was also connected to Cooper through the Hutchins Commission's report and the monopoly lawsuit against the AP. Cooper popularised several 'principles', as he calls them, that became influential concepts in international communication and in policy science related to it. They included: propaganda, the right to know, free flow, and freedom of information.

Cooper traces back the concept of propaganda to the Roman empire, but writes that a 'simple-non-aggressive, non-war-mongering form of *news* propaganda' was first used by Reuters in the 19th century (Cooper 1956, p.75). According to Cooper (1956, p.84), the Germans copied Reuters' model and put it into use in a more aggressive and militant way and it was later adopted in Russia, Eastern Europe and China. Cooper writes that propaganda has two functions: (1) to gain converts or patronage by teaching people that there is something for which they should yearn that would bring them personal, individual satisfaction and (2) to show all of those who yearn how to gain fulfilment (p.270). Cooper (1956, p.84) writes that:

> Germany was the first European nation to realize that propaganda for national unity, taught in school for the young and printed as news for adults, was essential in any country where the intellectual level of all the people had advanced almost to universal literacy.

However, for Cooper (1956, p.xii) the government suppression of news was worse than news propaganda, and he saw European government-controlled news agencies as propaganda vehicles, unlike the cooperative AP. According to Cooper, what follows from the US constitutional freedom of the press, 'the right to print', is 'the right to know', which extends the principle to people around the world (p.16). Cooper writes:

> The citizen is entitled to have access to news, fully and accurately presented. There cannot be political freedom in one country, or in the world, without respect for the 'right to know.' (Cooper 1956, p.xii)

To guarantee 'the right to know', as shown later in this chapter, resolutions were needed at national and international levels. To Cooper's disappointment, the freedom of the press was changed into freedom of information (Cooper 1956, p.184). As Lemberg (2019, pp.31–33) shows, one of Cooper's most well-known principles, 'free flow', was not invented by him but came from the dean of Columbia journalism school, Carl V. Ackerman (1890–1970), who used 'free flow of information to the American press' in his speech in 1934. Cooper referred to the 'purpose of obtaining freer flow of international news exchange' in the AP–UP contract signed at the Ritz–Carlton Hotel in New York to join their forces against Reuters in 1934 (Cooper 1942, p.252). Three years later it was used as 'free flow of words' by former president Herbert Hoover (1874–1964). The wording found its way to the mandate of the Office of War Information (OWI) in 1942 as 'accurate and consistent flow of information' and then was changed into the 'free flow of information' proposed by the US delegation for UNESCO in 1945 (Lemberg 2019, pp.31–33; Schiller 1975, p.80).

3.3 Cooper and his contemporaries

Cooper was 22 years older than Lasswell but they belonged intellectually to the same forefront generation, influenced by the two world wars. Professionally, Cooper and Lasswell lived in different, although not completely separate, worlds. Cooper's and Lasswell's ideologies were similar in reflecting US policy interests worldwide, although their views about the role of government in news transmission were different. They both became members of elites, albeit different ones, one scholastic and the other an organising elite, and each producing 'different patterns of culture in the various spheres of social life' (Mannheim 1934, p.108). My analysis of the two men's life stories shows how close these elites were to each other, even in a society as vast as that of the US.

The archival records show their paths crossing only a couple of times, most notably when Cooper gave a witness interview to the Commission on Freedom of the Press (Hutchins Commission), of which Lasswell was a member, in the early 1940s.[4] The Hutchins Commission's report on international mass communications, *Peoples Speaking to Peoples* (White and Leigh 1946), devoted a whole chapter to 'Merchants of Words and Images', where they reviewed the history of US press associations and their European counterparts. Cooper thought that the majority of the 'self-named' commission members were 'college professors, some of them quite liberal in their thinking' but 'not one of them was a newspaperman with current professional experience in the business or first-hand knowledge of the perplexities of collecting news or publishing newspapers' (Cooper 1956, pp.177, 295). According to Lemberg (2019, p.37), of the commission members 'Lasswell in particular insisted on what the government could do to promote press and speech freedoms'. The commission wrote in 1944 in its synopsis that:

> no government or private agency can be trusted to get at the truth. The purpose of society may be furthered if we have mixed institutions—both governmental and private. We may keep the aim of truth uppermost, and use all means to that available. The determination by private processes has the advantage that people can take it or leave it—no police back the statements of authenticity. The role of the state is kept at a minimum.[5]

Many newspapers saw the Hutchins Commission's suggestions as forms of governmental intervention in their operations (Blanchard 1977, p.9). This is why Cooper's attitude was not surprising, especially when the commission showed special interest in the AP. McIntyre (1987, p.149) observes that 'the public interest argument made at both Appeals Court levels in the AP decisions (*Associated Press v. United States* 1943; 1945) was relevant to the Hutchins Commission's thinking on the media as a public utility'. Some of its members questioned the AP's alleged monopoly. For example, one of them, Zechariah Chafee Jr. (1885–1957), had supported the Justice Department's antitrust case against the AP in 1942 (Lemberg 2019, pp.18, 35; Pickard 2014, pp.137–38).

The Hutchins Commission also discussed Cooper's *Barriers Down* (1942) (McIntyre 1987, p.155) but it was only one of their sources and was described as a 'readable, autobiographical account' (White and Leigh 1946, p.113). The commission's proposal to Congress and the State Department was rather general, stating that the 'U.S. seek, through negotiations of bilateral treaties with as many nations as possible' to:

guaranty for any authorized press associations, newspaper, news-picture agency, syndicate, magazine, book publisher, writer, radio station, or motion picture of one country of *the right to sell* its product directly any individual newspaper, radio station, motion-picture exhibitor, magazine, book publisher, or dealer in the in other country. (White and Leigh 1946, p.110, my emphasis)

If Cooper had hoped for a stronger statement from the commission to support his mission of the role of the AP in breaking international barriers, he may have been disappointed. However, he himself wrote: 'Don't Tell It—Sell It!' (Cooper 1956, p.273), implying that 'the right to know' meant 'the right to sell'.

In Chapter 2, I described Lasswell as an intergenerational figure who managed to avoid conflict between generations by shifting between utopias and ideologies. Cooper, in contrast, was not an intergenerational man and was known for a number of conflicts, both within and outside his own organisation: with company managers, with his predecessor Melville E. Stone, general manager of the AP between 1893 and 1921 (pictured, Figure 3.1),

Figure 3.1: Kent Cooper, Melville E. Stone, Frank B. Noyes and Frederick Roy Martin at AP's annual meeting, 1925

Source: Courtesy of Associated Press, AP Corporate/Alamy Stock Photo.
Notes: The first three general managers and president of the Associated Press at their annual meeting, Waldorf Astoria, New York, 1925. Left to right they are Kent Cooper (who was elected as general manager at the meeting and would serve until 1949), Melville E. Stone (general manager 1900–1920), AP president Frank B. Noyes (president 1900–1938) and Frederick Roy Martin (general manager 1920–1925) (AP Photo/Corporate Archives).

Figure 3.2: Roy W. Howard with Kent Cooper, *c.* 1920s or 1930s

Source: Roy W. Howard Photograph Collection, The Media School, Indiana University, Bloomington, Indiana. https://webapp1.dlib.indiana.edu/images/item.htm?id=http://purl.dlib.indiana.edu/iudl/media_school/VAD9735/VAD9735-001600&scope=media_school/VAD9735
Notes: Exact date unknown. Cooper pictured left; Howard right.

with Howard, president of the United Press Associations (UP) in 1912–1920 (with whom he is pictured in Figure 3.2), the AP's most important domestic competitor, and most famously (and made public by Cooper's own account in *Barriers Down* (1942)) with Sir Roderick Jones (1877–1962), general manager and chairman of Reuters (1915–1941) in the UK (see Figure 3.4).

3.4 Cooper as a liberal internationalist, 1914–1925

As a news agency manager, Cooper set himself the task of expanding the AP's activities abroad. Despite being a company man, he described himself an Outsider, not an Insider, in the AP, stating that between the years 1921 and 1924 there was only one person who believed in him, his secretary, Sarah A. Gibbs (1898–1993) (whom he later married, leaving his wife for her). Cooper claimed that he did not have a mentor: his relationship with Stone was strained, since he felt he was never one of the 'MS boys' and that Stone never wanted him to become his successor. When Stone retired in 1921 it was Frederick Roy Martin (1891–1952) who became general manager of the AP. Cooper had to wait four more years to achieve the top position (Rantanen 1998, p.18). Until 1925, when he finally became general manager, he could not improve the AP's international position independently since he did not have the power to do so. He is photographed in Figure 3.1 on the occasion with his two predecessors and AP's president.

Cooper fought hard against Stone, feeling even after he became general manager that he did not have the freedom he wanted. His relationship with Frank B. Noyes (1863–1948),[6] the long-time president of the AP (1900–1938), was not without problems either (Rantanen 1992, p.19). Stone and Noyes had been among the AP's founders in 1893, when they brought to an end its competitor, the forerunner of the first UP, largely thanks to their exclusive contract with Reuters, which gave them a monopoly in foreign news in the US. Both Noyes and Stone felt gratitude to Reuters, first to its founder, Baron Julius Reuter (1816–1899) and his son Herbert (1852–1915), who succeeded him, and then to Sir Roderick Jones (1877–1962), Reuters' general manager between 1915 and 1941.

In *Barriers Down* – and we must remember that this is Cooper's own narrative – he claimed that he had no previous knowledge about Reuters or the European news cartel and that in 1914 he found a cablegram from *La Nación* – 'the great Buenos Aires newspaper' – asking for AP news service, which had been left unanswered and copied to the Havas correspondent to whose exclusive territory South America 'belonged' (Cooper 1959, p.65). This was the same European news cartel about which Lasswell received detailed information in London in 1923, when he talked to a member of the news department of the British Foreign Office (see Chapter 2). Cooper claims he discussed this in 1914 with Stone, who described to him the nature of the cartel agreement that prevented the AP from selling its service to *La Nación* (Cooper 1942, pp.15–16).

Cooper's account seems doubtful, since the agreement with the cartel had already been a major issue in the news war that preceded the founding of the AP of Illinois (Knights 1967). In 1893, the AP had negotiated concessions with Reuters in South America. The AP Board discussed in 1914 whether to make an attempt to break through Havas' control over South America (Rantanen 1992, p.16). It also seems odd that Cooper, as a member of the AP's management team, even though he was responsible for internal matters, would be ignorant of the situation, when, for example, annual reports regularly included information about the agencies with which the AP had agreements.

South America became a market for the AP's competitor, the UP, who started selling UP news to several newspapers there in 1916. The AP could do nothing because of the contract with the cartel (Rantanen 1992, pp.15–18) but managed to extract, with Reuters' support, a major concession from the cartel by concluding a separate agreement with Havas in 1918 giving the AP access to the South American market, where the AP competed with the UP. A letter in the Newberry archive shows that in 1918 Stone was told in London that 'Sir Roderick Jones had no interest in South America'.[7] As a result, both US agencies now operated in South America, and both had been encouraged to do so by the State Department (Renaud 1985).

At the time of the World War I peace negotiations in Paris, Cooper was the AP's chief of traffic, while Stone was general manager and Noyes was chair of the board. Both Noyes and Stone supported a long-term relationship with Reuters, with whom Stone negotiated for the AP. Sir Roderick Jones of Reuters ran individual negotiations in Paris with Havas, Wolff and the AP in 1919, where all decided to continue the cartel without giving the AP a role as equal partner, agreeing 'that arrangements between the AP on the one hand and the three great European agencies on the other, had not been broken by the war'.[8] According to the new agreement, 'the U.S. shall be common to the Havas Agency and to Reuters Limited, and the profits shall be divided between them in equal parts,'[9] without giving the AP an equal role and dropping the Wolff agency from financially benefitting from the agreement. According to Jones, this happened without any objection from Stone, who said that 'we now happily could go on exactly as we did before the war'.[10]

When we explore Cooper's writings, we can see how he keeps on referring to World War I, although he was writing after the war's end. (See, for example, Figure 3.3, in which Cooper's *Life* magazine article from 1944 is illustrated with a diagram of world news cartels from 1919.) Like Lasswell, Cooper did not fight in the war, but he was a witness to victory celebrations in Paris in 1919 – the event that defined his generation. In his own words, Cooper was deeply influenced by what he saw in Paris at the Bastille Day military parade on 14 July, when he watched the Allied troops march down the Avenue des Champs-Élysées.[11] He later commented on this experience, writing that:

> the only time that millions of them had ever been near to other millions was when they were at death grips. They had come from all corners of the world for one purpose and it was to kill![12]

Cooper had also noticed the similarity between all those soldiers: 'the soldiers of most any one of the nations might seem to have fitted into the ranks of any other nation by the mere change of uniform'. Later he had the same thought when he was in Germany and saw discharged German soldiers,[13] writing:

> They only believed they had nothing in common with the enemy as life was going on in their separate spheres. Many governments had disseminated tainted news before that war, well aware that the decision as a result of their poison ultimately would rest on the number of dead in the field of battle.

> Prejudice, [when] once aroused, is indeed a consuming passion. It can be fed easily and people become slaves of it ... Prejudice takes on the color of hate. So, it must have been with what all those millions who fought in that war read in their newspapers; either they or those back home who sent them. So, it must be as to those who bring on any war.[14]

In this way, Cooper identified newspapers as a main cause of wars. But where did newspapers receive the news that caused this prejudice? For Cooper – and this became a main thesis in his later work – government sources were responsible for the untruthful news that in turn fed prejudice. He concluded that:

> many governments had disseminated tainted news before that war, well aware that the decision as a result of their poison ultimately would rest on the number of dead in the field of battle. (Cooper 1945b)

Figure 3.3: Diagram of the World News Cartel in 1919, as depicted by Cooper in a *Life* magazine article in 1944

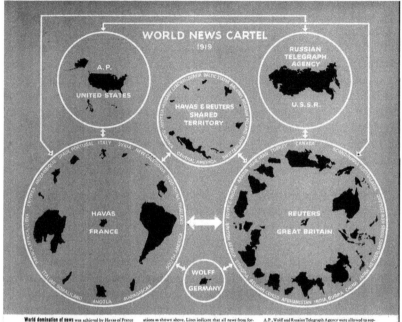

World domination of news was achieved by Havas of France and Reuters of Great Britain after World War I. Nations and continents were divided between these gigantic press associ- / ations as shown above. Lines indicate that all news from for- / eign countries passed through the central bureaus of the cartel / members where it could be suppressed or "properly angled." / A.P., Wolff and Russian Telegraph Agency were allowed to sup- / ply news to newspapers only in their home countries, except / that A.P. could supply news elsewhere in Western Hemisphere

Both party conventions last summer adopted resolutions in favor of worldwide freedom of information. Both houses of Congress have unanimously endorsed the idea. All this is largely due to the efforts of Kent Cooper, executive director and general manager of the Associated Press, who for years has made world-news freedom a personal crusade. Mr. Cooper explains the issue in this article.

FREEDOM OF INFORMATION

Head of Associated Press calls for unhampered flow of world news

by KENT COOPER

Before and during the first World War the great German news agency, Wolff, was owned by the European banking house of Rothschild, which had its central headquarters in Berlin. A leading member of the firm was also Kaiser Wilhelm II's personal banker, friend and loyal subject. Such an arrangement can be understood by supposing that a U. S. President, through his personal banker, controlled the Associated Press and thus could dictate what the A.P. would send to the U. S. press to print about him and his policies. What actually happened in Imperial Germany was that the Kaiser used Wolff to blind and excite his people to such a degree that they were eager for World War I.

Twenty years later, under Hitler, the pattern was repeated and enormously magnified. D.N.B., Wolff's successor, became the official Nazi news agency and spewed out the deceptions and propaganda that made the German people again ready to attack their neighbors. In Italy, Mussolini used Stefani, the official Fascist agency, for the same propagandistic ends. In Japan, where the news agency and daily press have always been subservient, the government leaders were careful to subvert it completely before starting the Japanese aggressions.

It has always been so: when a government wants to make war it first takes control of the news. In the peace conferences of World War I we overlooked this basic element of world peace. In the peace conferences of War II—even in the earliest discussions—we should not forget it.

"Freedom of the press" is a phrase that covers many arguments. Whatever it once meant, it is too limited to define the problem of international news in relation to world peace. A better phrase is "freedom of information." There should be freedom for journalists everywhere in the world both to seek out news—with equality of

CONTINUED ON NEXT PAGE   55

Source: Life, 13 November 1944, p.55. https://books.google.co.uk/books?id=3UEEAAAAM BAJ&q=cooper#v=snippet&q=cooper&f=false (also available in the Records of General Manager Kent Cooper, AP 02.1. Kent Cooper Papers, Box 49, The AP Archives).

Cooper's lifelong suspicion of governments' influence on news transmission can be traced back to World War I and to the role of news agencies in disseminating propaganda in news (Cooper 1956, pp.75–79).

In his writings and in reports of interviews he gave, Cooper repeatedly tells the story of how he, as an individual, brought his findings about the

European news cartel to the attention of the peacemakers at Versailles, but was told that press freedom would not be part of the peace treaty because all matters affecting news had been settled privately (Cooper 1945a). He writes:

> As a newspaperman I did so during the last war and found that the aggressor countries controlled the press and perverted truth in news. That plainly was one of the chief causes. (Cooper 1945a)

He also writes:

> So, in Paris, I sought out Colonel House. He seemed interested and promised to discuss the matter with President Wilson. Later, he explained that the President felt the League of Nations could satisfactorily deal with the problem of opening up new channels.[15]

I have not found any evidence for this except Cooper's own words, but he was in Paris at that time and it is very possible that this happened. At the same time, it may seem rather odd that Cooper would independently approach Colonel (Edward M.) House (1858–1938) at a time when his then superior, Stone, was negotiating a contract with Reuters. The American Peace Mission in Paris also had an adviser on the political aspects of international communication by telegraph, cable and radio, Walter S. Rogers (1877–1965) ('International Congress Will Consider Plans' 1919). There was nothing in the peace treaty about the role of media and communications, although the topic had been discussed in several documents. Wilson met journalists only twice at the conference (Coggeshall 1942, p.2), in Paris, and it is possible that Cooper asked his question on one of these occasions. According to James Lawrence (Larry) Fly (1898–1966), chairman of the Federal Communication Commission (FCC) (1939–1944) and chairman of the wartime Defence Communications Board (later Board of War Communications from 1940), Wilson did carry in his pocket a memorandum written at the peace negotiations by his communication adviser, Rogers, but it was never discussed.[16] The memorandum, according to Fly, emphasised:

> the important part which the distribution of the President's addresses and other American news had played in bringing the war to a conclusion and in clearing the way for a common understanding. Mr. Rogers pointed out plainly that when communication facilities are lacking the opportunity for growth of international misunderstanding is encouraged. He emphasized the need to avoid at all costs any extensive control of communications facilities by one nation which favors its own people and its own commerce. Mr. Rogers asserted that the ideal of a worldwide freedom of news and the breaking down of existing barriers, chauvinism, or lack of vision. He

called for adequate facilities, for the fair control thereof, and for the provision that there must be direct, unhampered communication.

As John (2020) has argued, Rogers, the US mission's adviser, was a liberal journalist who 'firmly believed that foreign press was systematically distorting U.S. news by foregrounding sensationalistic atrocity stories and underreporting uplifting accounts of current events'. Rogers' wartime experience led him to promote ideas of 'journalism-centric liberal internationalism' shared by many after World War I. Many of his ideas from the memorandum found their way into Cooper's writings, which emphasise the role of news in preventing prejudice. In his view, it was governments that spread tainted news, as Lippmann (1922) had argued in his *Public Opinion*. Cooper's thinking was aligned with that of Lippmann and of other forefront generation intellectuals, journalists and academics, who started for the first time to think of the role of news in causing and preventing wars. Unlike Lasswell, who concentrated on propaganda in general, Cooper borrowed the concept of propaganda and used it solely to refer to news, specifically to foreign news.

In retrospect, Cooper thought that what took place between news agencies in the negotiations of 1919 should rather have been a matter for the governments that signed the Versailles peace treaty. He saw this as a major mistake, later reflecting:

> At Versailles, the power that could have been exercised by the peace negotiators to bring the operations of the news cartel into the open and to establish arrangements by which the Germans and their neighbors could have truthful news of each other's activities was never utilized … This was done by the British and French news agencies exercising control of all the news in countries that bordered Germany … All this was fuel for the rapidly developing fire of Nazism.[17]

> … Barriers against freedom of news exchange and free press were erected in Europe trying to recover from the devastations of war. Without question the processes then set up to control news exchange contributed largely in bringing about the second war. (Cooper 1945a)

There is an interesting contradiction in Cooper's thinking. On the one hand, he criticised European news agencies for being controlled by governments and for controlling the news. On the other hand, he expected governments to have interfered in the negotiations held privately by the agencies and to have reflected the changes that had happened in world politics as a result of World War I. This did not happen, and Cooper, as a pragmatist, set himself the task of liberating the AP from Reuters, after which the former was free to expand its activities all over the world. Until 1925, Cooper's actions were restricted by his own position in the AP. He still felt an Outsider in the organisation, and increasingly that the AP was itself an Outsider in the transmission of international news by virtue of not having an equal position to Havas, Wolff and especially Reuters. All this was about to change when Cooper became general manager in 1925.

3.5 Cooper as a pragmatic policymaker, 1925–1934

Cooper started to be active internationally after World War I and before becoming general manager. In 1919 Stone sent him for two months to Europe to try to speed up the transmission of the AP's news dispatches. He visited both Reuters in London and Havas in Paris. Cooper wrote to Stone:

> While nations and people are seeking liberty, the agencies are actually tightening the cords of the form of domination of the press. If there is to be a new liberty in Europe the press will play no small part in it and the AP had no connection with the European press.[18]

While Cooper was critical of Reuters and Havas, he concluded his report by writing that 'I do not want to break with the agencies. I repeat that.'[19] He did, however, express doubt about the value of the European agencies to the AP, arguing that they were no longer indispensable, and that Reuters was more *dependent* (my emphasis) on the AP than the AP was on Reuters. In this report Cooper also started questioning the principle of exclusivity and of 'home territories', where no other agencies could operate except the one whose territory it belonged to. Cooper wrote that 'the ideal arrangement, of course, would be one as between *cooperative* agencies of the various nationalities' (my emphasis).[20]

The old AP generation to which both Stone and Noyes belonged felt gratitude to Reuters for the 1893 contract, but Cooper did not share those feelings. Cooper himself was still on good terms with Reuters in 1925, when he reported to have spoken of Jones and Reuters in a friendlier way than ever and of 'the two great agencies marching together hand in hand, like two comrades, to greater and greater fields of progress and development'.[21] (Figure 3.4 was taken at a dinner hosted by Stone and Cooper in honour of Sir Roderick Jones in 1926.) He was still in favour of exclusive territories in 1926, when writing about the AP's relationship with the European news cartel ('allied agencies'):

> It was my idea that you were going to continue your negotiations with Sir Roderick … since I made my first study of it in 1919, namely, that any allied agency could make its service contract with any allied agency that it might choose, all the allied agencies first to be signatory to a general contract that would designate some

Figure 3.4: Photograph of dinner given for Sir Roderick Jones of Reuters by Melville Stone and Kent Cooper, 18 October 1926

Source: Reuters Archive, 1/897905, LN321, PHO, reproduced with permission.
Notes: Complimentary dinner given to (Sir) R. Jones by M. Stone and K. Cooper in
New York. Guests include R. McLean, J.S. Elliott, J.J. Pulleyn, E. Root, F.B. Noyes, M.E. Stone,
J. Lamont, L.C. Probert, W.C. Cannon, M. Love, M. Garges, F.T. Birchall, P. Crawath,
F. Williams Douglas, T.J. O'Reilly, G. Enderis, J.G. Harbord, J.S. Mason, C. Brown, W.H. Hays,
J.L. Merrill, (Dr) N. Murray Butler, N. Carlton, W.S. Gifford, C.D. Gibson, C.S. Smith, J.R.
Youatt, L. Pickering, B. Rickatson-Hatt, O. Reid, A. Draper and N.A. Huse.

territories and unlimited activities therein, and, where a country
had no organized agency to enter the alliance, the country would
be open territory.[22]

One of the reasons for Cooper's changed attitude towards Reuters may have
concerned the UP. At the League of Nations press conference in 1926 in
Geneva, 16 of the news agencies attending belonged to the group of 'allied
agencies', i.e. were members of the European news cartel. The allied agencies,
most of them government-owned or government-run, included the AP, but
the UP belonged to the 'independent group'. The principal spokesman for the
independent agencies was Howard, who had already, in 1913, spoken at the
conference for press freedom ('Will seek laws to guard news property' 1926)

in terms very similar to those that Cooper would use in 1942 ('World Wire Services Meet at Geneva' 1926).

Under Cooper, the AP managed to achieve major concessions from the cartel, and in 1927 it signed a four-party contract with Havas, Reuters and Wolff. The AP was given North America and its possessions, with the 'reservation that Reuters and Havas shall have a free hand in Canada and Mexico and that the AP shall have a free hand in Central America, South America and Cuba'.[23] The four-party agreement was a significant achievement, for the first time acknowledging the AP as an equal partner with Reuters, Havas and Wolff. However, it still restricted the AP's operations and defined exclusive territories for each of the agencies.

Cooper's biggest generational conflict was with Jones, general manager and chairman of Reuters, the world's most powerful news agency of that time. Cooper and Jones were born just three years apart, but were separated by nationality, wealth and status. Jones was described as one of the influential men in the British empire, leading a news agency whose general managers in India, Australia and South Africa were known as Baron Reuter's proconsuls. Donald Read, Reuters' company historian, writes that 'Reuters regarded itself as an empire within the British empire, and was accepted as such by Ministers in London and by Governors and other imperial officers overseas' (Read 1990, p.175).

Jones's own background was rather modest. He was born in Dukinfield, England, as a hat salesman's only son and after his parents lost all their money could not attend public school or go to university (Read 1990, p.175). He later left the UK for South Africa, where he became general manager of the Reuters office for British South Africa in 1902. After Baron Herbert de Reuter (1852–1915), the founder's son, killed himself in 1915, Jones was appointed as general manager and continued in that role until he was forced to retire in 1941. He was knighted in recognition of his services to journalism in 1918, which could also be seen as a reward for Reuters' service to war propaganda during World War I (Read 1999, p.137). Jones was described as 'not being universally popular' and as being 'imperious and autocratic' (Entwisle no date). According to Read (1990, p.176), he:

> compensated for his modest background by dressing with excessive correctness, never missing a chance to make money and living in conspicuous style at Hyde Park Gate and in a country house. Bells at Reuters would ring to announce his comings and goings and the sidewalk was swept each morning, just before his chauffeured Rolls Royce pulled up the curb. ('The Press: Young Man with a Mission' 1946)

Although Jones and Cooper were as different in appearance and personal style, they were not so different from each other in their management styles.

At Reuters, Cooper was described as 'volatile and temperamental',[24] and as a 'conservative, ruthless, aggressive American businessman' (Rantanen 1994, p.21).[25] One Reuters employer wrote:

> Kent Cooper is an aggressive fighting type – so rough in fact that he finds it hard even to be tactful at times, and with him such tact is more in the nature of hypocrisy than anything else. He has a tremendous ego and so much vanity but with it all a certain ruthlessness which is no doubt most valuable to the AP. His power in the organization appears to be unlimited and I fully believe that Noyes gives him an entirely free hand, while Cooper is of course clever enough to exert such authority without disturbing Mr Noyes' dignity. His attitude towards his own staff is Czar-like and he makes and unmakes people with little consideration for them or their superiors.[26]

Archival documents show an increasing tension between Reuters and the AP and between Cooper and Jones that became very personal. Cooper was described as having almost a phobia about Jones.[27] Minutes from a Reuters board meeting reveal personal antipathy to Cooper.[28] What would have been seen as a 'normal' rupture between business partners became an ideological battlefield where views of news were to play the key role. This ideology again goes back to World War I, to utopian notions of how to prevent wars in the future.

Asia still 'belonged' to Reuters, which was reluctant to let the AP into its territory. After many years of difficult negotiations between the AP and Reuters, the cartel agreement was finally broken in 1934 through the efforts of Cooper, aligned with the UP, which refused to replace the AP in the cartel (the so-called Ritz–Carlton agreement; Silberstein-Loeb 2014, p.217), the Rengo agency in Japan (Iwanaga 1980) and the TASS agency in the Soviet Union (Rantanen 1994). The breaking of the European news agency cartel was thus far from purely a personal victory but was achieved in collaboration with other agencies and individuals. According to the new agreement, the AP was free to use any news without restrictions in the Western hemisphere and anywhere in the Eastern hemisphere outside the British empire.[29] This was a huge achievement, not only for the AP but also for the other national news agencies. However, because the world was in turmoil, these major changes only took place after World War II and the liberation and remained rather unnoticed outside the world of news agencies. Cooper himself writes:

> I never gave up my destination to see the international news cartel broken. That was not achieved until 1934 and by that time, Hitler was already in the saddle of Germany, and war lords of Japan were getting ready to send their arms marching. Indeed, the world was in no mood to embrace freedom of information.[30]

What Cooper does not say is that the Wolff agency was taken over by the Nazis in December 1933 and was renamed the Deutsches Nachrichtenbüro (DNB). It purged its Jewish employees, including those whose wives were Jewish, and they were replaced with Nazi supporters, and the AP replaced its own Jewish staff in Germany. DNB continued its collaboration with the former cartel members including the AP by making new agreements with them (Tworek 2019, pp.170, 183, 186–87; Scharnberg 2016, p.25). Understandably, neither Jones (1951) himself nor Storey (1951), in his authorised history of Reuters, shared Cooper's enthusiasm about the end of the cartel. In Jones's view, 'a new era in the relationship of the allied agencies to each other' was inaugurated (Jones 1951, pp.390). Jones thought that this would have happened in any case, at the latest with the outbreak of World War II. He also claims that at Reuters they believed (and Jones was satisfied with it) that

> by the release not only of ourselves but also of the Associated Press and our two international partners, Havas and the German Agency, from the stipulations, conditions, and restraints which ever since the 1914–1918 War had been proving less and less advantageous, less and less tolerable, at all events to Reuters and to the Associated Press, we had removed from the area of our mutual operations causes of misunderstanding and friction that had become seriously embarrassing to us; thereby we had given new life to an international league which, if not radically reformed, very soon would have broken down (Jones 1951, p.389).

The end of the European cartel was, however, over, but the rise of the US agencies, the AP, UP and INS, only took place after World War II. By 1952, these three agencies were listed together with Reuters, Agence France-Presse (AFP), which had succeeded Havas in France, and TASS as world agencies (UNESCO 1953).

3.6 Cooper as an ideologist, 1942–1956

Cooper's professional achievements may have been limited to the AP, but his book *Barriers Down* (Cooper 1942) made him famous outside the world of news agency operations. He himself called the book his 'crusade' against the European news cartel in which Reuters was the leading member and dominated the world's news market. *Barriers Down* was not based on thorough academic research, being without academic references or bibliography, even though there were already journalistic articles and research available (see, for example, Desmond 1937; Douglass and Bomer 1932; Stowe 1927). It was based on Cooper's own recollections and written documents and its aim was to improve the reputation of the organisation he worked for as well as his personal reputation. It is Cooper's recollection of how he discovered the nature of the international news cartel and how he personally broke it down in 1934, arguing that the AP was morally superior to European agencies because of its ownership form.

Cooper's *Barriers Down* was written at the request of the AP Board. All the royalties from the book were paid to the AP's Employees' Benefit Fund and its copyright belonged not to Cooper but to the AP for the benefit of the fund.[31] The AP also bought 5,000 copies of the book for educational and promotional purposes and had it translated into Spanish.[32] The book did not save the AP from the lawsuit by the US Department of Justice against its own monopoly in the US. After losing the case, the AP appealed to the Supreme Court, which in 1945 also ruled by five votes to three against it ('Special meeting of board is called' 1945). Finally, in the same year, the AP agreed to review its by-laws and accepted a new member earlier rejected. According to Cooper himself in 1959, his book influenced the members of the Supreme Court, whose decision destroyed neither the exclusive contract the AP had with the Canadian Press nor the exclusive right of the AP to news from its regular members (Rantanen 1998, p.25).

In *Barriers Down*, Cooper told a story of the 'overlordship' of Reuters over all national news agencies, and especially over the AP, and of how he liberated the AP from this:

> I personally believe that the overlordship of Reuters in the matter of consenting or denying agency connections between agencies … is not only antiquated but is wholly inconsistent with the progressive thought of today. Indeed, I personally believe that such overlordship may potentially lead to serious international misunderstandings. Certainly such overlordship can and I believe has, acted as a deferment to the widest possible development of news exchange upon salutary basis.[33]

Barriers Down has been described as 'breath-taking', 'inspiring', 'fascinating' and 'sensational' (Rantanen 1998, p.25; see also Figure 3.5). Its author was hailed as a 'crusader for the freedom of the press' (Willens 1951) and the book was to have a profound impact on future comparative communications studies, especially in international communication, as well as on actual news agency ownership worldwide. As one reviewer wrote (quoted by Rantanen 1998, p.25),

> perhaps no one but Kent Cooper could have done the job that he did, and this great fighter has the barriers come down one by one of his ideal, a truly American ideal, which, pray heaven, will always remain with us.

The reviews reveal the ideology of that period and how uniformly well received the book was. It is hard to understand this now, but only by contextualising the period during which it was written can we see why it happened.

Figure 3.5: Advertisement for Kent Cooper's *Barriers Down*, in *Editor & Publisher*, 12 December 1942

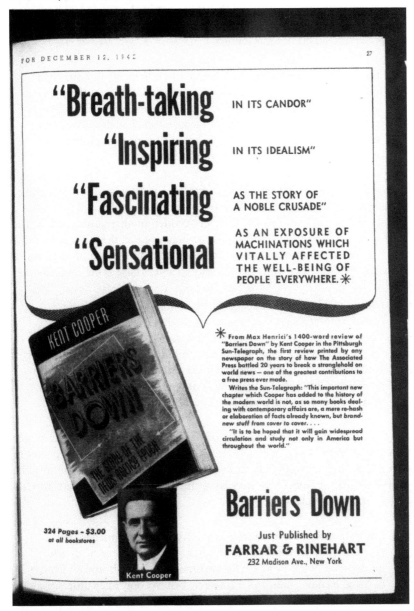

Source: *Editor & Publisher* 1942-12-12, vol. 75, no. 50, p.27. https://archive.org/details /sim_editor-publisher_1942-12-12_75_50/page/n28/mode/1up?q=Cooper

Cooper wrote several books in addition to *Barriers Down*, including one about Anna Zenger (Cooper 1946), the first female journalist in the US, and *The Right to Know* (1956). He was also a composer and lyricist of songs and marches (Cooper 1959). But none of his books after *Barriers Down* would become as famous. In *Barriers Down*, he was never shy about taking full credit for his achievements. He believed that if his personal crusade had been won within five years, instead of 20, World War II might have been averted.[34] Cooper described his book as follows:

> This book is not about the suit. It is about an activity of mine on behalf of the AP for 20 years that I consider the most important thing that I have ever done for the AP. Moreover, in all modesty, I think it's the most important thing that ever was accomplished on behalf of world journalism, provided the accomplishments are used as groundwork on which to build a free press for the civilized world.[35]

Barriers Down is an example of a generational story in which one member of the generation tells a story where his own role is emphasised over others. The success of the book made it difficult to offer an alternative version. The book clearly irritated Roy Howard, whose organisation, the UP, was founded to resist the AP's monopoly both at home and abroad. According to Howard, the book gave 'a picture … utterly misleading and as false as hell', and Cooper:

> had so thoroughly scrambled facts, fiction, sanctimony, and distorted or improperly emphasized truth, that it would be a ten year job and would take ten volumes to segregate the real truth from the false innuendo that have been combined to present an utterly inaccurate, unfair, and completely misleading picture of the press association business, and especially of the handling of foreign news to American consumption. (Rantanen 1998, p.26)

Howard thought that even the title of the book was ridiculous: 'the whole thing was phoney and a defensive fabrication in which he was doing a lot of things that he was compelled to do willy-nilly by us'. He made the mistake of thinking no response was necessary since few would ever read *Barriers Down*.[36] He also wrote:

> My opinion, not confidential, is that it [AP] is the damnedest, meanest monopoly on the face of the earth – the wet nurse of all other monopolies. It lies by day. It lies by night and it lies for the very lust of lying. Its news gatherers, I sincerely believe, only obey orders.[37]

Howard's view was privately shared by other UP men. One of them wrote, even 10 years after *Barriers Down* was published:

> It always struck me as an exhibition of supreme gall for Kent, or anybody else of the AP to lay any claim that he or the AP 'slew the

dragon'. Anybody who knew from personal observation anything about early news agency relationships ... especially relationships between Reuters and the AP ... must know that the AP was hand in glove with Reuter's idea of promoting a world news monopoly.[38]

Despite telling only one side of the story, in *Barriers Down* Cooper's starting point was comparative: Cooper compared the AP with Reuters, concentrating on the unfair nature of their relationship. It was based on Cooper's Insider knowledge about the cartel, his access to sources that were unavailable to Outsiders. It paved the way for his next book, *The Right to Know: An Exposition of the Evils of News Suppression and Propaganda* (Cooper 1956), but the ideas behind the latter were developed and put into action already after *Barriers Down* was published. As Schudson (2015, p.50) points out, in *The Right to Know* Cooper picked up on a phrase he claimed to have invented. Schudson (2015, p.50) writes:

> In the book, Cooper calls for a 'right to know' constitutional amendment because, he argues, what needs protecting is not the privileges of an industry (the 'free press') to write what they please but the rights of citizens to have access to the information they need. In his foreword, Cooper explains the sense of urgency in the book: government treatment of news was 'slowly pressing toward the totalitarian pattern.' He concludes the foreword by holding, 'Our government can more profitably accept the broader principle of the Right to Know and ardently maintain it for the benefit of its citizens than to continue totalitarian methods of news suppression and propaganda'.

Cooper had already argued, in *Barriers Down*, that the AP's cooperative ownership form ensured that its news was unbiased, since it was owned by newspapers and was a non-profit organisation. The basis for his argumentation was that:

> The membership of the AP includes persons of every conceivable political, economic and religious advocacy. The one thing upon which they are united, as far as the AP news service is concerned, is that it shall be wholly free from partisan activity, or even the expression of any opinion whatever.[39]

By combining the AP's ownership form with non-partisan news, Cooper developed an ideology that was later spread worldwide not least through the influence of the 1948 UN General Assembly's Universal Declaration of Human Rights, the preamble of which refers to 'the advent of a world in which humans shall enjoy freedom of speech' and is more fully elaborated in Article

19 Universal Declaration of Human Rights (Universal Declaration of Human Rights 1948). Governmental news agencies became the object of his criticism for propaganda in news because unlike the AP they were government-owned. This he then combined with the people's right to know, again going back to the situation before World War I. Cooper had visited Germany a year before World War II and found that:

> the peoples of other nations [were] being depicted by the German press and radio as so monstrously fictional as to seem like peoples from openly malignant. Not only were the large European agencies under government control or influence, but it was fashionable to serve the crown—not the people.[40]

During and after World War II, Cooper increasingly felt that what had happened in Versailles must not happen again, and he started actively campaigning for what he called the worldwide freedom of of the press (Cooper 1945b; Cooper 1956) without governmental interference. He wrote:

> If at Versailles we had insisted upon freedom of the press in Germany, and if we had compelled our French and English allies to put aside their selfish plans for the establishment of their own news hegemony over Germany, this war may not have occurred so soon, if at all ... In other words, the emphasis of the negotiators was on the material effects of the war rather than on the underlying cause of the war. There was not one word of discussion at any time as to how it happened that the people of the vanquished countries had been given mental food that bred their hatreds.[41]

Cooper was convinced that it was the cooperative ownership form that would guarantee the unbiased flow of news and had started advocating for a worldwide expansion of this ownership form. Meanwhile, however, Reuters' ownership form had been changed and Jones was forced to resign in 1941 (Read 1999, p.188). Cooper himself ceased to be general manager of the AP and became executive manager in 1943. More importantly, Great Britain was the US's ally in World War II. Cooper now started promoting the inclusion of the concept of a free flow of news in future peace negotiations and treaties again going back to Versailles:

> At Versailles, scarcely anyone dreamed that all means of communication in the new Germany would one day fall into the hands of a war-mad dictator. It did happen, as I feared it would, and it can happen again, if the rights to news and information are not set forth in treaties, and vigilantly protected.[42]

Cooper began actively campaigning for his proposal. His plan, according to his own words, was that future treaties should: (1) require that the vanquished nations guarantee their people a free press as known in the US; (2) require that any nation requesting help in re-establishing itself economically would guarantee such a free press; (3) leave to the press itself the missionary work to bring the same result in other countries; and (4) announce the determination of the US to foster and bring about news transmission facilities at a nominal rate that would guarantee the free flow of news between all the capitals of the world.[43]

The positive publicity that *Barriers Down* received resulted in promotion both for Cooper and for the AP. Cooper first made sure that he received his own organisation's backing in 1943. He also approached Reuters, which was now under new management and ownership and whose board of directors approved his proposal.[44] He then paid a personal visit to the Department of State, which started to investigate the proposal. He also approached individuals, prior to the Republican and Democratic Conventions in Chicago, with a view to the platform committees of both conventions being urged to adopt a position favouring freedom for news agencies (Forrest 1945). Cooper's influence was clearly shown in different documents from that period. Senator Tom Connally (1877–1963) writes:

> That the Congress of the United States believes in the world right of all men to write, send, and publish news at uniform communication rates and without interference by governmental or private monopoly and that right should be protected by treaty; that the representatives of the United States at the peace conference and at the conference called to create an international organization for the maintenance of peace be requested to urge that there be incorporated in the peace treaty or in the treaty creating the international organization for peace provisions to guarantee that each nation signatory to the treaty shall give to all responsible press and radio representatives the same access to information at the source and the same freedom from censorship as may be accorded to press services and radio representatives of such country; and that such agreements provide for the freedom of accredited press and radio representatives to write, transmit, and publish the news without private or governmental interference and at the same rates of charge for communications, national and international, as are given to the press and radio representatives of such nation.[45]

Cooper's dislike of any government interference was shared by Connally, even if they both must have known that communications technology was often governmentally owned in many countries. The importance of news agencies was however acknowledged, and the US Congress unanimously adopted a resolution in 1944:[46]

Resolved by the Senate (The House of Representatives concurring),
That the Congress of the United States expresses its belief in the
world-wide right of interchange of news by news-gathering and dis-
tributing agencies, whether individual or associate, by any means,
without discriminations to sources, distribution, rates, or changes;
and that right should be protected by international contract.

Cooper became increasingly anti-government in his battles concerning both
international and domestic markets (Cooper 1956). He saw government
interference in news everywhere, not only in Europe but also in his own country (Cooper 1947, 1956). Outside the US, his primary target had been Reuters,
which, although privately owned, like many other news agencies did have a
close relationship with the British government (Read 1990; 1999). Cooper
also claimed that the UP, in the same way as Reuters, was intimate with the
government.[47] In doing this he conveniently forgot that when the government-owned TASS in the Soviet Union failed to sign an agreement with the
European news cartel in 1934 this helped to bring down the cartel (Rantanen
1994). Cooper remained worried about government influence abroad, and
the AP again gave him its support by issuing a statement:

The AP stands committed to the principle of freedom of access
to the news and to the free flow of news throughout the world. It
holds that news disseminated by non-governmental news agencies is essential to the highest development of mankind and to the
perpetuation of peace between nations. It recognizes the possibility of useful purpose served by governments in the maintenance
throughout the world of official libraries of information. It applauds
the vigorous manner in which the present national administration
has advanced the doctrine of press freedom. It holds, however, that
government cannot engage in newscasting without creating the fear
of propaganda which necessarily would reflect upon the objectivity
of the news services from which such newscasts are prepared.[48]

In the US, Cooper opposed not only the lawsuit against the AP but also government control of the wireless telegraph, and even government war propaganda (Cooper 1947). At the same time, he did not find it problematic
that the AP served the US government with its news during the war, or that
many of its correspondents were located in embassies or US army headquarters.[49] In his view, the main enemy of the international flow of free news was
government-owned and/or government-controlled news. He writes:

While government control of the flow of news and information
must be prevented, major governments of the UN should lend their
benediction to the development of independent news agencies,

responsible only to the publications, radio stations and other outlets they serve, which in turn are responsible to their public.[50]

As the first of the world's news cooperatives, I say with humility that in my country the world ever has gotten any ethical standard to embrace, it consists of a method by which people assuredly can get the truth while freedom lasts. This method is the control of the collection of the news by the newspapers themselves rather than by opportunists or by governments.[51]

Cooper's *Barriers Down* and his other writings exceeded the life of his own biological generation and achieved a fame that crossed national boundaries. Despite the historical inaccuracies and biases of his writings, their deeply ideological tone seems to have spoken to succeeding generations who feel a need to justify the operations of their own organisations against those of other organisations, often their competitors or those owned or supported by governments. At a more general level, *Barriers Down* served as a tool for supporting US hegemony in news transmission on the basis of the nation's moral superiority. With an interesting generational twist, its ideas would go on to be used in the preparations of the New World Information and Communication Order (NWICO) debate in the 1970s and early 1980s, when US news agencies (including the AP) were themselves criticised on the same grounds as those on which the AP had criticised Reuters. As Cuthbert (1980, p.106; see also Renaud 1985, p.36) shows, the representatives of 59 non-aligned countries who drafted the New Delhi Declaration on Information Media in 1976 observed that 'the peoples of the world are forced to see one another, and even themselves, through the medium of the international news agencies' (Communicator 1976, quoted by Cuthbert 1980, p.106). Their declaration notes that:

In a situation where the means of information are dominated and monopolised by a few, freedom of information really comes to mean the freedom of these few to propagate information in the manner of their virtual denial to the rest of the right to inform and be informed objectively and accurately. (Non-aligned Conference of Ministers, New Delhi Declaration on Information Media, New Delhi, July 1976, quoted in Cuthbert 1980, p.99)

3.7 Conclusion

This chapter critically evaluates a non-academic book that has probably achieved more impact than many academically acclaimed works in comparative communications. I have tried to understand Cooper's books through the development of the organisation it was written for and whose values its author promotes throughout. *Barriers Down* is without doubt a book with many faults and, as I have shown using other materials, one that does not even present an accurate narrative but often twists the facts to serve a self-congratulatory project. However, there is something about it that has appealed to successive generations.

Anyone reading *Barriers Down* for the first time can see that the author paints a picture of himself as a hero, a veritable dragon-slayer – the dragon in this case being Sir Roderick Jones, managing director of Reuters. Theirs was a relationship where Jones saw other news agencies as children[52] he had nurtured, and therefore felt betrayed by Cooper. *Barriers Down* might thus almost be seen as a Shakespearean drama or analysed in terms of an Oedipal relationship where the son must kill his father in order to liberate himself. It can also be seen as depicting a transnational and intragenerational relationship, with the coloniser and oppressor (Great Britain) being defeated by its vibrant and more successful former colony, the United States. Cooper's book has a sense of drama that goes beyond what could otherwise be seen as the breakdown of a relationship between two long-time business partners – a rather mundane and commonplace event.

Cooper's other generational conflict was a domestic one, with the AP's competitor, the UP. Despite their age difference, Cooper and Howard belonged to the same generation. They both wanted to change things in their respective organisations but Cooper had less freedom and had to wait longer than Howard, who had an earlier start with a new organisation. They competed fiercely but also wanted the same things. With the AP's foreign expansion, Cooper followed Howard's path in the UP, and in the end it was the UP that, by not signing with Reuters, guaranteed the AP's independence from the cartel. They both signed up to the ideology of expanding American ideas abroad through news transmission. Despite being competitors, Howard and Cooper were influenced by similar utopias and ideologies concerning the role of US news worldwide.

Howard wrote as early as 1916, when the UP signed its first agreement with *La Nación* in Argentina, long before Cooper liberated the AP from the European news cartel:

> [that] America is destined to play a new part in things international is fully evidenced by the arrangements just concluded ... Summed up: these arrangements mean that New York is to become the news-gathering center, second to none – not even to London. ('New York to Be the News-Clearing House of the World' 1916)

The timing of Cooper's book was a key factor in its success. After Pearl Harbor and the US entry into World War II, the country needed all kinds of heroes and even news agency directors, not often seen as the most heroic characters, had to do their patriotic duty. Cooper certainly did his duty, at the right time but also potentially at the wrong time, since Great Britain and the US had now become allies fighting against a joint enemy, Nazi Germany.

Thus, although the timing of this was not right in terms of the military alliance, it was lucky for Cooper that Reuters' change of ownership and of director offered him a chance to return to London as a celebrated hero and a freedom fighter, whose values were now also Reuters' values (Willens 1951). The expansion of the cooperative ownership form into a Europe in ruins had just begun and was now adopted by many national news agencies, old and new, just as Cooper had envisioned in 1922.

Cooper's starting point was also undoubtedly comparative, since he compared his own news agency with agencies in Europe, and especially with Reuters. His work has similarities to propaganda studies, depicting a scenario of US propaganda versus enemy propaganda, discussed in Chapter 4. Not unlike much writing in propaganda studies, it takes sides – 'us versus them' and 'good versus evil'. Cooper's book wholly lacks any attempt to hide its biases, since in his thinking both the AP and the US represented freedom and other superlative values that other agencies and countries should adopt in order to join a worldwide free press community that would lead to lasting peace.

Was Cooper, then, an Insider or an Outsider? He was an Insider by virtue of his membership of an elite, of his running the biggest news agency in the United States, but his agency was not an equal member of the European news cartel. Cooper himself felt that not only his agency but he himself were underdogs in relation to Reuters and to Reuters' director, Sir Roderick Jones. By changing its position vis-à-vis the European news cartel the AP became an Insider, one of the biggest international news agencies, which would go on to dominate the world's news market for decades to come. Thus, Cooper showed, perhaps not intentionally, that, given it was possible for the AP to liberate itself from the dominance of the cartel, it was also possible for other news agencies that had become dependent on the big Western agencies to liberate themselves, an idea that was again taken up in the 1970s. In this way, it is also possible to analyse conflicts inside a transnational elite, often seen as homogenous and all-powerful Anglo-American hegemony by those outside it (Schiller 1969; 1976; Tunstall 1977). Since *Barriers Down* is not the story of a whole generation but mainly about Cooper himself, it has been crucial, in order to support or contradict his claims, to use materials from various different archives as well as previous research on his competitors.

Analysing Cooper's work at the AP, often seen by those outside the country as representative of the dominant US ideology and even at one time media imperialism (Mattelart 1979, pp.60, 149), also gives an opportunity to investigate generational conflicts inside organisations, where the struggle for power and for access to information may be even more atrocious than in academia. *Barriers Down* (1942) can be read as the story of national and international, intra- and intergenerational, conflict, which is rather unusual considering when it was published, just after the US entered World War II. The book is also an example of how utopias and ideologies are intertwined and how utopias are used to justify ideologies. It exemplifies what happens when the past is used to validate the future, and when utopias are transformed into new ideologies.

Intellectually, however, Cooper was an Outsider, since he did not have an academic position. Nonetheless, as the author of *Barriers Down* he outperformed his academic contemporaries by writing a book that reached both non-academic and academic audiences. By sharing some of the concepts, such as those of propaganda and of news flows, that academics were also using, he popularised them. The popularity of Cooper's work also shows how weak comparative communications then was, and how easy it was for him to have access to it, especially as a member of an elite. Since most of the work being done was applied, the boundaries between non-academic and academic work were extremely permeable – in practice there were no boundaries. Access to materials was one of the key features when defining an Insider or an Outsider. Cooper, as a member of an elite, had access to materials that very few people, including academics, had. His position as general manager of the AP also gave him an authority and status, especially outside academia, that few academics had.

Cooper's life and work reveal what it takes to transform utopias into ideologies. One has to question whether Cooper's utopias really originated in Paris in 1919, as he claimed in *Barriers Down* and in his various speeches, or whether this was just his rhetoric. Cooper's view that the AP could liberate itself from its contractual dependence on Reuters was certainly utopian even in the 1920s. He was not alone in his critique: for example, in German propaganda during World War I Reuters was called the headquarters of lies (Tworek 2019, pp.53–54). Of course, Cooper's ideas were not only his own individual ideas but reflected a change in international politics when Great Britain started losing its power of empire. Cooper not only conveniently forgot the UP's role in his struggle for liberation, but also how the US government offered discounts in wireless telegraph states and encouraged US news agencies to expand their activities. However, even taking all this into consideration, Cooper's pursuit of this utopia was successful. His methods may have been immoral and blameworthy but there is no doubt that he strongly believed in the superiority of the AP because of its cooperative ownership form.

Cooper's ideological thinking with regard to the supremacy of his own values was combined with utopian thinking about the role of news in maintaining and promoting peace. It reflects both the dominant ideology of the time, in the midst of World War II, and the emerging ideology of the role of news in the US and in the world at large. What Cooper and Howard together achieved was dominance by US news agencies, with the International News Service (INS) together with AFP in France, Reuters in the UK and TASS in the Soviet Union, as the new international news agencies that played a dominant role in the post-war world (UNESCO 1953). This was achieved only thanks to a US generation that shared a similar ideology of the supremacy of US news transmission. What Cooper did not know was that his generation's ideas would be turned against his own agency, all US agencies and the US itself in the 1970s by the movement for a New World Information and Communication Order, a new utopia.

Notes

1 Text of AP answer to Government monopoly suit. *The Chicago Sun* on 28 October 1942. Scrapbook, AP 39.07, Box 11, Folder 1. The Associated Press (AP) Corporate Archives.

2 According to Howard, he first went to London in 1913 'at the request of Baron Reuter to discuss with him a shift to the Reuter service from the AP to the UP that I first started dreaming of a rally international news agency that would compete around the world with Reuters and its satellites in the news cartel'. R.W. Howard to K. Bickel on 20 April 1950. Roy W. Howard Papers, The Media School Archive, Indiana University; Note by Sir Roderick Jones on conversation by Atlantic telephone with Mr. Karl Bickel. Private and Confidential on 24 January 1934. Section 2. Sir Roderick Jones Papers. Reuters Archives.

3 Draft report of Commission on Freedom of the Press. Box 2, Folder 2. Commission on Freedom of the Press Records. Hanna Holborn Gray Special Collections Research Center, University of Chicago Library.

4 Document No 33A, World Freedom of the Press & Mr. Cooper's Proposals on 24 January 1945. Box 2, Folder 2; Document No. 53, A Note on Sources. Reports on International Mass Communications, May 31, 1945. Box 2, Folder 11; Kent Cooper Statement, at luncheon meeting with the Commission; Associated Press Building, Rockefeller Plaza, on 5 June 1945; Document No. 66A, Addendum to Summary of Kent Cooper Statement, Document 66, pp.37–38. Based on Notes Made by Zechariah Chafee, Jr. Box 3, Folder 3. Commission on Freedom of the Press Records. Hanna Holborn Gray Special Collections Research Center, University of Chicago Library.

5 Commission of Freedom of the Press (1944) Document No 17. Synopsis of the meeting of 8–9 May 1944. Harold Dwight Lasswell Papers, General Files, Series I, Box 27, Folder 342. Manuscripts and Archives, Yale University Library.

6 R.W. Howard to K. Bickel on 11 May 1933. Roy Winston Howard Papers, the Collections of the Manuscript Division, Library of Congress.

7 M.E. Stone to R. Martin on 29 July 1918. Melville E. Stone Papers. The Newberry Library.

8 Memorandum by Sir Roderick Jones of conversation with Mr. Melville Stone on Friday morning on 19 December 1919, at the Hotel Mirabeau, Paris. Microfilms 186. Reuters Archives.

9 Havas-Reuters Treaty on 16 January 1919. R/1/8715530. Reuters Archives.

10 Memorandum by Sir Roderick Jones with Wolff (and AP's Mr Stone) on 20 December 1919. R/1/8715519. Reuters Archives.

[11] Cooper, K. Truthful news, a Basis for Peace. Address given at Congregation Emanu-el Temple on 21 January 1945. Records of General Manager Kent Cooper, AP 02.01, Box 44, Folder 1. The AP Archives.

[12] Cooper, K. Truthful news, a Basis for Peace. Address given at Congregation Emanu-el Temple on 21 January 1945. Records of General Manager Kent Cooper, AP 02.01, Box 44, Folder 1. The AP Archives.

[13] Cooper, K. Truthful News, a Basis for Peace. Address given at Congregation Emanu-el Temple on 21 January 1945. Records of General Manager Kent Cooper, AP 02.01, Box 44, Folder 1. The AP Archives.

[14] Cooper, K. Truthful News, a Basis for Peace. Address given at Congregation Emanu-el Temple on 21 January 1945. Records of General Manager Kent Cooper, AP 02.01, Box 44, Folder 1. The AP Archives.

[15] World Freedom of Press and Radio. Reprints of Cooper's address before the National Editorial Association on 21 October 1945. Records of General Manager Kent Cooper, AP 02.01, Box 45, Folder 2. The AP Archives.

[16] Document No. 68. Commission of the Freedom of the Press. Fly, J.L. Freedom of Communication. Roundtable discussion on The United Nations and the organization of Peace and Security before the Twenty-First Institute of the Norman Wait Harris Foundation, at Chicago, Illinois, 9–13 July, 1945. Box 3, Folder 4. Commission on Freedom of the Press. Records. Hanna Holborn Gray Special Collections Research Center, University of Chicago Library.

[17] Cooper, K. Truthful News, a Basis for Peace. Address given at Congregation Emanu-el Temple on 21 January 1945. Records of General Manager Kent Cooper, AP 02.01, Box 44, Folder 1. The AP Archives.

[18] K. Cooper to M. Stone on 1 September 1919. Cooper mss. Lilly Library, Indiana University.

[19] Cooper, K. Memorandum of agency contracts on 17 May 1920. Cooper mss. Lilly Library, Indiana University.

[20] Memorandum of agency contracts on 17 May 1920. Cooper mss. Lilly Library, Indiana University.

[21] D. Williams to Sir Roderick Jones on 2 July 1925. Box File 2. Sir Roderick Jones Papers. Reuters Archives.

[22] K. Cooper to F. Noyes on 19 May 1926. Cooper mss. Lilly Library, Indiana University.

[23] Copy of Treaty on 8 August 1927. R/1/864921. Reuters Archives.

[24] Report to the Board by Mr W.J. Healey on 1 July 1942. R/1/8746805. Reuters Archives.

25 Special meeting of the board on 20 June 1933. Box File 38, Sir Roderick Jones Papers. Reuters Archives.

26 F.D. Williams to Sir Roderick Jones on 7 July 1926. Box File 2, Sir Roderick Jones Papers. Reuters Archives.

27 Report to the Board by Mr W.J. Healey on 1 July 1942. R/1/8746805. Reuters Archives.

28 Mr Buchan: I doubt whether we shall have any peace as long as Kent Cooper is at the head of affairs. I have never liked the man. He is a low stamp American, of a different class altogether from the old AP man. Sir Roderick: He descends to methods which are enough to make Melville Stone turn in his grave. Special meeting of the board on 20 June 1933. Box 38. Sir Roderick Jones Papers. Reuters Archives.

29 Two-party contract between the AP and Reuters dated on 13 February 1934. R/1/871243412. Reuters Archives.

30 Cooper, K. So They Do Not Need to March Again, Manuscript, no date. Records of General Manager Kent Cooper papers, AP 02.01, Box 44, Folder 13. The AP Archives.

31 Meeting of the Board of Directors on 12 January 1943, p.4. The AP 44th annual volume for the year of 1943 (printed in 1944). Records of General Manager Kent Cooper, AP 02.01, Box 42, Folders 13–14. The AP Archives.

32 Meeting of the AP Board of Directors in New York on 12 January 1943. 44th annual volume for the year of 1943 (printed in 1944). Records of the Board & Annual Meetings, Charters & Bylaws 1922–1963, AP 01.01, Series 1, Box 2. The AP Archives.

33 K. Cooper to J.F.B. Livesay on 23 January 1934. Cooper mss. Lilly Library, Indiana University.

34 K. Cooper. A practical idealist, no date. Records of General Manager Kent Cooper, AP 02.01, Box 48, Folder 14. The AP Archives.

35 K. Cooper to multiple receivers on 27 November 1942. Records of General Manager Kent Cooper, AP 02.01, Box 43, Folder 7. The AP Archives.

36 R.W. Howard to W.W. Hawkins on 19 March 1952. Roy W. Howard Papers. The Media School Archive, Indiana University.

37 R.W. Howard to W.N. Bankhurst on 15 August 1938. Roy W. Howard Papers. The Media School Archive, Indiana University.

38 J.H. Furay to R.W. Howard on 28 March 1952. Roy W. Howard Papers. The Media School Archive, Indiana University.

39 Cartel members, the AP, on 1 July 1930. AP collections online. The AP Archives.

40 Cooper, K. Free Press – Antidote to Atomic Bomb. Address before the Boston Conference on Distribution on 16 October 1945. Records of General Manager Kent Cooper, AP O2.01, Box 43, Folders 14–15. The AP Archives.

41 Cooper, K. Truthful News a Basis for Peace. Address given at Congregation Emanu-el Temple on 21 January 1945. Records of General Manager Kent Cooper, AP 02.01, Box 44, Folder 1. The AP Archives.

42 Cooper K. Free News. First Step in Peace, 1944. Reprinted from *Free World*. Records of General Manager Kent Cooper, AP 02.01, Box 43, Folder 13. The AP Archives.

43 Cooper, K. Free Press – An Antidote to Atomic Bomb. Address before the Boston Conference on Distribution on October 16, 1945. Records of General Manager Kent Cooper, AP 02.01, Box 43, Folders 14–15. The AP Archives.

44 Cooper, K. World Freedom of Press and Radio. Address delivered before the National Editorial Association at Chicago on 21 October 1944. Records of General Manager Kent Cooper, AP 02.01, Box 45, Folder 2. The AP Archives.

45 Senate Concurrent Resolution 52 by Senator Tom Connally, of Texas, chairman, Committee on Foreign Relations. 1943. Records of General Manager Kent Cooper, AP 02.01, Box 43, Folder 6. The AP Archives.

46 Senate Concurrent Resolution 53 unanimously adopted on 21 September 1944 by the Senate and House of Representatives. Records of General Manager Kent Cooper, AP 02.01, Box 43, Folder 6. The AP Archives.

47 Cooper, K. Memorandum on Far Eastern news situation on May 27, 1933. Cooper mss. 1921–1935. Lilly Library, Indiana University.

48 The AP 47th annual volume for the year of 1946 (printed in 1947). Meeting of the Board of Directors, New York on 9 January 1946. Records of the Board and Annual Meetings, AP 01.01, Series 1, Box 2. The AP Archives.

49 Foreign service bureaus, January 1944. The AP Collections Online. The AP Archives.

50 Cooper, K. Free News: First Step in Peace, September 1944. Reprinted from *Free World*. Records of General Manager Kent Cooper, AP 02.01, Box 43, Folder 12. The AP Archives.

51 Reuters Centenary Address on 11 July 1951. Records of General Manager Kent Cooper, AP 02.01, Box 44, Folder 8. The AP Archives.

52 K. Cooper to F.B. Noyes on 23 July 1933. Cooper mss. Lilly Library, Indiana University.

References

'A.P. Called Greatest Cooperative Effort. News Service Formed to "Keep Pure the Channels of Public Information," Cooper Tells Insurance Presidents Group—Says It Has Contributed to Brotherhood of American Citizenship' (1926) *Editor & Publisher*, vol. 59, no. 29, 11 December. https://archive.org/details/sim_editor-publisher_1926-12-11_59_29/page/6/mode/2up

'AP Enjoined from Observing Membership Provision By-laws' (1944) *Editor & Publisher*, vol. 77, no. 3, 15 January. https://archive.org/details/sim_editor-publisher_1944-01-15_77_3

Associated Press v. United States (1943) 52 F. Sup 362. USA: US District Court for the Southern District of New York.

Associated Press v. United States (1945) 326 U.S. 1, 65 S. Ct 1416 (145). USA: U.S. Supreme Court.

Blanchard, Margaret A. (1977) 'The Hutchins Commission, the Press and the Responsibility Concept', *Journalism Monographs*, vol. 49, May, pp.1–59. http://www.aejmc.org/home/wp-content/uploads/2012/09/Margaret-A.-Blanchard.The-Hutchins-Commission.May-1977.pdf

Carlsson, Ulla (2003) 'The Rise and Fall of NWICO: From a Vision of International Regulation to a Reality of Multilevel Governance', *Nordicom Review*, vol. 24, no. 2, pp.31–67. https://doi.org/10.1515/nor-2017-0306

Coggeshall, Reginald (1942) 'Peace Conference Publicity: Lessons of 1919', *Journalism Quarterly*, vol. 19, no. 1, pp.1–11.

Cooper, Kent (1942) *Barriers Down: The Story of the News Agency Epoch*, USA: Farrar & Rinehart.

Cooper, Kent (1945a) 'Crusade for Truth. Kent Cooper Heads a Unique American Campaign for Worldwide Freedom of the Press, Meaning What?' *Fortune*, April, 13, pp.146–49.

Cooper, Kent (1945b) 'AP Put Under Court Control by Demand of FDR–Cooper', *Editor & Publisher*, vol. 78, no. 43, 20 October, p.11. https://rchive.org/details/sim_editor-publisher_1945-10-20_78_43

Cooper, Kent (1946) *Anna Zenger, Mother of Freedom*, USA: Farrar, Straus and Company.

Cooper, Kent (1947) 'Cooper Criticizes "Voice of America"; It Is Impotent, He Says at Medill School Jubilee, Speaking Not as AP Chief', *The New York Times*, 27 May. https://www.nytimes.com/1947/05/27/archives/cooper-criticizes-voice-of-america-it-is-impotent-he-says-at-medill.html

Cooper, Kent (1956) *The Right to Know: An Exposition of the Evils of News Suppression and Propaganda*, USA: Farrar, Straus and Cudahy.

Cooper, Kent (1959) *Kent Cooper and the Associated Press: An Autobiography*, USA: Random House.

Cuthbert, Marlene (1980) 'Reaction to International News Agencies: 1930s and 1970s Compared', *Gazette*, vol. 26, no. 2, pp.99–110.

Desmond, Robert W. (1937) *The Press and World Affairs*, USA: D. Appleton-Century.

'Directors and Members of the AP Join In Honoring Melville E. Stone' (1918) *Editor & Publisher*, vol 50, no. 46, 27 April, p.1. https://archive .org/details/sim_editor-publisher_1918-04-27_50_46/page/4/mode/2up

Douglass, Paul F. and Bomer, Karl (1932) 'The International Combination of News Agencies', *Annals of the American Academy of Political and Social Science*, vol. 162, pp.265–68. https://journals.sagepub.com/doi/pdf/10.1177/000271623216200138

Entwisle, John (no date) 'Sir Roderick Jones's Finest Hour', *The Baron*. https://www.thebaron.info/archives/sir-roderick-joness-finest-hour

Forrest, Wilbur (1945) 'Letter to Stettinius Outlines Mission', *Editor & Publisher*, vol. 78, no. 25, 18 June, p.4. https://archive.org/details/sim _editor-publisher_1945-06-16_78_25/page/n79/mode/2up

Gramling, Oliver (1940/1969) *AP (Associated Press): The Story of News*, USA: Kennikat Press.

Inter-Ocean Publishing Co. v. Associated Press (1900) 184 Ill. 438, USA: Illinois Supreme Court.

'International Congress Will Consider Plans for World-Wide News Service' (1919) *Editor & Publisher*, vol. 72, no. 7, 17 July, p.9. https://archive.org/details/sim_editor-publisher_1919-07-17_52_7

International Press Institute (1953) *The Flow of News: A Study by the International Press Institute*, Switzerland: International Press Institute.

Iwanaga, Shinkichi (1980) *Story of Japanese News Agencies: A Historic Account From Meiji Restoration (1868) to the End of World War II (1945)*, Japan: Institute of News Service Research.

John, Richard R. (2020) 'When Techno-diplomacy Failed: Walter S. Rogers, the Universal Electrical Communications Union, and the Limitations of the International Telegraph Union as a Global Actor in the 1920s', in Fickers, Andreas and Balbi, Gabriele (eds) *History of the International Telecommunication Union (ITU): Transnational Techno-diplomacy from the Telegraph to the Internet*, Germany: De Gruyter Oldenbourg, pp.55–76.

Jones, Roderick S. (1951) *A Life in Reuters*, UK: Hodder & Stoughton.

Knights, Peter R. (1967) 'The Press Association War of 1866–1867', *Journalism and Communication Monographs*, December, no. 6.

Komor, Valerie S. (2021) *AP at 175: A Photographic History*. https://apimag esblog.com/historical/2021/1/30/ap-at-175-a-photographic-history

Lasswell, Harold D. (1951a) 'The Policy Orientation', in Lerner, Daniel and Lasswell, Harold D. (eds) *The Policy Sciences: Recent Developments in Scope and Method*, USA: Stanford University Press, pp.3–15.

Lemberg, Diana (2019) *Barriers Down: How American Power and Free-flow Policies Shaped Global Media*, USA: Columbia University Press.

Lippmann, Walter (1922) *Public Opinion*, USA: Harcourt, Brace and Company.

Mannheim, Karl (1934) 'The Crisis of Culture in the Era of Mass-Democracies and Autarchies', *The Sociological Review*, vol. 26, no. 2, pp.105–29. https://doi.org/10.1111/j.1467-954X.1934.tb01902.x

Mattelart, Armand (1979) *Multinational Corporations and the Control of Culture: The Ideological Apparatuses of Imperialism*, UK: Harvester Press.

McIntyre, Jerilyn S. (1987) 'Repositioning a Landmark: The Hutchins Commission and Freedom of the Press', *Critical Studies in Media Communication*, vol. 4, no. 2, pp.136–60. https://doi.org/10.1080/15295038709360122

'New York to Be the News-Clearing House of the World' (1916) *Editor & Publisher*, vol. 49, no. 22, 11 November, p.1. https://archive.org/details /sim_editor-publisher_1916-11-11_49_22/page/n3/mode/2up

Pickard, Victor (2014) *America's Battle for Media Democracy: The Triumph of Corporate Libertarianism and the Future of Media Reform*, USA: Cambridge University Press. https://doi.org/10.1017/CBO9781139814799

Rantanen, Terhi (1990) 'Foreign News in Imperial Russia: The Relationship between International and Russian News Agencies, 1856–1914', *Annales Academiae Scientiarum Fennicae, Dissertationes humanarum litterarum*, Finland: Suomalainen tiedeakatemia. http://acadsci.fi/julkaisut/AASF_HumDiss_58_Rantanen.pdf

Rantanen, Terhi (1992) 'Mr. Howard Goes to South America. The United Press Associations and Foreign Expansion', Roy W. Howard Monographs in Journalism and Mass Communication Research, no. 2, USA: Indiana University. http://fedora.dlib.indiana.edu/fedora/get/iudl:2530612/OVERVIEW

Rantanen, Terhi (1994) 'Howard Interviews Stalin: How the AP, UP and TASS Smashed the International News Cartel', Roy W. Howard Monographs in Journalism and Mass Communication Research, no. 3, USA: Indiana University. http://fedora.dlib.indiana.edu/fedora/get/iudl:2530632/OVERVIEW

Rantanen, Terhi (1998) 'After Five O'clock Friends: Kent Cooper and Roy W. Howard', USA: Indiana University. Roy W. Howard Monographs in

Journalism and Mass Communication Research, no. 4.
http://fedora.dlib.ndiana.edu/fedora/get/iudl:2530662/OVERVIEW

Rantanen, Terhi (2006) 'Foreign Dependence and Domestic Monopoly: The
European News Cartel and US Associated Presses, 1861–1932', Media History, vol. 12, no. 1, pp.19–35. https://doi.org/10.1080/13688800600597145

Rantanen, Terhi (2012) 'Quickening Urgency: The Telegraph and Wire
Services in 1846–1893', in Valdivia, Anharad N. (ed.) The International
Encyclopedia of Media Studies, vol. 1: Media History and the Foundations
of Media Studies, USA: Wiley-Blackwell.
https://doi.org/10.1002/9781444361506.wbiems015

Rantanen, Terhi (2019) 'News Agencies from Telegraph Bureaus to Cyberfactories', in Communication. Oxford Research Encyclopedias, UK: Oxford
University Press. https://oxfordre.com/communication/view/10.1093
/acrefore/9780190228613.001.0001/acrefore-9780190228613-e-843

Read, Donald (1990) 'Sir Roderick Jones and Reuters: Rise and Fall of a
News Emperor', in Fraser, Derek (ed.) Cities, Class and Communications:
Essays in Honour of Asa Briggs, UK: Harvester Wheatsheaf, pp.175–99.

Read, Donald (1999) The Power of News: The History of Reuters (2nd ed.),
UK: Oxford University Press.

Renaud, Jean-Luc (1985) 'US Government Assistance to AP's World-Wide
Expansion', Journalism Quarterly, vol. 62, no. 1, pp.10–36.
https://doi.org/10.1177/107769908506200102

Rosewater, Victor (1930) History of Cooperative News-Gathering in the
United States, USA: D. Appleton.

Scharnberg, Harriet (2016) 'The A and P of Propaganda: Associated Press
and Nazi Photojournalism', Zeithistorische Forschungen / Studies in
Contemporary History, vol. 13. https://doi.org/10.14765/zzf.dok-1414

Schiller, Herbert I. (1969) Mass Communications and American Empire,
USA: Beacon Press.

Schiller, Herbert I. (1975) 'Genesis of the Free Flow of Information Principles: The Imposition of Communications Domination', Instant Research
on Peace and Violence, vol. 5, no. 2, pp.75–86.
http://www.jstor.org/stable/40724768

Schiller, Herbert I. (1976) Communication and Cultural Domination, USA:
M.E. Sharpe.

Schudson, Michael (2015) The Rise of the Right to Know: Politics and the
Culture of Transparency 1945–1975, USA: Belknap Press.

Schwarzlose, Richard A. (1989a) Kent Cooper, USA: Greenwood Press.

Schwarzlose, Richard A. (1989b) *The Nation's Newsbrokers, Vol. 1: The Formative Years From Pretelegraph to 1865*, USA: Northwestern University Press.

Schwarzlose, Richard A. (1989c) *The Nation's Newsbrokers, Vol. 2: The Rush to Institution From 1865 to 1920*, USA: Northwestern University Press.

Silberstein-Loeb, Jonathan (2014) *The International Distribution of News: The Associated Press, Press Association, and Reuters, 1848–1947*, UK: Cambridge University Press.

Stone, Melville E. (1921) *Fifty Years a Journalist: Line Cuts by Paul Brown*, USA: Doubleday, Page & Company.

Storey, Graham (1951) *Reuters' Century, 1851–1951*, UK: Parrish.

Stowe, Leland (1927) 'Tainted News in Peace', *New Republic*, 10 August.

'Supreme Court Rules against AP, 5–3. Special Meeting of Board Is Called' (1945) *Editor & Publisher*, vol. 78, no. 26, 23 June, p.5. https://archive.org/details/sim_editor-publisher_1945-06-23_78_26

'Text of Federal Court's Decision in the Government's Suit against the Associated Press' (1943) *The New York Times*, 7 October. https://www .nytimes.com/1943/10/07/archives/text-of-federal-courts-decision-in -the-governments-suit-against-the.html

'The Press: Young Man with a Mission' (1946) *Time*, 11 February. https://content.time.com/time/subscriber/article/0,33009,854150-1,00.html

Tunstall, Jeremy (1977) *The Media Are American: Anglo-American Media in the World*, UK: Constable.

Tworek, Heidi (2019) *News from Germany. The Competition to Control World Communications, 1900–1945*, USA: Harvard University Press.

UNESCO (1953) *News Agencies: Their Structure and Operation*, France: UNESCO. https://unesdoc.unesco.org/ark:/48223/pf0000073446

United Nations General Assembly (1948) Universal Declaration of Human Rights. https://www.un.org/en/about-us/universal-declaration-of -human-rights#:~:text=Article%2019,media%20and%20regardless%20 of%20frontiers

White, Llewellyn and Leigh, Robert D. (1946) *Peoples Speaking to Peoples: A Report on International Mass Communication from the Commission on Freedom of the Press*, USA: University of Chicago Press.

'Will Seek Laws to Guard News Property' (1926) *Editor & Publisher*, vol. 59, no. 14, 4 September, p.9. https://archive.org/details/sim_editor-publisher_1926-09-04_59_15

Willens, Doris (1951) 'Reuters Celebrates Its 100th Anniversary, London, July 11. World Press Leaders to Attend with Kent Cooper Honoured', *Editor & Publisher*, vol. 84, no. 24, 9 June, p.9. https://archive.org/details/sim_editor-publisher_1951-06-09_84_24

'World Wire Services Meet at Geneva. Commission Called by League Preparing Agenda for 1927 Press Conference – Howard, Named Executive Committee Head, Wins Plea for Public Sessions and Moves Keynote Resolution' (1926) *Editor & Publisher*, vol. 59, no. 13, 21 August, p.5. https://archive.org/details/sim_editor-publisher_1926-08-21_59_13

4. World War II comparative communications: the institutionalisation of ideology by policy scientists, émigré scholars and the military, 1940–1943

> In war, men suffer pain, hunger, sorrow; the specific source of pain, the specific sensation of one's specific object of sorrow, may be very private. In contrast, the key symbol enters directly into the focus of all men and provides an element of common experience. (Lasswell 1949, pp.51–52)

This chapter picks up where Chapter 2 left off, with Lasswell, but it brings in new actors who were working with him during World War II on content analysis in order to study war propaganda. Lasswell was, from 1940 to 1943,[1] director of the Experimental Division for the Study of War Time (sometimes War-Time) Communications at the US Library of Congress (hereafter the Wartime Communications Project), funded by the Rockefeller Foundation, whose purpose was to conduct a 'World Attention Survey' through analysis of major newspapers (Berelson and Lazarsfeld 1948, pp.23–24; Lasswell 1941a; Lasswell and Goldsen 1947; Lasswell, Leites and Associates 1949). It did pioneering work on the methodological development of quantitative and qualitative content analysis, and most of it was done in pairs and groups. The chapter gives me an opportunity to analyse how policy science was conducted and to emphasise the role of non-academics and of émigré scholars from Europe who worked collectively during World War II to collect data and provide analysis that contributed to propaganda research. I argue that wartime comparative communications made its participants into a unified generation, where Insiders and Outsiders temporarily came together, leaving aside their non-shared utopias, united by the same ideology but separated by their status.

This chapter also problematises the concepts of ideology and utopia by questioning the concept of time (ideologies being about the past, utopias about the future). I explore how collective comparative communications was

---

How to cite this book chapter:

Rantanen, Terhi (2024) *Dead Men's Propaganda: Ideology and Utopia in Comparative Communications Studies*, London: LSE Press, pp. 125–165.
https://doi.org/10.31389/lsepress.wmf.d. License: CC BY-NC 4.0

carried out primarily within the Wartime Communications Project and in other government departments. I concentrate here especially on those émigré scholars whose names have been largely forgotten, specifically Nathan Leites (1912–1987) and Paul Kecskemeti (1901–1980), together with US researchers who themselves came from migrant families and many of whom were Lasswell's students or colleagues from the University of Chicago. The networks among the men who together analysed war propaganda often lasted their whole lifetimes. These men not only became colleagues who continued their work together at RAND Corporation after World War II but often also became friends, who, with their families, socialised outside of work. They became a generation that shared memories of fighting the propaganda war together. In this chapter, I analyse some of their projects, showing what kinds of theories they used, what kinds of methodological problems these researchers faced and how they solved them.

The chapter also touches on parallel work done in other government departments in the US at the same time or after the project was finished, since researchers often worked in pairs or in groups across institutions. There were other projects funded by private foundations, such as the Research Project on Totalitarian Communication under the direction of Ernst Kris and Hans Speier (Kris and Speier 1944) at the New School for Social Research in New York. The Office of Radio Research at Columbia University used content analysis. The Media Division of the Office of War Information (OWI) conducted content studies of war-related problems in newspapers, magazines, radio programmes, newsreels and comic strips. Another major application of content analysis was in the Analysis Division of the Foreign Broadcast Intelligence Service of the Federal Communications Commission (FCC), which prepared weekly special reports on broadcasts to and within the US from foreign countries (see, for example, Berelson and de Grazia 1947, Berelson and Lazarsfeld 1948, pp.10–12). Yet another was the Organization and Propaganda Analysis Section of the Special War Policies Unit, Department of Justice, which employed content analysis techniques in its investigation of the propaganda output of various suspect organisations or individuals. This attempted to:

> establish parallelisms between such propaganda and the propaganda of enemy countries and it took into court exhibits based upon content analysis and had them accepted as legal evidence requiring testimony of experts. (Berelson and Lazarsfeld 1948, p.24)

Other agencies included the Office of Strategic Services, the Board of Economic Warfare, and the War, Navy and State departments.[2] This chapter is divided into three parts. The first deals with Lasswell's role as director of the project at the US Library of Congress and the Rockefeller Foundation as a funder, while the second part moves on to émigré scholars and their US colleagues, and the final part considers the research and its evaluation.

4.1 The nature of research

The research done during World War II marks the beginning of a new period of group research, of collaboration between US and foreign researchers, and between academics, policy scientists and the military. This was also the period when future academics (many of whom were PhD or even undergraduate students when working for the project) became full-time policy scientists, for some paving the way for future careers at RAND Corporation (see, for example, Davison 2006; Chapter 5 in this book). Much of their research was published in reports of the Wartime Communications Project during World War II and was later in academic books, articles and chapters after the war. According to Smith (1943, p.2), research included:

> 'semi-scientific literature', meaning the writings of responsible newspaper men, radio commentators, public officials and others who have earned the respect of the scientific community not only for their accuracy, comprehensiveness and detachment in covering assignments but for their insight into the total social context.

Thus, World War II opened up new, unforeseen opportunities for individual men and research groups who achieved access to materials for their propaganda studies. The young Heinz Eulau (1915–2004), who had just received his PhD, remembered what happened when he joined Lasswell's project as a research associate in 1943 (Eulau 1968, pp.9–10):

> Moreover, the seemingly endless coding, all the pluses for strength and the minuses for weakness in the flow of symbols, and the poring over Lasswellian prose were richly rewarded by the company that Lasswell was keeping at the Library of Congress. He had assembled a research team of young men, including anthropologists, psychologists, sociologists and political scientists, almost all of whom were to influence the course of behavioral science after the war. Among the political scientists and political sociologists were David Truman, Ithiel Pool, Alexander George [1920–2006], Edward Shils, Nathan Leites, Bruce Lannes Smith, Morris Janowitz, Sebastian de Grazia and others. From Shils, walking me under an inevitable umbrella down Pennsylvania Avenue, I heard about Toennies, Simmel, Mannheim and other European sociologists I had never heard of. From Leites, giving a seminar in a language that combined Freud and Lasswell and was at first quite incomprehensible, I heard about the relevance of culture and personality for political science.

All the individuals recruited to Lasswell's project as researchers (fellows) were men, while women worked only as research assistants. The telephone directory and letters in the archival materials reveal that many women were, for example, carrying out the coding of content analysis in several govern-ment departments,[3] but their names never appeared in publications. They included Miss Brockett, Louise Baker, Elizabeth Beitz,[4] Phyllis Preston,[5] Clara J. Kretzinger, Sophia Ramm, Grace De Palma, Frances A. McCarter and M. Lubow Hansen.[6] Very little is known about them. Their names never appeared as authors, nor were they thanked in the acknowledgements in various works published during and after World War II. My findings support the existence of what Ashcraft and Simonson (2016, p.65) call a 'homosocial work practice', where 'works typically refer to published research or sometimes, by extension, to the investigative labor of an author whose name is affixed to a publication' (p.49). The Library of Congress project offered new opportunities for men, both US and non-US nationals, but not usually for women, except in this role of nameless research assistants.

Two academic publications were published under Lasswell's name alone (Lasswell 1941; 1942), although they were the result of collective work, and even work done in groups or in pairs is credited to Lasswell alone (see, for example, Levyatan 2009). The Wartime Communications Pro-ject, as collective research carried out by groups or pairs of academics, PhD students, consultants and civil servants, together with the army, was policy science in its purest form.[7] This pioneering work and served as an example for future comparative communications that would use research groups often consisting of researchers from different countries, funded by foundations, governments and international organisations. Some earlier studies have already concentrated on the ideological aspects of wartime psy-chological studies (Glander 1999; Simpson 1994; Sproule 1997) and their influence on the future of communications studies in the US in general. Simp-son, for example, has shown that US psychological warfare studies carried out during World War II became part of an applied form of mass communication theory (Simpson 1994, p.115). As a consequence, according to Simpson,

> Despite its claims, communication studies in the United States have not been typically neutral, objective, or even held at arm's length from the political and economic powers of the day. Instead, communication studies entwined themselves with the existing institutions of power, just as have, say, the mainstream study of economics or atomic phys-ics, whose inbreeding with the political and military establishment are so extensive as to have become common knowledge. (p.116)

Simpson (1994) and Glander (1999) agree that World War II was a water-shed, when communication studies in the US started to come of age. There is also research on the work carried out in wartime by individual academics, especially Lazarsfeld, and on how this has been used (see, for example, Mor-rison 1988, 2008, 2022), but not much research has focused on *how* wartime collective comparative communications on the content of propaganda was conducted. This is probably because academic research is often seen as an individual achievement rather than as something done by a group, but also because so much of established scholarship on émigré scholars has concentrated on the Frankfurt School (Jay 1973/1996) with its different ideologies and utopias.

Further, history of the field of communication studies has often structured as being either 'administrative' or 'critical'. This distinction seems first to have been made by Lazarsfeld (1941), who famously defined administrative research as 'carried through the service of some kind of administrative agency of public or private character' and as being of a more 'practical character', while critical research:

> develops a theory of the prevailing social trends of our times, general trends which yet require consideration in any concrete research problem; and it seems to imply ideas of basic human values according to which all actual or desired effects should be appraised. (pp.8–9)

Rogers (1981, p.25) writes that the empirical school in communication research has usually relied on empiricism, functionalism and positivism, while the critical school emphasises its philosophical approach, its connections with Marxism, the socio-structural contexts and the control systems of communication. Even if the administrative versus critical research division has been debated extensively (see, for example, 'Ferment in the Field' 1983; Katz and Katz 2016), the division has resulted in a bias in who is remembered in generational narratives. The émigré researchers at the Wartime Communications Project, Paul Kecskemeti and Nathan Leites, fell in the 'administrative category': they worked for an administrative agency, they were not Marxists, they were anti-communists, they worked with and for the military and for pragmatic and interested objectives rather than, disinterestedly, for knowledge's own sake. Still, they made a significant contribution to critical research, as did non-academics, another neglected group in the disciplinary histories of communication studies.

Before and after the beginning of World War II, there was suddenly a demand not only for propaganda analysis but also for researchers with language skills and experience of non-US political systems and cultures. In many ways this was a remarkable period, when substantial collective comparative communications was carried out for the first time, bringing together foreign- and native-born US academics and researchers. This was policy science that served the wartime goals of the US government. It was also a period when Outsiders received access to Insiders' information and themselves temporarily became Insiders, all united by the same ideology of the US versus the enemy. They shared a utopia: the end of World War II and possibly even the end of all wars. The difference between 'how it is' and 'how it ought to be' (Lasswell 1968, p.11) was immaterial as a goal of research: they came as one. There was no question about the deeply ideological aspect of the research; it was intended to benefit the propaganda war that needed to be won. However, what in my view needs to be emphasised is the ways in which this research influenced future comparative communications in terms of its funding, the composition of research groups, its methodology and materials, using the criteria set out by Merton in Chapter 1.

4.2 The organisation and funding of the Wartime Communications Project

The organisation of propaganda research was somewhat chaotic. Sobel (1976, p.201) observes that 'Roosevelt delegated the same responsibilities to several offices and executives, often without informing one of the existence of the others, or the limits of authority'. Lasswell, as director of the Wartime Communications Project with the Reference Department of the Library of Congress (Library of Congress (no date), p.43), worked as a consultant funded by the Rockefeller Foundation, which paid his salary. He was one of four: other consultants included Hadley Cantril (1906–1969) (radio), Paul Lazarsfeld (radio), and Saul Padover (1905–1981) (history).[8] They all worked under Frank Stanton (1908–2006), first under the Bureau of Intelligence within the Office of Facts and Figures (OFF), then with the Office of War Information (OWI), the Office of Strategic Services, the Office of Censorship, the Foreign Broadcast Information Service, the Psychological Warfare Division of the Supreme Headquarters Allied Expeditionary Force, and other intelligence and morale offices within the military and the federal government (Farr, Hacker and Kazee 2006, p.580).

In this chapter I do not argue that Lasswell's project was the most important of all research projects conducted during World War II but I do argue that it is crucial to our understanding of how the content of propaganda was studied, as we try to understand how comparative communications research was done in groups, a feature that is now commonplace in international communication studies. Since much of the research so far has been about psychological warfare studies, this chapter concentrates on the content of propaganda rather than on its reception. Lasswell made this distinction by defining 'psychological warfare [as] concerned with influencing the attitudes and habits of nations and other groups', while propaganda is concerned with habits and skills.[9]

Since the project collaborated with individual researchers, both from the US and from abroad, under the auspices or different government offices, this chapter also considers some individuals who were not working in the Wartime Communications Project but who worked *with* it and whose work was covered in its publications. These included both émigré scholars and researchers from migrant families, both consultants and academics. As Chapter 2 recounted, Lasswell left Chicago in 1938 and worked outside academia until he received his chair at Yale in 1946. This was the period when he worked for the Wartime Communications Project and for the Hutchins Commission. Chapter 2 also emphasised Lasswell's networking skills, both inside and outside academia, with funders such as the Rockefeller Foundation and notably with John Marshall (1903–1980), director of the Rockefeller

Foundation Division of Humanities. Lasswell's project was funded by the foundation with a grant of $85,400 from 1940 to 1943 (Rogers 1994, p.224) and was yet another example of how he was with the right people at the right time. As Buxton (2003, p.134) has shown, the Rockefeller Foundation was one of the largest funders of communication-related studies in the 1930s and 1940s, while Marshall had spent considerable time in Europe visiting several countries and cultural institutions (for example, the BBC) in the 1930s in his attempt to create 'international transatlantic community', especially between the UK and the US. His interest in Europe led later to the decision to bring émigré scholars from Europe to the US, working together with the Ford Foundation. Like Lasswell, he knew Europe better than many of his colleagues and also encountered there the rise of Nazism (Buxton 2003, p.147).

In 1939 Marshall organised an informal Communications Group, which had regular meetings (10 altogether). The academic members of the original Communications Group included Lasswell, Robert Stoughton Lynd (1892–1970), Paul Lazarsfeld, Hadley Cantril (1906–1969), Geoffrey Gorer (1905–1985), Donald Schlesinger, I.A. Richards (1893–1979) and Douglas Waples (1893–1978). Together they produced over 30 working papers (two of them written by Lasswell) and a final unpublished report entitled *Needed Research in Mass Communications* (Gary 1992, p.106). One of the papers was *Public Opinion and Emergency*[10] in 1939, published to turn attention to the role of communications in the emergency and mobilisation after the outbreak of war in Europe. The group emphasised the need to advance research methods including straw polling and short interviews, panel interviews, community studies, content analysis and source analysis (Simpson 1994, pp.22–23; Gary 1992, p.117). Lasswell was invited by the Rockefeller Foundation to submit a project. He received a two-year grant (later extended) to direct a programme that was to (1) develop the methods of 'content analysis' in communications research, as well as organisational analysis; (2) train technical personnel for agencies of the government that could be expected to become more actively involved in propaganda and intelligence activities; and (3) make Lasswell available in Washington so that he could serve as a consultant on developing the government's various propaganda and intelligence programmes[11] (Sproule 1997, pp.193–94). Gary (1996, p.142) writes that:

> the Rockefeller Foundation generously financed defence research, supported promising American scholars and European refugee scholars in their collaborative efforts, and helped set in motion vitally important exchanges of information and personnel between allied intelligence and American ones.

The foundation funded: 'the Princeton Radio project, the Princeton Public Opinion Project, the Office of Radio Research at Columbia, the Princeton Shortwave Listening Center, the Graduate Library Reading Project at the University of Chicago, the Film Library of the Museum of Modern Art, the Library of Congress Radio Project, the American Film Center, the Totalitarian Communications Research Center at the New School of Social Research and the Experimental Division for the Study of Wartime Communications' (Gary 1996, p.125).

Cmiel (1996, p.91) writes:

> The war was the ultimate triumph of Lasswell's vision. Lasswell himself proved to be at the center of much of the government's extensive communication research during the war (Gary 1996; Simpson 1994, pp.26–27). Lasswell managed to push out the 'fact' crowd at the Office of War Information, arguing that propaganda had to have 'a large element of fake in it.' To use only 'truthful statements,' Lasswell argued, 'seems … an impractical maxim'. (in Blum 1976, p.26)

Previous research emphasises Lasswell's role but now it is time to look at those who did much of the work, his collaborators, and especially those who came to the US as émigré scholars. It is not entirely clear how Lasswell recruited the people who worked for the project he directed, although there is some evidence that he ran the candidates past Marshall.[12] The realisation that there are some projects one person cannot carry out alone came with the wartime need for quick propaganda analysis focused not only on enemy countries such as Germany, Italy or Japan, but also on Allied countries such as the UK and the Soviet Union. The quest for language skills led to the recruitment not only of émigré scholars but also of researchers from migrant families, who, while perhaps lacking direct experience of the enemy countries in question, were nonetheless culturally familiar with them. As a result, the researchers had varied backgrounds and were of different ages. The oldest in my sample was born in 1901 and the youngest in 1920.

4.3 Nazi terror: European intellectuals run for their lives

Thousands of European academics and intellectuals had to flee for their lives after Hitler became chancellor of Germany in 1933. A new 'Law for the Restoration of the Professional Civil Service' was introduced in order to 're-establish a national and professional civil service', and members of certain groups of tenured civil servants were dismissed (Cox 2021). By 1936, about 1,300 university teachers had been dismissed for reasons of racial origin or of suspected political sympathies (Dale 1936, p.1). During the 1930s about 60 per cent of the scholars who had been fired emigrated. As a consequence, the number of émigré scholars who arrived in the UK and the US approached 2,000 if other, younger academics and non-university research scientists are included (Lamberti 2006, p.159).

Five distinct sets of contributors established programmes to help émigré scholars leave their countries and to relocate them to the US. They included (1) individual academics and administrators; (2) aid and self-help organisations; (3) foundations; (4) colleges and universities; and (5) the Roosevelt Administration (Lässig 2017, p.779). For example, the Rockefeller Foundation Refugee Scholar Programs awarded aid amounting to almost $1.4 million for 303 scholars and their families (Iacobelli 2021; Krohn 1996/2013, pp.15, 28). Most of those who went to the US stayed, and by 1947 around 77 per cent of them had obtained faculty positions (Lamberti 2006, p.158). According to Leff (2019, pp.3–4; emphasis in the original), in order to receive a US visa via these routes 'immigrants had to establish that they *had been* professors in a higher education institution and that they *would be* professors in such an institution in the United States'. Émigré scholars therefore needed American universities to offer them jobs 'in order to establish that their purpose in immigrating to the United States was to carry on the vocation of professor' (Leff 2019, p.3). As a result, only '944 professors, 451 wives and 348 children received non-quota visas between 1933 and 1941, when most emigration from Europe ended' (Leff 2019, p.4).

The records of the American Council for Émigrés in the Professions[13] show how difficult it was to secure a visa. US universities could pick and choose the ones they wanted. Among those they considered were Raymond Aron (1905–1983), Bertolt Brecht (1898–1956), Norbert Elias, Friedrich Hayek, Hermann Mannheim (1889–1974), Karl Mannheim, and Jean-Paul Sartre (1905–1980). Together with general information about the candidates, two recommendation letters from colleagues at US universities were required, and sometimes they were not all favourable. For example, Aron 'should be saved at once and without fail', Brecht was considered to be a communist or a 'fellow traveller', Elias a 'convinced democrat', Hayek had 'no communist sympathies', Hermann Mannheim 'proved his capacity to adjust himself to a new situation', Mannheim was 'no communist' but 'tends to be extreme in order to be brilliant', and there was some uncertainty about who Sartre was.[14] Mannheim, of course, did not migrate to the US but to the UK. Mannheim may well have been regarded as *persona non grata* by the US, not least for his association with Greta Kuckhoff (née Margareta Lorke, 1902–1981), who had studied at the University of Wisconsin. She worked as a scientific secretary (research assistant) at the Institute for Social Research, University of Frankfurt, and worked for Mannheim while pursuing her doctorate. When, in March 1933, Kuckhoff was doing doctoral research at LSE and in the British Library, the Nazis closed the institute and burned its books in public. She returned to Germany and helped with Mannheim's move to LSE. Kuckhoff was a member of the resistance movement known as the Rote Kapelle and of the German Communist Party (KPD). She was imprisoned, sentenced to death and then reprieved, while her husband, Adam, was murdered by the Nazis. Subsequently, Kuckhoff became president of the post-war East German (DDR) state bank (Kuckhoff 1972; 'Kuckhoff, Greta' (no date); Nachlass Greta Kuckhoff (no date); Sayner 2013, p.4).

Those who started their new life in the US found that was not easy. According to Kurzweil (1996, p.140), the experiences of émigré scholars included: (1) becoming victims of a virulent, racially based anti-Semitism and so being forced to emigrate leaving their families and friends behind; (2) being delegitimated as human beings and starting a new life in a country whose political culture and system they were unfamiliar with and being forced to leave their former radical politics behind; (3) losing their professional, social and economic status and being forced to relegitimate themselves by adjusting to the American culture of research including writing in English; and (4) being expected to provide the intellectual tools to help defeat Hitler. Leff (2019, p.4) concludes:

> Overall, to be hired by American universities, refugee scholars had to be world class and well connected and working in disciplines for which the American academy had a recognizable need. They could not be too old or too young, too right or too left, or, most important, too Jewish. Having money helped; being a woman did not.

Academically, émigré scholars' backgrounds differed from their American colleagues. As Neumann (1953, p.19) observes about German émigré scholars, they came from different intellectual traditions, namely German idealism, Marxism and historicism, and their way of thinking was primarily theoretical and historical, rarely empirical or pragmatic. He (Neumann 1953, p.19) sums up:

> thus, on the whole, the German exile, bred in the veneration of theory and history, and contempt for empiricism and pragmatism, entered a diametrically opposed intellectual climate: optimistic, empirically oriented, ahistorical, but also self-righteous.

Before the outbreak of World War II their reception had not been entirely positive. Many US political scientists were not critical of all aspects of Nazism (Oren 2003, p.47) and émigré scholars had been arriving in the United States at a time when universities were struggling financially and student fees declining sharply (Lamberti 2006, p.159). While many émigré scholars eventually gained faculty positions, they struggled as new migrants in a country where they did not know the language, culture and educational system, far away from their families, often not understanding what had happened to them.

Among those whose names are often mentioned were Theodor Adorno, Franz Alexander (1891–1964), Hannah Arendt, Erich Fromm (1900–1980), Herta Herzog (1910–2010), Horkheimer, Marie Jahoda (1907–2001), Otto Kirchheimer (1905–1965), Wolfgang Kohler (1887–1967), Siegfried Kracauer (1889–1966), Ernst Kris (1900–1957), Paul Lazarsfeld (1901–1976), Kurt Lewin, Leo Löwenthal (1900–1993), Herbert Marcuse, Hans Morgenthau

(1904–1980), Franz Neumann (1900–1954), Hans Speier (1905–1990), Leo Strauss (1899–1973) and many others (see, for example, Lang 1979, p.89). As Lang (1979, p.88) writes, they played an important role in propaganda studies including the Research Project on Totalitarian Communication at the New School for Social Research, the Foreign Intelligence service at the US Office of War Information, and the Wartime Communications Research Project at the Library of Congress, directed by Lasswell. Among those who were not mentioned on this list were Paul Kecskemeti and Nathan Leites.

European émigré intellectuals: Paul Kecskemeti and Nathan Leites

Paul Kecskemeti and Nathan Leites played an important part in World War II, carrying out research on propaganda, and both brought with them to the US their European intellectual traditions, especially their interest and expertise in psychoanalysis. Both were experts on totalitarian communication, and later especially on communism. Kecskemeti and Leites had academic qualifications, considered comparable to those of most of the US colleagues they worked with during World War II. I concentrate here only on some, most notably on those who were central in developing content analysis and/or who collaborated with Kecskemeti and Leites, namely Ithiel de Sola Pool, Alexander L. George, Joseph M. Goldsen and Jacob Goldstein. De Sola Pool and George were students at that time, Goldstein finished his PhD in 1942, and Goldsen was a man of experience. Their research, along with others who worked in different departments, was published in a series called 'Documents' from the Library of Congress (Experimental Division for the Study of Wartime Communications. Harold D. Lasswell: Chief).

Paul Kecskemeti (né Pál Kecskeméti; 1901–1980) was among the last of the émigré scholars to reach the US, although it is unclear how he got his visa (he came as a journalist). He was born in Makó, Hungary, the son of rabbi and scholar Dr Ármin Kecskeméti (1874–Strasshof, 1944), who died in a concentration camp (Ármin Kecskeméti 2008) and Irma (née Magyar) Kecskeméti (1884–circa 1944). Figure 4.1 is a photo of him taken in Hungary, as a boy. Kecskemeti had a twin brother, Dr György Kecskeméti, who also died in a concentration camp (1901–Auschwitz, 1944), who was an academic and journalist (György Kecskeméti 2008).[15] After Paul Kecskemeti had studied philosophy in Pecs and Budapest, he worked in Budapest as a journalist. In the 1920s, he joined the *Századunk* (Circle of Our Century) magazine.[16] Kecskemeti published his first article on Mannheim in 1926 (Kecskeméti 1926) and became Mannheim's literary executor after Mannheim's death (Meja and Kettler 1993, p. xi; Némedi 1992).

Kecskemeti moved in 1927 to Berlin, where he spent a decade reporting on the Third Reich and worked for the United Press (see Chapter 3), reporting news (Kecskemeti 1931), sometimes using the name Péter Schmidt (1933a; b; 1935), arguing that the main factor leading to the Nazi victory was the

Figure 4.1: A young Paul Kecskemeti in Hungary

Source: Image courtesy of Ilana Burgess.
Notes: Date unknown, though possibly his Bar Mitzvah photo.

division of the working-class movement (Némedi 1992, p.165). Kecskemeti had to leave Germany for France (the UP was seen by the Nazis as a Jewish agency).[17] In 1938 in Budapest,[18] he married Elisabeth (née Erzsébet) Láng (1889–1959), a concert artist who had been a piano student of Béla Bartók (1881–1945) and a harpsichord student of Alice Ehlers (née Ehlersnél) (1887–1981) and was a sister of Dr Júlia Láng (who was married to Mannheim). They later emigrated to the US, where they arrived in August 1942, allegedly managing to take one of the last ships from Casablanca.[19] In the US during the war, he worked in various roles in the Office of War Information, notably with Leites on the psychological aspects of Nazi Germany. Kecskemeti was said to have predicted the break in US–Soviet relations, which did not make him popular among his colleagues at the OWI, who were 'aglow with the heroics of the Red Army and wishfully fantasised away the essence of political realities,'[20] as one of his colleagues testified 20 years later.

Nathan Constantin Leites (1912–1987) was born in St Petersburg, Russia. His family was of Sephardic Jewish origin, his mother, Nichama Leites (1882–year of death unknown), was a medical doctor and his father, Kussiel (Constantin) Leites (1881–year of death unknown),[21] an economist and journalist associated with the Mensheviks (Marwick 1988, p.705). Both parents studied at German and Swiss universities. His father received a PhD from the University of Zurich and worked as a journalist and a publisher of social science books.[22] The family left Russia soon after the Bolsheviks took power, when Nathan Leites was three years old, for Denmark, where they lived until he was nine. Leites went to different schools, mainly in Germany, and then studied at the University of Berlin.[23] Like many other young socialists, he had come to attend the seminar of mathematician Ladislaus von Bortkiewicz (né Ladislaus Josephovich Bortkiewicz; 1868–1931) at the University of Berlin before going to Heidelberg (1929–1933), where he studied under Emil Lederer (1882–1939) (Krohn 1996/2013, p.172). The rise to power of the Nazis made it clear to him that there was no professional future for him in Germany (Marwick 1988, p.705). Leites then moved to the University of Lausanne (1933–1934), and the University of Fribourg (1934–1935), Switzerland, where he earned his doctorate[24] on monetary problems. After stopovers in other European countries, including the UK, Leites emigrated to the United States in 1935[25] to take up a fellowship at Cornell University (Marwick 1988, p.705).[26] He then went to the university of Chicago as a student and a researcher for Lasswell (Krohn 1996/2013, p.185).[27] Leites was married to Dr Martha Wolfenstein (1911–1976), who was a psychoanalyst and with whom he co-wrote a pioneering book on psychoanalytical film analysis (Wolfenstein and Leites 1947; 1950), but they later divorced.

In 1937 Leites joined the Department of Political Science at the University of Chicago as an instructor and was naturalised as a US citizen in 1941 He worked as an analyst in the Special War Policies Unit at the Department of Justice from 1941 to 1942. He then served, from 1942 to 1943, as chief of the French Section at the Foreign Broadcast Intelligence Service (FBIS). From 1943 to 1945 he was a regional specialist at the Office of War Information and he also served from 1943 to 1944 as a visiting lecturer during winter semesters at the New School for Social Research in New York. He spoke and wrote fluently in German, Russian, English and Italian and could read Danish, Swedish and Norwegian.[28]

Together, Kecskemeti and Leites wrote a report, *Some Psychological Hypotheses on Nazi Germany*,[29] in 1944, which was published by the Wartime Communications Project (Kecskemeti and Leites 1945) and was once described as the 'earliest major psychopolitical work and the first fully to reveal the method he [they] would employ in most of his [their] later prodigious and original contributions to this field' (Marwick 1988, p.705). This work was later published, in four parts, in the *Journal of Social Psychology* (Kecskemeti and Leites 1947; 1948a; 1948b; 1948c).

Some of their US colleagues

Leites authored one of the earliest publications of the Wartime Communications Project on content analysis with Ithiel de Sola Pool (1917–1984)[30] and on communist propaganda and the Third International (1942), an analysis of Communist International congresses, of *International Press Correspondence* and of the *Daily Worker*.[31] De Sola Pool had been Leites' student at the University of Chicago and became his research assistant at the Wartime Communications Project between 1940 and 1942.[32] He was born in New York City in 1917. His father, David (Eleazer) de Sola Pool (1885–1970), was a rabbi with a PhD from Heidelberg and his mother, Tamar Hirschensohn (1890–1981), the Palestinian-born daughter of a rabbi, had degrees from Hunter College and the Sorbonne. De Sola Pool received a BA in 1938, MA in 1939 and PhD in 1952 from the University of Chicago, where he was known during his student days on campus as a student organiser and a Trotskyite (Frederick 1981; 'Guide to the Ithiel de Sola Pool Papers 1935–1948' 2011). During his time at the University of Chicago he went to Washington to work for the Wartime Communications Project. In 1949 he moved to Stanford's Hoover Institution under Daniel Lerner (1917–1980) (see Chapter 5) ('Ithiel de Sola Pool' 1997). In later life, de Sola Pool would become a member of the Council on Foreign Relations and an adviser to the United States government during the Cold War (Frederick 1981; 'Guide to the Ithiel de Sola Pool Papers 1935–1948' 2011).

The career of Alexander L. George (1920–2006) is another example of how difficult it is to define who actually worked for the Wartime Communications Project (Simpson 1993, p.321). His published CV lists him as working as a Rockefeller Fellow for the project in 1942, a research analyst for the Federal Communications Commission (FCC) from 1942 to 1944, and he served as a civil affairs officer and deputy chief, Research Branch, Information Control Division, OMGUS in post-war Germany from 1945 to 1948. George (né Alexander L. Givargis) was born in Chicago to impoverished Syrian Christian parents who had fled from pogroms in Persia (George 2008, p.477). He earned undergraduate and graduate degrees at the University of Chicago, where he received his doctorate in political science in 1958. In Figure 4.2 he is pictured as a student here (and member of the fencing team) in around 1938–1940. His doctoral dissertation (George 1959) was based on his work for the FCC, where his task was to analyse Nazi propaganda (Bennett 2008, p.491). He married Juliette L. George (1922–death year unknown), a graduate of the University of California at Berkeley and Columbia University who served during World War II as a propaganda analyst for the OWI in Washington and London, and later in Berlin and Munich, and edited political affairs reports for the Intelligence Branch of the Office of Military Government for Germany (US). She became a senior scholar at the Institute for International Studies at Stanford University from 1984 until her retirement in 1990 and they published together ('Alexander and Juliette George' no date). George started working for RAND in 1948 and worked there for 20 years until he became professor of political science at Stanford University in 1968 (Palmer 2006).

Figure 4.2: Alexander George, photographed when a student at the University of Chicago, *c.* 1938–1940

Source: University of Chicago Photographic Archive, apf5-00785, Hanna Holborn Gray
Special Collections Research Center, University of Chicago Library.
https://photoarchive.lib.uchicago.edu/db.xqy?one=apf5-00785.xml
Notes: George is photographed as a member of the fencing team, around 1938–1940.

One of the early pioneers in content analysis was Bernard Reuben Berelson (1912–1979, pictured Figure 4.3), who published *The Analysis of Communication Content* together with Lazarsfeld in 1948 (Berelson and Lazarsfeld 1948) and as the only author in 1952 (Berelson 1952). He was born in Spokane, Washington, to Max (1875–1950) and Bessie (née Shapiro, 1877–1942) Berelson, both Jewish migrants from Russia. He studied library science at the University of Washington, received his PhD from the University of Chicago in 1941 and joined the Foreign Broadcast Service of the FCC. During the war Berelson worked in Washington as an analyst of German opinion and morale with the Foreign Broadcast Intelligence Service (FBIS) under the Office of War Information (OWI). In 1944 he became a project director at the Columbia University Bureau of Applied Social Research, then directed by its founder, Lazarsfeld. Shils writes that:

> it is fair to say that Berelson learned how to categorize from Lasswell and how to cross-tabulate from Lazarsfeld, and he applied these skills with imagination and distinction during the rest of his working life. (Shils 1980, p.174)

Berelson co-authored the analysis of the famous Erie County panel study of the 1940 presidential election and was a co-author of *The People's Choice* (Lazarsfeld, Berelson and Gaudet 1944). Other projects in this phase of Berelson's career were a reader on public opinion and communication (edited with Morris Janowitz 1950) and a text on content analysis (Berelson and Lazarsfeld 1948; Sills 1980).

Figure 4.3: Bernard R. Berelson

Source: University of Chicago Photographic Archive, apf1-00626, Hanna Holborn Gray
Special Collections Research Center, University of Chicago Library.
https://photoarchive.lib.uchicago.edu/db.xqy?one=apf1-00626.xml
Notes: Date unknown.

Joseph (Joe) M. Goldsen (1916–1998) was born in Passaic, New Jersey, to
a migrant from Russia, Herman (né Goldstein) and Tinie (née Pitzele) Goldsen, and educated at the City College of New York and the American University. Before the war he worked as research director for the Norman Bel
Geddes Company from 1938 and joined the Wartime Communications Project in 1941 for two years as research director. He then worked in different
consultancy, public relations and management counselling roles for bodies
including the Commission on Freedom of the Press and the city of New York,
before joining RAND Corporation as senior social scientist in the Social Science Division in 1948 (pictured during his time at RAND in Figure 4.4).[33]
After joining RAND Corporation he married Lucille Gibbons, who worked
as director for communications, stenographic filing and library services in the
Social Science Division at RAND Corporation, but left her job after marrying
Goldsen. He spent his early years at RAND Corporation as an administra-
tor and researcher and then in Washington, where he worked as executive
to Speier. He became a specialist in the politics and legal implications of
activities in outer space and published *Outer Space in World Politics* in 1959
(Goldsen 1959).[34]

Jacob Goldstein (1914–2009) was born in Poland and later emigrated with
his parents to the US. His PhD dissertation, 'Content Analysis: A Propaganda
and Opinion Study',[35] carried out under the sponsorship of Max Wertheimer
(1880–1943) and Hans Speier, was submitted to the Graduate Faculty of

Figure 4.4: Joseph M. Goldsen at RAND Corporation

Source: Biographical file for Joseph M. Goldsen, RAND Corporation Archives, Santa Monica, CA.
Notes: Date unknown.

Political and Social Science at the New School for Social Research in 1942. It was based in part on material collected by the Research Project on Totalitarian Communication led by Speier and Ernst Kris. Goldstein's dissertation chapter, 'Some Methodological Problems in Content Analysis', is probably one of the first attempts to address methodological problems of quantitative content analysis in propaganda analysis. After serving in the army, Goldstein joined the Wartime Communications Project and then became an analyst with the Foreign Broadcast Intelligence Service of the FCC.[36] One of the chapters of his thesis was later published as an article entitled 'An Exploratory Analysis of Opinion Trends with Special Reference to Conscription in the United States' (Goldstein 1943). Its materials had been made available by Lazarsfeld, whose cooperation 'at all stages of the study' was acknowledged (p.156). It analysed, using content analysis, 701 letters pertaining to conscription received by two Midwestern senators during the summer of 1940 (Goldstein 1943, p.157). Goldstein later became a psychologist and published mainly in academic journals of his field.

4.4 Quantitative and qualitative content analysis

Attempts to quantify symbols

Lasswell's earlier writings around content analysis had been influenced by Freud's concept of a symbol, focusing on its latent meaning. When Lasswell started his work for the Wartime Communications Project his inspiration still came from psychoanalytic theory (see Chapter 2), although his thinking started to change even before the war. His article from 1938, 'A Provisional Classification of Symbol Data' (Lasswell 1938), is about psychoanalytic interviews with patients and establishing categories for the words they used, described in these interviews as 'symbolic events'. He wrote that 'references used in interviews may be quantified by counting the number of references which fall into each category during a selected period of time (or per thousand words uttered)' (p.198) but the main problem for Lasswell in this article was their classification. The quantification of symbols became one of the main objects of research for the Wartime Communications Project.

One of the early and most quoted research papers published on content analysis that still reflected the importance of symbols was one jointly written by Leites and de Sola Pool.[37] In this paper they state that there had been a considerable ambiguity in the meaning of content analysis. In their view, content analysis had to satisfy the following requirements:

(1) It must refer either to syntactic characteristics (such as the presence of certain logical fallacy, e.g. *petitio principii*) or to semantic characteristics (such as the characteristic of having reference to material objects as against persons) of symbols.

(2) It must indicate *frequencies* of occurrence of such characteristics with a high degree of precision. One could perhaps define it more narrowly: it must assign *numerical* values to such frequencies.

(3) It must refer to these characteristics by terms which are general (i.e. the definitions of which do not place their referents within time–space regions or which are, by definition subsumable under such general terms). A general term-sequence in this sense would be 'predictions of success', whereas a term 'predictions of military victory in World War II' would be a term-sequence not general in itself but subsumable in the language adopted under a general term-sequence (i.e. the first mentioned one).

(4) It must refer to these characteristics by terms that occur, or that it is intended to make occur, in universal propositions of social science.

They also added another requirement: a high degree of *precision* in the terms used to refer to the symbol characteristics studied. But according to them, this did not mean that 'objectivity' should be contrasted with 'subjectivity' or with 'impressionistic ways of talking about symbols'. Leites and de Sola Pool then combined symbols with propaganda, defining these as 'symbolic occurrences behind which there are certain manipulative intentions'. They distinguished among (1) the intentions of propagandists; (2) symbols that emitted themselves; (3) the responses of 'propagandees'.

As this early and much quoted paper by contemporaries shows, its authors were trying to combine the tradition from which Leites, at least, came with the practical needs of the US government, which required them to quantify content analysis. Goals set for the new method were to 'anticipate the enemy' (Lasswell 1949, p.48), and to 'predict' the future (Lasswell 1949, pp.49–51). George (1956, p.334) describes their aims as follows:

> the possibility of predicting an opponent's initiatives was generally regarded as requiring discovery of a regular pattern, or relationship, in the opponent's past behavior, which would serve as a rule of inference in new instances. Regular relationships were sought between the opponent's intention to initiate a certain line of action and (1) some type of *content characteristic* in his propaganda; or (2) some type of *propaganda strategy* pursued by him prior to the initiative.

There was a shift from latent to manifest content, and from qualitative to quantitative analysis. Krippendorff writes that the early work of the Wartime Communications Project 'addressed basic issues of sampling, measurement problems, and the reliability and validity of content categories, continuing the tradition of early quantitative analysis of mass communications' (Krippendorff 1980/2004, p.9). This included the training of staff when producing analyses on a tight schedule,[38] which made the team look for a new form of content analysis that could be taught. Lasswell later evaluated how he had trained more than 60 people in different departments during World War II.[39] The aim was to develop quantitative methods for studying the content of propaganda.

Goldsen seems to have played a key role in preparing content analysis and solving methodological issues. His many memoranda addressed to Lasswell tackle questions like coding efficiency (reliability, economy), symbol frequency, and how to prepare a detailed coding book. One of the main concerns was coders' application of the rules and their shared understanding of symbol expressions, referred to as 'unreliability'.[40] An early report used content analysis to study British and German newspapers at two-week intervals from the start of the war until March 1941. The researchers found that it was the factor of inactivity, rather than 'events', that in certain periods produced significant symbol fluctuations. By a symbol, they meant a 'word standing for some group, idea, or some other definable field of reference', and they were interested in 'those word-symbols of supreme importance which are characterised and joined by other words as subordinates'.[41] This was one of the first studies where they analysed retabulated data, but they ran into problems with the unreliability and inadequacies of the original coding procedures. They concluded that it was imperative to be just as analytical in planning the collection of the data as in studying the product.[42]

Goldsen was also responsible for developing a handbook of coding instructions. These were to 'provide a uniform, systematic scheme for the collection and presentation of politically significant symbols in the press'. Much of the work went into writing instructions and training the coders to code in a uniform manner. Many members of the research team, including Leites and de Sola Pool (1959; 1969)[43] and George (1949),[44] wrote about the methodological aspects of content analysis; some also published their work after the war, most notably Berelson (Berelson 1952; Berelson and Lazarsfeld 1948) but also de Sola Pool (1959) and Morris Janowitz[45] (1968; 1969). Their research focused both on the US and on foreign countries, but not necessarily comparing these to one other, at least simultaneously. Some studies concentrated on one country only. They mainly concentrated on newspapers, although they also researched Hitler's speeches, posters and broadcasting. In short, most research was comparative in the sense that it compared two objects, that is, comparing, for example, the US to Germany.

Perhaps the most ambitious project was what was called the 'World Attention Survey: World Press', prepared by Goldsen and Goldstein. Its aim was to 'describe the frequency in the use of selected lists of political symbols in the world press considered as a whole', although several nations were not represented. For the survey, 47 newspapers were selected, one from each political entity, for the period from 28 August 1939 to June 1941, using eight-week periods. The study analysed the distribution of 100 symbols, including names of countries and their leaders, ideologies such as fascism, communism or democracy, and words such as 'war', 'nation' and 'people'. The data for each newspaper was obtained from headlines on the major world news pages and from editorials. The statistical treatment primarily involved an analysis of the distribution of arithmetic means, through the use of rank-order correlations. These correlations 'suggested that the use of ideological symbols in editorials is less dependent on the changes in the political environment than is the use of the same symbols in headlines'.[46]

Lasswell published the results of this collective work in 1941 as *The World Attention Survey* (Lasswell 1941), without any acknowledgement of Goldsen's and Goldstein's work. The article was based on the idea that 'we gain insight into the lives of others when we know what they read, see and hear' (p.456), and that it had been difficult to objectively discuss the connection between 'material and ideological' factors due to the lack of data on ideological changes through time (p.459). In the article, four newspapers were compared: *Pravda*, the official paper of the Communist Party in the Soviet Union, *Völkischer Beobachter*, the main Nazi newspaper in Germany, *Excélsior*, then published by a workers' cooperative in Mexico, and *Il Giornale d'Italia*, at the time a supporter of Mussolini's fascism in Italy, and particularly the attention these gave to foreign as compared with domestic politics, and to the United States as a symbol. The purpose of the technique was 'to describe the field of attention, to show the relative prominence of selected symbols like the names of the leaders, nations policies, institutions' by 'showing the percentage of words containing significant symbols' (pp.459–60). The article emphasised that objectivity was achieved by giving coders regular tests in order to 'verify the comparability of their results' (p.460). At the end of the article, Lasswell suggests that symbols may be either positive or negative.

Lasswell's article 'The Politically Significant Content of the Press: Coding Procedures' (1942) was published under the name Lasswell and Associates. In this article, Lasswell writes that there is no comprehensive list of political symbols that can be applied to all research, but he then lists symbols such as persons (for example, Roosevelt, Churchill, Hitler, Stalin), groups (for example, US, Germany, Great Britain, Russia), agencies (for example, Congress, Parliament, Fuhrer, Premier), policies (for example, war, peace, income tax), participations (for example, enlisting, bond-buying, food-saving) and ideas (for example, statements of aims, future expectations) (p.15) and suggests measuring their frequency of presentation. The article includes detailed coding instructions that also address the tone of the symbols (positive, negative, neutral).

Other articles were also published that concentrated on methodology, such as 'A Coefficient of Imbalance for Content Analysis', an article by Irving Janis (1918–1990) and Raymond H. Fadner (1917–1996) (Janis and Fadner 1943a) and 'The Reliability of Content Analysis Technique' by Janis, Fadner and Janowitz (1943b), both working at the time of these publications for the special policies unit at the Department of Justice. Janis and Fadner, after acknowledging the importance of psychoanalysis for studying content, suggested that:

> Impressionistic judgments suffice for broad classification of symbol data and description of gross temporal changes in the content of mass communications. Thus, we may report reliably that a certain movie is manifestly anti-Nazi, or that the contents of a certain newspaper changed from pro-isolation to pro-intervention. But if we wish to develop precise hypotheses concerning mass communications, here is a need for quantitative analysis of symbols. (Janis and Fadner 1943, p.106)

The work that was done to develop content analysis in order to study propaganda during World War II was pioneering and was to have a long-term influence on so-called news flow studies, as shown in Chapter 5. There were several innovations that were developed in a relatively short period in the early 1940s, including focus on the source of news stories, their country of origin, tone (positive, negative, neutral), and topics of news stories. While the theories and concepts still came mainly from psychoanalysis and the study of symbols, the need to quantify the analysis meant that there was a gradual shift from studying latent content to studying manifest content. This shift took place in the period when governmental needs started increasingly to define what kind of research was required.

Research using psychoanalysis

It would be wrong to conclude that all the work was about developing quantitative content analysis. Leites was described as being 'deeply committed to psychoanalysis'[47] and he even published work together with lead-ing psychoanalyst Ernst Kris (1900–1957), who had worked with Freud on an article. It was later considered a should-be classic (Lang 1979, p.88). Kecskemeti published an early article in Freud's journal *Imago* as early as 1933.[48] Leites and de Sola Pool's report on the Third International (Com-munist International, 1919–1935) and its propaganda was produced as early as 1942.[49] It was a study of the frustration and setbacks of the Com-munist International after several defeats. Leites and de Sola Pool were perplexed as to why, despite defeats, a loyal group of followers remained. They studied the Third International's propaganda and constructed a typology of modes of the symbolic treatment of setbacks consisting of approximately 1,000 statements. Their aim, again, was to illustrate the applicability of quantitative methods of content analysis to the study of communications.[50]

Leites also collaborated with Kecskemeti, for example in their already-men-tioned study published by the Wartime Communications Project in 1945[51] on psychological hypotheses concerning Nazi Germany,[52] which was written in the second half of 1944 and published after the war in the *Journal of Social Psychology* as four articles (Kecskemeti and Leites 1947; 1948a; 1948b; 1948c). In this study they thank Kris and Lasswell for 'their researches applying psy-choanalytic hypotheses to social phenomena' and 'the OWI for permission to use German press and radio material collected under its auspices' when they were on its staff (Kecskemeti and Leites 1947, p.141). Their aim was to study the Nazi variant of German culture, using the concept of compulsive character from psychoanalytic theory, and most of the references in their bibliography were about it. This was a completely *qualitative* study, where they analysed cultural products including films and speeches in order to find indicators of German culture. They write:

> this study, then, contains many hypotheses about the role of certain 'indicators' (of a compulsive character structure) in German cul-ture. But here two further points must be noted: (1) These hypoth-eses refer, by implication or explicitly, to frequencies–e.g., to fre-quencies of use of 'life-with-a-capital-*l*' terms in certain contexts in German culture. But we are at this point in the development of psycho-cultural analysis unable to be rather specific about the fre-quencies involved–hence we use ambiguous terms like 'very large,' etc. (2) Even if we were in a position to say '78.7 per cent' instead of 'very large,' there still would be the task of performing the appropri-ate 'counting' operations to correct 'impressionistic' errors. This the authors of the study have not done. (Kecskemeti and Leites 1947, p.143; emphasis in the original)

In this extract, the tension between quantitative and qualitative approaches is already out in the open. Kecskemeti and Leites felt that they needed to justify their approach, probably after comments from their reviewers. What was in all likelihood acceptable before and during the war had now come under criticism.

How useful was content analysis?

It would be easy to argue that for ideological reasons the research was forced to follow the needs of the military, and so be part of the war effort. However, the answer is not necessarily so simple. The usefulness of content analysis became a debated issue, not only among the military and civil servants but among the academics themselves, especially after World War II. The Wartime Communications Project ended by autumn 1943, and was not continued at the Library of Congress, although several members of the team continued to work for different government departments in different roles. Perhaps it was the military that was most disappointed with content analysis. Doob writes:

> Many social scientists employed by the government or in the armed services during the war found their research and scientific wisdom was not eagerly accepted, wisely interpreted, or sensibly followed by policy-makers. Unlike some of the old-line departments, the war agencies had no established procedure for utilizing social science. Social scientists had a place on the ever-changing organization charts, sometimes merely because it was somewhat vaguely felt that all kinds of brains, even academic, were necessary to win a total war. Often they had to carve out for themselves the specific roles they wished to play. They functioned, not in accordance with the charts, but within what Mansfield and Marx call informal organizations of their own making. (Doob 1947, p.649)

Many of those identified in this quotation as social scientists evaluated the usefulness of the method of content analysis on several occasions (see, for example, Berelson 1952; Committee on International Communications Research 1952; Davis 1951; de Sola Pool 1959; 1969; Doob 1947; George 1949; 1956; Kaplan 1943; Kracauer 1952; Kris and Speier 1944), and the overall verdict could be described as lukewarm or even critical. According to George (1956, p.335), there was:

> implicit recognition in the ... work that some modification would be necessary in the early assumption that the ability to predict Nazi initiatives rested upon the discovery of a single, regularly recurring relationship of intended action with propaganda strategy.

Berelson summarised the critique after World War II: 'Content analysis, as a method, has no magical qualities – you rarely get out of it more than you put in, and sometimes you get less' (Berelson 1952, p.198).

There was another, more philosophical, tension in the work of those who studied propaganda. Abraham Kaplan (1918–1993),[53] a migrant and Lasswell's future collaborator and colleague at RAND Corporation, recognised this difference as early as 1943 (Kaplan 1943), writing that 'Lasswell and his associates have developed a technique known as content analysis, which attempts to characterise the meanings in a given body of discourse in a systematic and quantitative fashion' (p.230). In his article Kaplan then discusses the similarities and differences between semiotics and content analysis and concludes that these could complement each other, and that the contribution of content analysis can make the 'provision of empirical proposition about symbol data' and 'is simply a part of semiotic' (Berelson 1952, p.25), and his view was shared by Janis and Fadner (1942; see also Janis 1943).

They thus recognised Lasswell's original idea. Janowitz writes that, for Lasswell,

> meaning depends upon the superimposition of some frame of reference, and his conception of content analysis is much broader, including both manifest and latent content. Latent content includes tacit meanings and associations as well as the more readily verbalized expressions, and for Lasswell, content analysis involved the application of historical, cultural, psychological, and legal frames of reference with various levels of meaning, subtleties, and efforts at explication of ambiguities. In the broadest sense, content analysis is a system for objectifying the process of inference, since the meaning of the symbolic environment can be derived only by a process of inference. (Janowitz 1968, pp.647–48)

Lasswell's goals, however, were not achieved. Most of the research, especially after World War II, defined content analysis, as Berelson and Lazarsfeld (1948, p.18) did, as 'a research technique for the *objective, systematic*, and *quantitative* description of the *manifest* content of communication' (my emphasis). According to Berelson and Lazarsfeld (1948, p.19), 'there is no guarantee that the meanings in the "manifest content" are the same as the meanings actually understood by the different readers or intended by the writer'. Lasswell's formula of 'who says what to whom, how and with what effect' (Lasswell 1948, p.216) recognises that studying only manifest content does not say anything about intentions or effect. When content analysis was defined as the study of manifest content, psychoanalytic theories became obsolete since intentions and meanings were no longer the object of study.

Many of the results from the work done for the Wartime Communications Project were published after the war. *Language of Politics. Studies in Quantitative Semantics* (Lasswell, Leites and Associates 1949) is probably the most comprehensive example. Most of the work included in the book was done with the project at the University of Chicago (Lasswell 1947, p.v), and the emphasis was clearly on quantitative techniques and applications. Perhaps the most quoted chapter from this edited book is Lasswell's own, 'Why Be Quantitative?', which summarises the book's key point that the 'study of politics can be advanced by the quantitative analysis of political propaganda' (Lasswell 1949, p.41). Lasswell (1949, p.520) writes:

> Why, then to be quantitative about communication? Because of the scientific and *policy* gains that can come of it. The social process is one of *collaboration* and *communication*; and quantitative methods have already demonstrated their usefulness with the former. (my emphasis)

The results may not have been the most convincing, or therefore the most useful for policymakers or for the army, since at its best content analysis could not but show that the use of different symbols in propaganda varied over time. But the main focus was on the process, on how content analysis could be used when studying propaganda. By carrying out this study the Wartime Communications Project opened up an avenue for the further development of quantitative content analysis, and a door to the development of the behaviouralism that, in the 1950s, would sweep not only through political science but also comparative communications.

4.5 Conclusion

The Experimental Division for the Study of War Time Communications at the Library of Congress (the Wartime Communications Project), led by Lasswell, contributed significantly to comparative communications. In fact, many of the features we take for granted and recognise in contemporary comparative communications were formulated during a relatively short and exceptional period at the beginning of World War II. It is easy to ignore this period because the research was not principally carried out by academics in universities or research institutes but under the government and its ministries, and financed by private foundations. Most of the credited work was done by young men in their 20s or 30s and by academics with diverse education and backgrounds. The women remained unrecognised.

These young men became temporary Insiders by doing propaganda research. Simpson (1994, p.9) writes that the government agencies:

> sought scientific data on the means to manipulate targeted populations at home and at abroad, and they were willing to pay well for it at a time when there was very little other funding available for large-scale communication studies.

However, the Wartime Communications Project was funded by the Rock-efeller Foundation, not by the US government, and provided unforeseen opportunities for a new generation of propaganda researchers who suddenly received access to data – 'big' data of that time – that they could previously only have dreamed of. Some of this data was confidential or difficult to access and was coded by female research assistants paid by foundations or the government. Several men who worked as researchers later became acknowledged experts in their fields and received university chairs. This was an unequal process that academically benefitted some of them, but not all, as the next chapter shows.

What needs to be emphasised is that this was pioneering comparative research. Even though Lasswell's project was not funded by the US government, its goals served that government, and it was carried out in close cooperation with different government offices. It would be too simple, however, to conclude that the government forced the researchers to do something against their will in that research. Rather, it appears that the researchers were eager to take part in the war effort, but that they also continued to do the research they were themselves interested in. There was a hidden intergenerational conflict concerning the method of content analysis, as to whether it should become qualitative or quantitative. The quantitative side won, perhaps to Lasswell's regret, but by this point he had become a pragmatist and given up psychoanalysis (Eulau 1968, p.11), obliged to worry about where the next research grant would come from. When this happened, one of the topics for the next chapter, it also meant that the European psychoanalytic tradition, carried forward by Kecskemeti and Leites, was no longer in demand.

Did all these researchers belong to the same generation? Yes and no. They were brought together, with all their differences and different experiences, to work together for the same goal: to win the war. Many of them had traumatic pasts, with family members and friends killed in concentration camps while they themselves survived. They formed a *cross-generation* on the basis of a shared experience of the war, brought together almost randomly by world politics. This created a temporary transnational generation consisting of academics and researchers with different educational backgrounds and from different countries. Their experience was life-forming and many of them went on to work together for decades, as the next chapter shows.

We might say that, in a number of ways, the formation of these research groups was a result of both known and unknown factors. Many of the researchers had a connection with the University of Chicago and through Lasswell, a networker who would rapidly turn his network into an effective 'old boys' club' that would support its members for the rest of their lives by finding positions and securing jobs for them. They also shared an intellectual agenda of promoting the comparative study of symbols using psychoanalysis and different types of content analysis. At the same time, Lasswell welcomed new members who had come to the US as émigré scholars. There is something open about any new type of research before disciplinary boundaries are established. When new skills are needed and cannot be found close to home, new opportunities open up for Outsiders, who then may become Insiders. This is what happened to émigré scholars such as Kecskemeti, Leites and others. They not only found employment but later became defence scholars who voluntarily took the position of defending US interests at home and abroad. It is important to remember that these men saw this as their patriotic duty. There was no question about whose side they were on, all coming together to fight the enemy. This is when ideology explains a lot but not everything. If an ideology is defined as something referring to the past and a utopia as referring to the future, the difference between ideology and utopia is problematic. Winning the war may have been a utopian project in 1941, but it required a strong ideology of moral superiority, of 'us against them'.

Although the studies discussed here opened up the world to communication from other countries, which would seldom otherwise have received attention, they would not have been pursued without the deep patriotism and nationalism of men who were convinced that the US had to win the war and that their duty was to help their government to do that. This sentiment was shared by the émigré scholars, who often continued to work for the US government, army or intelligence services even after the war. Speier, himself an emigrant from Germany, has written (1989, p.17) of his own experiences:

> After Pearl Harbor, U.S. Government agencies tried to obtain the service of German-born anti-Nazis who had sought refuge in the United States, become citizens, and possessed useful area knowledge. Nevertheless, I expected to encounter occasional distrust or at least reservation in government service, but I was wrong. My German origin led to difficulties only once, and this unimportant episode occurred in Europe after the fighting had ceased.

It was the unforeseen and unexpected element of research groups combining different nationalities that had one of the most lasting influences on comparative communications, which continues today. It would be almost impossible to carry out comparative research, at least qualitatively, without the expertise and experience of specialists from the country or area in question. The feeling that such men were 'one of us' did not last. Speier himself became a suspect after the war as McCarthyism took root (see Chapter 5), as did Lasswell himself and many others. The camaraderie that the team shared during the wartime project lasted and took many of them to California to work for RAND Corporation, but it did not help them to obtain academic appointments in universities, at least not immediately. Their shared mission of winning the war against Nazism also disappeared, and was gradually turned against a new enemy, communism. In short, their professional lives were influenced by the dominant ideologies of the time: the youthful idealism that carried these men through the war was soon to be absorbed into a profession defined by US interest in expanding its own ideology around the world.

Notes

1. Summary of Activities on 19 October 1951. Harold Dwight Lasswell Papers, Biographical/Memorabilia Files 1043, Series V, Box 213, Folder 15. Manuscripts and Archives, Yale University Library.

2. George, A.L. (1949) The intelligence value of content analysis. RAND, D419, Copy No 10 on 13 February 1949. Harold Dwight Lasswell Papers, General Files 1043, Series I, Box 80, Folder 1001. Manuscripts and Archives, Yale University Library.

3. J.M. Goldsen to P. Lewis. Analysis of tests to measure internal consistency of coders and reliability. Memorandum. Experimental Division for the Study of War Communications on 22, 23, 24 October 1941. The coders included Misses DePalma, Kretzinger and McCarter. Harold Dwight Lasswell Papers, General Files 1043, Series I, Box 38, Folder 516. Manuscripts and Archives, Yale University Library.

4. J.M. Goldsen to H.D. Lasswell on 31 December 1942. Experimental Division for the Study of War-Time Communications. Harold Dwight Lasswell Papers, General Files, 1043, Series I, Box 38, Folder 518. Manuscripts and Archives, Yale University Library.

5. J.M. Goldsen to H.D. Lasswell on 3 August 1942. Memorandum. Experimental Division for the Study of War-Time Communications. Harold Dwight Lasswell Papers, General Files 1043, Series I, Box 38, Folder 517. Manuscripts and Archives, Yale University Library.

6. J.M. Goldsen to P. Lewis. Analysis of Tests to Measure Internal Consistency of Coders and Reliability. Memorandum. Experimental Division for the Study of War-Time Communications; Personnel trained in whole or in part by the War Communications Research Project on 30 December 1941. Harold Dwight Lasswell Papers, General Files 1043, Series I, Box 38, Folder 516. Manuscripts and Archives, Yale University Library.

7. Lasswell H.D. A summary of activities dictated on 19 October 1951. Harold Dwight Lasswell Papers, General Files 1043, Series V, Box 213, Folder 15. Manuscripts and Archives, Yale University Library.

8. Office of Facts and Figures. Bureau of Intelligence, no date. Harold Dwight Lasswell Papers, General Files 1043, Series I, Box 95, 1160. Manuscripts and Archives, Yale University Library.

⁹ H.D. Lasswell to Legislative Services on 9 April 1941. Harold Dwight Lasswell Papers, General Files 1043, Series I, Box 56, Folder 797. Manuscripts and Archives, Yale University Library.

¹⁰ Public opinion and emergency on 1 November 1939. Harold Dwight Lasswell Papers, General Files 1043, Series I, Box 81, Folder 1018. Manuscripts and Archives, Yale University Library.

¹¹ Lasswell, H.D. Affidavit. Subscribed and sworn to before me on 23rd day of October 1951. Harold Dwight Lasswell Papers, General Files 1043, Series V, Box 213, Folder 14. Manuscripts and Archives, Yale University Library.

¹² Correspondence between H.D. Lasswell and J. Marshall. Harold Dwight Lasswell Papers, Biographical & Personal, General Files 1043, Series V, Box 213, Folder 15. Manuscripts and Archives, Yale University Library.

¹³ American Council for Émigrés in the Professions Records, 1930–1974. M.E. Grenander Department of Special Collections and Archives, University Libraries, University at Albany, State University of New York.

¹⁴ Annual reports 1940–1950, Individual files, Box 1, Folder, 26 (Brecht); Box 2, Folder 21 (Aron); Box 2older 121 (Elias); Box 3, Folder 108 (Hayek); Box 4, Folder 202 (Mannheim); Box 4, Folder 201 (Manheim), Box 5, Folder 84 (Neumann); Box 6, Folder 68 (Sartre). American Council for Émigrés in the Professions Records, 1930–1974. M.E. Grenander Department of Special Collections and Archives, University Libraries, University at Albany, State University of New York.

¹⁵ Litvan, G. (1980) In memoriam P. Kecskemeti on 25 October 1980. Hans Speier Papers. Box 3. German and Jewish Intellectual émigré Collection. M.E. Grenander Department of Special Collections and Archives, University Libraries, University at Albany, State University of New York.

¹⁶ According to the online Hungarian Encyclopaedia of Ethnography (Magyar Néprajzi Lexikon), *Századunk (Our Century)* was a radical social sciences journal established in 1926. It specialised in sociology, political science and ethnography. The journal harshly criticised the Horthy government (1920–1944) and was banned and ceased publication in 1939. It was considered a highly intellectual bourgeois radical monthly that was interested in Marxism (Gabel 1991, p.27).

¹⁷ K. Bickel to R.W. Howard on 28 June 1933. Roy W. Howard Papers. The Media School Archive, Indiana University.

¹⁸ Marriage certificate on 1 June 1938. Paul Kecskemeti Papers. The Robert D. Farber University Archives & Special Collections Department at Brandeis University.

¹⁹ His diary, held at Brandeis, tells a thrilling story about their escape from Paris. He writes when leaving Paris on 10 June 1940: 'Farewell journey

through Paris … I have the feeling that I shall never see all this again.'
Paul Kecskemeti Papers. The Robert D. Farber University Archives &
Special Collections Department at Brandeis University.

[20] Testimonial dinner for P. Kecskemeti on 20 September 1966. J.M. Goldsen presiding. Harold Dwight Lasswell Papers, General Files 1043, Series
I, Box 38, Folder 532, Manuscripts and Archives, Yale University Library.

[21] A memo from N.C. Leites concerning his father (no date). Harold
Dwight Lasswell Papers, General Files 1043, Series I, Box 57, Folder 790.
Manuscripts and Archives, Yale University Library.

[22] 'Among the émigré professional economists was a remarkably large group
of Russians, who as young Mensheviks had fled to Germany after the
October Revolution. They not only shared a political profile but were also
highly qualified younger people who gave critical impetus to the field of
mathematical analysis and statistics in particular … It is interesting to
note that many of these young Russian socialists, among them Paul
Baran [1909–1964], Georg Garvy (Bronstein), Nathan Leites, Jacob
Marschak [1898–1977], Mark Mitnitzky [1908–1984] and Wladimir
Woytinski [1885–1960], came together in the Berlin seminar of the
ultra-reactionary mathematician Ladislaus von Bortkiewicz in order to fin-
ish their previous studies before going to either Heidelberg or Kiel, where
they then studied economics. Bortkiewicz was also a Russian by birth
(born in St. Petersburg in 1868), but he had been working in Germany
since the 1890s and had come to Berlin in 1901' (Krohn 1996/2013, p.181).

[23] Fellowship application to the John Simon Guggenheim Memorial Foundation on 1 August 1946. Nathan Leites Papers, Box 1. Hanna Holborn
Gray Special Collections Research Center, University of Chicago Library.

[24] Fellowship application to the John Simon Guggenheim Memorial Foundation on 1 August 1946. Nathan Leites Papers, Box 1. Hanna Holborn
Gray Special Collections Research Center, University of Chicago Library.

[25] Fellowship application to the John Simon Guggenheim Memorial Foundation on 1 August 1946. Nathan Leites Papers, Box 1. Hanna Holborn
Gray Special Collections Research Center, University of Chicago Library.

[26] Leites does not mention this in his fellowship application. Fellowship
application to the John Simon Guggenheim Memorial Foundation on 1
August 1946. Nathan Leites Papers, Box 1. Hanna Holborn Gray Special
Collections Research Center, University of Chicago Library.

[27] Fellowship application to the John Simon Guggenheim Memorial Foundation on 1 August 1946. Nathan Leites Papers, Box 1. Hanna Holborn
Gray Special Collections Research Center, University of Chicago Library.

[28] Fellowship application to the John Simon Guggenheim Memorial Foundation on 1 August 1946. Nathan Leites Papers, Box 1. Hanna Holborn
Gray Special Collections Research Center, University of Chicago Library.

[29] Kecskemeti, P. and Leites, N. (1945) *Some Psychological Hypotheses on Nazi Germany*. Document No. 60, on 30 July 1945, the Library of Congress, Washington, DC, Experimental Division for the Study of Wartime Communications, Harold D. Lasswell, Chief. Harold Dwight Lasswell Papers, General Files 1043, Series III, Box 57, folder 790. Manuscripts and Archives, Yale University Library,

[30] Leites, N.C. and de Sola Pool, I. (1942) *On Content Analysis*. Document No. 26, on 1 September 1942. The Library of Congress, Washington, DC, Experimental Division for the Study of Wartime Communications; Harold D. Lasswell, Chief. Harold Dwight Lasswell Papers, General Files 1043, Series VII, Box 57, Folder 790. Manuscripts and Archives, Yale University Library.

[31] Leites, N.C. and de Sola Pool, I. (1942) *Communist Propaganda in Reaction to Frustration*. Document No. 27, on 1 December 1942. The Library of Congress, Washington, DC, Experimental Division for the Study of Wartime Communications; Harold D. Lasswell, Chief. Harold Dwight Lasswell Papers, General Files 1043, Series VII, Box 57, Folder 790.

[32] MacKenzie Pool, J. (1988) 'Nathan and Ithiel', in RAND (ed.) *Remembering Nathan Leites, An Appreciation: Recollections of Some Friends, Colleagues, and Students*, p.34, RAND Corporation Archives.

[33] Biography. Joseph M. Goldsen. Harold Dwight Lasswell Papers, General Files 1043, Series I, Box 38, Folder 529. Manuscripts and Archives, Yale University Library.

[34] Joseph Goldsen Profile, Biographical Files, RAND Corporation Archives.

[35] Goldstein, J. (1942) Content analysis. A Propaganda and opinion study. Unpublished PhD thesis. New School for Social Research, New York. New School Faculty Vertical Files. The New School Archives and Special Collections.

[36] H. Speier to K. Lewin on 25 August 1945. Hans Speier Papers, German and Jewish Intellectual émigré Collection, Box 3, Folder 9. M.E. Grenander Department of Special Collections and Archives, University Libraries, University at Albany, State University of New York.

[37] Leites, N.C. and de Sola Pool, I. (1942) *On Content Analysis*. Document No. 26, on 1 September 1942. The Library of Congress, Washington, DC, Experimental Division for the Study of Wartime Communications; Harold D. Lasswell, Chief on 1 September 1942. No 26. Confidential. Harold Dwight Lasswell Papers, General Files 1043, Series I, Box 57, Folder 790. Manuscripts and Archives, Yale University Library.

[38] H.D. Lasswell to J.M. Goldsen. Memorandum regarding research program on coding method. Experimental Division for the Study of War Time Division on 16 February 1942. Harold Dwight Lasswell Papers, General Files 1043, Series I, Box 38, Folder 516. Manuscripts and Archives, Yale University Library.

39 Affidavit. Harold D. Lasswell on 23 October 1951. Harold Dwight Lasswell Papers, Biographical/Memorabilia Files, 1043, Series I, Box 213, Folder 15. Manuscripts and Archives, Yale University Library.

40 J.M. Goldsen to H.D. Lasswell. Memorandum on 16 February 1942. Harold Dwight Lasswell Papers, General Files, Series I, Box 8, Folder 516. Manuscripts and Archives, Yale University Library.

41 J.M. Goldsen to H.D. Lasswell. Memorandum. Re: Handbook of coding instructions on 9 May 1942. Harold Dwight Lasswell Papers, General Files 1043, Series I, Box 8, Folder 517. Manuscripts and Archives, Yale University Library.

42 A. Geller, A. George, D. Kaplan and J.M. Goldsen to H.D. Lasswell. Memorandun regarding analysis of the coded British and German newspapers on 10 June 1942. Harold Dwight Lasswell Papers, General Files 1043, Series 1, Box 8, Folder 517. Manuscripts and Archives, Yale University Library.

43 Leites, N.C. and de Sola Pool, I. (1942) *On Content Analysis*. Document No. 26, on 1 September 1942. The Library of Congress, Washington, DC, Experimental Division for the Study of Wartime Communications; Harold D. Lasswell, Chief. Document No. 26. Harold Dwight Lasswell Papers, General Files 1043, Series VII, Box 57, Folder 790. Manuscripts and Archives, Yale University Library.

44 George, A.L. (1949) The Intelligence value of content analysis. A preliminary progress report. US Air Force Project. RAND on 15 February 1949. D-419. Harold D. Lasswell Papers, General Files 1043, Series I, Box 89, Folder 1095. Manuscripts and Archives, Yale University Library.

45 Morris Janowitz was born to Samuel and Rose Janowitz, both Polish immigrants, and raised in Paterson, New Jersey. He earned a bachelor's degree from Washington Square College of New York University in 1941. After World War II started, he went to work for the Department of Justice Special War Policies Unit until he was drafted in 1943. Janowitz was assigned to the Research and Analysis Branch of the Office of Strategic Services (OSS) and sent to work for the Psychological Warfare Division at the Supreme Headquarters of the Allied Expeditionary Forces in London, where he analysed German radio broadcasts. He completed his PhD in sociology at the University of Chicago in 1948 and received a chair in the department of sociology in 1961 ('Guide to the Morris Janowitz Collection 1940–1989' 2009).

46 J.M. Goldsen and J. Goldstein to H.D. Lasswell. Preliminary analysis of World Attention Survey on 1 October 1943. Harold Dwight Lasswell Papers, General Files, 1043, Series I, Box 58, Folder 519, Manuscripts and Archives, Yale University Library.

47 MacKenzie Pool, J. (1988) 'Nathan and Ithiel', in RAND (ed.) *Remembering Nathan Leites. An Appreciation: Recollections of Some Friends, Colleagues, and Students*, p.34, RAND Corporation. RAND Corporation Archives.

48 Kecskeméti, P. (1933) 'Psychologie und Ontologie'. *Imago*, Band XIX, Heft 2. Paul Kecskemeti Papers. The Robert D. Farber University Archives & Special Collections Department at Brandeis University.

49 Leites, N.C. and de Sola Pool, I. (1942) Communist propaganda in reaction to frustration. The Library of Congress, Experimental Division for the Study of Wartime Communications, No 27 Harold D. Lasswell, Chief. Document on December 1, 1942. Harold Dwight Lasswell Papers, General Files 1043, Series VII, Box 57, Folder 790. Manuscripts and Archives, Yale University Library.

50 Leites, N.C. and de Sola Pool, I. (1942) Communist propaganda in reaction to frustration. The Library of Congress, Experimental Division for the Study of Wartime Communications, No 27 Harold D. Lasswell, Chief. Document on December 1, 1942. Harold D. Lasswell Papers, General Files 1043, Series VII, Box 57, Folder 790. Manuscripts and Archives, Yale University Library.

51 Kecskemeti, P. and Leites, N. (1945) Some Psychological Hypotheses on Nazi Germany. The Library of Congress, Experimental Division for the Study of Wartime Communications; Harold D. Lasswell, Chief. Document No 60 on 30 July 1945. Harold Dwight Lasswell Papers, General Files 1043, Series VII, Box 57, Folder 790. Manuscripts and Archives, Yale University Library.

52 Kecskemeti, P. and Leites, N. (1945) Some Psychological Hypothesis on Nazi Germany. Document No. 60, 30 July 1945. The Library of Congress, Experimental Division for the Study of War Time Communication; Harold D. Lasswell, Chief. Harold Dwight Lasswell Papers, General Files 1043, Series III, Box 57, Folder 790. Manuscripts and Archives, Yale University Library.

53 Abraham Kaplan was born in Odessa, Ukraine, in 1918 to Joseph J. Kaplan, a rabbi, and Chava (née Lerner) Kaplan. In 1923, Kaplan and his family immigrated to the United States and he became a naturalised citizen in 1930. He studied at the University of Chicago in 1937–1940 but received his PhD in 1942 from UCLA, where he became a professor of philosophy in 1952. He described himself as 'by training a positivist, by inclination a pragmatist, in temperament a mystic, in practice a democrat; my faith Jewish, educated by the Catholics, an habitual Protestant; born in Europe, raised in the Midwest, hardened in the east, and softened in California' (Casebier and Copi 1994; Kaplan (Abraham) Papers (no date)).

References

'Alexander and Juliette George' (no date).
http://plunkettlakepress.com/ajg.html

'Ármin Kecskeméti' (2008).
https://www.jewishvirtuallibrary.org/kecskem-x00e9-ti-x00c1-rmin

Ashcraft, Karen L. and Simonson, Peter (2016) 'Gender, Work, and the History of Communication Research', in Park, David W. and Simonson, Peter (eds) *The International History of Communication Study*, USA: Taylor & Francis, pp.47–68.

Bennett, Andrew (2008) 'Building Communities, Bridging Gaps: Alexander George's Contributions to Research Methods', *Political Psychology*, vol. 29, no. 4, pp.489–507. http://www.jstor.org/stable/20447141

Berelson, Bernard (1952) *Content Analysis in Communication Research*, USA: Hafner.

Berelson, Bernard and de Grazia, Sebastian (1947) 'Detecting Collaboration in Propaganda', *Public Opinion Quarterly*, vol. 11, no. 2, pp.244–53. https://doi.org/10.1093/poq/11.2.244

Berelson, Bernard and Janowitz, Morris (1950) *Reader in Public Opinion and Communication*, USA: Free Press.

Berelson, Bernard and Lazarsfeld, Paul F. (1948) *The Analysis of Communication Content*, Norway: Universitetets studentkontor.

Blum, John M. (1976) *V Was for Victory: Politics and American Culture during World War II*, USA: Harcourt Brace.

Buxton, William J. (2003) 'John Marshall and the Humanities in Europe: Shifting Patterns of Rockefeller Foundation Support', *Minerva*, vol. 41, no. 2, pp.133–53.
https://www.jstor.org/stable/41821239#metadata_info_tab_contents

Casebier, Allan and Copi, Irving (1994) 'Abraham Kaplan 1918–1993', *Proceedings and Addresses of the American Philosophical Association*, vol. 67, issue. 4, pp.137–40. http://www.jstor.org/stable/3130752

Cmiel, Kenneth (1996) 'On Cynicism, Evil, and the Discovery of Communication in the 1940s', *Journal of Communication*, vol. 46, no. 3, pp.88–107. https://doi.org/10.1111/j.1460-2466.1996.tb01491.x

Cox, Michael (2021) '"His Finest Hour": William Beveridge and the Academic Assistance Council'. https://blogs.lse.ac.uk/lsehistory/2021/04/28/his-finest-hour-william-beveridge-and-academic-assistance-council

Dale, Henry (1936) *The Protection of Science and Learning*, UK: Society for Protection of Science and Learning.

Davis, Elmer (1951) 'War Information', in Lerner, Daniel (ed.) *Propaganda in War and Crisis: Material for American Policy*, USA: George W. Stewart, pp.274–313.

Davison, W. Phillips (2006) *A Personal History of World War II: How a Pacifist Draftee Accidentally Became a Military Government Official in Postwar Germany*, USA: iUniverse.

de Sola Pool, Ithiel (ed.) (1959) *Trends in Content Analysis*, USA: University of Illinois Press.

de Sola Pool, Ithiel (1969) 'Content Analysis and the Intelligence Function', in Rogow, Arnold A. (ed.) *Politics, Personality, and Social Science in the Twentieth Century: Essays in Honor of Harold D. Lasswell*, USA: University of Chicago Press, pp.197–224.

Doob, Leonard W. (1947) 'The Utilization of Social Scientists in the Overseas Branch of the Office of War Information', *American Political Science Review*, vol. 41, no. 4, pp.649–67. https://doi.org/10.2307/1950646

Eulau, Heinz (1968) 'The Behavioral Movement in Political Science: A Personal Document', *Social Research*, vol. 35, no. 1, pp.1–29. https://www.jstor.org/stable/40969896

Farr, James; Hacker, Jacob S.; and Kazee, Nicole (2006) 'The Policy Scientist of Democracy: The Discipline of Harold D. Lasswell', *American Political Science Review*, vol. 100, no. 4, pp.579–87. https://doi.org/10.1017/S0003055406062459

'Ferment in the Field. Introduction' (1983) *Journal of Communication*, Vol. 33, no 3, pp.4–5. https://doi.org/10.1111/j.1460-2466.1983.tb02400.x

Frederick, Howard H. (1981) *The Life Work of Ithiel De Sola Pool: An Assessment and Bibliography*. Colloquium in International Communication, USA: The American University. https://www.academia.edu/30119424/The_Life_and_Work_of_Ithiel_de_Sola_

Gary, Brett J. (1992) *American Liberalism and the Problem of Propaganda: Scholars, Lawyers, and the War on Words, 1919–1945*, USA: University of Pennsylvania.

Gary, Brett J. (1996) 'Communication Research, the Rockefeller Foundation, and Mobilization for the War on Words, 1938–1944', *Journal of Communication*, vol. 46, no. 3, pp.124–48. https://doi.org/10.1111/j.1460-2466.1996.tb01493.x

George, Alexander L. (1956) 'Prediction of Political Action by Means of Propaganda Analysis', *Public Opinion Quarterly*, vol. 20, no. 1, pp.334–45. https://doi.org/10.1086/266623

George, Alexander L. (1959) *Propaganda Analysis: A Study of Inferences Made from Nazi Propaganda in World War II*, USA: Row, Peterson & Co.

George, Juliette (2008) 'Recollections of Alex George', *Political Psychology*, vol. 29, no. 4, pp.475–87. https://doi.org/10.1111/j.1467-9221.2008.00645.x

Glander, Timothy R. (1999) *Origins of Mass Communications Research during the American Cold War: Educational Effects and Contemporary Implications*, USA: Routledge.

Goldstein, Jacob (1943) 'An Exploratory Analysis of Opinion Trends with Special Reference to Conscription in the United States', *Sociometry*, vol. 6, no. 2, pp.156–81. https://doi.org/10.2307/2785355

Goldsen, Joseph (1959) (ed.) *Outer Space in World Politics*, USA: Frederick A. Praeger.

'Guide to the Ithiel de Sola Pool Papers 1935–1948' (2011) *Biographical Note*. University of Chicago Library. https://www.lib.uchicago.edu/e/scrc/findingaids/view.php?eadid=ICU.SPCL.POOLI

'Guide to the Morris Janowitz Collection 1940–1989' (2009) https://www.lib.uchicago.edu/e/scrc/findingaids/view.php?eadid=ICU.SPCL.JANOWITZM

'György Kecskeméti' (2008). https://www.jewishvirtuallibrary.org/kecskem-x00e9-ti-gy-x0151-rgy

Iacobelli, Teresa (2021) *The Rockefeller Foundation's Refugee Scholar Program*. https://resource.rockarch.org/story/the-rockefeller-foundations-refugee-scholar-program-world-war-ii-nazi-europe

'Ithiel de Sola Pool' (1997). https://web.mit.edu/m-i-t/profiles/profile_ithiel.html

Janis, Irving L. (1943) 'Meaning and the Study of Symbolic Behavior', *Psychiatry*, vol. 6, no. 4, pp.425–39. https://doi.org/10.1080/00332747.193.11022475

Janis, Irving L. and Fadner, Raymond H. (1943a) 'A Coefficient Imbalance for Content Analysis'. Library of Congress, Experimental Division for the Study of War-Time Communication, Document No 31.

Janis, Irving L. and Fadner, Raymond H. (1943b) 'A Coefficient of Imbalance for Content Analysis', *Psychometrika*, vol. 8, no. 2, pp.105–19. https://doi.org/10.1007/BF02288695

Janis, Irving L.; Fadner, Raymond H.; and Janowitz, Morris (1942a) 'The Reliability of a Content Analysis Technique'. Experimental Division for the Study of War-Time Communication, Document No 32.

Janis, Irving L.; Fadner Raymond H.; and Janowitz, Morris (1942b) 'Content Analysis Technique'. Library of Congress, Experimental Division for the Study of War-Time Communication, Document No 33.

Janis, Irving L.; Fadner, Raymond H.; and Janowitz, Morris (1943) 'The Reliability of a Content Analysis Technique', *The Public Opinion*

Quarterly, vol. 7, no. 2, pp.293–96.
https://www.jstor.org/stable/2745657#metadata_info_tab_contents

Janowitz, Morris (1968) 'Harold D. Lasswell's Contribution to Content Analysis', *Public Opinion Quarterly*, vol. 32, no. 4, pp.646–53.
https://doi.org/10.1086/267652

Janowitz, Morris (1969) 'Content Analysis and the Study of the "Symbolic Environment"', in Rogow, Arnold A. (ed.) *Politics, Personality, and Social Science in the Twentieth Century: Essays in Honor of Harold D. Lasswell*, USA: University of Chicago Press, pp.155–70.

Jay, Martin (1973/1996) *The Dialectical Imagination: A History of the Frankfurt School and the Institute of Social Research, 1923–1950*, USA and UK: University of California Press.

Kaplan, Abraham (1943) 'Content Analysis and the Theory of Signs', *Philosophy of Science*, vol. 10, no. 4, pp.230–47.

'Kaplan (Abraham) Papers' (no date).
https://oac.cdlib.org/findaid/ark:/13030/c86q1z11

Katz, Elihu and Katz, Ruth (2016) 'Revisiting the Origin of the Administrative versus Critical Research Debate', *Journal of Information Policy*, vol. 6, pp.4–12. https://doi.org/10.5325/jinfopoli.6.2016.0004

Kecskeméti, Pál (1926) 'A szociológia történetfilozófiai megalapozása: Mannheim Károly', *Századunk*, vol. 1, pp.447–57.

Kecskemeti, Paul (1931) 'Communists Demand Hitler's Arrest'.
https://www.upi.com/Archives/1931/10/12/Communists-demand-Hitlers-arrest/7781144211301

Kecskemeti, Paul (1952) *Meaning, Communication, and Value*, USA: University of Chicago Press.

Kecskemeti, Paul and Leites, Nathan (1947) 'Some Psychological Hypotheses on Nazi Germany: I', *The Journal of Social Psychology*, vol. 26(2), pp.141–83. https://doi.org/10.1080/00224545.1947.9921742

Kecskemeti, Paul and Leites, Nathan (1948a) 'Some Psychological Hypotheses on Nazi Germany: II', *The Journal of Social Psychology*, vol. 27, no. 1, pp.91–117. https://doi.org/10.1080/00224545.1948.9918914

Kecskemeti, Paul and Leites, Nathan (1948b) 'Some Psychological Hypotheses on Nazi Germany: III', *The Journal of Social Psychology*, vol. 27, no. 2, pp.241–70. https://doi.org/10.1080/00224545.1948.9918929

Kecskemeti, Paul and Leites, Nathan (1948c) 'Some Psychological Hypotheses on Nazi Germany: IV', *The Journal of Social Psychology*, vol. 28, no. 1, pp.141–64.

Kettler, David and Meja, Volker (1995) *Karl Mannheim and the Crisis of Liberalism: The Secret of These New Times*, USA: Transaction.

Kracauer, Siegfried (1952) 'The Challenge of Qualitative Content Analysis', *The Public Opinion Quarterly*, vol. 16, no. 4, pp.631–42. https://doi.org/10.1086/266427

Krippendorff, Klaus (1980/2004) *Content Analysis: An Introduction to Its Methodology*, UK: Sage.

Kris, Ernst and Leites, Nathan C. (1947) 'Trends in the 20th Century Propaganda', in Roheim, Geza (ed.) *Psychoanalysis and Social Sciences – An Annual, Vol. 1*, UK: Imago, pp.393–41.

Kris, Ernst and Speier, Hans (1944) *German Radio Propaganda: Report on Home Broadcasts during the War*, USA: Oxford University Press.

Krohn, Claus-Dieter (1996/2013) *Intellectuals in Exile: Refugee Scholars and the New School for Social Research*, USA: University of Massachusetts Press.

Kuckhoff, Greta (1972) *Vom Rosenkraz zur Roten Kapelle*, Germany: Verlag Neues Leben.

'Kuckhoff, Greta' (no date) 'Biographische Angaben aus dem Handbuch "Wer war wer in der DDR?"'. https://www.bundesstiftung-aufarbeitung.de/de /recherche/kataloge-datenbanken/biographische-datenbanken/greta -kuckhoff

Kurzweil, Edith (1996) 'Psychoanalytic Science: From Oedipus to Culture', in Ash, Mitchell G. and Söllner, Alfons (eds) *Forced Migration and Scientific Change: Émigré German-Speaking Scientists and Scholars After 1933*, UK: Cambridge University Press, pp.139–55.

Lamberti, Marjorie (2006) 'The Reception of Refugee Scholars from Nazi Germany in America: Philanthropy and Social Change in Higher Education', *Jewish Social Studies*, vol. 12, no. 3, pp.157–92. https://www.jstor.org/stable/pdf/4467750.pdf

Lang, Kurt (1979) 'The Critical Functions of Empirical Communication Research: Observations on German-American Influences', *Media, Culture & Society*, vol. 1, no. 1, pp.83–96. https://doi.org/10.1177/016344377900100107

Lässig, Simone (2017) 'Strategies and Mechanisms of Scholar Rescue: The Intellectual Migration of the 1930s Reconsidered', *Social Research: An International Quarterly*, vol. 84, no. 4, pp.769–807. https://doi.org/10.1353/sor.2017.005

Lasswell, Harold D. (1938) 'A Provisional Classification of Symbol Data', *Psychiatry*, vol. 1, no. 2, pp.197–204. https://doi.org/10.1080/00332747.1938.11022172

Lasswell, Harold D. (1941) 'The World Attention Survey: An Exploration of the Possibilities of Studying Attention Being Given to the United States by Newspapers Abroad', *Public Opinion Quarterly*, vol. 5, no. 3, pp.456–62. https://doi.org/10.1086/265515

Lasswell, Harold D. (1942) 'Analyzing the Content of Mass Communication. Brief Introduction'. Library of Congress, Experimental Division for the Study of War-Time Communication, Document No 11.

Lasswell, Harold D. (1948) 'The Structure and Function of Communication in Society', in Bryson, Lyman (ed.) *The Communication of Ideas*, USA: Institute for Religious and Social Studies, pp.37–51.

Lasswell, Harold D. (1949) 'Why Be Quantitative?' in Lasswell, Harold D. and Leites, Nathan (eds) *Language of Politics: Studies in Quantitative Semantics*, USA: G.W. Stewart, pp.40–52.

Lasswell, Harold D. (1968) 'The Future of the Comparative Method', *Comparative Politics*, vol. 1, no. 1, pp.3–18. https://www.jstor.org/stable/421372#metadata_info_tab_contents

Lasswell, Harold D. and Associates (1942) 'The Politically Significant Content of the Press: Coding Procedures', *Journalism Quarterly*, vol. 19, no. 1, pp.12–23. https://doi.org/10.1177/107769904201900102

Lasswell, Harold D. and Goldsen, Joseph M. (1947) 'Public Attention, Opinion, and Action', *International Journal of Opinion and Attitude Research*, vol. 1, no. 1, pp.3–11.

Lasswell, Harold D.; Leites, Nathan; and Associates (1949) *Language of Politics: Studies in Quantitative Semantics*, USA: George W. Stewart.

Lazarsfeld, Paul F. (1941) 'Remarks on Administrative and Critical Communications Research', *Studies in Philosophy and Social Science*, vol. 9, no. 1, pp.2–16. https://doi.org/10.5840/zfs1941912

Lazarsfeld, Paul F.; Berelson, Bernard; and Gaudet, Hazel (1944) *The People's Choice: How the Voter Makes Up His Mind in a Presidential Campaign*, USA: Duell, Sloan and Pearce.

Leff, Laurel (2019) *Well Worth Saving: American Universities' Life-And-Death Decisions on Refugees from Nazi Europe*, USA: Yale University Press.

Levyatan, Yaniv (2009) 'Harold D. Lasswell's Analysis of Hitler's Speeches', *Media History*, vol. 15, no. 1, pp.55–69. https://doi.org/10.1080/13688800802583299

Library of Congress (no date) *Annual Report of the Librarian of Congress 1941/1942–1943/1944*, USA: Library of Congress. https://babel.hathitrust.org/cgi/pt?id=mdp.39015036841743&seq=53&q1=wartime+communications

Magyar Néprajzi Lexikon (Hungarian Encyclopaedia of Ethnography) (no date). http://mek.niif.hu/02100/02115/html/

Marwick, Arthur (1988) *Total War and Social Change*, UK: Palgrave Macmillan.

Meja, Volker and Kettler, David (1993) 'Cultural Politics in Karl Mannheim's Sociology: Introduction to the Transaction Edition', in Wolff, Kurt H. (ed.) *From Karl Mannheim*, USA: Routledge, pp.vii–xxxvi.

Morrison, David (1988) 'The Transference of Experience and the Impact of Ideas: Paul Lazarsfeld and Mass Communication Research', *Encyclopaedia of Communication*, vol. 10, pp.185–209.

Morrison, David E. (2008) 'Opportunity Structures and the Creation of Knowledge: Paul Lazarsfeld and the Politics of Research', in Park, David W. and Pooley, Jefferson (eds) *The History of Media and Communication Research. Contested Memories*, USA: Peter Lang, pp.179–204.

Morrison, David (2022) 'Lazarsfeld's Legacy| Paul Lazarsfeld: Living in Circles and Talking around Tables', *International Journal of Communication*, vol. 16, pp.616–25. https://ijoc.org/index.php/ijoc/article/view/18891/3664

'Nachlass Greta Kuckhoff' (no date). http://www.argus.bstu.bundesarchiv.de/N2506-35612/index.htm

Némedi, Dénes (1992) '"Sociologists", Sociographers, and "Liberals": Hungarian Intellectuals Respond to Fascism', in Turner, Stephen P. and Käsler, Dirk (eds) *Sociology Responds to Fascism*, UK: Routledge, pp.151–67.

Neumann, Franz L. (1953) *The Cultural Migration: The European Scholar in America*, USA: University of Pennsylvania Press.

Oren, Ido (2003) *Our Enemies and US: America's Rivalries and the Making of Political Science*, USA: Cornell University Press.

Palmer, Barbara (2006) 'Alexander George, "Giant" in International Relations, Dead at 86', *Stanford News*, https://news.stanford.edu/news/2006/august23/obitgeorge-082306.html

Committee on International Communications Research (1952) 'Proceedings of the Committee on International Communications Research', *Public Opinion Quarterly*, vol. 16, no. 4, pp.705–08. https://doi.org/10.1086/266434

Rogers, Everett M. (1981) 'The Empirical and the Critical Schools of Communication Research', *Annals of the International Communication Association*, vol. 5, no. 1, pp.125–44. https://doi.org/10.1080/23808985.181.11923842

Rogers, Everett M. (1994) *A History of Communication Study: A Biographical Approach*, USA: Free Press.

Sayner, Joanne (2013) *Reframing Antifascism: Memory, Genre and the Life Writings of Greta Kuckhoff*, UK: Palgrave Macmillan.

Schmidt, Péter (1933a) 'Az ellenforradalom gyözelme Németországban', *Századunk*, vol. 9, pp.97–105.

Schmidt, Péter (1933b) 'A harmadik birodalomból', *Századunk*, vol. 8, pp.229–33.

Schmidt, Péter (1935) 'Hitler három éve', *Századunk*, vol. 10, pp.74–82.

Sills, David L. (1980) 'In Memoriam: Bernard Berelson, 1912–1979', *The Public Opinion Quarterly*, vol. 44, no. 2, pp.274–75. http://www.jstor.org/stable/2748438

Simpson, Christopher (1993) 'U.S. Mass Communication Research, Counterinsurgery, and Scientific "Reality"', in Solomon, William S. and McChesney, Robert W. (eds.) *Ruthless Criticism: New Perspectives in U.S. Communication History*, USA: University of Minnesota Press, pp.313–48.

Simpson, Christopher (1994) *Science of Coercion: Communication Research and Psychological Warfare, 1945–1960*, USA: Oxford University Press.

Smith, Bruce L. (1943) 'Scientific and Semi-scientific Literature on War Information and Censorship', *Journalism Quarterly*, vol. 20, no. 1, pp.1–20. https://doi.org/10.1177/107769904302000101

Sobel Robert (1976) *The Manipulators. America in the Middle Age*, USA: Anchor Press/Doubleday.

Speier, Hans (1989) *The Truth in Hell and Other Essays on Politics and Culture, 1935–1987*, USA: Oxford University Press.

Sproule, J. Michael (1997) *Propaganda and Democracy: The American Experience of Media and Mass Persuasion*, UK: Cambridge University Press.

'The United States and the Founding of the United Nations, August 1941–October 1945' (2005) US Department of State Archive. https://2001-009.state.gov/r/pa/ho/pubs/fs/55407.htm

Wolfenstein, Martha and Leites, Nathan C. (1947) 'An Analysis of Themes and Plots', *The Annals of the American Academy of Political and Social Science*, vol. 254, no. 1, pp.41–48. https://doi.org/10.1177/000271624725400108

Wolfenstein, Martha and Leites, Nathan (1950) *Movies: A Psychological Study*, USA: Free Press.

5. From togetherness to separation: comparative communications in the 1950s

> Everyone has the right to freedom of opinion and expression; this right includes freedom to hold opinions without interference and to seek, receive and impart information and ideas through any media and regardless of frontiers. (Universal Declaration of Human Rights, Article 19, United Nations General Assembly 1948)

Given that comparative communications had been attached so closely to US war efforts, what would become of it in the post-war period? In this chapter, I argue that a unified generation became divided, following not only the ideological clashes of the time, marked by the Cold War and McCarthyism, but also by the advent of the new discipline of communication studies. In this period, this 'independent' new discipline of communication studies, increasingly focusing on domestic issues, did not promote international communication as a new subfield but buried it. However, comparative communications continued in separate projects led mostly by World War II propaganda researchers in political science, rather than in communication studies.

What happened after World War I was repeated in the immediate aftermath of World War II. There was a brief period of internationalism in which there emerged a new utopian vision of comparative communications research as a mindset of increasing mutual understanding between peoples so as to prevent future war (see Chapter 3). For example, the Commission on Freedom of the Press, the Hutchins Commission (see Chapters 2 and 3), in its report *Peoples Speaking to Peoples* (White and Leigh 1946, p.vi), urged that 'the government and people of the U.S. should recognise the importance of a mutual understanding between peoples'. However, internationalistic sentiment would be challenged by a global ideological war, the Cold War between former military allies the US and the Soviet Union, accompanied by an intense US-based anti-communism, spearheaded by Senator Joseph McCarthy's (1908–1957) investigations to uncover alleged domestic communist sympathisers. Although Mannheim writes about a pre-World War II era, his concepts of utopias and ideologies

How to cite this book chapter:

Rantanen, Terhi (2024) *Dead Men's Propaganda: Ideology and Utopia in Comparative Communications Studies*, London: LSE Press, pp. 167–208.
https://doi.org/10.31389/lsepress.wmf.e. License: CC BY-NC 4.0

can be applied to the post-war US era when analysing the growing influence of these rival ideologies.

In this chapter I explore why comparative communications did *not* emerge after World War II as a field of its own, like comparative politics in political science, but was dispersed into several fields including mainstream communication studies. Rajagopal (2020) calls the years of 1945–1955 in communication studies 'the first period of interest—and, in retrospect, ingenuous curiosity, shaped by wartime euphoria, about the power of communications technology'. The early communication scholars included political scientists, psychologists and sociologists (Schramm 1980), who had studied communication long before it became a distinct field of study. These included Lazarsfeld and Merton (Lazarsfeld and Merton 1943; 1948/1964; Merton and Lazarsfeld 1950), whose work illustrates how the new field of communication emerged both from military propaganda research and from advertising market research (Lazarsfeld 1948, p.218; Merton 1949/1968, p.505) and how these interests influenced research funding (Stanton and Lazarsfeld 1949, p.xviii).

Wahl-Jorgensen (2004, p.560) argues that the US field of communication research began not with Wilbur Schramm at the Illinois Institute of Communication Research (see, for example, Schramm 1957; 1959; 1963; 1985; Rogers 1994), but emerged in many places including Harvard, Cornell, Yale, Columbia and Berkeley in the post-war years (Berelson 1959; Glander 2000, pp.62–63), and that there is evidence of extensive collaboration between researchers at these institutions. Berelson's (1959) and Schramm's (1959; 1963) are examples of the stories told by the generation of so-called founders themselves and repeated by the following generations, before being challenged by Wahl-Jorgensen (2004). Her argument can be extended to apply also to comparative communications, and this chapter gives various examples of studies at Stanford and MIT. I also look at the environment – academic and societal, national and international – in which this research was being carried out when communication studies was becoming institutionalised (Rantanen 2017). I further explore the later careers of scholars, who had worked together as well as separately during World War II and who continued their careers as policy science researchers and academics. I also note that émigré scholars Kecskemeti and Leites, while securing careers for themselves as policy scientists, did not become full professors in academia like many of their native US World War II colleagues (for example, Lasswell, George, de Sola Pool and Berelson) but made their contributions to the emerging field at RAND Corporation.

This chapter uses Mannheim's key concepts to analyse these materials. It was the members of what I described earlier as the forefront generation who started comparative communications, and this brings us back to the concept of a generation and of generational conflicts, as well as to Merton's concepts of Insider/Outsider, in addition to Mannheim's concepts of ideology and of utopia. The forefront generation lived through ideological changes

from pessimism to optimism and back to pessimism. Some forefront generation research, such as effect studies, became so dominant that it would not be
challenged for more than a decade (see, for example, Klapper 1960). Simpson
(1994, p.16) writes: 'the psychological warfare projects of World War II left
their strongest legacy in academic circles, particularly in the then embry-
onic field of communication research', especially emphasising Lasswell's role
in this. Thus, the forefront generation actively contributed to what Simpson
(1994, p.115) calls the US government's psychological warfare programmes,
which lasted until 1960. However, the role of many members of this generation has so far been invisible and they became Outsiders in various attempts
to construct historical accounts of communication studies in the US which
emphasised a national context. Those who followed, starting from the 1960s
generation, mainly reviewed the forefront generation's work critically in order
to justify their own, different, approach.

This chapter is divided into five parts. The first part analyses the societal
environment, both national and international, within which comparative
communications was carried out and compares post-World War I and post-
World War II environments. The second part explores post-World War II projects carried out by those who had come to know each other when working
at the Library of Congress and who continued their policy science thereafter.
The third part reviews attempts to define international communication as a
new and emerging field. The fourth part investigates those who worked for
RAND Corporation. Finally, I address the question of the main features of
new international communications studies in the 1950s.

5.1 Post-World Wars I and II communications compared

World War I has often been called the first propaganda war, where both the
old media of leaflets and newspapers and the new media of wireless and cin-
ema were used on a mass scale. At its outset, on the order of President Wilson (1856–1924), the US Navy Department seized all wireless stations in the
US and in its possessions (Mock and Larson 1939) and these were used for
governmental news dissemination abroad – America's worldwide news service (Creel 1920, pp.251, 254). The periods before and after the war saw the
emergence of modern mass media, including mass-circulation newspapers,
magazines, photos, films and the wireless telegraph, which carried what Creel
(1920) referred to as 'the gospel of Americanism' to every corner of the globe.
As early as the mid-1920s, US filmmakers were producing an estimated 90 per
cent of the movies shown around the world (Read 1976, p.7).

However, World War I was still a minor propaganda war compared with
World War II when it came to the use of mass media, especially the electronic
media. World War II also provided the conditions for the international expansion of US media. For example, the US news agencies Associated Press (AP)
and United Press (UP)[1] had already started their worldwide expansion in the

late 1930s, after the European news cartel was broken, and continued their expansion into foreign markets during and after World War II (UNESCO 1953). The US film industry continued to benefit from its dominance in overseas markets during and after World War II (Guback 1969) and reached its third export peak in the late 1940s (Tunstall 1977, p.143). In 1950, the US consumed 51 per cent of the world's newsprint (Lemberg 2019, p.53). The US had in 1950 over 10 million television sets – while the rest of the world had fewer than one million – and half the world's radio sets (Tunstall 1977, p.92). Tunstall (1977, p.137) calls the years 1943–1953 the high tide of American media, closely connected with the new status of the US as the dominant military power, and defines the years 1947–1948 as the highest peak of the dominant US position in the world market (Tunstall 2008, p.70).

In a joint article, Kris and Leites (1947, pp.395–96) conclude that propaganda in World War II exhibited, on the whole, a higher degree of sobriety than propaganda in World War I and that World War II propaganda was (1) less emotional; (2) less moralistic; and (3) more fact-based than World War I propaganda. However, the need for this type of comparative communications was now diminishing because of a rapidly changing international political climate.

The US government's role in promoting freedom of information after World War I and World War II

The peace negotiations at Versailles in 1919 showed the newly active role of the US in international politics. However, the final peace treaty came to be widely seen as punitive towards Germany and as having led directly to World War II. There were those who put their trust in the new League of Nations in Geneva, founded in 1919 as a forum for attempting to solve international disputes, but the US did not take part in this, even though the League was based on the Fourteen Points introduced by President Wilson at Versailles. US public opinion was very much divided between those who supported the League of Nations and those who were critical of it. Seidelman and Harpham (1985, pp.101, 105) write that 'the aftermath of the Great War seemed to show that elites and masses had gone somewhat mad. No one wanted to listen to political science vanguards', who 'had themselves rejected their pre-war optimism'. Academics were themselves divided into those who supported pre-war pragmatism and optimism and those critical of these, as exemplified in the debate between Walter Lippmann (1889–1974) and John Dewey (1859–1952) (see, for example, Gary 1999; Schudson 2008). Bateson (1966) summarises some of these sentiments by quoting the Bible:

> the sins of the fathers shall be visited on the children even to the third and fourth generation of those that hate me. We all live in the same crazy universe whose hate, distrust, and hypocrisy relates

back (especially at the international level) to the Fourteen Points and the Treaty of Versailles.

The forefront generation, albeit divided, nonetheless had an effect on the establishment of new academic fields. Brown (2001, p.214) writes about the foundation of international relations, characterised in its early days by what he calls idealism or utopianism, which was dominated by liberal internationalist thinking and was largely the product of World War I. He argues (2001, p.214) that international relations was founded as an academic discipline/discourse in the immediate post-1918 world by British and American 'liberal internationalists' and upon a liberalism 'peculiar to, or at least highly characteristic of, the English-speaking peoples'. One of the post-World War I liberal internationalists was Lasswell, who, as shown in Chapter 2, came to play a major role both in political science and in comparative communications studies during and after World War II. Lasswell (1927, p.216) described Wilson as World War I's 'great generalissimo on the propaganda front' (Cmiel 1996, p.90), and under him greater importance started to be given to research on public opinion when it was realised how much communication mattered, especially with the appearance of the 'new' media of the time: radio and motion pictures. Early research institutes and projects were founded, such as the Institute for Propaganda Analysis, the Payne Fund studies, and the Princeton Office of Radio Research (Lazarsfeld 1952, p.482). As a contemporary wrote,

> [the] ignorance of the character, objects and purposes, doings, and intentions of other people, is the most prolific cause of misunderstanding and ill-feeling between such peoples, tending to generate suspicions and produce friction and disagreement, and is, therefore, one of the principal causes of war. (Bleyer 1926, p.7)

Compared to the situation after World War I, the US government was much more active in participating in the post-World War II international order. Mowlana (1986/1997, p.2) writes that post-World War II theorists of international relations drew a distinction between domestic and international politics and viewed nation states and their decision makers as the most important actors in international relations. Chapter 3 explored how Cooper promoted his idea of the freedom of news in the US and abroad. After World War II, the US government actively promoted the idea of the United Nations, which was physically located in New York City rather than in Geneva, the site of the League of Nations. The US had surpassed Europe as the site for the premier global institution. Learning from what was by this time seen as Wilson's mistake of not participating in the League of Nations after World War I, both President Franklin D. Roosevelt (1882–1945) and President Harry S. Truman (1884–1972) supported US participation in the United Nations (UN) and associated bodies ('The United States and the Founding of the United Nations, August 1941–October 1945' 2005). The UN Charter was signed in 1942, in the midst of

World War II. The Charter states that 'we the peoples of the United Nations determined to save succeeding generations from the scourge of war, which twice in our lifetime has brought untold sorrow to mankind' (United Nations, no date). The UN as an institution was established in a meeting on 24 October 1945, hosted by the US, in San Francisco.

Cooper's advocacy on behalf of the role of news in fostering and maintaining peace was very much in line with the mission of the United Nations. Communication became a primary concern for the United Nations Educational, Scientific and Cultural Organization (UNESCO), founded on 16 November 1945. Its constitution followed the spirit of the UN but referred explicitly to the role of the media in maintaining peace by 'desiring to improve understanding between their peoples through the *free flow* of information and opinion' (my emphasis) ('Draft Convention of the Gathering and International Transmission of News' 1948). In 1948, one of the first special conferences organised by the UN was devoted to freedom of information. News was given a special status in the flow of ideas and was considered 'the most serious information as a fundamental human right and essential in the cause of peace and for the achievement of political, social and economic progress' (UN Economic and Social Council 1948, p.24; see also Rantanen 2010, p.28).

The new interest in comparative communications was strongly supported by researchers' commitment to promoting international understanding through their work. Smith (1956, p.183) argued that 'it is plainly urgent to develop an art and science of international and cross-cultural communication, in the hope of reducing international confusion and irritation'. Mowlana (1986/1997, p.6) calls this an idealistic-humanistic approach embraced as a 'means of bringing nations and people together and as a force for assisting international organisations in the exercise of their services to the world community'. There was a strong utopian sentiment, shared by academics, policy researchers and politicians, in favour of a new kind of internationalisation that was close to becoming an ideology, being supported by institutions and individuals alike.

This idealistic-humanistic approach is clearly visible in various US documents from the period that emphasised a need for a 'unified programme that we Americans might, as a beginning, seek to carry out in this country' (Angell 1950/1953, p.380), and that would:

(1) Encourage further study of international communications problems;
(2) Increase the flow of international communication;
(3) Foster a greater sense of international responsibility among those performing communications functions;
(4) Foster particularly the exchange of creative works of literature, both fiction and non-fiction;
(5) Foster exchange of students, professors, and other professional men;
(6) Support UNESCO.

In the post-World War II period, the close collaboration between the US government and private foundations established in wartime continued. Comparative communications became mostly policy research that was funded primarily outside academia, both nationally and internationally. Between 1945 and 1955, the major sponsors of studies in communications research, which in the US and in other countries was now increasingly being called international communication studies, were national governments. According to Smith, one of the striking trends of the decade was the willingness of policymakers to commission important research on international communication and opinion, and to pay attention to its results (Smith 1956, p.184). In the US, after the war, the Ford Foundation replaced Rockefeller as the principal patron of communication research (Pooley 2011, p.226), and many of the wartime comparative researchers went on to participate in new comparative communications projects, as detailed in the subsequent sections of this chapter.

Changing ideologies: the Cold War and McCarthyism

The initial post-war spirit of internationalism changed rapidly under the external influences of the Cold War and of McCarthyism, which affected both individual researchers and their funding. Recent research on the Cold War and its influence on academic research has been divided (Isaac 2007), but, while the evidence is open to debate, we see an example of how utopias and ideologies follow each other, when:

> ruling groups can in their thinking become so intensely interest-bound to a certain situation, that they are simply no longer able to see certain facts which would undermine their sense of domination. (Mannheim 1960, p.36)

The combination of the Cold War and McCarthyism created an atmosphere of new fear that heightened ideological battles over the concept of 'truth'. According to President Eisenhower (1890–1969),

> our aim in the Cold War is not conquering of territory or subjugation by force. Our aim is more subtle, more pervasive, more complete. We are trying to get the world, by peaceful means, to believe the truth. (quoted by Saunders 2000, p.148)

The US Congress began to reauthorise worldwide propaganda, and significant funding was given both to propaganda work and to research that would pre-test and post-evaluate its effectiveness (Smith 1956, p.184). The CIA, like other national state security agencies, funded a significant number of communications and social science programmes at US universities throughout the Cold War period (Glander 2000, p.63). There was new interest in what Almond and Coleman once called 'exotic and uncouth' parts of the world (Almond and Coleman 1960, p.10). The new enemy was the Soviet Union and other communist countries and there was a perceived need, again supported both by the government and by private funders, to know more about them. A new interest was also found in comparative communications following the tradition that had started in World War II.

In 1947, President Truman promulgated Executive Order 9835, the so-called 'Loyalty Order', to eliminate communists from all areas of the US government including universities, despite the fact that the Communist Party in the US was thought to be one of the tiniest in the world (Saunders 2000, pp.8, 191). This meant that the international organisations that the US had become actively involved in now also came under suspicion. Tiede (2022, p.647) writes:

> The period from 1948 to the mid-1950s—the 'difficult years' (Lazarsfeld and Thielens 1958, p.35), as *The Academic Mind* called them—was an era of sustained attack on academic freedom in U.S. higher education. Anti-communist hysteria led to legislative investigative hearings, in which faculty members were asked about their political allegiances and those of their friends and colleagues; to mandatory loyalty oaths, imposed by legislatures or governing boards; and to individual denunciations of faculty members over their past associations with the Communist Party, communist front organizations, or other left-liberal causes.

The UN had been a target of the American Right from its inception (Caute 1978, p.325) and, for example, 15 Americans employed by UNESCO in Paris were ordered to appear before the International Organizations Employees Loyalty Board (IOELB) established by the Eisenhower Administration in 1953 to screen Americans serving an international organisations (Caute 1978, pp.330–31; Preston 1989, pp.63–64). During the 'Great Fear' (Caute 1978), many were interrogated and some lost their jobs. This fear emphasised loyalty to the US government and any international activity could potentially be seen as communist. At the same time, as Saunders (2000) has shown in her work, many US and European intellectuals, writers and artists started working closely with the CIA and other US governmental organisations.

It is difficult to find evidence of how the 'Great Fear' influenced individuals, because accusations of communist sympathies and/or activism are part of a secret history *ad usum Delphini*, in the same way as Kirchick (2022) argues with regard to sexual orientation (see Chapter 2). As Farr, Hacker and Kazee (2006, p.586) observe, the political scientists of democracy were clearly anti-fascist (as was Lasswell during World War II) in the 1930s and anti-communist (as was Lasswell during the Cold War) in the 1950s, although Lasswell's anti-communism had already started in the 1930s. Lasswell had to undergo a government security check because of his earlier research on communism. Lazarsfeld came under attack for his work funded by the Ford Foundation, which was the 'most exposed to charges of support for communism' (Morrison 2008, p.191). As detailed in Chapter 6, George Stoddard lost his job as president of the University of Illinois. He had been a member of the US delegation to the first general meeting of UNESCO in Paris in 1946 (Sproule 1997, p.245; 'George Stoddard Dies at the Age of 84' 1981). From the Wartime Communications Project, and from among those in addition to Lasswell who did propaganda research during World War II (see Chapters 2 and 4), Speier (Bessner 2018), de Sola Pool (and his parents)[2] and Sebastian de Grazia[3] had to go through security checks. Kecskemeti was interviewed as early as 1944 by the Civil Service Commission after somebody had made accusations against him.[4] We also know that de Sola Pool felt that Leites did not give him his support when he and his family were accused and that this resulted in a break in their friendship that lasted until de Sola Pool was on his deathbed.[5] One can only imagine the distress these individuals went through at a time when anybody could be accused of being communist.

Oren (2003, pp.126, 130) argues that in the 1950s American political science swung strongly towards ideological nationalism but also simultaneously towards ideological internationalisation. Blyth (2006, p.493) writes of political science after World War II that it was required to become positive and predictive, as 'a conscious instrument of social engineering' (Loewenstein 1944) in order to achieve status and acknowledgement as a field. Lasswell had promoted the idea of 'policy science' (see Chapters 1 and 2), in which policy scientists would find 'a solution to the major problems of our epoch' (Gilman 2003, p.167). The same applies to comparative communications of that period and as a result, as Glander (2000, p.204) points out, during the Cold War 'mass communication research units were established on university campuses that profited from the needs of national security apparatus to control and shape opinions about foreign and domestic policy'. In short, there was funding available, but it came with strings attached.

5.2 The continuation of World War II studies

Comparative communications research continued in several projects funded by private foundations, the research sponsor next in importance to the national government. According to Shah (2011, p.18),

> between 1946 and 1958, private foundations alone gave $85 million for social science research (nearly half of that money going to just three universities: Harvard, Columbia, and University of California–Berkeley). The three largest foundations—Carnegie, Ford, and Rockefeller—viewed themselves as supporting important aims of U.S. foreign policy.

In this section I look at different projects, all relevant comparative communications. The first is the Revolution and the Development of International
Relations (RADIR) project at the Hoover Institute at Stanford University
(Lasswell, Lerner and de Sola Pool 1952a). This was inspired by the theories
of Lasswell on world revolutionary developments, and the project was in
some respects the successor to work done at the Library of Congress in the
Wartime Communications Project (Eulau 1977, p.392) in the study of 'current
revolution and its influence on the development of international relations'. For
the second project, the Massachusetts Institute of Technology (MIT) received
$875,000 for a programme of 'Studies in International Communication' from
the Ford Foundation, reports from which focused largely on 'elite attitudes'
and 'elite communications' (de Sola Pool 1954; 1955; Mowlana 2004, pp.7–8;
Planning Committee of the Center for International Studies at the Massachusetts Institute of Technology 1954). Both projects were much influenced by
Lasswell's earlier work.

The third category of projects is the Committee on Comparative Politics,
funded by the US Social Science Research Council (SSRC), which funded
Wilbur Schramm's (1907–1987) study on *One Day in the World's Press* (1959b)
and News Flow Studies by UNESCO and International Press Institute (IPI).
These projects became influential in their respective fields, the first in comparative politics and the second and third in international communication.
There were, however, overlapping methodologies, objects of study and personnel between these projects.

The Revolution and the Development of International Relations (RADIR) project at Stanford

Lasswell (who had become a professor in the Yale Law School in 1946) continued to develop content analysis as a research technique including on the
RADIR project, which ran from 1949 to 1953 at the Hoover Institution at
Stanford University. It was funded by the Carnegie Corporation to study
major political changes between 1890 and 1950 and became a many-volumed
analysis of several countries' institutions ('General Studies'), leadership ('Elite
Studies') and communications ('Symbol Studies') from 1890 and in relation
to 'the world revolution of our time' (Smith 1956, p.186). The symbols study
examined nine elite (prestige) newspapers in the US, the UK, the Soviet
Union, France and Germany over 60 years. The modified list of symbols used
in this study was drawn from the World Attention Survey (Lasswell 1941),
directed by Lasswell at the Library of Congress. It included a study of symbols,
which were the 'names of political units, including nations, encompassing key
symbols of the major ideologies contending in the world political arena over
the preceding century' (Lerner, de Sola Pool and Lasswell 1951, p.720). Newspaper editorials were examined 'to ascertain the rise and fall of major political
concepts, particularly those pertaining to democracy and authoritarianism,

violence and peace, and self and other (i.e., identity)' (de Sola Pool 1969, p.208). Their results showed that the variety of symbols used is reduced under conditions of political crisis; in other words, that there is greater attention at such times to fewer symbols (Lerner, de Sola Pool and Lasswell 1951, p.733). *The Prestige Papers. A Survey of Their Editorials* (1952), for which de Sola Pool was credited as a leading author for the first time together with Lasswell, also, unlike the World War II reports, included the names of the women who did the coding as additional contributors. They were Mary Chapman, Barbara Conner, Barbara Lamb, Barbara Marshall, Eva Meyer, Elena Schueller and Marina S. Tinkoff. The introduction was written by Berelson, another wartime collaborator (see Chapter 4).

The authors involved in the RADIR project, included and credited as such, were Lasswell, Lerner and de Sola Pool (1952b), but none of the émigré scholars. Daniel Lerner (1917–1980; pictured Figure 5.1) was born in Brooklyn, New York, to Russian émigré parents Louetta (Yetta) (née Swiger, 1895–year of death unknown) and Louis Lerner (1891–year of death unknown). He attended New York City public schools and earned a bachelor's degree in English literature in 1938, a master's degree in English in 1939 and a PhD in 1948, all from New York University. Lerner fought in Normandy, was wounded in action in 1944 and transferred to the Psychological Warfare Division (PWD),

Figure 5.1: Daniel Lerner

Source: The MIT History Collection, Massachusetts Institute of Technology, Cambridge, MA; reproduced courtesy MIT Museum.
https://mitmuseum.mit.edu/collections/object/GCP-00014581#people
Notes: Date unknown.

where he served as chief editor in the Intelligence Branch. His PhD dissertation at New York University was later published with the title *Sykewar: Psychological Warfare against Germany, D-Day to V-E Day* (Lerner 1949; Shah
2011, p.26). He started working for RADIR at Stanford in 1946 and married
his schoolfriend from Brooklyn Jean Weinstein (1918–2001). Lerner regularly
thanked her for typing and retyping his manuscripts (Shah 2011, p.27).

In 1949, de Sola Pool, one of Lasswell's collaborators on propaganda
research in World War II, moved to Stanford's Hoover Institution to become,
under Lerner, assistant director of research of the RADIR project. His primary academic appointments were at Stanford University and MIT, where
he spent 30 years, having initially joined the new MIT Center for International Studies to direct a research programme on the effects of communication technology on global politics ('Ithiel de Sola Pool' 1997) (pictured at
MIT in Figure 5.2). In later life, de Sola Pool would become a member of
the Council on Foreign Relations and an adviser to the United States government during the Cold War (Frederick 1981; 'Guide to the Ithiel de Sola
Pool Papers 1935–1948' 2011). However, de Sola Pool later became critical of
this project, in which he himself had participated. He thought that, although
'the designers of the project certainly thought that they were clarifying the
central issues of our time', it had not become relevant to policy (de Sola Pool
1969, p.209). Although the RADIR project produced a report, *The Policy
Sciences* (see Chapter 2), de Sola Pool considered that this in fact contained

Figure 5.2: Ithiel de Sola Pool in front of a chalkboard at MIT

very little policy, since, while 'recording 105,000 instances of occurrence of 416 symbols in some 20,000 editorials' (de Sola Pool 1969, p.209), its theoretical contribution remained undeveloped. With reference to Lasswell, de Sola Pool later wrote that 'timeless generalizing science is a young man's game' and 'understanding time and development takes a more mature kind of development' (de Sola Pool 1969, p.222). This may have been a polite way of saying that, although the project produced a large amount of data, its theoretical contribution was less significant.

The Center for International Studies at MIT

The Lasswell papers at Yale University contain several applications for research grants in international communication submitted to different private funders such as the Ford Foundation. One of the early examples is from the summer of 1952, when the Behavioral Sciences Division of the Ford Foundation gave a grant to the Center for International Studies at MIT for a four-year programme of research in international communication. The Center appointed a Planning Committee to advise it on the use of this grant. The committee consisted of Speier as chairman, Jerome Bruner (1915–2016), Wallace Carroll (1906–2002), Lasswell, Lazarsfeld, Shils, and de Sola Pool as secretary. They wrote in their application that:

> 'International communication' viewed in this way is indeed a broad area—so broad, in fact, that it embraces most of the social processes. Yet, in approaching a research program, it is best to reject the alternative view of communication research as the specialized study of the mass media. Such a program would be relatively unfruitful if it segregated for study one particular group of human actions concerning mass communication as if they were governed by principles unlike the rest. The study of communication is but one way to study man, and the study of international communication is but another way to study international relations. (Planning Committee of the Center for International Studies at the Massachusetts Institute of Technology 1954, pp.358–59)

By international communication they understood: (1) communications which cross-national boundaries, such as radio broadcasts from any country to another country; (2) communications among persons and agencies of different nationality, for example at international conferences; and (3) communications on international agencies that include governmental communications; the international contacts of labour unions, political parties, churches, voluntary organisations, and so on.[6] Their priority was to study elite communication, defined as 'messages to or among persons who wield considerable influence in society', including political, economic and cultural elites (p.360). In their view, there is, therefore, every reason why a communication program, in selecting its research projects, should keep in mind such issues of major political significance as the conflict between the Kremlin and the free world, the integration and disintegration of Europe, and the rise of new nationalisms in countries that have in the past been colonial areas of European powers. (p.365)

They saw international communication, as a new potentially emerging field of study, as very close to the study of international relations, emphasising that there was no need to separate the two. Mowlana (2004 p.8) retrospectively underlines the importance of the group's work:

By focusing on the study of elite communication relationships, and the impact of mass media and the structure of communication systems in various countries, this research orientation had various policy impacts. Even the language of the report reflected American political situations in the world at the time, showing a world divided between East and West, an eagerness bordering on obsession with knowing how Third World elites are recruited and how they think, and an interest in knowing about European elites after World War II during the Marshall Plan period. The language also emphasised policy implications despite a stated academic purpose.

The grant was used to fund the Institute of International Communications, and Speier was hired by the Ford Foundation to determine what social science projects the foundation should fund at that time (Bessner 2018, p.196). After consulting colleagues such as Kecskemeti, Leites, Lerner and Margaret Mead (1901–1978), the institute was merged with MIT's Center for International Studies (CIS), with de Sola Pool as its first director (Bessner 2018, pp.198–200). Lerner was appointed the Ford Professor of International Communication at MIT in 1957 ('Daniel Lerner appointed' 1957). According to Bessner (2018, p.201), between 1956 and 1961, members of the communications programme consulted or worked for the Department of Defence, the Departments of State, Army, Navy and Air Force, the US Information Agency and other governmental organisations. Bessner (2018, p.196) notes that 'international communications became an often-used euphemism for psychological warfare during the early Cold War'.

The Committee on Comparative Politics

The most successful long-term comparative project to receive funding was not in international communication but in political science. The Committee on Comparative Politics (1954–1970) was first chaired by Gabriel Almond and then by Lucian W. Pye[7] (1921–2008, pictured Figure 5.3), both of whom

Figure 5.3: Lucian Wilmot Pye leading a senior seminar at MIT

Source: The MIT History Collection, Massachusetts Institute of Technology, Cambridge, MA; reproduced courtesy MIT Museum.
https://mitmuseum.mit.edu/collections/object/GCP-00020845
Notes: Pye is second from right; four unidentified students flank Pye on either side.

worked for and were funded by the Social Science Research Council (SSRC).[8] Almond had received his PhD from the University of Chicago and worked at the Office of War Information, where he analysed foreign propaganda. The Committee on Comparative Politics, which produced 296 written reports, helped to establish comparative research as a legitimate field of study in political science and was also to influence academics in the new field of political communication, a subfield of media and communication studies. As documents in the Rockefeller archive reveal, the purpose of this ambitious project was 'to bring to the center of comparative politics the study of the *non-Western* world and the problems of political development of the new states that emerged with the *end of colonialism*' (my emphasis). A total of 245 people (almost exclusively men), representing six disciplines and working in 21 countries, participated.[9]

The project, which started with the concept of a political system, famously included the concept of political culture, because – as Almond put it – every political system is 'embedded in a particular pattern of orientations to *political action*. I have found it useful to refer to this as the "political culture"' (my emphasis) (Almond 1956, p.396). The project led to one of the most pioneering books in comparative politics, *The Civic Culture: Political Attitudes and Democracy in Five Nations* (Almond and Verba 1963) to systematically study political cultures using cross-national surveys. According to the authors, '*civic culture is based on communication and persuasion*', emphasising the role of communication in culture (Almond and Verba 1963, p.8). Although most of the research was in comparative politics, there was some in interest in comparative communications. Schramm received a grant from the Committee on Comparative Politics to study 'the nature and dynamics of national communications systems and especially those of developing countries'.[10] The Stanford International Communication Grant ($100,000) was part of a larger grant to Stanford for international studies for a period of six years including student scholarships for 40 students from India, Pakistan, Indonesia, Taiwan, Japan, Thailand, France, the UK, Germany, the Netherlands, Poland and Yugoslavia. The publications included Schramm's *One Day in the World's Press* (1959b), a study of the events of 2 November 1956, in Suez and Hungary as reported in the prestige papers of 14 countries, and *Mass Media and National Development* (1964). The committee also commissioned Lucian Pye's (1963) *Communications and Political Development*, which included chapters from Schramm, Shils, de Sola Pool and Lerner under 'Studies in Political Development'. Many of these studies including the flow of news studies conducted collaboratively with the University of Paris were only published in the early 1960s.[11] Communication was not the main object of study for the committee, although the initial programme submitted to the SSRC already included a programme of improved communication to:

> encourage higher standards among scholars studying these problems in different parts of the world … The Committee hopes to improve communication among those specializing in the major areas of Europe, Asia, the Middle East, Latin America and Africa.[12]

From the beginning, the Committee on Comparative Politics was all-male, and the very few first female contributors appeared much later.[13] It would probably be fair to conclude that the Committee on Comparative Politics became much more influential in comparative politics than the RADIR and MIT projects became in comparative communications. Perhaps one of the main reasons was that they were embedded in political science rather than in the field of communication studies. In academia, there are Insiders and Outsiders, depending on how old, how large and how established disciplines are.

The significance of news flow studies

News flow studies played a significant role, not only in emphasising the role of news but also in making content analysis internationally popular. Mowlana (1985, p.11) defines flow studies as 'the study of the movement of messages across national boundaries between and among two or more national and cultural systems, which should combine both a national and an international dimension'. He argues that:

> international communication in general and information flows in particular, like other areas of inquiry in the social sciences, largely acquire their *legitimacy* and *consistency* from the perspectives and methods of analysis used by those who study the subject. (Mowlana 1985, p.12)

Mowlana thus suggests that these are achieved in terms of the theories and methods primarily used in the field, namely content analysis and flow studies. News flow studies on which US scholars collaborated with their European colleagues were funded by the International Press Institute (IPI) (International Press Institute 1953) and by UNESCO (Kayser 1953; Rantanen 2010; Smith and Smith 1956, p.11).

One example of these studies, *One Week's News* (Kayser 1953), was conducted in Europe using content analysis. The author was Jacques Kayser (1900–1963), assisted by Fernand Terrou (1905–1976), who had also been actively involved in drafting Article 19 during the UN Conference on Freedom of Information in 1948 ('In Remembrance of Jacques Kayser' 1963). The study covered 17 newspapers published in different countries in the week of 5–11 March 1951. The author acknowledged the difficulty of carrying out a comparative study of newspapers that varied in size, wealth and political orientation, but nevertheless argued that it was possible to draw some conclusions of value from a study of national customs, cultural development and political psychology (Kayser 1953, p.11).

Kayser's UNESCO study is strikingly similar to a study by the IPI and shares the same faith in the power of information and news. The IPI was not (and is not) a governmental organisation. It was founded in October 1950, when 34 editors from 15 countries met at Columbia University in New York City to form an international organisation dedicated to the promotion and protection of press freedom and the improvement of the practices of journalism. Its constitution states:

> World peace depends on understanding between peoples and peoples. If peoples are to understand one another, it is essential that they have good information. Therefore, a fundamental step towards understanding among peoples is to bring about understanding among the journalists of the world. (Lemberg 2019, p.617)

This quantitative study sought to discover how much foreign news the news agencies were supplying to newspapers, what areas of the world were covered in that news, what kind of news it was, and what use was made of it by newspapers. A total of 177 newspapers in 10 countries and 45 wire service reports were examined daily over periods of one week in October–December 1952 and in January 1953. Editors, news agency executives and foreign correspondents were asked for their views on how their countries were covered by the press in the countries where they were stationed. Finally, audiences were also interviewed (International Press Institute 1953, pp.8–9).

Content analysis was thus imported and rapidly adopted by researchers in countries beyond the US. These developments can be credited to Lasswell and the research groups carrying out propaganda research and came to be widely used in communication studies, not only in comparative communications. International communication studies continued to rely on concepts like those of news flows and domination, earlier mobilised by Cooper, which in the 1970s gave way to concepts of dependency and imperialism (Rantanen 2019).

5.3 Attempts to define international communication

There was great enthusiasm for establishing a new field of international communication. As Lowenthal wrote, 'the baptism of this new science as a specific discipline was a deliberate attempt to establish some means of systematically observing the infant's rapid growth' (Lowenthal 1952, p.vi). The Committee on International Communications Research was created at Lazarsfeld's request; the chairman of the Committee on Research Development of the American Association for Public Opinion Research (AAPOR) wrote to Lowenthal on 2 November 1951, asking him 'to form and chair a sub-committee on communications research in the international field'. The committee's contribution was made public in a special issue on international communication of *Public Opinion Quarterly*. Lazarsfeld (1952, p.483) was concerned by the:

> discrepancy between the amount of research activity going on in this new field and the relative inaccessibility of the methods and findings, particularly of pertinent studies done for the government. Other social scientists, also pioneering in this area, agreed that the concern expressed was fully warranted.

According to Lazarsfeld:

> First, it can be assumed that international communications research will have most of the talent, funds and interest which domestic communications research has commanded for the past twenty years. Consequently, since the domestic area will not have many opportunities in the years to come, the new ideas in communications research which made their appearance after the end of World War II will have to be picked up and developed in the international field if they are not to be neglected altogether. Secondly,

there are certain comparative possibilities in the sphere of international communications research which will open up new and
rather exciting subjects for investigation. So long as communications research struggled in one country only, to wit, the United
States, it was difficult for it to 'bracket out' the pervasive features of
American culture. Now, in the international field, where comparative studies between various countries will be made, these cultural
variables and their role can better be discerned. Finally, there are a
number of methodological problems, left relatively in the domestic field, which might be more expeditiously explored nationally.
(Lazarsfeld 1952, p.483)

According to Lowenthal, Lazarsfeld had felt that such a committee would
provide occasion and means for the accumulating findings of international
communications research to be 'collected, interrelated, and made available to
the research fraternity' (Lowenthal 1952, p.vi). Lowenthal undertook to form
and chair the committee, which, at the time of its first meeting, consisted of
the following members: Raymond Bauer (1916–1977), Robert Bower (1919–
1990), Leo Crespi (1916–2008), W. Phillips Davison (1918–2012), Helen Dinerman (1920–1974), Ben Gedalecia (1913–year of death unknown), Alexander George, Charles Y. Glock (1919–2018), Herta Herzog, Arno Georg Huth
(1905–1986), Alex Inkeles (1920–2010), Marie Jahoda, Morris Janowitz,
Patricia Kendall (1922–1990), Joseph T. Klapper (1917–1924), Marjorie Fiske
(1914–1992), Daniel Lerner, Leo Lowenthal, William A. Lydgate (1909–1998),
Paul Massing (1902–1979), James N. Mosél (1918–year of death unknown),
John W. Riley Jr. (1908–2002), Richard C. Sheldon, Frederick Williams
and John F. Zuckerman (Lowenthal 1952, p.vii; 'Proceedings of the Committee on International Communications Research', 1952, p.705). The composition of this group was somewhat different from the wartime studies group.
Although there were some members, such as Lerner, Davison and George,
who worked with Lasswell, many members of the group were sociologists. It
is also surprising how many women there were (Dinerman, Herzog, Jahoda,
Kendall and Fiske) and how many émigré scholars (Herzog, Jahoda and Massing). On the basis of my own archival research, it is difficult to know whether
this was a conscious attempt to counterbalance political scientists, or what
happened to the group after they produced the special issue of *Public Opinion
Quarterly* in 1952/1953.

Following a public discussion that lasted five hours ('Proceedings of the
Committee on International Communications Research' 1952, p.706), this
group was:

convinced that international communications research will eventually
stand on its own feet as a self-respecting discipline, and that in the long
run it may even serve as an integrating force among many branches of
the social sciences and humanities. (Lowenthal 1952, p.vii)

However, the group also identified problems derived from 'attempts to conceptualise or define both the field of international communications research and the role of the researcher'. These included:

(1) the difficulty of so conceiving the field of international communications research as to include such pertinent areas as attitude psychology, cultural and demographic characteristics of target audiences, etc., without at the same time equating the field with all human thought and behaviour.

(2) the role of the researcher vis-à-vis policy and production, i.e. whether the researcher either could or should restrict himself to the description of findings, or whether it is also part of his responsibility to translate findings into recommendations for policy or production personnel.

(3) the possibility that researchers were emphasising mass media of communication to such a degree as to exclude proper consideration of such other types of communication as literature, graphic art, face-to-face discourse, and the like.

The approach of Lowenthal's group was thus clearly different from that of the political scientists in Lasswell's wartime project. Davison and George, for example (1952, pp.501–02), defined international political communication as 'the use by national states of communications to influence the politically relevant behaviour of people in other national states'. In other words, comparative communications, according to their approach, was about comparing countries, states or people in different countries to one another, with the nation state taken for granted as the starting point of analysis, which explains why the label 'cross-national' has often been synonymous with comparative research. This, of course, was one of the influences of World War II studies, as shown in Chapters 2 and 4.

5.4 RAND Corporation and the work of émigré scholars after the war

Émigré scholars had played an important role in studying propaganda during World War II. They brought with them, as Lowenberg has testified:

> their knowledge, interdisciplinary training, passage through inter-disciplinary institutions such as LSE, the New School and the Institute for Social Research at Columbia, first-hand experience of Nazism, their understanding of totalitarianism and their commitment to resistance. (Loewenberg 2006, p.597)

These skills found their use in research teams during World War II, when there was a shared goal of defeating Nazism. Funding had opened up US comparative research by including non-US researchers in work on non-US topics. This also meant that research became highly normative, since everything about the US was seen as positive, while the enemy was seen purely in negative terms. But what happened to these émigré scholars after the war?

Their lives did not become any simpler. As Neumann (1953, p.20) notes, émigré scholars had three choices (he himself preferred the third of these, as the most difficult but also the most rewarding solution): (1) the exiled scholar might (and sometimes did) abandon his previous intellectual position and accept without qualification the new orientation; (2) he might (and sometimes did) retain completely his old thought structure and either believe himself to have the mission of totally revamping the American pattern, or withdraw (with disdain and contempt) into an island of his own; and finally (3) he might attempt an integration of his new experience with old traditions. Many émigré scholars remained in the US, simply because there was nowhere to go back to. The researchers whose work is studied in Chapter 4 found new employment, primarily at RAND Corporation in Santa Monica, California. RAND Corporation was a think tank established by the US Army Airforce and the Douglas Aircraft Company in 1946, which that was transformed into a free-standing non-profit private research organisation with a loan in 1948 from the Ford Foundation (Hounshell 1997, pp.241–42). Much of the work carried out in the Social Science Division of RAND Corporation was concentrated on the politics of the Cold War (Bessner 2018) and shifted away from the study of comparative communications. Under the leadership of Speier, George, Kecskemeti, Leites, de Sola Pool, de Grazia and Lerner joined RAND Corporation for shorter or longer periods of employment and Lasswell joined as a consultant. They became, using Bessner's (2018, p.3) term, defence intellectuals, who:

> during the Cold War researched, analysed and advised decision makers on national security while moving between a newly created network of think thanks, government institutions, and academic centres that historians have termed the 'military-intellectual complex'.

Many RAND researchers were only given university positions, for example as visiting professorships, relatively late in their careers, in some cases after they had retired.

Leites and Kecskemeti both joined RAND Corporation. Leites had first, in 1947, joined the staff of UNESCO in Paris to help set up a research project entitled 'Tensions Dangerous to Peace'. He became an associate at RAND Corporation from 1947 until 1962, afterwards remaining as a consultant (see Figure 5.4, taken during this period). Finally, he returned to serve on the faculty of the Department of Political Science at the University of Chicago from 1962 until 1974, when he retired and lived the rest of his life in France, where he continued to publish on various topics including French politics (Leites

Figure 5.4: Nathan Leites, 1950

Source: Courtesy RAND Corporation, photographed by J. Richard Goldstein, 1950.

1959; Wirth Marvick 1979). At RAND Corporation, he continued to publish academic journal articles and books. Leites did not leave psychoanalysis behind but expanded his interests to encompass Hollywood films (Wolfenstein and Leites 1947), Politburo members (Leites 1951a; 1951b; Leites, Bernaut and Garthoff 1951) and the Moscow trials (Leites and Bernaut 1954).

Leites increasingly felt that the academic community failed to recognise his accomplishments despite the extraordinary scope of his published work, which was, as Speier wrote, successful by academic standards. According to Speier, Leites expressed the view to him many times that his work was neglected if not ostracised.[14] Leites' work was, in my view, like Kecskemeti's, exceptional and in many ways ahead of its time, but was not recognised as such by his academic contemporaries. The work of both Leites and Kecskemeti was interdisciplinary and deeply rooted in European scholarly traditions, bringing in expertise that very few people had at that time. One of their areas of expertise was in studies of communism, to which both of them contributed in their monographs and research reports for RAND Corporation. One of the most interesting uses of content analysis was a study by Leites, Bernaut and Garthoff (1951) on the images of Stalin used by different Politburo members. The researchers constructed two images, which they labelled as Stalin the Party Chief (the Bolshevik image) and Stalin the People's Leader (the popular image). They concluded, albeit cautiously, that the Politburo members who stressed the Bolshevik image could be assumed to be politically closer to Stalin than those who did not (p.338).

Kecskemeti (1950, pictured, Figure 5.5) argues in his article 'Totalitarian Communications as a Means of Control: A Note on the Sociology of

Figure 5.5: Paul Kecskemeti, c. 1951

Source: Courtesy RAND Corporation.

Propaganda' that audiences in totalitarian countries were able to read between the lines and discussed the differences between rumours and news. In this article, he thus defines audiences as active, something that communication scholars did only much later. In 1952, Kecskemeti published a significant monograph, *Meaning, Communication, and Value* (Kecskemeti 1952), in which he discussed the value of meaning and argued for the importance of interpretation. This is a highly original book that shows Kecskemeti's wide reading as a European intellectual from Thucydides (*c.* 460–400 bc) to Rudolf Carnap (1891–1970), with quotations in original languages. He writes that:

> the idea that communication—insofar as it is recognized as a legitimate means of influencing the decision-process—must be limited to 'factual' matters breaks down because factual communication is life-less and meaningless without communication in terms of values. (pp.87–88)

The book received some positive reviews (see, for example, Arrow 1955), but was not recognised in the emerging field of communication studies, where it did not fit well with the quantitative turn that marked the field in the US in the 1950s and the 1960s. In the late 1950s and early 1960s Kecskemeti's work focused more on totalitarian communication, the politics of surrender, and on Hungary after the 1956 uprising (see for example, Kecskemeti 1953a; 1956; 1958a; 1959b).

One of the interesting papers Kecskemeti wrote at RAND Corporation was 'Sociological Aspects of the Information Process', originally presented as a Ford seminar paper in New York (Kecskemeti 1953b). In this paper Kecskemeti combines sociology of knowledge (Merton 1949), Lasswell's 'who gets what when and how' (1936) with cybernetics (Wiener 1948). He suggests that in the sociology of knowledge there are always originators, sources and receptors. The originator is a person who holds a belief because the content of the belief corresponds directly to a normal integrated element of his experience, the receptor of a belief is a person who holds a belief because he trusts someone who communicates it to him, and the transmitter of the belief is called the source. Kecskemeti is here more interesting than Lasswell's (1948) later model of communication. According to Kecskemeti, the source does not need to be the originator; he may be the receptor who is passing on a belief received from another source (Kecskemeti 1953b, pp.10–11). In short, Kecskemeti's 'model' is much more complex than Lasswell's but more thought-provoking and may be even more relevant to our times.

During the years 1946–1962, RAND Corporation became the leading centre for the development of game theory (Hounshell 1997, p.253). Kecskemeti,[15] along with de Sola Pool and Walter Phillips Davison (1918–2012) ('Walter Phillips Davison '39' 2013), were among those who developed political games. Kecskemeti directed a game about Poland that came to be widely played by senior faculty at MIT, Harvard, Yale and Columbia (Bessner 2018 p.223; Emery 2021, p.28). Emery quotes Bessner (2018, p.205) when he writes about Mannheim's influence on Speier in developing political games:

> This immersive environment that engages the players on a more holistic level — a better representation of decision-making under stress and uncertainty — comes from Speier's mentor Karl Mannheim. Bessner places the origins of the idea for the game with Mannheim, Speier's professor at Heidelberg University in Weimar, Germany. Mannheim believed that the idea of an immersion activity 'imbued students with political empathy and the skills to act as effective political agents'. (Emery 2021, p.29)

Mannheim's influence came not only through Speier but also through Kecskemeti, who at the time was not only married to Elisabeth Láng, Julia Mannheim-Láng's sister, but also translating and editing Mannheim's work (Kecskemeti 1952/1997). Developing political games is yet another example of group work where it is difficult to separate each individual's work. Both Leites and Kecskemeti survived the McCarthy years. They became decisively anti-communist, to the extent that Leites was described as a fervent anti-Bolshevik (Hounshell 1997, p.263) and Kecskemeti as 'having venomous hatred of the remaining totalitarian power', as he so much hated the Soviet Union.[16] Their attitudes to the US government may have been very close to what Bessner wrote about Speier and his loyalty to the US government:

> For the entirety of his career, Speier retained a profound loyalty to the nation that had saved him and his family. Even when the U.S. officials violated the principles for which the nation supposedly stood, Speier never questioned America's fundamental goodness. Such devotion perhaps helps to explain why Speier remained silent in the face of McCarthyism, the U.S.-backed groups in Guatemala and Iran, and most dramatically the 'Vietnam war'. The U.S. protected Speier and his family, and for this he was eternally grateful (Bessner 2018, p.71) … Working with or for the U.S. state – which, after all, had saved them – was the proper means by which émigré social scientists could fulfil their duty to make proper use of their exile. (Bessner 2018, p.72)

Later, Speier and Kecskemeti felt that their generation's 'basic outlook took a terrible beating in the "sixties"'. According to Kecskemeti, the main reason was neither a generational conflict nor the war in Vietnam, but the fact that the 'world history entered a new stage', that 'the era of western world domination is over'.[17] However, he was pleasantly surprised by the reawakened interest of the 1960s generation in German philosophy. Kecskemeti's and Speier's letters to each other in the 1970s reveal melancholy, if not sadness, that they were not understood by the new radicals they once thought they themselves to be. Speier had sent Kecskemeti his review (Speier 1976) of Jay's (1973/1996) book, and Kecskemeti shared Speier's view that Jay neglected 'the diversity of views and approaches existing with the institute, and the changes that the theoretical position of various members has undergone over time' and disapproved of Jay's 'polemical stance'.[18] They both felt that their generational story had been neither acknowledged nor fully written.

5.5 What were the main features of new international communication studies in the 1950s?

How, then, does one define the new international communication studies that was to replace comparative communications? What kind of criteria do we use when trying to name something that had not existed before but that clearly carried on many of the features of earlier research? Some academics even argue that all research is naturally comparative and that there is thus no reason to separate comparative research from other research (Beniger 1992, p.35). If this is the case, there is no need to separate international communication studies from any other kind of communication research. However, proponents of its separateness belong to at least three schools of thought, arguing that comparative research is defined mainly (1) through the methods it uses; (2) through its objects of study; or (3) through its theoretical contribution.

Lijphart (1971, p.682) famously argues that the term comparative politics indicates *the how* but does not specify *the what* of the analysis. In the first case, comparative research is about *how* materials/data are collected, the methods used to analyse them. We can see the contribution of Lasswell's work and of the wartime comparative communications to this in the form of content analysis. The popularity of content analysis, especially through news flow studies, spread even outside the US and became the one method that has not lost its popularity even to this day. The second case, where comparative research is defined through its objects and its cross-sited nature, also continues comparative communications into international communication studies. All of these had cross- or multi-sited objects, bringing in new objects of study, namely the media in other countries. In this case, comparative research is defined through *the what*, as having two or more objects of research on different sites, that is, concerning different data sets, and through the comparison between these. Eisenstadt (1968, p.423) argued that the definition of comparative social sciences can also include 'a special focus on cross-societal, institutional, or macro-societal aspects of societies and social analysis', emphasising the multi-character and multi-object nature of comparative research. If understood in this way, international communication studies must include two or more objects on different geographical sites. In most cases, this meant countries and their media systems, as shown in Chapter 6.

There was nothing distinctive about the theories or methods in international communication studies. It was its multi-object character (these objects mainly being foreign newspapers) that set it apart from domestic communication studies. Lazarsfeld (1952) turned out to be wrong in his prediction that international communication studies would attract significant funding and resources. Much of what we now understand as international communication research continued for decades largely to be funded by UNESCO (see, for example, Schramm 1959b) and concentrated on news (Rantanen 2010).

The inability to create new theoretical approaches different from those of non-comparative research soon became apparent. For example, according to Stevenson (1992, p.550), international communication:

> lacks a common method as well as a body of knowledge, and seems more prone than most of its companion fields towards disagreement over what is good—or even minimally competent research.

This critique is not unheard of in other fields of study: academics in comparative politics and international relations often testify that their fields lack theory-building. As Halliday (1985, p.408) points out, in terms of theory international relations has always been 'an absorber and importer, not a producer in its own right'. Berelson (1959, p.5) writes of international communication as early as in the 1950s that 'most such work, however, seems to have been in the nature of geographical rather than conceptual or intellectual extensions'. In his critical review of the state of communication research in 1959, Lasswell's and Blumenstock's *World Revolutionary Propaganda* (1939) and *The Language of Politics* (1949, p.2) were the only examples of comparative communications recognised, along with other studies by Lazarsfeld, Lewin and Hovland, all tackling domestic issues.

5.6 Conclusion

The move from utopia to ideology was fast, and academics and men of practice sailed with the new wind, becoming almost overnight Cold War warriors who not only accepted US ideology but also contributed to it. Utopias crashed and everybody suffered. But is this the only 'truth'? Is it so simple? It would be easy to conclude that the post-World War II period is the ultimate example of how ideology works. Many authors have shown how difficult the 'Great Fear' was for many. At the same time, underneath this, there were several factors that promoted new avenues of comparative communications. First, of course, there was research funding available and helped academics to follow their research interests as long as their projects fitted within the general framework of the Cold War ideology. With this funding, for the first time, large-scale research projects in comparative politics and in comparative communications became achievable. The interest in enemy propaganda that started during World War II was now widened to other countries where the US government showed interest. This research could not be done by the military, which was why social scientists had the opportunity of their lifetimes to do research that had not been possible before. There were also opportunities for non-academics such those hired by RAND Corporation, which seems to have provided almost ideal circumstances for interdisciplinary researchers who passed security checks and were ready to align with the military. There were even new opportunities for women, although male domination continued to be strong.

Breiner (2004, p.138) asks an important question:

> how did other emigres influenced by the Weber-Mannheim approach to political science avoid having their own political project stall with the disappearance of the context that served as the ground for its meaning?

Kecskemeti was translating Mannheim and developing war games with Speier while working at RAND Corporation. However, several authors have raised the question of how useful social scientists actually were to the military. As Isaac (2007, p.731) writes,

Some historians of science have taken a more cautious line. In pains-taking case studies, they have shown how the military's attempts to instrumentalize scientific research often failed or, at the very least, left scientists enough room to shape research agendas according to their own interests. Despite their divergence on the issue of how state-science relations should be conceived, however, all of these studies explore the acute tension between the national security establishment's demand for secrecy and applied technologies, and the scientific community's need for open debate and basic research.

After World War II, the forefront generation that had been united in fighting for the same cause became divided. It was divided by many things, including new disciplinary boundaries. When communication studies was founded as a discipline, many researchers left the study of communication to move on to other topics. As Schramm (1959, p.8) famously said of communication research,

> in the study of man, it is one of the crossroads where many pass but few tarry. Scholars come into it from their own disciplines, bringing valuable tools and insights, and later go back, like Lasswell, to the more central concerns of their disciplines.

In Berelson's view, of the four 'founding fathers' of communication studies, Hovland, Lasswell, Lazarsfeld and Lewin,

> Lazarsfeld was the only one of the four who centered on communi-cations problems *per se*; Lasswell was interested in political power, Lewin in group functioning, and Hovland in cognitive processes, and they all utilized this field as a convenient entry to those broader concerns. (Berelson 1959, p.5)

In short, what Schramm and Berelson were more or less directly saying was that the so-called 'founding fathers' had used resources available for study-ing communication, but then moved back to the core questions of their own respective fields. The new field of communication studies had its own new makers. As Simonson (2016, p.65) has observed, communication research was still a marginal field and still arguing for its own legitimacy. At the same time, the forefront generation was also divided by the professionalisation of communication research, which meant that academics such as Peterson, Schramm and Siebert, as shown in Chapter 6, chose to publish with each other, that is, with fellow academics, rather than with consultants or men of experience. However, many academics including Schramm became consult-ants working closely with UNESCO or with military or intelligence organi-sations such as the US Army and Navy or the CIA. They divided their time between their academic and policy science work, publishing the latter as frequently as the former. This tradition, which started during World War II, has continued until today. Many comparative communications researchers have wanted to carry out policy science and to influence the world and seen no difference between their personal goals and the goals of the organisations they worked for.

They were also divided by their nationalities. Often university positions went to candidates born in the US, while many émigré scholars started working for RAND Corporation or on short-term research contracts. Originally educated in various different fields, they had collaborated on US wartime projects. They belonged to an intergenerational and transnational cohort that had brought together men who, without the war, would in all likelihood have remained in their home countries. However, the influence of émigré scholars became less important in communication studies, where they remained more Outsiders than in political science. When the new field of communication studies was institutionalised, the émigré scholars studied in Chapter 4 were not among those who were part of that institutionalisation. It was no longer a transnational generation but became a national and international generation where the national had an upper hand.

There were characteristic features of communication studies at its foundation that contributed to its isolation from political science and from the European influences that were notable on the latter. Perhaps the most influential of these was the 'old boys' network', consisting mostly of male US scholars, mainly from the University of Chicago, who had worked together during World War II to study propaganda and who now continued to work together, but not in the field of communication studies. The institutionalisation of communication research as a whole contributed to the deinstitutionalisation of comparative communications, which largely continued to be conducted in projects financed by governments or foundations in different fields.

Many émigré scholars and some women, although able to find jobs in political science, were less able to do so in the field of communication studies. They had been useful in collecting and interpreting data, but university chairs were now given to American (male) citizens born in the US. Those who had worked on the propaganda projects suffered from a lack of recognition and their work still awaits rediscovery. They remained in the US, having given up their first languages and cultures and unable to go back, but moved often now outside academia. They received professorships relatively late, if at all. The new field of communication studies, and within it international communication, was from the start becoming nationalised. Those who were Insiders during the war in propaganda studies became Outsiders in the new field of communication studies. They were respected, but nevertheless remained Outsiders and did not achieve the positions of kingmakers – those Insiders, *éminences grises*, who operated behind the scenes and decided who were worthy of professorships and scholarships, though Lasswell did acquire such a role and continued to support his wartime brothers in arms when they applied for jobs and scholarships.

Émigré scholars, especially during the Cold War, had to show their uncon-
ditional loyalty to their new home country. I would not argue that they were
always forced to do so, and in most cases I would think they were glad to do
so when their former home countries were taken over by communist regimes
and they often felt there was no way of going back to an impoverished Europe
where their family members and friends had died in concentration camps. It
was also a testing time, with ideologies rapidly changing. The post-World War
II atmosphere, with its utopian belief in the possibility of world peace if nations
would only understand each other, and belief that research conducted by working closely together across borders would best help in this endeavour, was soon
transformed into Cold War ideology. In the Cold War atmosphere, foreign
countries, foreign researchers and collaboration with them were seen as suspicious and even dangerous. As a result, the atmosphere also became more normative, since the difference between good (the US) and evil (the enemy) remained
unquestionable. It is also important to remember that it was not only academics
who conducted such research. Kent Cooper's deeply ideological contribution to
promoting the role of news (agencies) in international politics influenced this as
much as did content analysis. It is somewhat ironic that in the following decades
it was Cooper's own agency, the AP, that was seen to practise dominance of the
world's news flows, together with Reuters, its former arch-enemy.

The interdisciplinary character of propaganda research had been essential to the research teams working during World War II. The comparative
communications of the 1930s and 1940s mainly responded to the needs of
the non-academic institutions who also funded it. Now it was time to find
new homes for that wartime research. The World War II projects that had
brought together academics and practitioners with different backgrounds
were now completed and funding had to be sought from different sources,
both public and private. As Schramm himself (1949, p.vii) notes, 'by bringing
together anthropologists, psychologists, political scientists, economists and
media men, this approach has attempted to combine diversity of approach
with unity of target' (Delia 1987, p.72). The interdisciplinarity of earlier
research teams was now changing. The US was to become the 'home of comparative politics' (Blyth 2006, p.494; Griffiths and O'Callaghan 2001, p.188)
and a 'birthplace of communication studies' (Katz 1977, p.22; Tunstall 1977,
pp.203–08) but not of comparative communications. However, political science was a much older discipline. When the first PhD programme in communication was founded in 1947, in Urbana-Champaign, political science
had already marked its sixtieth anniversary as a discipline. Munck (2006, p.8)
argues that political science was initially conceived of as practically synonymous with the study of comparative politics. This had a long-lasting effect on
research and on publications. Hence, in the early stage of the development of
political science, comparative research was not seen as a separate field but as
something accepted as a naturalised element in any research. This may have
happened with comparative communications: with the move to international
communication studies, the word comparative was lost and it became part
of communication studies.

Notes

¹ The UP would become United Press International (UPI) in 1958 after amalgamation with International News Service (INS).

² De Sola Pool joined the Young Peoples Socialist League in 1934 and later the Socialist Party prior to its breach with the Trotskyites, and thereafter was a member of the Socialist Workers Party, from which he withdrew in about 1940. He was a member of the American Student Union between 1935 and 1937. He reportedly joined these organisations because of his pacifist and idealist views. He went through FBI security investigations in 1946, 1951 with his parents,1962, 1963, 1965, and 1969. Ithiel de Sola Pool FBI files.

³ Affadavit concerning Sebastian de Grazia, 1954. Harold Dwight Lasswell Papers, General Files 1043, Series I, Box 30, Folder 392. Manuscripts and Archives, Yale University Library.

⁴ Report of interview and special hearing on 25 February 1944 in New York by Investigator Jack Zimmerman. Kecskemeti had been working as a script editor for OWI in New York since 1942. When he arrived in Baltimore from Casablanca he had been interviewed by a panel consisting of Immigration, FBI and Naval Intelligence officers. Paul Kecskemeti Papers. The Robert D. Farber University Archives & Special Collections Department at Brandeis University.

⁵ MacKenzie Pool, J. (1988) 'Nathan and Ithiel', in RAND (ed.) *Remembering Nathan Leites, An Appreciation: Recollections of Some Friends, Colleagues, and Students*, pp.45–46, RAND Corporation Archives.

⁶ Report of the Advisory Committee. The Research Center on International Communications, no date. Harold Dwight Lasswell papers, General Files 1043, Series I, Box 89, File 1096. Manuscripts and Archives, Yale University Library.

⁷ Lucian W. Pye (1921–2008) was born to Gertrude Chaney Pye (1885–1966), a graduate of Oberlin College, who travelled independently to China where she met and married Watts O. Pye (1878–1926). They were both missionaries of the American Board of Commissioners for Foreign Missions in Fenzhu, Shanxi, China. He primarily lived there before attending high school in the US. Pye returned to China at the end of World War II to serve as an intelligence officer in the 5th Marine Corps. He attended graduate school at Yale University, where he met Lasswell and Almond and received his PhD in 1951. Pye married Mary Toombs Waddill (1924–2013), who played a key role as his editor, typist and sounding board for all his works. In 1956, Pye joined MIT, where he taught for 35 years and became one of the leading China experts in the US. His most well-known book in communication studies is *Communications and Political Development* (Pye 1963). ('MIT Professor Lucian

W. Pye, Leading China Scholar, Dies at 86' 2008; Vogel 2008; Pye Family China Album (no date)).

8   The Social Science Research Council (SSRC) is a private, not-for-profit organisation established in 1923 to advance research in the social sciences in the US (Social Science Research Council records (no date)).

9   Pye, L.W. and Ryland, K.K. *Activities of the Committee on Comparative Politics*, 1954–1970. The Social Science Research Council (SSRC) Collection, Research Group 1–2, Series 1, FA021, Box 736, Folder 8882. Rockefeller Archive Center.

10 Final Narrative Report by Wilbur Schramm, 1958–1964. Stanford International Communications Grant. Received 29 May 1964. SSRC Collection, Record Group 1–2, Series 1, FA021, Box 739. Rockefeller Archive Center.

11 Final Narrative Report by Wilbur Schramm, 1958–1964. Stanford International Communications Grant. Received 29 May 1964. SSRC Collection, Record Group 1–2, Series 1, FA021, Box 739. Rockefeller Archive Center.

12 A Programme of Research on Comparative Politics submitted by the Comparative Politics Social Science Research Council, no date. SSRC, Record Group 1–2, Series 1, FA021, Box 736, Folder 8882. Rockefeller Archive Center.

13 Members, Committee on Comparative Politics, 1954–1970. SSRC Collection, Record Group 1–2, Series 1, FA021, Box 736, Folder 8882. Rockefeller Archive Center.

14 Speier, H. (1988) 'Nathan Leites: An Uncompromising Intellect', in RAND (ed.) *Remembering Nathan Leites, An Appreciation: Recollections of Some Friends, Colleagues, and Students*, pp.63–66, RAND Corporation Archives.

15 Kecskemeti, P. (1955) *War Games and Political Games*, RAND Corporation Archives.

16 Susan to Marty on 15 August 1981. Paul Kecskemeti Papers. The Robert D. Farber University Archives & Special Collections Department at Brandeis University.

17 P. Kecskemeti to H. Speier on 21 January 1975. Hans Speier Papers, Box 3. German and Jewish Intellectual émigré Collection. M.E. Grenander Department of Special Collections and Archives, University Libraries, University at Albany, State University of New York.

18 P. Kecskemeti to H. Speier on 20 March 1977. Hans Speier Papers, Box 3. German and Jewish Intellectual émigré Collection. M.E. Grenander Department of Special Collections and Archives, University Libraries, University at Albany, State University of New York.

References

Almond, Gabriel A. (1956) 'Comparative Political Systems', *The Journal of Politics*, vol. 18, no. 3, pp.391–409. https://doi.org/10.2307/2127255

Almond, Gabriel A. and Coleman, James S. (1960) *The Politics of The Developing Areas*, USA: Princeton University Press.

Almond, Gabriel A. and Verba, Sidney (1963) *The Civic Culture: Political Attitudes and Democracy in Five Nations*, USA: Princeton University Press.

Angell, Robert C. (1950/1953) 'International Communication and World Society', in Berelson, Bernard and Janowitz, Morris (eds) *Reader in Public Opinion and Communication*, USA: Free Press of Glencoe, pp.369–80.

Arrow, Kenneth J. (1955) 'Review of *Meaning, Communication, and Value*, by P. Kecskemeti', *Econometrica*, vol. 23, no. 1, pp.103–04. https://doi.org/10.2307/1905585

Bateson, Gregory (1966) *From Versailles to Cybernetics*. https://archive.org/details/css_000051

Beniger, James R. (1992) 'Comparison, Yes, but—The Case of Technological and Cultural Change', in Blumler, Jay G.; McLeod, Jack M.; and Rosengren, Karl E. (eds) *Comparatively Speaking: Communication and Culture Across Space and Time*, USA: Sage, pp.35–52.

Berelson, Bernard (1959) 'The State of Communication Research', *Public Opinion Quarterly*, vol. 23, no. 1, pp.1–17. https://doi.org/10.1086/266840

Bessner, Daniel (2018) *Democracy in Exile: Hans Speier and the Rise of the Defense Intellectual*, USA: Cornell University Press.

Bleyer, Wollard G. (1926) 'The Press and Public Opinion in International Relations', *Journalism Quarterly*, vol. 3, no. 2, pp.7–20. https://doi.org/10.1177/107769902600300203

Blyth, Mark (2006) 'Great Punctuations: Prediction, Randomness, and the Evolution of Comparative Political Science', *The American Political Science Review*, vol. 100, no. 4, pp.493–98. https://doi.org/10.1017/S0003055406062344

Breiner, Peter (2004) 'Translating Max Weber: Exile Attempts to Forge a New Political Science', *European Journal of Political Theory*, vol. 3, no. 2, pp.133–49. https://doi.org/10.1177/1474885104041043

Brown, Chris (2001) 'Fog in the Channel: Continental International Relations Theory Isolated (or an Essay on the Paradoxes of Diversity and Parochialism in IR Theory)', in Crawford, Robert and Jarvis, Darryl S. (eds) *International Relations: Still an American Social Science?* USA: State University of New York Press, pp.203–20.

Caute, David (1978) *The Great Fear: The Anti-Communist Purge under Truman and Eisenhower*, USA: Simon & Schuster.

Cmiel, Kenneth (1996) 'On Cynicism, Evil, and the Discovery of Communication in the 1940s', *Journal of Communication*, vol. 46, no. 3, pp.88–107. https://doi.org/10.1111/j.1460-2466.1996.tb01491.x

Creel, George (1920) *How We Advertised America: The First Telling of the Amazing Story of the Committee on Public Information that Carried the Gospel of Americanism to Every Corner of the Globe*, USA: Harper & Brothers.

'Daniel Lerner Appointed Professor of International Communication December 10' (1957) MIT Press release. https://cdn.libraries.mit.edu /dissemination/diponline/AC0069_NewReleases/NewsRelease_1950 /AC0069_1957/AC0069_195712_007.pdf

Davison, W. Phillips and George, Alexander L. (1952) 'An Outline for the Study of International Political Communications', *Public Opinion Quarterly*, vol. 16, no. 4, pp.501–11. https://doi.org/10.1086/266413

de Sola Pool, Ithiel (1952) *The 'Prestige Papers': A Survey of Their Editorials*, USA: Stanford University Press.

de Sola Pool, Ithiel (1954) *Research in International Communication*, USA: Massachusetts Institute of Technology. Center for International Studies.

de Sola Pool, Ithiel (1955) *Progress of the International Communications Program*, USA: Massachusetts Institute of Technology. Center for International Studies.

de Sola Pool, Ithiel (1969) 'Content Analysis and the Intelligence Function', in Rogow, Arnold A. (ed.) *Politics, Personality, and Social Science in the Twentieth Century: Essays in Honor of Harold D. Lasswell*, USA: University of Chicago Press, pp.197–224.

Delia, Jesse (1987) 'Communication Research: A History', in Berger, Charles R. and Chaffee, Steven H. (eds) *Handbook of Communication Science*, USA: Sage, pp.20–98.

'Draft Convention of the Gathering and International Transmission of News' (1948) United Nations Conference on Freedom of Information. https://igitallibrary.un.org/record/212470

Eisenstadt, Shmuel N. (1968) 'Social Institutions: Comparative Study', in Sills, David L. (ed.) *International Encyclopedia of the Social Sciences, Vol. 14*, USA: Macmillan & Free Press, pp.421–28.

Emery, John R. (2021) 'Moral Choices without Moral Language: 1950s Political-Military Wargaming at the RAND Corporation', *Texas National Security Review*, vol. 4, no. 4, pp.12–31. http://dx.doi.org/10.26153/tsw/17528

Eulau, Heinz (1977) 'The Hoover Elite Studies Revisited', *Social Science History*, vol. 1, no. 3, pp.392–400. https://doi.org/10.1017/S0145553200022136

Farr, James; Hacker, Jacob S.; and Kazee, Nicole (2006) 'The Policy Scientist of Democracy: The Discipline of Harold D. Lasswell', *American Political Science Review*, vol. 100, no. 4, pp.579–87. https://doi.org/10.1017/S0003055406062459

Frederick, Howard H. (1981) *The Life and Work of Ithiel De Sola Pool: An Assessment and Bibliography*, USA: The American University.

Gary, Brett J. (1999) *The Nervous Liberals: Propaganda Anxieties from World War I to the Cold War*, USA: Columbia University Press.

'George Stoddard Dies at the Age of 84 in 1981. Educator Led 4 Universities' (1981) *The New York Times*, 29 December. https://www.nytimes.com/1981/12/29/obituaries/george-stoddard-dies-at-84-educator-led-4-universities.html

Gilman, Nils (2003) *Mandarins of the Future: Modernization Theory in Cold War America*, USA: Johns Hopkins University Press.

Glander, Timothy (2000) *Origins of Mass Communications Research During the American Cold War: Educational Effects and Contemporary Implications*, USA: Routledge.

Griffiths, Martin and O'Callaghan, Terry (2001) 'The End of International Relations?' in Griffiths, Martin and O'Callaghan, Terry (eds) *International Relations—Still an American Social Science? Toward Diversity in International Thought*, USA: State University of New York Press, pp.187–202.

Guback, Thomas H. (1969) *The International Film Industry: Western Europe and America Since 1945*, USA: Indiana University Press.

'Guide to the Ithiel de Sola Pool Papers 1935–1948' (2011) *Biographical Note*. University of Chicago Library. https://www.lib.uchicago.edu/e/scrc/findingaids/view.php?eadid=ICU.SPCL.POOLI

Halliday, Fred (1985) 'Book Reviews: A "Crisis" of International Relations?' *International Relations*, vol. 8, no. 4, pp.407–12. https://doi.org/10.1177/004711788500800

Hounshell, David (1997) 'The Cold War, RAND, and the Generation of Knowledge, 1946–1962', *Historical Studies in the Physical and Biological Sciences*, vol. 27, no. 2, pp.237–67. https://doi.org/10.2307/27757779

'In Remembrance of Jacques Kayser' (1963) *Gazette*, vol. 9, no. 4, pp.1–3. https://doi.org/10.1177/001654926300900407

International Press Institute (1953) *The Flow of News: A Study by the International Press Institute*, Switzerland: International Press Institute.

Isaac, Joel (2007) 'The Human Sciences in Cold War America', *The Historical Journal*, vol. 50, no. 3, pp.725–46.
https://doi.org/10.1017/S0018246X07006334

Jay, Martin (1973/1996) *The Dialectical Imagination: A History of the Frankfurt School and the Institute of Social Research, 1923–1950*, USA: University of California Press.

Katz, Elihu (1977) *Social Research on Broadcasting, Proposals for Further Development: A Report to the British Broadcasting Corporation*, UK: British Broadcasting Corporation.

Kayser, Jacques (1953) *One Week's News: Comparative Study of 17 Major Dailies for a Seven-Day Period*, France: UNESCO.
https://unesdoc.unesco.org/ark:/48223/pf0000062870

Kecskemeti, Paul (1950) 'Totalitarian Communications as a Means of Control', *Public Opinion Quarterly*, vol. 14, no. 2, pp.224–34.
https://doi.org/10.1086/266181.

Kecskemeti, Paul (1952/1997) 'Introduction', in Kecskemeti, Paul (ed.) *Mannheim, Karl, Essays on the Sociology of Knowledge*, UK: Routledge and Kegan Paul, pp.1–32.

Kecskemeti, Paul (1953a) *Totalitarianism and the Future*, USA: RAND Corporation.

Kecskemeti, Paul (1953b) *Sociological Aspects of the Information Process*, USA: RAND Corporation.

Kecskemeti, Paul (1956) 'The Soviet Approach to International Political Communication', *Public Opinion Quarterly*, vol. 20, no. 1, pp.299–308.
https://doi.org/10.1086/266618

Kecskemeti, Paul (1958a) 'Limits and Problems of Decompression: The Case of Hungary', *The Annals of the American Academy of Political and Social Science*, vol. 317, pp.97–106. https://www.jstor.org/stable/1031082

Kecskemeti, Paul (1958b) *Strategic Surrender: The Politics of Victory and Defeat*, USA: Stanford University Press.

Kirchick, James (2022) *Secret City: The Hidden History of Gay Washington*, USA: Henry Holt and Company.

Klapper, Joseph T. (1960) *The effects of mass communication*, USA: Free Press of Glencoe.

Kris, Ernst and Leites, Nathan C. (1947) 'Trends in the 20th Century Propaganda', in Roheim, Geza (ed.) *Psychoanalysis and Social Sciences, Vol. I*, UK: Imago, pp.393–409.

Lasswell, Harold D. (1927) *Propaganda Technique in the World War*, USA: A.A. Knopf.

Lasswell, Harold D. (1941) 'The World Attention Survey: An Exploration of the Possibilities of Studying Attention Being Given to the United States by Newspapers Abroad', *Public Opinion Quarterly*, vol. 5, no. 3, pp.456–62. https://doi.org/10.1086/265515

Lasswell, Harold D. (1948) 'The Structure and Function of Communication in Society', in Bryson, Lyman (ed.) *The Communication of Ideas*, USA: Institute for Religious and Social Studies, pp.37–51.

Lasswell, Harold D. and Blumenstock, Dorothy (1939b) *World Revolutionary Propaganda: A Chicago Study*, USA: Alfred A. Knopf.

Lasswell, Harold D.; Leites, Nathan; and Associates (1949) *Language of Politics: Studies in Quantitative Semantics*, USA: George W. Stewart.

Lasswell, Harold D.; Lerner, Daniel; and de Sola Pool, Ithiel (1952a) *The Comparative Study of Symbols: An Introduction*, USA: Stanford University Press.

Lasswell, Harold D.; Lerner, Daniel; and de Sola Pool, Ithiel (1952b) 'Scope and Methods of the RADIR Project', in Lasswell, Harold D.; Lerner, Daniel; and De Sola Pool, Ithiel (eds) *Comparative Study of Symbols: An Introduction*, USA: Stanford University Press, pp.26–28.

Lazarsfeld, Paul F. (1952) 'The Prognosis for International Communications Research', *Public Opinion Quarterly*, vol. 16, no. 4, pp.481–90. https://doi.o1952-1953g/10.1086/266411

Lazarsfeld, Paul F. and Merton, Robert K. (1943) 'Studies in Radio and Film Propaganda', *Transactions of the New York Academy of Sciences*, vol. 6, no. 2, pp.58–74. https://doi.org/10.1111/j.2164-0947.1943.tb00897.x

Lazarsfeld, Paul F. and Merton, Robert K. (1948/1964) 'Mass Communication, Popular Taste and Organized Social Action', in Bryson, Lyman (ed.) *The Communication of Ideas*, USA: Institute for Religious and Social Studies, pp.95–118.

Lazarsfeld, Paul F. and Thielens, Wagner Jr (1958) *The Academic Mind: Social Scientists In a Time of Crisis*, USA: Free Press.

Leites, Nathan C. (1951a) *The Operational Code of the Politburo*, USA: McGraw Hill.

Leites, Nathan C. (1951b) *A Study of Bolshevism*, USA: Free Press.

Leites, Nathan C. (1959) *On the Game of Politics in France*, USA: Stanford University Press.

Leites, Nathan C. and Bernaut, Elsa (1954) *Ritual of Liquidation: The Case of the Moscow Trials*, USA: Free Press.

Leites, Nathan C.; Bernaut, Elsa; and Garthoff, Raymond L. (1951) 'Politburo Images of Stalin', *World Politics*, vol. 3, no. 3, pp.317–39. https://doi.org/10.2307/2009118

Lemberg, Diana (2019) *Barriers Down: How American Power and Free-flow Policies Shaped Global Media*, USA: Columbia University Press.

Lerner, Daniel (1949) *Sykewar: Psychological Warfare Against Germany, D-Day to VE-Day*, USA: G.W. Stewart.

Lerner, Daniel; de Sola Pool, Ithiel; and Lasswell, Harold D. (1951) 'Comparative Analysis of Political Ideologies: A Preliminary Statement', *Public Opinion Quarterly*, vol. 15, no. 4, pp.715–33. https://doi.org/10.1086/266356

Lijphart, Arendt (1971) 'Comparative Politics and the Comparative Method', *The American Political Science Review*, vol. 65, no. 3, pp.682–93. https://doi.org/10.2307/1955513

Loewenberg, Gerhard (2006) 'The Influence of European Emigré Scholars on Comparative Politics, 1925–1965', *The American Political Science Review*, vol. 100, no. 4, pp.597–604. https://doi.org/10.1017/S0003055406062472

Loewenstein, Karl (1944) 'Report on the Research Panel on Comparative Government', *The American Political Science Review*, vol. 38, no. 3, pp.540–48. https://doi.org/10.2307/1948903

Lowenthal, Leo (1952) 'Introduction', *The Public Opinion Quarterly*, vol. 16, no. 4, pp.v–x. https://doi.org/10.1093/poq/16.4.481-a

Merton, Robert K. (1949/1968) *Social Theory and Social Structure* (1968 enlarged ed.), USA: Free Press.

Merton, Robert K. and Lazarsfeld, Paul F. (1950) *Continuities in Social Research: Studies in the Scope and Method of 'The American Soldier'*, USA: Free Press.

'MIT Professor Lucian W. Pye, Leading China Scholar, Dies at 86' (2008) MIT News. https://news.mit.edu/2008/obit-pye-0908

Mock, James R. and Larson, Cedric (1939) *Words that Won the War: The Story of the Committee on Public Information, 1917–1919*, USA: Princeton University Press.

Morrison, David E. (2008) 'Opportunity Structures and the Creation of Knowledge: Paul Lazarsfeld and the Politics of Research', in Park, David W. and Pooley, Jefferson (eds) *The History of Media and Communication Research. Contested Memories*, USA: Peter Lang, pp.179–204.

Mowlana, Hamid (1985) *International Flow of Information: A Global Report and Analysis*, France: UNESCO.

Mowlana, Hamid (1986/1997) *Global Information and World Communication: New Frontiers in International Relations*, USA: Longman.

Mowlana, Hamid (2004) 'International Communication. The Journey of a Caravan', *The Journal of International Communication*, vol. 10, no. 2, pp.7–32. https://doi.org/10.1080/13216597.2004.9751972

Munck, Gerardo L. (2006) *The Past and Present of Comparative Politics*, USA: Helen Kellogg Institute for International Studies. https://kellogg.nd.edu/sites/default/files/old_files/documents/330_0.pdf

Neumann, Franz L. (1953) 'The Social Sciences', in Neumann, Franz L.; Peyre, Henri; Panofsky, Erwin; Köhler, Wolfgang; and Tillich, Paul (eds) *The Cultural Migration: The European Scholar in America*, USA: University of Pennsylvania Press, pp.4–26.

Oren, Ido (2003) *Our Enemies and US: America's Rivalries and the Making of Political Science*, USA: Cornell University Press.

Planning Committee of the Center for International Studies at the Massachusetts Institute of Technology (1954) 'A Plan of Research in International Communication: A Report', *World Politics*, vol. 6, no. 3, pp.358–77. https://doi.org/10.2307/2009069

Pooley, Jefferson (2011) 'From Psychological Warfare to Social Justice: Shifts in Foundation Support for Communication Research', in Jansen, Sue C.; Pooley, Jefferson; and Taub-Pervizpour, Lora (eds) *Media and Social Justice*, USA: Palgrave Macmillan, pp.211–40.

Preston William (1989) 'The History of U.S.-UNESCO Relations', in Preston, William; Herman, Edward S.; and Schiller, Herbert I. (eds) *Hope and Folly: The United States and UNESCO 1945–1985*, USA: Minnesota University Press, pp.3–188.

'Proceedings of the Committee on International Communications Research' (1952) *Public Opinion Quarterly*, vol. 16, no. 4, pp.705–08. https://doi.org/10.1086/266434

'Pye Family China Album' (no date). https://www.virginiapye.com/album

Pye, Lucian W. (1963) *Communications and Political Development*, USA: Princeton University Press.

Rajagopal, Arvind (2020) Communicationism: Cold War Humanism. *Critical Inquiry*, vol. 46, no. 2, pp.353–80. https://doi.org/10.1086/706683

Rantanen, Terhi (2010) 'Methodological Inter-nationalism in Comparative Media Research: Flow Studies in International Communication', in Roosvall, Anna and Salovaara-Moring, Inka (eds) *Communicating the Nation: National Topographies of Global Media Landscapes*, Sweden: Nordicom Publications, pp.25–40. https://www.nordicom.gu.se/sv/publications/communicating-nation

Rantanen, Terhi (2017) 'A "Crisscrossing" Historical Analysis of Four Theories of the Press', *International Journal of Communication*, vol. 11, pp.3454–75. https://ijoc.org/index.php/ijoc/article/view/6253

Rantanen, Terhi (2019) 'News Agencies from Telegraph Bureaus to Cyberfactories', in *Oxford Research Encyclopedias of Communication*, UK: Oxford University Press.

Read, William H. (1976) *America's Mass Media Merchants*, USA: Johns Hopkins University Press.

Rogers, Everett (1994) *A History of Communication Study: A Biographical Approach*, USA: Free Press.

Saunders, Frances (2000) *Who Paid the Piper? The CIA and the Cultural Cold War*, UK: Granta.

Schramm, Wilbur (1949) *Mass Communications: A Book of Readings Selected and Edited for the Institute of Communications Research in the University of Illinois*, USA: University of Illinois Press.

Schramm, Wilbur (1957) 'Twenty Years of Journalism Research', *Public Opinion Quarterly*, vol. 21, no. 1, pp.91–107. https://doi.org/10.1086/266689

Schramm, Wilbur (1959a) 'Comments on "The State of Communication Research"', *The Public Opinion Quarterly*, vol. 23, no. 1, pp.6–9. https://doi.org/10.1086/266841

Schramm, Wilbur (1959b) *One Day in the World's Press: Fourteen Great Newspapers on a Day of Crisis*, USA: Stanford University Press.

Schramm, Wilbur (1963) 'Communication Research in the United States', in Schramm, Wilbur (ed.) *The Science of Human Communication*, USA: Basic Books, pp.1–16.

Schramm, Wilbur (1980) 'The Beginnings of Communication Study in the United States', *Annals of the International Communication Association*, vol. 4, no. 1, pp.73–82. https://doi.org/10.1080/23808985.1980.11923795

Schramm, Wilbur (1985) 'The Beginnings of Communication Study in the United States', in Rogers, Everett M. and Balle, Francis (eds) *The Media Revolution in America and in Western Europe*, UK: Ablex Publishing, pp.200–11.

Schudson, Michael (2008) 'The "Lippmann-Dewey Debate" and the Invention of Walter Lippmann as an Anti-Democrat 1985–1996', *International Journal of Communication*, vol. 2, pp.1031–42.

Seidelman, Raymond and Harpham, Edward J. (1985) *Disenchanted Realists: Political Science and the American Crisis*, USA: State University of New York Press.

Shah, Hemant (2011) *The Production of Modernization: Daniel Lerner, Mass Media, and the Passing of Traditional Society*, USA: Temple University Press.

Simonson, Peter (2016) 'Herta Herzog and the Founding Mothers of Mass Communication Research', in Klaus, Elizabeth and Seethaler, Josef (eds) *What Do We Really Know about Herta Herzog?* Germany: Peter Lang, pp.61–84.

Simpson, Christopher (1994) *Science of Coercion: Communication Research and Psychological Warfare, 1945–1960*, USA: Oxford University Press.

Smith, Bruce L. (1956) 'Trends in Research on International Communication and Public Opinion, 1945–1955', *Public Opinion Quarterly*, vol. 20, no. 1, pp.182–95. https://doi.org/10.1086/266607

Smith, Bruce L. and Smith, Chitra M. (1956) *International Communication and Political Opinion: A Guide to the Literature*, USA: Princeton University Press.

'Social Science Research Council records' (no date). https://dimes.rockarch .org/collections/iNo7dbyWw2GwSwKsC3nDj3?category=&limit= 40&query=The%20Social%20Science%20Research%20Council%20

Speier, Hans (1976) '"The Dialectical Imagination: A History of the Frankfurt School and the Institute of Social Research, 1923–1950. By Martin Jay". (Boston, Mass.: Little, Brown & Co., 1973. Pp. 382. $3.95, paper.)', *American Political Science Review*, vol. 70, no. 4, pp.1276–78. https://doi.org/10.2307/1959402

Sproule, J. Michael (1997) *Propaganda and Democracy: the American Experience of Media and Mass Persuasion*, UK: Cambridge University Press.

Stanton, Frank N. and Lazarsfeld, Paul F. (1949) *Communications Research: 1948–1949*, USA: Harper & Brothers.

Stevenson, Robert L. (1992) 'Defining International Communication as a Field', *Journalism Quarterly*, vol. 69, no. 3, pp.543–53. https://doi.org/10.1177/107769909206900302

'The United States and the Founding of the United Nations, August 1941– October 1945' (2005). US Department of State Archive. https://2001-2009.state.gov/r/pa/ho/pubs/fs/55407.htm#:~:text=of %20Public%20Affairs-,The%20United%20States%20and%20the %20Founding%20of%20the%20United%20Nations,of%20the%20Second %20World%20War

Tiede, Hans-Joerg (2022) 'Lazarsfeld's Legacy. Paul Lazarsfeld and the Limited Effect of McCarthyism on the Academic Mind', *International Journal of Communication*, vol. 16, pp.646–54. https://ijoc.org/index.php/ijoc/article/view/18661

Tunstall, Jeremy (1977) *The Media Are American: Anglo-American Media in the World*, UK: Constable.

Tunstall, Jeremy (2008) *The Media Were American: U.S. Mass Media in Decline*, USA: Oxford University Press.

United Nations (no date) 'United Nations Charter: Preamble'. https://www.un.org/en/about-us/un-charter/preamble

United Nations Economic and Social Council (1948) *United Nations Conference on Freedom of Information*, Switzerland: United Nations. https://igitallibrary.un.org/record/212470

United Nations General Assembly (1948) *The Universal Declaration of Human Rights*, France: United Nations. https://www.un.org/en/about-us/universal-declaration-of-human-rights#:~:text=Article%2019,media%20and%20regardless%20of%20frontiers

Vogel, Ezra F. (2008) 'Lucian Pye, 1921–2008'. *The China Quarterly*, vol. 196, December, pp.912–18. http://www.jstor.org/stable/20192274

Wahl-Jorgensen, Karin (2004) 'How Not to Found a Field: New Evidence on the Origins of Mass Communication Research', *Journal of Communication*, vol. 54, no. 3, pp.547–64. https://doi.org/10.1111/j.1460-2466.2004.tb02644.x

'Walter Phillips Davison '39' (2013) *Princeton Alumni Weekly*. https://paw.princeton.edu/memorial/walter-phillips-davison-'39

White, Llewellyn and Leigh, Robert D. (1946) *Peoples Speaking to Peoples. Report from the Commission on Freedom of the Press*, USA: University of Illinois Press.

Wiener, Norbert (1948) *Cybernetics: or control and communication in the animal and the machine*. France: Hermann & Co.

Wirth Marvick, Elizabeth (1979) *Psychopolitical Analysis. Selected Writings of Nathan Leites*, USA: Sage.

Wolfenstein, Martha and Leites, Nathan C. (1947) 'An Analysis of Themes and Plots', *The Annals of the American Academy of Political and Social Science*, vol. 254, no. 1, pp.41–48. https://doi.org/10.1177/000271624725400108

6. Ideological utopias: Fred S. Siebert, Theodore Peterson and Wilbur Schramm and their *Four Theories of the Press*

> All scholarship must be inevitably adapted to the time and place of its creation. That relationship is either unconscious, disguised, and indirect or reflexive, explicit, and avowed. (Carey 1989, p.148)

My final empirical chapter turns to a book of only four chapters and 153 pages, which was published in 1956 by the University of Illinois Press. This little book has a grand title: *Four Theories of the Press: The Authoritarian, Libertarian, Social Responsibility, and Soviet Communist Concepts of What the Press Should Be and Do* (hereafter *Four Theories*). Its three authors, Fred(e)rick (Fred) S. Siebert (1901–1982), Theodore (Ted) B. Peterson (1918–1997) and Wilbur Schramm (1907–1987), had all worked before the book's publication in the Institute of Communications Research (ICR) and/or the Department of Journalism at the University of Illinois Urbana-Champaign (UIUC).

Four Theories became a canonical book (selling more than 90,000 copies) that combines ideologies and utopias. It is not about the content of propaganda but is a comparative study of press systems used to understand why the press is different 'from our own' in different countries. As the authors argue in their introduction, 'the press always takes the form and the coloration of the social and political structures within which it operates' (Siebert, Peterson and Schramm 1956, p.1). The four theories are: authoritarian, liberal, totalitarian and social responsibility. They constitute authoritarian 'rationale' with 16th- and 17th-century England, 'practiced in many places', libertarian after 1686 in England and in the US but influential elsewhere, social responsibility in the 20th-century US, and Soviet totalitarian with the Soviet Union but also with Nazis and Italian fascism (p.7). Since its publication the book has become not only 'the bible of comparative media studies' (Curran 2011, p.28) but also that of international communication and political communication.

In this chapter I argue that the book was a compromise between the diverse interests of its authors, their backgrounds, ideas and national and international politics. It lies at, and exemplifies, the intersection of contradictory elements, and gave rise to new concepts of a press system and of press theory in an

---

How to cite this book chapter:

Rantanen, Terhi (2024) *Dead Men's Propaganda: Ideology and Utopia in Comparative Communications Studies*, London: LSE Press, pp. 209–243.
https://doi.org/10.31389/lsepress.wmf.f. License: CC BY-NC 4.0

international and comparative context. However, because of the changes in the international and domestic political climate, academics who participated in international networks came under the suspicion of the US government, as explored in Chapter 5. In order to rescue themselves, the authors may have felt that they needed to show their loyalty to their domestic government and funders, especially in relation to communism. In the end, *Four Theories* itself became a disguised battlefield of the ideologies and utopias of its time. The book also reflects the battles inside the emerging field of communication studies, where historical communication research gave way to more present-oriented research.

Four Theories is an example of intergenerational work done by academics who each belonged to a different biological and intellectual generation, but who came together only once to write a book. The archival materials available at the University of Illinois give us a glimpse of how they worked, allowing us to analyse the relationships and dispersal of power between the authors. If any book is intergenerational it is *Four Theories*, which brings together what was seen as 'old' (history) and as 'new' (modern communication research) in an international comparative study. In addition to Merton's concept of how to evaluate research, including its funding, the concepts of Mannheim's generation can also be applied to the book's audiences in the way that Merton did when he compared communication research to the sociology of knowledge (see Chapter 1). *Four Theories* extended generational memory beyond the lifetime of the generation of its authors against all expectations.

This chapter also uses the concepts of ideology and of utopia, since these were not only present in the circumstances in which the academics worked but are also present in the text of *Four Theories*. Two of its chapters, Peterson's on social responsibility theory and Schramm's on Soviet communist theory, are outcomes of policy science research, and are related indirectly either to propaganda research done during World War II or to the Hutchins Commission on Freedom of the Press. The changing ideologies and utopias of the time also directly influenced the university where its authors worked. This is why George D. Stoddard (1897–1981), president of the University of Illinois from 1946 to 1953, who hired Schramm, is included here. The university's archive materials show the pressure he was under following accusations of communism and atheism from politicians and religious leaders in the name of the people of Illinois. Stoddard's and Schramm's careers, and their involvement with UNESCO and other international organisations, also show how they were caught up with the utopias of a relatively short period following World War II.

The concepts of Insiders and Outsiders are also important for this chapter, where they can be applied both to academics and institutions. Schramm was an Outsider who was hired by Stoddard and became an Insider by editing several books in new communication studies and deciding who was then 'in' and who was 'out' in this new field. Later, and even more clearly, by naming the founding fathers of the field, he contributed to the dominant story of his generation, a story of the origins of communication research told by a generation about itself that was then repeated by following generations. Schramm's story about his own generation became a dominant story that is still alive.

This chapter is organised in the following way. First, it introduces the key characters: Stoddard, Schramm, Siebert and Peterson. Second, it explores how *Four Theories* was written and the power relationships between the authors. Third, it analyses the key theories, concepts and empirical materials used in the book. Fourth, it describes how future generations received the book.

6.1 The key characters – authors and colleagues at the University of Illinois

George D. Stoddard

Without Stoddard, Schramm's move to Illinois would not have happened. Stoddard himself was headhunted and appointed as president of the University of Illinois (UIUC) in 1946 with the aim of transforming a 'sleeping giant' into a world-class university (Solberg and Tomilson 1997, p.57; Stoddard 1981, p.104). Schramm had been Stoddard's colleague at the University of Iowa and when Stoddard joined the Office of War Information (OWI) during World War II he brought in Schramm (Glander 2000, p.16; Nerone 2004, p.23) and later invited Schramm to establish the Institute of Communications Research (ICR) at UIUC (Rogers 1994, p.449).

Stoddard (pictured in Figure 6.1) was born in in Carbondale, Pennsylvania, the fourth child of Eugene Anson Stoddard (1852–1929), an insurance agency owner and a Methodist, and Charlotte Elizabeth Dinsmore Stoddard (1858–1937). He interrupted his studies at the Pennsylvania State University to serve as a second lieutenant in World War I. After the war he studied psychology at the University of Paris and received his PhD at the University of Iowa. Stoddard became a child psychologist at the University of Iowa, where he served as professor, head of the department and dean of the Graduate College (Stoddard 1981). There he met Schramm and became friends with him (Cartier 1988, pp.112, 117). In 1945 he was a member of the US delegation to the London conference for the establishment of an educational and cultural organisation, a predecessor of UNESCO, and a year later he was chairman of the US education mission to Japan. He was deputy chairman of the US delegation to UNESCO and for three years chairman of the US National Commission for UNESCO.[1] In July 1946 President Truman made him a member of the President's Commission on Higher Education (Solberg and Tomilson 1997, p.56). Stoddard also became a member of the Board of Trustees of RAND Corporation for 15 years (1948–1963) (Stoddard 198, p.193).

Stoddard's appointment at the University of Illinois was severely criticised from the start. A leaflet was published stating that 'in the light of his past public utterances of disrespect for religious people, not acceptable to the citizens of Illinois as president-elect of the state university'[2] and he was accused

Figure 6.1: George Stoddard at his desk, University of Illinois, *c.* 1950

Source: Courtesy of the University of Illinois at Urbana-Champaign Archives, image
000780, Photographic Subject File, 1868-, RS 39/2/20, Box 171, Folder Stoddard, G.D.,
1950–1953. https://archon.library.illinois.edu/archives/index.php?p=digitallibrary
/digitalcontent&id=11071

of 'godlessness' in 1945 by a Roman Catholic Bishop of Springfield. Stoddard
regarded the required affidavit of allegiance applied to university personnel as
'annoying' and 'degrading' (Stoddard 1981, p.120). It read:

> I….., do solemnly swear (or affirm) that I believe in and pledge my
> allegiance to the Constitution of the United States and the system
> of free representative government founded thereon; that I do not

nor will I advocate the overthrow of the Government of the United States by force or violence; and that I am not a member of nor will I join any political party or organization that advocates the over-throw of the Government of the United States by force or violence. (Stoddard 1981, p.119)

In 1946, after taking office, Stoddard was accused of taking his first trip abroad on the United Nations business to help organise a global group, which had 'produced many controversial proposals'. He was again accused in 1949 of allowing an allegedly 'pink' professor to remain in the faculty and was required to carry out an investigation to get 'Russia lovers' out of the school. According to these accusations, there were 150 'reds', 'pinks' and socialists on the university staff and the university was 'being used to indoctrinate youth with radical political philosophies' (Stoddard 1981, pp.159–60). Stoddard replied that he was 'against Communists as teachers but socialists were all right if they advocated the replacement of capitalism with socialism by legal means'. However, he did ask J. Edgar Hoover (1895–1972) of the FBI to make an enquiry about Dallas W. Smythe's (1907–1992) loyalty and whether Smythe had communist or pre-communist form before his appointment at UIUC.[3] Smythe himself believed that it was Schramm who made the request to the FBI (Pickard 2014, p.201). According to Stoddard,[4]

those of us in charge have worked quietly, through our own security officers, the military establishment, to make sure that no Communists are on the staff. This is important for we have a number of classified and secret research projects at the University. All staff members at the University of Illinois have signed a standard loyalty oath, and the Security Officer has announced publicly that there is not, to his knowledge, a single Communist in the University of Illinois.

Schramm is said to have been Stoddard's friend and ally, but the archival materials at UIUC have no record that suggests a special relationship. Siebert claims in his memoirs that Schramm's departure from UIUC happened because 'Schramm understandably felt handicapped without Stoddard's support' after Stoddard's own departure from UIUC.[5] While the new Cold War atmosphere increased interest in comparative communications, it was also increasingly unfavourable to US scholars who had been active in international organisations. The Board of Trustees gave Stoddard a vote of no confidence and he was forced to leave the university in 1953 (with a demonstration held in support of Stoddard; see Figure 6.2), three years before *Four Theories* was published ('The Rise and Fall of President George D. Stoddard' 2022). After his departure, Schramm was released from his non-academic duties at UIUC (Stoddard 1981, p.127; Rogers 1994, p.436).

Figure 6.2: A demonstration held in support of Stoddard, on either 24 or 25 July 1953

Source: Courtesy of the University of Illinois at Urbana-Champaign Archives. Image 0011529, RS 2/10/20, Box 32, Folder Photographs July 24-25, 1953. https://archon.library .illinois.edu/archives/index.php?p=digitallibrary/digitalcontent&id=14188

Wilbur Schramm

Wilbur Lang Schramm (pictured Figure 6.3) has been seen as the prime mover behind *Four Theories*. Peterson described the book as a spin-off from Schramm's work on the responsibility of the media.[6] The US National Council of Churches had asked Schramm (Schramm 1957a) to undertake a project on the responsibilities of mass communicators and he used money left over from that project to produce *Four Theories*.[7] He was clearly the organiser behind the book, even if he himself only wrote one chapter.

Schramm was the son of Archibald A. Schramm (1880–1945), who was a lawyer, and Louise M. Lang (1880–1971), both of German descent and from the small town of Marietta in Ohio. After studying in Marietta and at Harvard, he joined the AP in 1928 and worked as a reporter and correspondent. He received his PhD in English at the University of Iowa in 1932 and started working as an instructor in the English department,[8] where he met Stoddard, George Gallup (1901–1984) and Kurt Lewin, whose seminar he took while working at Iowa (Cartier 1988, p.174). Stoddard and Schramm became friends and 'mutual admirers while at Iowa' (Rogers 1994, pp.448–49). Shortly after the bombing of Pearl Harbor in 1941, Schramm volunteered to work for the Office of Facts and Figures (OFF) (Cartier 1988, p.158).

Figure 6.3: Wilbur Schramm photographed in his office at the University of Illinois, c. 1940s

Source: Courtesy of the University of Illinois at Urbana-Champaign Archives, image 0005605, Institute of Communications Research Subject File, 1947–1983, RS 13/5/1, Box 4. https://archon.library.illinois.edu/archives/index.php?p=digitallibrary/digitalcontent&id=7044

During the war he worked as director of the Division of Educational Service in the Office of War Information (OWI), as an educational consultant to the Navy Department and as an educational adviser to the War Department[9] (Cartier 1988, p.159).

In Washington Schramm also attended regular meetings in the Library of Congress with a group consisting of 20 to 25 staff members and advisers. The group included Carl Hovland (1912–1961) and Berelson, as well as, in an advisory capacity and present when possible and when needed, such figures as George Gallup, Elmo Roper (1900–1971), Lazarsfeld and Frank Stanton (Cartier 1988, p.170). Although Schramm was not working as a researcher, he had plenty of opportunities to meet with and learn from them. As Cartier (1988, pp.169–70) wrote, drawing on her interviews with Schramm and his contemporaries, 'discussions, informal and formal, were frequent and they learned a great deal from one another'. Cartier quoted a contemporary:

> The group of academics who came to staff the OWI and to conduct research for the branches of government quickly discovered an added benefit: each other's company, and concomitant intellectual and personal vitalization ... 'So many of us were together. I mean, everybody knew everybody ... We were all acquainted, and worked together'. (quoted by Cartier 1988, p.170)

As shown in Chapters 2 and 4, lifelong relationships were formed among those who worked in propaganda analysis, even in different departments. This sense of camaraderie was facilitated by the generous resources the researchers had available. The government and the foundations were paying for everything: salaries, facilities, research assistance and publications, among other things. It was quite an experience, as a contemporary testified, 'for researchers used to working in obscurity. It was much like a very busy sabbatical year.' According to an interview conducted by Cartier, there was a sense of loyalty that was universal: given the nature of the war and its significance, the academics 'were so eager to be used by the government, rather than [having] fear of being used by the government' (Cartier 1988, p.169). This had to do the with the dominant political ideology of the period, not only with the war effort but with the New Deal. As Cartier writes,

> Thus, for an academic to be invited to come to Washington was to be associated with the New Deal Establishment, the shining stars not only of intellect but also of practical wisdom, and virtue besides. It was to sense the laurel wreath descending toward one's brow. (p.169)

However, Schramm was not entirely happy in Washington, finding his OWI department 'tangled, messy, busy', and that 'the tasks were routine'. He also found that, although there was innovative interdisciplinary scholarship, it was only with a practical orientation, unlike at the University of Iowa. Schramm returned to Iowa in March 1943, was appointed director of the School of Journalism and founded there in the same year the first doctoral programme in mass communication in the US (Cartier 1988, p.174; Rogers 1994, p.4).

In 1947, Schramm moved to the University of Illinois (UIUC) as director of the University of Illinois Press, director of the Institute of Communications Research (ICR), research professor of journalism and assistant to President Stoddard.[10] While at UIUC, Schramm worked as a consultant to the Department of Defense, for the Air Force on research assignments, and in consulting work on the theory of psychological warfare[11] for the Operations Coordinating Board, the Human Relations Research Office, the Operations Research Office, the US Information Agency (USIA) and other branches of government. He also served as a US delegate to the international communication meetings organised by UNESCO in Paris in 1949, conducted research in Europe in the following year, and participated in a UNESCO study of international news agencies and in an International Press Institute (IPI) study of news flows[12] (International Press Institute 1953).

The University of Illinois Press published several key books in communication (Chaffee 1974, p.7) edited by Schramm (see, for example, 1948; 1949; 1954). Chaffee (1974, p.7) writes about them that:

These are not merely books. They define the boundaries and the substance of the field for many purposes. And to say that they were 'edited' by Schramm is to grossly understate the contribution. Nothing like them had existed before.

Schramm thus became chief organiser of the newly founded field of communication studies, founding new institutional programmes in several universities. He played a key role in institutionalising communication as an independent discipline, as well as in defining key concepts and theories. The field started moving, according to Schramm (1957b, p.107), from 'the stage of literary and philosophical speculation to the stage of laboratory and field research'. Much of Schramm's influence is credited to his role as an organiser, synthesiser, explainer and disseminator (Chaffee 1974, pp.3–4) as the 'definer of the field' (Tankard 1988). After his wartime projects came to an end, his new collaborators were in journalism schools and speech communication departments (Delia 1987, p.21; Sproule 2008, p.166).

In 1950 the US Air Force sent Schramm to Korea on a wartime research assignment, and the following year the army sent him to Japan to study psychological warfare practices.[13] At UIUC, Schramm was also contracted to provide a series of textbooks for use by the US army in instructions on psychological warfare.[14] During 1954 he was on leave for five months to direct a worldwide research project at the request of the National Security Council, visiting several universities,[15] and half of his salary came from the USIA.[16] Schramm became the self-nominated expert on Soviet theory for *Four Theories*. His work on psychological warfare and his empirical research in Korea (Schramm and Riley 1951a; Schramm and Riley 1951b) gave him the most expertise on communist countries among his colleagues at UIUC.[17] His teaching and his research reports show how the concept of a system had started to influence his thinking. In Schramm's outline for the Theory of Communications course he taught at UIUC he lists three systems: (1) totalitarian; (2) socialist-paternal; and (3) democratic-free enterprise system.[18] His *Four Working Papers on Propaganda Theory* (1955), written for the USIA with Hideya Kumata (1921–1972), includes four case studies either co-authored or written separately by the two on: (1) the Japanese concept of propaganda (Kumata); (2) the propaganda theory of the German Nazis (Kumata); (3) the British concept of propaganda (Schramm); and (4) the Soviet concept of psychological warfare (Schramm) (Kumata et al. 1955). In this way, Schramm had already outlined the structure of what was to become *Four Theories*, which would be written without a conclusion – as was his *Four Working Papers*.

Berelson (1959, p.2) and Schramm (1980) later named four of their wartime colleagues, Hovland, Lewin, Lasswell and Lazarsfeld, as founders of communication studies. This is one way to extend the lifetime of a generation, by extending generational memory beyond the lifetime of a generation. Long after nominating these 'founding fathers' of communication research,

218   DEAD MEN'S PROPAGANDA

Schramm was himself given that title (Rogers 1994, p.xi). When nominating those 'founding fathers', Schramm famously left out several others, including women, members of the Frankfurt School in exile and other émigré scholars such as Leites and Kecskemeti. Schramm later justified his choices:

> The four men who might be thought of as founding fathers for communication research are a political scientist interested in psychoanalytic approaches, the study of power, and the analysis of political content; a sociologist interested in mass phenomena, political campaigns, and mathematical models; an experimental psychologist, known originally for his studies of animal learning; and a Gestalt psychologist, interested in the study of group decision and child rearing. These men ... more than any others set the traditions of communication research, and their influence continues in many students and followers. (quoted in Cartier 1988, p.175)

Schramm recognised another set of common characteristics:

> These 'fathers' of our field had strikingly similar backgrounds. All of them had rich early experiences, went to excellent universities, and came into contact with great minds. Three of them had all or part of their academic training in Europe. All four were interdisciplinary in their interests. Each was trained in another discipline and turned to communication study through the experience of confronting 'real world' problems ... And all except one of them founded a research institute or program that attracted bright young people and able colleagues. (quoted in Cartier 1988, p.176)

In this way, Schramm became, in the same way as Cooper but less egoistically, the man who told the story of his generation and of those he chose to name as the founders of the field. He acknowledged the émigré scholars Lazarsfeld and Lewin, but at the same time had a problem with the Frankfurt School. While Schramm (1963; 1980) named the 'founding fathers', as Pooley (2017, p.13) argues by quoting Chaffee and Rogers (1997: x–xi), 'Communication scholars today may debate who their forefathers were, but no one disputes that Schramm was the founder and the "finest storyteller".

Fred S. Siebert

While Schramm was seen as the initiator behind *Four Theories*, two of the book's four chapters were written by Fred (Fred(e)rick) Siebert (pictured, Figure 6.4). He was born in 1902 in Tower, a village in northern Minnesota, the son of a German migrant, Frank F. Siebert (Seibert) (1859–1940), and Sarah A. Paine Siebert (1861–1940), the daughter of an Irish immigrant who

Figure 6.4: Fred S. Siebert, c. 1940

Source: Courtesy of the University of Illinois at Urbana-Champaign Archives, image 0012200. Record Series 39/2/20, Box 135, Category FAC-4, Folder Siebert, Frederick S. https://archon.library.illinois.edu/archives/index.php?p=digitallibrary/digitalcontent&id=17923

had travelled to the Minnesota territory by covered wagon.[19] Siebert was first educated in journalism at the University of Minnesota, then in law at the University of Illinois, and was admitted to the Illinois Bar in 1927. Having worked as an instructor and assistant professor since 1927, in 1941 he was appointed professor in journalism and director of the School of Journalism and Communications. When he joined UIUC he saw the faculty as 'somewhat moribund and opposed to change' and hired two new colleagues, Jay Jensen (1937–1997) and Theodore Peterson.[20] Siebert defined himself as a 'legal historian in journalism'.[21] His magnum opus was *Freedom of the Press in England, 1476–1776* (1952), on which he had worked for 20 years including eight months of library research in the UK[22] (Schwarzlose 1978, pp.106–07). The book introduced three theories seen as likely to influence the press in any society: (1) the Tudor–Stuart; (2) the Blackstone–Mansfield; and (3) the Camden–Erskine Jefferson theories.

Siebert also did policy science. He was called as a consult by the Chicago law firm that the *Chicago Tribune* had hired in relation to the antitrust suit against the AP (see Chapter 3). The *Chicago Tribune* owner, Robert McCormick (1880–1955), was the only member of the AP Board to file a separate defence, an appeal to the Supreme Court and to Congress to amend antitrust laws to exempt the AP (Blanchard 1987, pp.57, 66). In his statement Siebert dismissed the AP monopoly argument (Picard 1985, p.138) and concluded that the 'first Amendment offered little or no protection for the practises of the AP'. He was also critical of the argument that opening the AP to new members would stimulate the establishment of new and competing newspapers since their number had steadily been in decline. Siebert pointed out that there were many economic factors limiting competing newspapers and that opening up the AP would have little effect. According to Siebert, the competing news agencies, the UP and the INS, would be seriously affected by the expansion of AP membership. Siebert's conclusions were incorporated in the briefs with the Supreme Court, which, however, ruled in 1945 after a vote that the by-laws of the AP were in violation of the federal antitrust laws[23] (*Associated Press v. United States* 1945; Blanchard 1987, p.77).

Siebert also shared a utopian view of communications. In 1948 he wrote that the objective of communication media was:

> to make available to the peoples of the world the kind of communications content which will enable them to maintain a peaceful and productive society and which will also provide them with personal satisfactions. (Siebert 1960, p.219)

Even if he was critical of some recommendations of the Commission on Freedom of the Press, he also provided a useful classification of government activities: they were government as (1) restrictive agency; (2) as regulating agency; (3) facilitating agency; and (4) participating agency. This was a much more sophisticated and nuanced version of the strictly anti-government line Cooper was shown to take in Chapter 3.

The use of the word theory in *Four Theories* clearly came from Siebert's book, in which he used the term in order to separate historical periods one from another, carrying out comparative research over time. The idea of using theories to separate periods from one another for comparison purposes also came from Siebert's work, although in *Four Theories* he used them primarily for purposes of comparison over space. According to Siebert, 'philosophical principles played a secondary, but important, role in the development of the freedom of expression' (Marler 1990, p.193), indicating that another concept was needed, that of a press system.

There was also a research assistant, Eleanor Blum (1909–2011), whose contribution remained invisible, as often happened to female academics at that time (see, for example, Rowland and Simonson 2013). Blum was herself to receive a PhD in communications in 1958 at UIUC ('Eleanor Blum Papers, 1962–1991' no date).

Theodore Peterson

The third author was Theodore (Ted) Peterson (pictured, Figure 6.5). He was born in 1918 in Albert Lea, Minnesota, to Theodore B. and Emelia

Figure 6.5: Theodore Peterson presenting Linnea Pearson with the College of Journalism, Harold Roettger Award, 1960

Source: Courtesy of the University of Illinois at Urbana-Champaign Archives, image 0000175, Photographic Subject File, 1868, RS:39/2/20, Box COL – 4, Folder COL 4-1 Communications, 1952–1971. https://archon.library.illinois.edu/archives/index.php?p =collections/controlcard&id=4014
Notes: Linnea Pearson is presented the Harold Roettger memorial as outstanding graduating senior of the University of Illinois College of Journalism and Communications by Dean Theodore Peterson.

(Emelie) C. (Jensen) Peterson, who were of Danish origin. He received his BA from the University of Minnesota in 1941. During his 30 months with the US Army Air Force in England, Sergeant Peterson gathered material for two articles on British journalism history, which were published after the war (Peterson 1945; 1948). Siebert had invited him to join the faculty at UIUC in 1948 as an instructor and Peterson also became a PhD student there. He recalled that in 1955, after defending his thesis on magazines (published as a book in 1964),[24] as the most junior author he was allocated social responsibility theory for *Four Theories*.[25] Since Schramm, Siebert and Peterson had only one meeting, where the division of labour was made between them, and Peterson was left alone with his chapter without further guidance, the report of the Hutchins Commission, *A Free and Responsible Press* (Commission on Freedom of the Press 1947) became his primary source. Siebert, as director of the School of Journalism, had organised a series of seminars within the faculty to consider their implications.[26] Peterson formulated the main results of the Hutchins report into the social responsibility theory of the press (McIntyre 1987, p.136).

Siebert and Peterson appeared to be close, with Peterson describing them as having a 'father–son relationship',[27] but there appears to have been no great affection between these two and Schramm. Both Siebert and Schramm were on Peterson's doctoral committee.[28] Schramm was seen by Peterson as a 'brilliant guy'[29] but was not as close to him as Siebert was. However, all three authors shared similar backgrounds in migrant families from small Midwestern towns and universities. Siebert had worked for eight months in British archives in 1936[30] and Peterson had carried out archival research during his 30 months in the UK while serving in the US Army Air Force during World War II (Peterson 1945). Schramm had been to Korea and Japan and possibly to other places on US army missions. They had all worked as journalists and none of them was a social scientist by education. They all became early members of the International Association for Mass Communication Research (IAMCR), an international organisation founded in Paris for communication researchers in 1957, as did Lasswell.[31]

Four Theories could probably have been written without Peterson, who described his chapter as a 'term paper',[32] but not without Siebert. However, Schramm was quite the academic entrepreneur, editing several books at the same time and bringing in big research grants. He was also the one at that time who was internationally oriented, even if with the interests of the US government primarily in mind. Without Schramm's initiative, *Four Theories* might easily not have been put together, but it could certainly not have been written without Siebert. Whenever Peterson was asked how *Four Theories* came to be written, his answer was always 'Casually. Very casually.'[33] Siebert said that the book grew out of a graduate course he had been teaching at UIUC, and that after Schramm had visited Siebert's class he suggested to Siebert that he should write out 'that part with the four theories' (Schwarzlose 1978, p.109). Peterson confirmed that the book was Schramm's idea, and that it was based on a seminar that Siebert had been teaching on government and the press.[34] Siebert did not want to write all the chapters himself, although he later wondered if he should have done so (Schwarzlose 1978, p.109). Instead, he was reported to have said, 'I'll do two parts of it and get Peterson to do one part, and you do the other, Schramm' (Schwarzlose 1978, p.109). Peterson was then stopped one day 'while using the drinking fountain outside Siebert's office by Schramm, who asked him whether he was interested in helping to write a book'.[35] He agreed and was given Chapter 3 to write. Siebert later suggested to Schramm that Peterson's name should go after his and before Schramm's.[36]

The title of the book was briefly discussed at their only meeting, which lasted no more than an hour. Instead of *Four Theories*, the authors decided to call it just 'Theories' without 'The', thus accepting the possibility that other theories existed. After the meeting Schramm produced a single sheet headed 'These questions (and probably others) should be answerable from each of our chapters'.[37] *Four Theories* was written in five weeks in the summer of 1956, after that one meeting. Peterson does not even remember whether, after finishing their individual chapters independently, they commented on one another's.[38]

However, none of the authors could foresee the future success of their book, which happened after it was reprinted in paper copy in 1963. The University of Illinois Press, directed by Schramm, published the book in hardback only in 1956. According to Peterson, it received a couple of favourable reviews and the Kappa Tau Alpha award for research on journalism from UIUC.[39] Both Peterson and Siebert felt that, compared with their other works, which took up anything from six to 20 years of their lives, the success of *Four Theories* was unfair[40] (Schwarzlose 1978). Around the time the book was published, Schramm had already left for Stanford and Siebert was to leave for Michigan State University in 1957.[41]

6.2 New intellectual ideas: the inspirations for *Four Theories*

Ironically, there is not much theory in *Four Theories*. The introduction is six pages long and the four chapters are followed by no conclusion. None of the authors was particularly interested in developing theory, perhaps reflecting their own education and background, and the result was more policy-oriented than theoretical. The subtitle included the phrase 'What the Press Should Be and Do'. Partly this has to do with the field of communication studies itself, which was just being established and emerging from the shadows of political science and propaganda studies. If theories and concepts were used, they were borrowed from other disciplines. However, what *Four Theories* did, even if this was not made explicit, was to introduce the concept of a press system and combine this with theories (philosophies) of the press to produce a systematic comparative study. In the book, these two very different traditions were brought together.

The concept of a system

The concept of a system was suddenly 'found' by many academics in different fields after World War II. They were influenced by the works of Talcott Parsons (1951), who adopted the concept of a system from Max Weber, Émile Durkheim (1858–1917), T.H. Marshall (1893–1981) and Vilfredo Pareto (1848–1923), and from general system theorists (Rogers 1994, pp.132–35). The introduction to Norbert Wiener's (1894–1964) *Cybernetics* had come out in 1948, and Claude Shannon (1916–2001) and Warren Weaver's (1894–1978) *Mathematical Theory of Communication* was published a year later, in 1949, followed by Parsons' *The Social System* (1951) and David

Easton's (1917–2014) *The Political System* (1953). Rather surprisingly, anthropology seems to have played a key role, especially through the works of George Bateson (1904–1980) and Margaret Mead (1901–1978). Many of the early system theorists attended the so-called Macy Conferences (1946–1953) on cybernetics funded by the Josiah Macy Jr. Foundation. However, none of the authors of *Four Theories* attended these conferences ('Summary: The Macy Conferences' no date; Rogers 1994, pp.401–05). Schramm seemed to be more influenced by Shannon and Weaver than by Parsons. According to Chaffee, it was Schramm who persuaded Shannon of Bell System Laboratories and Weaver of the Rockefeller Foundation to publish their book *A Mathematical Model of Communication* collaboratively (Chaffee 1974, p.3).

When Siebert, Peterson and Schramm introduced the concept of a press system in *Four Theories*, they clearly knew Parsons' *The Social System* (1951) and used his concept in their book. One can see the influence of Parsons' system theories in *Four Theories* when the authors write at the beginning of the book: 'To see the differences between press systems in full perspective, then, one must look at the social systems in which the press functions' (Siebert, Peterson and Schramm 1956, p.2). The great achievement of *Four Theories* is that it uses the idea of a system, introduces the concept of a press system, and suggests using the same criteria in comparing different press systems with each other.

However, when it comes to definitions of a press system, it is hard to find one in *Four Theories*. According to McQuail (1994, p.133), 'the theories were also formulated in very general terms and did not describe or underlie any factual media system, except, perhaps, in the case of the Soviet model'. *Four Theories* clearly focuses on the philosophies that lie behind 'different kinds of press'. As its authors (Siebert, Peterson and Schramm 1956, p.2) write,

> in the last analysis the difference between press systems is one of philosophy, and this book is about the philosophical and political rationales or theories which lie behind the different kinds of press we have in the world today.

In a way, indirectly, this looks as if they were suggesting that Parsons' social system be replaced by philosophical theories, thus acknowledging that there was something other than the system. This is also problematic, since, as Nerone (1995, p.18) points out with regard to *Four Theories*,

> its theory is that in its structure, policy, and behavior the communications system reflects the society in which it operates and that society can be categorically defined by a coherent philosophy.

This is, of course, a valid point, but at the same time what made *Four Theories* unique was precisely the fact that it compared philosophies and not only material circumstances as many of the early system theorists did.

Although *Four Theories* uses the concept of a press system, it does so sparsely. It is also remarkable that the book uses the word 'system' only 58 times and only twice with reference to the concept of a press system (pp.2, 5). Most of the references are generic, such as those to a system of social control or of principles. The first reference in *Four Theories* to a mass-media system can be found on page 18, where it is used under the subtitle of 'authoritarian control systems', referring to the 'operation of the system of mass media control'. Like Almond (1956), whose article came out in the same year, *Four Theories* combined systems with countries. As Hallin and Mancini note,

> every theory was related to a particular country: the United States to which they trace the Libertarian and Social responsibility theories; Britain, to which they trace both the Authoritarian and along, with United States, Libertarian theories, and the Soviet Union, the Soviet theory. (2004, p.10)

Press theories

In *Four Theories*, the authors combined systems with four press theories, although they themselves were unsure as to whether there should have been only three theories. The social responsibility theory did not exist anywhere, it was a 'should be' rather than a 'how it is' theory, a utopian theory. Nerone correctly argues that the *Four Theories* are not all theories in the same sense, that only two of the theories are grounded in historical realities (Nerone 1995, pp.18–19), and that the book defines the *Four Theories* from within one of the *Four Theories* of classical liberalism (Nerone 1995, p.21). According to Sparks and Reading (1998, p.50), the *Four Theories* turn out in practice to be only two – the 'Libertarian' and the 'Soviet Communist'.

The authoritarian and libertarian theories of the press

The idea behind Siebert's *Freedom of the Press in England* originated with his interest in the American Constitution and the First Amendment. When Siebert worked on the colonial period, he discovered that 'all the concepts originated in England' and this led him to carry out archival and library research in London (Schwarzlose 1978, p.106). Siebert's authoritarian and libertarian theories were the only ones among those introduced in the book that were based on research into primary sources, unlike Peterson's and Schramm's chapters, which were based on secondary sources.

Siebert clearly saw the government as the greatest threat to press freedom. This was partly because of the historical period he was interested in, which preceded the rise of modern media, and partly because of what was happening in the United States at that time. In his address at New York University, Siebert listed four challenges the US media had recently faced: (1) the growth of the role of the federal government; (2) the leading role the US had in world politics; (3) the aggressiveness of Soviet communism and its implications for 'our way of life'; and (4) the 'amazing growth of productivity in the USA' (Siebert 1956, pp.5–6). However, Siebert was primarily a legal historian and most comfortable when writing about history even if he bowed to the dominant ideology of the time.

The social theory of the press

Peterson considered himself lucky when he was invited to co-author the book, especially when Siebert insisted that his name should come before Schramm's.[42] Siebert may have been unhappy about Schramm's contribution, since, according to Siebert, he had given Schramm his own materials on the Soviet press (Schwarzlose, 1978, p.109). The young Peterson tried to seek help from his senior authors but was left very much alone to write his chapter on social theories. He had, like other members of the faculty, attended the seminars organised by Siebert and Schramm on the Hutchins Commission report (officially the Commission on Freedom of the Press).[43] Peterson, in his dual role as instructor and PhD student, had less freedom and experience than his co-authors.

The Hutchins Commission was set up in 1942 to study whether the freedom of the press was in danger (see Chapters 2 and 3). It listed 13 recommendations, ranging from guaranteeing institutionalised freedom of the press (and of radio broadcasting and motion pictures) to maintaining competition through antitrust laws (Commission on Freedom of the Press 1947). These recommendations were seen by many in the industry as increasing government control (Blanchard 1977). In its first recommendation, the commission (p.94) recommended that 'agencies of mass communication accept the responsibility of common carriers of information and discussion', which became the basis of the concept of social responsibility. In a way, the commission indirectly introduced here, in the form of social responsibility theory, the role of the press as a kind of a public sphere (McIntyre 1987; Nerone 1995).

As McIntyre (1987, p.137) argues, the Hutchins Commission's concept of responsibility was intended as a guide to policy and was a practical proposal for dealing with specific social conditions in the US. Within the context of the report, it achieved a status it was never intended to have and came to be seen as a yardstick for the media around the world. It included severe criticism of the state of the media in the US that not everybody shared (including Cooper, see Chapter 3) and by choosing to make it the subject of one of the chapters in *Four Theories* the authors made a statement that could also be interpreted as progressive in the US context (Blanchard 1977; McIntyre 1987). As Peterson writes three decades after its publication,

> the work of the commission was the basis for a chapter called 'Social responsibility' in *Four Theories of the Press*, a slender volume by

Siebert, Schramm and Peterson, which appeared in 1956, a decade after the report, and which since then has introduced the ideas of the Commission to several generations of journalism students.[44]

Although, as Peterson testifies, generations of US journalism students were introduced to the social responsibility theory, a normative, utopian theory empirically supported by a committee report, it became an almost universal ideology of how the press should be. This happened, although when the report was published the press attacked it in 1947[45] and, as shown in Chapter 3, Cooper was also very critical of it. Peterson gives credit to Cooper for introducing the concept of 'right to know'. He writes:

> The right-to-know movement goes back to World War 2, when Kent Cooper of the AP in books, articles, and talks pleaded for a toppling of the barriers impeding international communications. He coined the phrase 'the people's right to know' in 1945. It turned up as the title of a book prepared for the American Society of Newspaper Editors in 1953 by Harold Cross, an attorney who stated his premises in its first three sentences 'Public business is the public's business. The people have a right to know. Without that the citizens of a democracy have not changed their kings.' His premise broke sharply with classical libertarian theory, which had no affirmative aspects about it.[46]

The Soviet theory of the press

Perhaps the chapter of *Four Theories* that has received most criticism is Schramm's. Altschull (1995, p.108), for example, argues that:

> the problem with Schramm's analysis was that it was hostile. Its approach was within the 'us-versus-them' framework. There could be little doubt of the good guys and the bad guys in Schramm's analysis.

Like Peterson, Schramm did not collect his own materials for this chapter. As Siebert says, 'Schramm was a facile, agile writer and never did very much research himself' (Schwarzlose 1978, p.109). Schramm did not speak Russian and was dependent on research published in English. He used many émigré scholars' published work on the Soviet Union, as well as Andrei Vyshinsky's *The Law of the Soviet State*, which had been translated into English in 1948. Schramm's footnotes (1956, pp.152–53) refer to the works of Frederick Barghoorn (1911–1991), Raymond Bauer (1916–1977), Merle Fainsod (1907–1972), Alex Inkeles (1920–2010) and Philip Selznick (1919–2010), all working in US universities, and to the work of Kecskemeti and Leites.

The concept of a system is more frequently used Schramm's chapter than in any other. More than 30 per cent of the uses of the word 'system' occur in the section where Schramm refers to the Soviet system in general, to the communication system (p.122) or to the mass communication system (p.130) of the Soviet Union. There is also one reference to the Nazi system (p.143). In sum, it is fair to say that the system was not a key concept for Siebert and Peterson, but that it was primarily Schramm, who used it in his formulation of the Soviet Communist theory. If any of those outlined in *Four Theories* could be seen as a system *par excellence*, it was the Soviet system, although this was the one most heavily criticised. It was seen as a system within which a social system and political system collided, and thus the most powerful – the system of systems. Schramm (Siebert, Peterson and Schramm 1956, p.146) famously ends this chapter and the book by writing:

> To the Soviets, the multidirectional quality, the openness, the unchecked criticism and conflict in our media represent a weakness in our national armor. To us, they seem our greatest strength. The next few decades will tell which is the better estimate.

What made Four Theories a pioneering book?

The first contribution of *Four Theories* is that it was a pioneering attempt to carry out systematic comparative international research by applying the concept of a press philosophy to comparison of the press (and in some cases also of radio) in different parts of the world. This is an achievement in itself, taking into account the fact that most research on media and communications had been primarily national, especially in the journalism research tradition from which both Siebert and Peterson came. Journalism research had mainly concerned the history of great American journalists, and *Four Theories* is a clear attempt to break away from that tradition, even if it still carries some if its traits. The field was even introducing courses in foreign and or comparative journalism to journalism schools. Still, only 36 per cent of journalism schools taught international journalism in 1955, when *Four Theories* was published (Markham 1956).

Second, *Four Theories* was clearly influenced by system theories, which had become fashionable within US academia at the time. Since the book is not very theoretical and does not show which system theories it is using, the use of the concept of a system remains rather vague. The book shows some originality in its use of the concept of a system because it combines this with press philosophies rather than with political systems. By so doing it also indirectly argues for the independent existence of a press system, which had not been properly conceptualised before *Four Theories* came out. Even after its publication, political scientists continued to conceptualise the media as part of a political system (see, for example, Almond and Powell 1966).

Third, by using the concept of a press philosophy (theory), the book suggested that there was something more powerful than a system itself as a material form. The idea that there was some notion of how the media should be, and not just how they actually are, originates from *Four Theories*. In its strong historical approach, the book acknowledges the importance of journalism history, although this is not consistent throughout.

6.3 Generational conflicts over *Four Theories*

There were two generational disputes behind *Four Theories of the Press*. One of these was the intragenerational conflict between the academics who wrote the book, the main topic for this chapter, while the other was the intergenerational conflict between the authors and the generations to come. The latter particularly is one of the reasons why *Four Theories of the Press* is included in this book. Its influence has been exceptional, even considering the critical response it received. This is why Mannheim's concept of a generation has been particularly useful here, and especially the concept of generational memory. In this chapter, I argue that *Four Theories* united, albeit temporarily, three generations of men with different backgrounds. Lasswell once noted that,

> if you want a book to become a classic, there are two strategies. One strategy is to have it published in very small quantity by an obscure university press that has no budget for advertising. That will soon make your book an addition to a 'rare book room' in some university library and guarantee something out of it being repeatedly quoted without having been read, like Havelock Ellis on sexuality. The other one was to mass-market your opus. A notorious Athenian, Socrates by name, was rather good at that. Originally his messages were spread by word of mouth, until some entrepreneur by the name of Plato—one of his students—came along, and then there was no end to the fame of *The Republic*. (Eulau and Zlomke 1999, p.89)

While the University of Illinois Press was not obscure, when *Four Theories* was published it did not receive much attention. Probably, nobody could anticipate that after its publication *Four Theories* would sell over 90,000 copies worldwide, making it an all-time bestseller in the field of communication studies. It has been translated into several languages, including German, Japanese, Chinese, Russian and Latvian. It is generally agreed that *Four Theories* had a tremendous impact not only on US communication studies but also on international communication studies and political communication studies around the world. However, at the same time, there are very few books that have provoked as much criticism. Numerous media and communication scholars[47] have been critical of *Four Theories*. Sparks and Reading (1998, p.179), for example, conclude that the book should be 'relegated forthwith to the gloomiest recess of the Museum of the Cold War and visited only by sensible graduate students of a historical persuasion'. Hallin and Mancini (2004, p.10) write that the book has 'stalked the landscape of media studies like a horror-movie zombie for decades beyond its natural lifetime'. All these authors criticised the book from their own diverse perspectives, most of them concentrating on its US-centrism and anti-communism, but the book is still viewed as a starting point for comparative communications research using the concept of a media system.

Despite all the criticism *Four Theories* received from Western scholars, the book remained popular among academics in communist and post-communist countries. Schramm visited China in 1982 and *Four Theories* was translated into Chinese soon after his visit. His Soviet Communist theory did not encounter any criticism in China and gained considerable and widespread recognition from readers there (Huang 2003, p.445). *Four Theories* was translated into Russian only in 1998 but it soon became the foundation text for media and journalism theory in Russia (Vartanova 2009, pp.121, 125). As Vartanova (2009, p.126) writes, the book became very popular because it:

> addressed the most up-to-date issues in Russian political life of that time, i.e., a freedom of speech concept based on ideals of the 'free' market, a complete opposite of the previous Soviet theory that viewed the media as pure instruments of politics and ideology.

This is an important aspect that many critical media scholars have missed. *Four Theories* potentially provided inspiration by outlining the different options available when a system collapses.

6.4 Conclusion

One of the distinctive features of *Four Theories* is that its authors were all working at the same time at the University of Illinois. When it comes to the set of criteria set out in Chapter 1 to evaluate comparative communications (funding, the composition of research groups, theory, methodology and materials), *Four Theories* is a curious mixture. It introduces new concepts and uses empirical materials to support its arguments. At the same time, there is no explicit methodology and the materials used to support its analysis vary chapter by chapter. It was written by individual academics, but at the same time it is not an edited book but one where all three authors were responsible for their own chapters with almost no interaction with each other, and it paved the way for many edited books in international communication. The institution provided them with an environment where they could develop their ideas, but at the same time expected at least Schramm, as director, to also bring in money. Schramm brought in much-needed revenue from his government contracts, amounting to $225,000 annually for the newly founded Institute of Communication Research. His own salary at UIUC was a rather modest $10,000.[48] Thus, most of the work done by Schramm was policy science that also funded other projects such as *Four Theories*.

When carrying out my archival research on the complex situation in which the book was written, it became evident that it was a combination of the diverse interests of its authors and of their aims. This chapter shows that, although *Four Theories* was born almost accidentally and written casually, it brought together two different academic traditions: humanistic journalism research and emerging social-science-influenced comparative research. While domestically oriented journalism research had been dominant, international communication was about to be born out of the traditions of wartime propaganda studies and Cold War propaganda studies. The book reflects the struggles between these different traditions with its different chapters, which are not consistent in their approaches but together make a powerful argument about the need to do comparative research beyond one's own country even if this is with the clear bias of one's own country. *Four Theories* also shows the limitations of these authors, with each of them concentrating on his own chapters rather than contributing to an overall theoretical framework.

The book also shows the struggle between different societal strategies. Peterson's social theory is closely connected to the Hutchins Committee's report, with its cautious recommendations that communication should not be left solely to the free markets, outside any regulatory control, since it has a social, societal function. Unlike Cooper, who was fiercely anti-government, the committee and Peterson took a different view, even if a mild one. *Four Theories* also fought another ideological battle in Schramm's chapter on communist press theories. Here the author aligned with the government's hard line in the battle against communism. It would have been very difficult not to do so, considering the circumstances both at the University of Illinois and outside it. When the changes took place in the international and domestic political climate, academics who had participated in international networks came under the suspicion of the US government. In order to rescue themselves, they may have felt that they needed to show their loyalty to their domestic government and funders, especially in relation to communism. We are also talking about a divided generation when it comes to their academic orientations. Despite the fact that they were all academics and worked at the same institution, the three authors were very different in their research interests. Schramm was 'brought' to Illinois by Stoddard, a member of the forefront generation who like many others came under suspicion from McCarthyism because of his alleged liberalism.

Four Theories is also about winners and losers, Insiders and Outsiders. Siebert and perhaps Peterson represented 'old' journalism research, while Schramm brought in the 'new', 'modern' communication research with its international networks. Schramm clearly felt that he was on the winning side when he jubilantly wrote in 1957 about the transformation in journalism research:

> From almost wholly non-quantitative research, to a fairly even balance between quantitative and non-quantitative; from an almost exclusive preoccupation with the methods and viewpoints of the humanities, to a concern with the methods and problems of the behavioral sciences as well; from a view of the printed media as shadows of the great personalities, to a view of them as part of the social process; and from a local or national to a world-wide focus. (Schramm 1957b, p.91)

Even if *Four Theories* did not completely break away from the old tradition and did not use quantitative methods, it presents a clear attempt to go beyond research on the media only in the US and to begin comparative research. All its authors were educated in the humanities tradition, but it was Schramm who brought in his wartime experience and sometimes dubious government connections in order to fund the newly founded Institute of Communication Research. The publication of *Four Theories* can be seen as a crossroads where journalism studies, with its emphasis on history and philosophies, meets the social sciences, with their new concept of a system and international policy orientation. In this generational conflict, journalism history became a loser, an Outsider, that gradually lost its position in communication studies as the dominant subfield and gave way to modern communication studies.

The book's enduring success remains a conundrum. It caught the dominant ideology of the time, the battle against communism, but at the same time it also presented a cautious utopia, at least in the US, with the social responsibility theory of the press suggesting that the media should have some responsibility for their actions. *Four Theories* was a combination of the past (authoritarian and libertarian theories), the present (communist theory) and a possible future (social responsibility theory). When the book's critics called it a Cold War relic they missed the fact that it was actually an example of the ideological battle of the period and that its authors were caught in this battle. The critics of the book reviewed it from the perspective of their own period, when they could see what the authors of *Four Theories* could not: the power of ideology in the period they lived through. Only the generations who came after them could see the biases of *Four Theories*, which were taken as 'natural' by its authors. This shows how powerful ideologies are, how difficult it is to criticise them when they are dominant, and how new ideas take a long time to emerge.

At the same time, the success of *Four Theories* shows how influential its authors' generation was and how little progress has been made since the book was published. Many of its key ideas, for example the concept of a press (media) system as a naturalised starting point in international communication, have not disappeared but become even stronger as dominant concepts that cannot be criticised. Philosophies may have changed into political economies, but despite its critics the influence of *Four Theories* carries on. One of the ironies is that the book has become so powerful in former and present communist countries, where its systemic approach appeals to those who have collective or personal memories from the communist era. Many of the critics who criticised the ideology of *Four Theories* were no less ideological but represented a different ideology and/or utopia. They were not less utopian either, but believed in a different utopia, that of liberation. Many of them belonged to another generation, that of 1968, and to the generations that followed it. This again shows how powerful ideologies and utopias are and how they even when they are transformed live through generational conflicts. As Merrill (2002, p.133) once wrote, 'it seems that this formidable little book will never die. It shows no signs of even fading away'.

Notes

[1] Stoddard, G.D. Remarks on a series of controversies involving the University of Illinois. Press release for release on 3 August 1953. George D. Stoddard Papers, 1915–2001, Record Series 2/10/20, Box 16, University of Illinois Archives.

[2] Stoddard, G.D. Remarks on a series of controversies involving the University of Illinois. Press release for release on 3 August 1953. George W. Stoddard Papers, 1915–2001, Record Series 2/10/20, Box 16, University of Illinois Archives.

[3] G.D. Stoddard to E. Hoover on 11 August 1948. Federal Bureau of Investigation (FBI): Dallas Walker Smythe File.

[4] Remarks on a series of controversies involving the University of Illinois. Press release for release on 3 August 1953. George W. Stoddard Papers, 1915–2001, Record Series 2/10/20, Box 16, University of Illinois Archives.

[5] Siebert, F.S. Memoirs, manuscript on 13 March 1979. Frederick S. Siebert Papers, 1932–1948, 1979, Record Series 13/1/21, Box 1, University of Illinois Archives.

[6] T.B. Peterson to S.H. Chaffee on 23 September 1988. Theodore B. Peterson Papers, 1933–2001, Record Series 13/1/22, Box 20, University of Illinois Archives.

[7] W. Schramm to President Morey, no date. Annual Reports, Office of the University President, 1954–1955, Record series 2/11/3, Box 184. University of Illinois Archives.

[8] Appointment of Dr Schramm. Board meeting on 24 April 1947. Journalism and Communications, Institute of Communications Research Subject File, 1947–1953, Record Series 13/5/1, Box 3, University of Illinois Archives.

9   Appointment of Wilbur Schramm. Press release of 24 April 1947. Journalism and Communications, Institute of Communications Research Subject File, 1947–1953, Record Series 13/5/1, Box 3, University of Illinois Archives. According to an FBI report from 1962 (Federal Bureau of Investigation (FBI): Wilbur Lang Schramm File) his various consultancies included: the US Information Agency, Washington, DC; the Department of Defense, Washington, DC; and the Navy Department, Air Force and State Department, and Agency for International Development.

10   Appointment of Dr W. Schramm. Board Meeting on 24, April 1947. Journalism and Communications, Institute of Communications Research Subject File, 1947–1953, Record Series 13/5/1, Box 3, University of Illinois Archives.

11   W. Schramm to H. Kellerman on 6 September 1951. Journalism and Communications, Institute of Communications Research Subject File, 1947–1953, Record Series 13/5/1, Box 7, University of Illinois Archives.

12   W. Schramm to H. Kellerman on 6 September 1951. Journalism and Communications, Institute of Communications Research Subject File, 1947–1953, Record Series 13/5/1, Box 7, University of Illinois Archives.

13   'Wilbur Schramm to Leave U.I on 4 April 1955'. *Stanford Post*. President's Office, Staff Appointments File, 1905–2000, Record Series 2/5/15, Box 183, University of Illinois Archives.

14   R.A. McClure to G.D. Stoddard, on 16 May 1952. Journalism and Communications, Institute of Communications Research Subject File, 1947–1953, Record Series 13/5/1, Box 8, University of Illinois Archives.

15   President L. Morey to W. Schramm on 15 April 1955. Annual Reports, 1954–1955, Record Series 2/11/3, Box 3, University of Illinois Archives; Schramm was reviewed by FBI on several occasions. FOIPA [Freedom of Information/Privacy Acts] Request No. 1592121-000. Federal Bureau of Investigation (FBI): Wilbur Lang Schramm File.

16   From C.E. Osgood to staff of the Institute of Communications Research on 30 September 1952. Journalism and Communications, Institute of Communications Research Subject File, 1947–1953, Record Series 13/5/1, Box 8, University of Illinois Archives.

17   The Soviet Concept of 'Psychological Warfare.' Four Theories of a working paper by W. Schramm, no date. Annual Reports, 1954–1955, Record Series 2/11/3, Box 3, University of Illinois Archives.

18   Theory of Communications course outline, Instructor Schramm, no date. Journalism and Communications, Institute of Communications Research Subject File, 1947–1953, Record Series 13/5/1, Box 6, University of Illinois Archives.

19 Siebert, F.S. A Belated Diary, 1979. Frederick S. Siebert Papers, 1932–1948, 1979, Record Series 13/1/21, Box 1, University of Illinois Archives.

20 Siebert, F.S. A Belated Diary, 1979. Frederick S. Siebert Papers, 1932–1948, 1979, Record Series 13/1/21, Box 1, University of Illinois Archives.

21 Hudson, R.V. Interview with Fredrick Seaton Siebert, 1970. Association for Education in Journalism and Mass Communication Papers (A.E.J.). Michigan State University, School of Journalism (MCHC70-65). Wisconsin Historical Society.

22 Hudson, R.V. Interview with Fredrick Seaton Siebert, 1970. Association for Education in Journalism and Mass Communication Papers (A.E.J.). Michigan State University, School of Journalism (MCHC70-65). Wisconsin Historical Society.

23 Siebert, F.S. A Belated Diary, 1979. Frederick S. Siebert Papers, 1932–1948, 1979, Record Series 13/1/21, Box 1, University of Illinois Archive.

24 T.B. Peterson to S.H. Chaffee on 23 September 1988. Theodore B. Peterson Papers, 1933–2001, Record Series, 13/1/22, Box 20, University of Illinois Archives.

25 T.B. Peterson to S.H. Chaffee on 23 September 1988. Theodore B. Peterson Papers, 1933–2001, Record Series 13/1/22, Box 20, University of Illinois Archives.

26 Hudson, R.V. Interview with Fredrick Seaton Siebert, 1970. Association for Education in Journalism and Mass Communication Papers (A.E.J.). Michigan State University, School of Journalism, MCHC70-65. Wisconsin Historical Society.

27 T.B. Peterson to S.H. Chaffee on 23 September 1988. Theodore B. Peterson Papers, 1933–2001, Record Series 13/1/22, Box 20, University of Illinois Archives.

28 T.B. Peterson to S.H. Chaffee on 23 September 1988. Theodore B. Peterson Papers, 1933–2001, Record Series 13/1/22, Box 20, University of Illinois Archives.

29 T.B. Peterson to S.H. Chaffee on 23 September 1988. Theodore B. Peterson Papers, 1933–2001, Record Series 13/1/22, Box 20, University of Illinois Archives.

30 Siebert, F.S. A Belated Diary, 1979. Frederick S. Siebert Papers, 1932–1948, Record Series 13/1/21, Box 1, University of Illinois Archive.

31 From F. Terrou to H.D. Lasswell on 28 July 1959. Harold Dwight Lasswell Papers. Bibliographical/Memorabllia Files 1043, Series V, Box 213, File 17. Manuscripts and Archives, Yale University Library.

32 T.B. Peterson to S.H. Chaffee on 23 September 1988. Theodore B. Peterson Papers, 1933–2001, Record Series 13/1/22, Box 20, University of Illinois Archives.

33 T.B. Peterson, untitled and undated memo. Theodore B. Peterson Papers, 1933–2001, Record Series 13/1/22, Box 20, University of Illinois Archives.

34 T.B. Peterson, untitled and undated memo. Theodore B. Peterson Papers, 1933–2001, Record Series 13/1/22, Box 20, University of Illinois Archives.

35 T.B. Peterson, untitled and undated memo. Theodore B. Peterson Papers, 1933–2001, Record Series 13/1/22, Box 20, University of Illinois Archives.

36 T.B. Peterson at the Memorial service to F. Seaton on 28 April 1982. Theodore B. Peterson Papers, 1933–2001, Record Series 13/1/22, Box 4, University of Illinois Archives.

37 These questions (and probably others) should be answerable from each of our chapters, undated and unsigned memo. Theodore B. Peterson Papers, 1933–2001, Record Series 13/1/22, Box 4, University of Illinois Archives.

38 T.B. Peterson, untitled and undated memo. Theodore B. Peterson Papers, 1933–2001, Record Series 13/1/22, Box 20, University of Illinois Archives.

39 T.B. Peterson to S.H. Chaffee on 23 September 1988. Theodore B. Peterson Papers, 1933–2001, Record Series 13/1/22, Box 20, University of Illinois Archives.

40 T.B. Peterson, untitled and undated memo. Theodore B. Peterson Papers, 1933–2001, Record Series 13/1/22, Box 20, University of Illinois Archives.

41 T.B. Peterson, untitled and undated memo. Theodore B. Peterson Papers, 1933–2001, Record Series 13/1/22, Box 20, University of Illinois Archives.

42 T.B. Peterson at F. Seaton's Memorial Service on 28 April 1982. Theodore B. Peterson Papers, 1933–2001, Record Series 13/1/22, Box 4, University of Illinois Archives.

43 Hudson, R.V. Interview with Fredrick Seaton Siebert, 1970. Association for Education in Journalism and Mass Communication Papers (A.E.J.). Michigan State University, School of Journalism (MCHC70-65). Wisconsin Historical Society.

44 Peterson, T.B. Social Responsibility Theory Thirty Years after the Hutchins Commission. Essays in honour of Jay W. Jensen and Theodore

B. Peterson. Editors James W. Carey and Clifford G. Christians. Manuscript, 1979. Theodore B. Peterson Papers, 1933–2001, Record Series 13/1/22, Box 21, University of Illinois Archives.

45 Peterson, T.B. Social Responsibility Theory Thirty Years after the Hutchins Commission. Essays in honour of Jay W. Jensen and Theodore B. Peterson. Editors James W. Carey and Clifford G. Christians. Manuscript, 1979. Theodore B. Peterson Papers, 1933–2001, Record Series 13/1/22, Box 21, University of Illinois Archives.

46 Peterson, T.B. Social Responsibility Theory Thirty Years after the Hutchins Commission. Essays in honour of Jay W. Jensen and Theodore B. Peterson. Editors James W. Carey and Clifford G. Christians. Manuscript, 1979. Theodore B. Peterson Papers, 1933–2001, Record Series 13/1/22, Box 21, University of Illinois Archives.

47 See, for example, Altschull 1995; Blumler 1981; Blumler and Gurevitch 1995; Christians et al. 2009; Curran 2011; Guback 1995; Gunaratne 2005; Hachten and Hachten 1992; Hallin and Mancini 2004, 2012; Hanitzsch 2008; Hardt 1988; Jones and Pusey 2010; Lowenstein and Merrill 1990; Martin and Chaudhary 1983; McIntyre 1987; McKenzie 2006; McQuail 1994; Meng and Rantanen 2015; Merrill 1974; 2002; Merrill and Lowenstein 1979; Mundt 1991; Nerone 1995, 2004; Picard 1985; Sparks and Reading 1998; Thomass 2007; Toepfl 2016; Rantanen 2017; Vaca-Baqueiro 2017.

48 G.D. Stoddard to W. Schramm on 1 September 1947. Journalism and Communications, Institute of Communications Research Subject File, 1947–1953, Record Series 13/5/1, Box 4, University of Illinois Archives.

References

Almond, Gabriel A. (1956) 'Comparative Political Systems', *The Journal of Politics*, vol. 18, no. 3, pp.391–409. https://doi.org/10.2307/2127255

Almond, Gabriel A. and Powell, G. Bingham (1966) *Comparative Politics: A Developmental Approach*, USA: Little, Brown and Company.

Altschull, Herbert J. (1995) *Agents of Power: The Media and Public Policy*, USA: Longman.

Associated Press v. United States (1945) 326 U.S. 1, 65 S. Ct 1416 (145). USA: U.S. Supreme Court.

Berelson, Bernard (1959) 'The State of Communication Research', *Public Opinion Quarterly*, vol. 23, no. 1, pp.1–17. https://doi.org/10.1086/266840

Blanchard, Margaret A. (1977) 'The Hutchins Commission, the Press and the Responsibility Concept', *Journalism Monographs*, vol. 49, no. May, pp.1–59. http://www.aejmc.org/home/wp-content/uploads/2012/09/Margaret-A.-Blanchard.The-Hutchins-Commission.May-1977.pdf

238   DEAD MEN'S PROPAGANDA

Blanchard, Margaret A. (1987) 'The Associated Press Antitrust Suit: A Philosophical Clash over Ownership of First Amendment Rights', *The Business History Review*, vol. 61, no. 1, pp.43–85. https://doi.org/10.2307/3115774

Blumler, Jay G. (1981) 'Mass Communication Research in Europe: Some Origins and Prospects', in Burgoon, Judee K. (ed.) *Communication Yearbook 5*, USA: Transaction Books, pp.145–56.

Blumler, Jay G. and Gurevitch, Michael G. (1995) 'Towards a Comparative Framework for Political Communication Research', in Chaffee, Steven H. (ed.) *The Crisis of Public Communication*, UK: Sage, pp.165–93.

Carey, James W. (1989) *Communication as Culture: Essays on Media and Society*, USA: Unwin Hyman.

Cartier, Jacqueline M. (1988) *Wilbur Schramm and the Beginnings of American Communication Theory: A History of Ideas*. PhD thesis, USA: University of Iowa.

Chaffee, Steven H. (1974) 'The Pathways of Proteus', in Westley, Bruce H. (ed.) *Contributions of Wilbur Schramm to Mass Communication Research. Journalism Monograph, No.36*, USA: Association for Education in Journalism, pp.1–8. https://files.eric.ed.gov/fulltext/ED099879.pdf

Chaffee, Steven H. and Rogers, Everett M. (1997) 'Institutionalization of Advanced Communication Study in American Universities', in Schramm, Wilbur *The Beginnings of Communication Study in America: A Personal Memoir*, USA: Sage, pp.155–80.

Christians, Clifford G.; Glasser, Theodore L.; McQuail, Denis; Nordenstreng, Kaarle; and White, Robert A. (2009) *Normative Theories of the Media: Journalism in Democratic Societies*, USA: University of Illinois Press.

Commission on Freedom of the Press (1947) *A Free and Responsible Press. A General Report on Mass Communication: Newspapers, Radio, Motion Pictures, Magazines, and Books*, USA: University of Chicago Press.

Cross, Harold and American Society of Newspaper Editors (1953) *The people's right to know; legal access to public records and proceedings*, USA: Columbia University Press.

Curran, James (2011) *Media and Democracy*, UK: Routledge.

Delia, Jesse G. (1987) 'Communication Research: A History', in Berger, Charles R. and Chaffee, Steven H. (eds) *Handbook of Communication Science*, USA: Sage, pp.20–98.

Easton, David (1953) *The Political System: An Inquiry into the State of Political Science*, USA: Alfred A. Knopf.

'Eleanor Blum Papers, 1962–1991' (no date) University of Illinois Archives. https://archon.library.illinois.edu/archives/index.php?p=collections /controlcard&id=4635

Eulau, Heinz and Zlomke, Susan (1999) 'Harold D. Lasswell's Legacy to Mainstream Political Science: A Neglected Agenda', *Annual Review of Political Science*, vol. 2, pp.75–89. https://doi.org/10.1146/annurev.polisci.2.1.75

Federal Bureau of Investigations (FBI): Dallas Walker Smythe File. https://www.muckrock.com/foi/united-states-of-america-10/fbi-dallas -walker-smythe-110668

Glander, Timothy (2000) *Origins of Mass Communications Research during the American Cold War: Educational Effects and Contemporary Implications*, UK: Routledge.

Guback, Thomas H. (1995) 'Marxism', in Nerone, John (ed.) *Last Rights: Revisiting Four Theories of the Press*, USA: University of Illinois Press, pp.125–52.

Gunaratne, Shelton A. (2005) *The Dao of the Press: A Humanocentric Theory*, USA: Hampton Press.

Hachten, William A. and Hachten, Harva (1992) *The World News Prism: Changing Media of International Communication*, USA: Iowa State University Press.

Hallin, Daniel C. and Mancini, Paolo (2004) *Comparing Media Systems: Three Models of Media and Politics*, USA: Cambridge University Press.

Hallin, Daniel C. and Mancini, Paolo (2012) *Comparing Media Systems Beyond the Western World*, USA: Cambridge University Press.

Hanitzsch, Thomas (2008) 'Comparing Media Systems Reconsidered: Recent Development and Directions for Future Research', *Journal of Global Mass Communication*, vol. 1, no. 3/4, pp.111–17.

Hardt, Hanno (1988) 'Comparative Media Research: The World According to America', *Critical Studies in Mass Communication*, vol. 5, no. 2, pp.129–46. https://doi.org/10.1080/15295038809366693

Huang, Chenju (2003) 'Transitional Media vs. Normative Theories: Schramm, Altschull, and China', *Journal of Communication*, vol. 53, no. 3, pp.444–59. https://doi.org/10.1111/j.1460-2466.2003.tb02601.x

International Press Institute (1953) *The Flow of News: A Study by the International Press Institute*, Switzerland: International Press Institute.

Jones, Paul K. and Pusey, Michael (2010) 'Political Communication and "Media System": The Australian Canary', *Media, Culture & Society*, vol. 32, no. 3, pp.451–71. https://doi.org/10.1177/016344370936117

Propaganda*, USA: University of Illinois Press.

Lowenstein, Ralph L. and Merrill, John C. (1990) *Macromedia: Mission, Message and Morality*, USA: Longman.

Markham, James W. (1956) 'Journalism School Courses in International Communications', *Journalism Quarterly*, vol. 33, no. 2, pp.201–06. https://doi.org/10.1177/107769905603300207

Marler, Charles (1990) 'Fredrick Siebert and the Legal Method', in Sloan, David Wm (ed.) *Makers of the Media Mind Journalism Educators and their Ideas*, USA: Lawrence Erlbaum, pp.187–94.

Martin, L. John and Chaudhary, Anju G. (1983) *Comparative Mass Media Systems*, USA: Longman.

McIntyre, Jerilyn S. (1987) 'Repositioning a Landmark: The Hutchins Commission and Freedom of the Press', *Critical Studies in Media Communication*, vol. 4, no. 2, pp.136–60. https://doi.org/10.1080/15295038709360122

McKenzie, Robert (2006) *Comparing Media from around the World*, USA: Pearson.

McQuail, Denis (1994) *Mass Communication Theory: An Introduction*, UK: Sage.

Meng, Bingchun and Rantanen, Terhi (2015) 'A Change of Lens: A Call to Compare the Media in China and Russia', *Critical Studies in Media Communication*, vol. 32, no. 1, pp.1–15. https://doi.org/10.1080/15295036.2014.997831

Merrill, John C. (1974) *The Imperative of Freedom: A Philosophy of Journalistic Autonomy*, USA: Hastings House.

Merrill, John C. (2002) 'The Four Theories of the Press Four and a Half Decades Later: A Retrospective', *Journalism Studies*, vol. 3, no. 1, pp.133–36. https://doi.org/10.1080/14616700120107374

Merrill, John C. and Lowenstein, Ralph L. (1979) *Media, Messages, and Men: New Perspectives in Communication*, USA: Longman.

Mundt, Whitney R. (1991) 'Global Media Philosophies', in Merrill, John C. (ed.) *Global Journalism: Survey of International Communication*, USA: Longman, pp.11–27.

Nerone, John (1995) *Last Rights: Revisiting Four Theories of the Press*, USA: University of Illinois Press.

Nerone, John (2004) 'Four Theories of the Press in Hindsight: Reflections on a Popular Model', in Semat, Mehdi (ed.) *New Fronters in International Communication Theory*, USA: Rowman and Littlefield, pp.21–32.

Parsons, Talcott (1951) *The Social System*, UK: Routledge and Kegan Paul.

Peterson, Ted (1945) 'British Crime Pamphleteers: Forgotten Journalists'. *Journalism & Mass Communication Quarterly*, vol. 22, no. 4, pp.305–16. https://doi.org/10.1177/107769904502200401

Peterson, Ted (1948) 'The Fight of William Hone for British Press Freedom', *Journalism Quarterly*, vol. 22, no. 2, pp.132–38. https://journals.sagepub.com/doi/10.1177/107769904802500203

Picard, Robert (1985) *The Press and the Decline of Democracy: The Democratic Socialist Response in Public Policy*, UK: Greenwood Press.

Pickard, Victor (2014) *America's Battle for Media Democracy: The Triumph of Corporate Libertarianism and the Future of Media Reform*, USA: Cambridge University Press.

Pooley, Jefferson (2017) 'Wilbur Schramm and the "Four Founders" History of U.S. Communication Research', *Коммуникации. Медиа. Дизайн*, vol. 2, no. 4, pp.5–16. http://dx.doi.org/10.17613/M6Q859

Rantanen, Terhi (2017) 'A "Crisscrossing" Historical Analysis of *Four Theories of the Press*'. *International Journal of Communication*, vol. 11. https://joc.org/index.php/ijoc/article/view/6253

'The Rise and Fall of President George D. Stoddard' (2022) Illinois Library. https://guides.library.illinois.edu/c.php?g=348250&p=2350903

Rogers, Everett (1994) *A History of Communication Study: A Biographical Approach*, USA: Free Press.

Rowland, Allison L. and Simonson, Peter (2013) 'The Founding Mothers of Communication Research: Towards History of a Gendered Assemblage', *Critical Studies in Mass Communication*, vol. 31, no. 1, pp.3–26. https://doi.org/10.1080/15295036.2013.849355

Schramm, Wilbur (1948) *Communications in Modern Society: Fifteen Studies of the Mass Media Prepared for the University of Illinois Institute of Communications Research*, USA: University of Illinois Press.

Schramm, Wilbur (1949) *Mass Communications: A Book of Readings Selected and Edited for the Institute of Communications Research in the University of Illinois*, USA: University of Illinois Press.

Schramm, Wilbur (1954) *The Process and Effects of Mass Communication*, USA: University of Illinois Press.

Schramm, Wilbur (1957a) *Responsibility in Mass Communication*, USA: Harper & Brothers.

Schramm, Wilbur (1957b) 'Twenty Years of Journalism Research', *Public Opinion Quarterly*, vol. 21, no. 1, pp.91–107. https://doi.org/10.1086/266689

Schramm, Wilbur (1963) 'Communication Research in the United States', in Schramm, Wilbur (ed.) *The Science of Human Communication*, USA: Basic Books, pp.1–16.

Schramm, Wilbur; Chaffee, Steven H.; and Rogers, Everett M. (1997) *The Beginnings of Communication Study in America: A Personal Memoir*, USA: Sage.

Schramm, Wilbur and Riley, John W. (1951a) 'Communication in the Sovietized State, as Demonstrated in Korea', *American Sociological Review*, vol. 16, no. 6, pp.757–66. https://doi.org/10.2307/2087502

Schramm, Wilbur and Riley, John W. (1951b) *The Reds Take a City: The Communist Occupation of Seoul, with Eye-Witness Accounts*, USA: Rutgers University Press.

Schwarzlose, Richard A. (1978) 'A Conversation with Fredrick S. Siebert', *Journalism History*, vol. 5, no. 4, pp.106–23. https://doi.org/10.1080/0094679.1978.12066894

Siebert, Fred S. (1948) 'Communications and Government', in Schramm, Wilbur (ed.) *Mass Communications* (2nd ed.), USA: University of Illinois Press, pp.219–26.

Siebert, Fred S. (1952) *Freedom of the Press in England, 1476–1776: The Rise and Decline of Government Control*, USA: University of Illinois Press.

Siebert, Fred S. (1956) *The Mass Media in a Free Society*, USA: New York University School of Commerce Accounts and Finance Department of Journalism.

Siebert, Fred S.; Peterson, Theodore; and Schramm, Wilbur (1956) *Four Theories of the Press: The Authoritarian, Libertarian, Social Responsibility, and Soviet Communist Concepts of What the Press Should Be and Do*, USA: University of Illinois Press.

Solberg, Winton U. and Tomilson, Robert W. (1997) 'Academic McCarthyism and Keynesian Economics: The Bowen Controversy at the University of Illinois', *History of Political Economy*, vol. 29, no. 1, pp.55–81. https://doi.org/10.1215/00182702-29-1-55

Sparks, Colin and Reading, Anna (1998) *Communism, Capitalism, and the Mass Media*, UK: Sage.

Sproule, J. Michael (2008) '"Communication": From Concept to Field to Discipline', in Park, David W. and Pooley, Jefferson (eds) *The History of Media and Communication Research. Contested Memories*, USA: Peter Lang, pp.143–62.

Stoddard, George W. (1981) *The Pursuit of Education: An Autobiography*, USA: Vantage Press.

'Summary: The Macy Conferences' (no date) *American Society for Cybernetics.* http://www.asc-cybernetics.org/foundations/history/MacySummary.htm

Tankard, James W. (1988) 'Wilbur Schramm: Definer of a Field', *The Journalism Educator*, vol. 43, no. 3, pp.11–16. https://doi.org/10.1177/107769588804300303

Thomass, Barbara (2007) 'Comparing Media Systems: The Development of Analytical Tools and Theoretical Concepts Over the Last 50 years'. Paper presented at the IAMCR Conference, France: Paris.

Toepfl, Florian (2016) 'Beyond the Four Theories: Toward a Discourse Approach to the Comparative Study of Media and Politics', *International Journal of Communication*, vol. 10, pp.1530–47. https://ijoc.org/index.php/ijoc/article/view/4669

Vaca-Baqueiro, Maira T. (2017) *Four Theories of the Press: 60 Years and Counting*, USA: Routledge.

Vartanova, Elena (2009) *Mass Media Theory: Current Issues*, Russia: MediaMir.

Wiener, Norbert (1948) *Cybernetics: or control and communication in the animal and the machine.* France: Hermann & Co.

7. Conclusion: can the circle be broken?

Those who do not believe in the ideology of the United States, shall not be allowed to stay in the United States.

Attorney General Tom Clark, addressing the Cathedral Club of Brooklyn, 15 January 1948 (Caute 1978, p.15)

My five empirical chapters have explored the work of the individual researchers and men of practice from the forefront generation. Many of the actors discussed in this book were Outsiders because of their race, nationality, class, religion or location, or even simply because of their academic training and background. Most of them worked on policy science and many, but not all, were academics. One of my key tasks was to explore their personal journeys, both physical and spiritual, through the dominant structures of that period and how they themselves changed during those journeys.

My argument throughout the book is that in order to understand how ideologies and utopias work we need to study the life histories of individuals, which are often neglected when only macro-level phenomena are studied. As Mannheim (1993, p.71) reminds us, 'historical life is made of the lives of human beings (a commonplace, which nevertheless is routinely forgotten by historians)' – and I would add by social scientists. According to Mannheim,

> what really counts in history is not the transformation of individuals but that of associated human beings bound together by specific and determinate group relationships and conflicts in concrete social situations (in general, such groups do not coincide with nations, and even less with humanity as a whole). (1932/1993, p.71)

That is why this book focuses not only on individuals but also on research groups whose members were of different nationalities. I have called them the forefront generation.

How to cite this book chapter:

Rantanen, Terhi (2024) *Dead Men's Propaganda: Ideology and Utopia in Comparative Communications Studies*, London: LSE Press, pp. 245–276.
https://doi.org/10.31389/lsepress.wmf.g. License: CC BY-NC 4.0

The backgrounds of each of these actors were different, and they did not necessarily know one another personally. However, they all encountered, and even contributed to, the structures promoting an overall ideology of the time, that of US nationalism and patriotism. Despite the fact that they were motivated by utopias of their own – political or personal, conservative or radical – they ended by supporting, at least superficially, the same ideologies. It was, for example, a long journey from being an intellectual in Budapest to becoming a war or Cold War specialist in Santa Monica working for RAND Corporation, or from being a newspaper boy in Columbia, Indiana, to becoming general manager in New York of the Associated Press, the country's biggest news agency. Their world was turned upside down and during this process their thinking changed radically. They were all seeking 'the truth' and were often convinced that their truth was the right one.

Having studied personal histories of individuals and their work, it is time to return to Mannheim's key concepts of ideology and utopia, and to the generation defined at the beginning of this book, and to ask how useful these notions are for understanding the origins of comparative communications. I return here also to Merton's concepts of Insider and Outsider, before using his four criteria to analyse the origins of comparative communications and its early development.

This chapter mirrors the structure of my first chapter, drawing again on the concepts of ideology and utopia, the concept of a generation, Merton's concepts of Insiders and Outsiders, and finally his criteria for the evaluation of research.

7.1 Ideology and utopia

Mannheim's distinction between ideologies and utopias is important, but also troubling. Breiner (2013, p.7) argues that the difference between utopias and ideologies is that only utopias 'seek to radically break with historical and social realities to achieve forms of society that historical and social tendencies have not yet made possible', and that only ideologies 'inhibit our understanding of the social and political possibilities within the dynamic trends that constitute historical "reality"'. I am not convinced that this is the case. Having researched the origins of comparative communications in the US, I argue that both ideologies and utopias sometimes prevent researchers from seeing 'reality'. Academics and men of practice have often been blinded by their own utopias and have not engaged with ideologies that oppose these. Speier, among others, was very critical of liberals in Weimar whose anti-propaganda moralism represented a 'fallacy of misplaced righteousness' (Bessner 2018, p.86), but he was unable to accept the criticism by the 1960s generation of his own political views (see Chapter 5). The deep scars left by having been wrong about politics in Weimar and having failed to prevent the rise of Nazism never completely healed, affecting the émigré scholars discussed in this book for the rest of their lives and making them cling to the dominant US ideology of the time. That same ideology was shared by all the members of the forefront generation studied in this book, whatever their former ideologies and/or utopias.

The 1960s generation that came after the forefront generation saw their predecessors as conservative, and themselves as radical (Gitlin 1978, p.230; Malherek 2022) in following a radical utopia of 'no war'. It is too easy to think that ideologies are always 'conservative' and utopias are always 'radical'. It is also tempting to argue that while ideologies are always based on false consciousness utopias are not and are thus almost impossible to change. According to Breiner, a change can come about in three ways.

> First, a set of ethical norms may no longer correspond to the imperatives of a new social structure. Second, the human agent may be deceived or deceive him/herself regarding both self and others either through reifying or idealizing certain human characteristics at the expense of others. And lastly, an agent's everyday orientation to the world fails to comprehend changes in social structure. (Breiner 2013, p.7)

In my introduction to this book, I raised four proposals from Mannheim that I then sought to explore while studying the role of ideologies and utopias in research on the forefront generation and its members. These were: (1) a loosening of the relationship between class and ideology, especially in relation to intellectuals; (2) a recognition that ideology is sometimes hidden, especially from those living through it; (3) a widening of the definition of ideology beyond traditional politics; and (4) an argument that ideologies and utopias are so interwoven that one cannot exist without the other.

(1) The relationship between class and ideology

One of the most famous and most often criticised of Mannheim's concepts is that of free-floating intellectuals (*freischwebende Intelligenz*). We need to ask how free-floating the men I have studied in this book really were. They seemed to have floated between utopias and ideologies such as internationalism and nationalism synchronously, almost like travelling waves. This is why I find it crucial to acknowledge the importance not only of the concepts of ideology and utopia but also of their interrelationship and changing natures. Consideration of the empirical chapters included in this book underlines how theoretically close these concepts are. They show how the motivation of both academics and men of action shifted from utopias to ideologies, and sometimes back. When we compare, for example, the young Lasswell with the older Lasswell, we can see the shift from a young man influenced by the League of Nations to an old man who had not only left behind his idealistic view of international understanding but even changed his own research interests to focus on law and order.

But we also see Cooper's utopia becoming an ideology, which in turn gave birth, in the 1960s and 1970s, to a new utopia. I chose him as an example of a non-academic, a man of action, in order to see why he was influenced by those same ideologies and utopias, as well as to study his role in promoting these. When we compare Lasswell with Cooper, we can see similarities in their lives. They were born 22 years apart but the careers of both were marked by the two world wars. Both were disillusioned by the outcome of World War I, and both ended by aligning themselves with the Cold War ideologies that gave a leading role to the US in promoting worldwide freedom after World War II. At the same time, they were very different in terms of their education and professional careers. Both were caught up with the ideologies and utopias of the time, although they disagreed about the role of government in relation to news. When Cooper retired, his writings no longer served his organisation but his book became an inspiration to future generations outside the US, while Lasswell went on publishing for 30 more years, and *Four Theories*, the subject of Chapter 6, still lives on. This shows how long-lasting ideologies and utopias are.

Does my empirical research, then, support the notion of a loosening of the relationship between class and ideology, especially in relation to intellectuals? All the men I studied ended up supporting the same ideologies, having partly shared different utopias and despite their different backgrounds. Defined as intellectuals or elites, and taking into account that they included men of practice, they become surprisingly uniform in their ideology. At the same time, one has to remember that academics, at least, were a divided generation, and in this book I have concentrated on some of those who were not included as members of the Frankfurt School, though some, such as Mannheim, held office in the Frankfurt Institut für Sozialforschung. The men I studied in this book were policy scientists whose close relationship to the government was justified by their research serving wider social goals, not only academic purposes. Policy science brought researchers closer to other elites and it became harder for them to conduct independent critical research.

(2) Recognising that ideology is sometimes hidden

By raising this point, I argue that ideologies are naturalised to the extent that they do not require further thinking. This may be an oversimplified statement, especially in relation to the academics featured in this book, many of whom were familiar with Mannheim's work and his insistence on the social sitedness of knowledge and intellectual labour. They were very aware of the dominant *political* ideology of their time, often bending to it because they were constantly reminded of it. There was no uncertainty about what was expected from them during World War II and in the late 1940s and early 1950s, especially when they worked on policy science. However, Cooper's campaign against Reuters, and especially its timing, was not a textbook example of how ideologies work; on the contrary, he was going against the tide, and against the UK, a military ally of the US.

I include émigré scholars in order to see whether their careers had been affected by the same ideologies. We have Leites, an émigré originally from Russia, who became a critical researcher on Soviet Communism. We also have Kecskemeti, an émigré originally from Hungary, who shared Leites' interest in studying communism. Both were marked by their escape from fascism and from their former home countries taken over by communism. Both were doubly displaced by the two European dictatorships of Soviet Communism and Nazism. They chose was to support US government ideology during and after World War II. One could question whether they had any other choice, but during the war and the 'Silent Decade' (Horowitz 1996, p.357) of McCarthyism choices were very few. RAND Corporation may have been a safe place for émigré scholars who did not oppose US military ideology. One of the great ironies is that many of RAND Corporation researchers and consultants, notably Lasswell, Kecskemeti, Leites and Speier (who had been Mannheim's PhD student at Heidelberg), shared an admiration for Mannheim and used his ideas when working with the military (Bessner 2018, p.227). Kecskemeti edited and translated Mannheim's writings while working at RAND Corporation (Kecskemeti 1952/1997; Mannheim 1953). This is yet another example of how what was largely seen as a bastion of US military ideology can also be seen as a haven for émigrés from Europe.

Even the 'Illinois Three' of Siebert, Peterson and Schramm could not avoid, during that decade, the influence of McCarthyism. They encountered the change from a short-lived government ideology of internationalism to government suspicion of internationalism. Schramm was brought to the University of Illinois by its president, Stoddard, whose role in UNESCO opened up new opportunities for collaborative international research. When the Cold War started this was no longer supported by the university's governing body, which found a reason to fire him (Stoddard 1981). The change took place within a short period, between 1947 and 1956, and *Four Theories* reflects this change in its critical, if not hostile, view of the Soviet Communist press theory. Schramm was also rumoured to have worked for the CIA, although evidence remains circumstantial (Glander 1996, p.156). However, at the same time, the book's chapter on the social theory of the press marks a departure from Cooper's anti-government interference campaign and follows the ideas of the Hutchins Committee on Freedom of the Press. Again, it is possible to see the interplay between ideology and utopia in *Four Theories*.

Ideologies also became naturalised for many if not all of these men, who began to think that everybody supported the same ideologies as they did. The shock expressed by Kecskemeti and Speier, in their correspondence, at what they saw as the disloyalty of the 1960s and 1970s generations towards the US showed how deeply they were embedded in their own ideologies.[1] Writers of the 1960s and 1970s generations blamed them not only for standing for US militarism but also for accepting its capitalist and consumerist values. As Gitlin (1978, p.245) writes, referring to Lazarsfeld's work,

By ignoring the systemic and institutionalized nature of these processes, and by fusing its administrative, commercial, and social-democratic impulses, the mainstream of American media sociology has done its share to consolidate and legitimize the cornucopian regime of mid-century capitalism. That the dominant paradigm is now proving vulnerable to critique at many levels is a measure of the decline of capitalist legitimacy, commercial values, and the political self-confidence of the rulers.

This is yet another example of how one's own ideology becomes hidden from oneself and so taken for granted that only when confronted by the ideology of another person who belongs to a succeeding generation does one becomes aware of it. This is reinforced by the stories told by a generation itself and by following generations.

(3) Widening the definition of ideology beyond traditional politics

By widening the definition of ideology beyond the realm of traditional politics – for example, anti-communism versus communism, McCarthyism versus anti-McCarthyism – I explore issues around gender and race. Here ideology is, by comparison, hidden and naturalised. It was taken for granted that academics, researchers and company directors would all be men, while secretaries and research assistants were not. It was taken for granted that all academics were white, that Jewish émigré scholars were almost all men, and that their spouses did not need a job even if they often had equal qualifications. All academic texts used 'he' as the only pronoun and the term 'mankind' went unquestioned.

Rogers (1994, p.474) argues that 'Schramm's gender attitudes were somewhat typical of his times'. According to him, Schramm did not treat women students as equal to men. He, for example, referred to a female assistant professor as a 'pretty little thing'. He even titled his book *Men, Messages, and Media* (1974), and only reluctantly later changed it. His attitude was no different from that of Lerner, who requested '1 man of knowledge, 1 man of power, 1 man of affairs and 1 woman of indigenous qualities' for his Itinerary.[2] Sentiments of male 'camaraderie' between 'brothers in arms', albeit arising not from fighting on the front but from work on analysing propaganda, also excluded women. Not only were women not hired as researchers or company managers but they were simply not considered 'one of us'. In academia, the personal affection between those who worked together for long hours, days, weeks and years was replicated professionally in job offers, invitations to write chapters in edited books, applying for grants together, collaborating on research projects, and writing reference letters and positive book reviews, among other things. Those who worked in the Library of Congress were able to use the materials after the war and to publish books or articles in academic journals. Women simply did not have that opportunity.

CONCLUSION: CAN THE CIRCLE BE BROKEN?   251

The personal letters that I studied in the archives reveal the important role played in their private lives by the women married to the men who feature in this book. Their shared interests are reflected in letters where their names are routinely added by their spouses and best wishes sent from both, revealing that the various couples saw each privately outside work. Speier referred to the 'Santa Monica higher society' when he gossiped about Leites' new female friend in a letter to Kecskemeti.[3] But we know very little about these women and this is, of course, an issue when one seeks to analyse the structure of feeling (Williams 1977) of a period when women's independent role was largely hidden. There are so many secrets, hidden sexual and political orientations included that the stories told about this generation by themselves or others, simply do not reveal.

There was also an issue of race, which is rarely discussed in archival documents. As Bessner showed (see Chapter 4), this was clearly a factor in the selection of émigré scholars and in general. When I write about race here I only concentrate on Jewishness and leave aside all other ethnic minorities, who were even further excluded. According to interviews conducted by Simonson, for example, Merton and Lazarsfeld never discussed their Jewishness and Merton even changed his name (Peters 2006, p.9). Gitlin writes of Lazarsfeld:

> Lazarsfeld's insecurity about being Jewish in America was well grounded in the reality of academic anti-Semitism. His memoir (pp. 300–301) gives evidence of some of the social bases of his sense of marginality. It is worth noting that John Marshall of the Rockefeller Foundation, Stanton, Lynd, and Cantril were all white Anglo-Saxon Protestants: the most reliable sponsors to accumulate. (Gitlin 1978, p.250)

This highlights the extent to which Jewish migrants were expected to accommodate to their new life in the US. Lazarsfeld was mentioned as the most successful of all the émigré scholars at this. One of Lazarsfeld's fellow migrants said of him: 'He was very American – the most successful of us all' (Gitlin 1978, pp.230, 250). At the same time, according to Berelson, Lazarsfeld's fellow academics did not like him because he was 'too pushy, he was foreign, he was too bright, he was too self-confident, arrogant – sometimes to them – and too tied-in with the business and commercial world' (quoted in Rogers 1994, p.312). Lasswell (1937, p.311) presented six scenarios (in his view authentic, although they were anonymised) of émigré scholars in the US. The final option, and the most undesirable in Lasswell's thinking, was that of 'Dr. F':

> Dr. F had been engaged upon one aspect of culture; in exile he dropped systematic work, and collected memoir and other material which was intended to prove that his native land had been victimized by conspiracies of a secret society; he also engaged in propaganda and conspiracy.

There was an expectation of becoming American, not only through citizenship but in thinking and manners, by becoming 'one of us', a good American citizen with shared values. This meant dropping one's European intellectual identity and/or at least not overemphasising one's ethnic and/or religious identity and testifying on demand that one was not a communist or a homosexual.

(4) Ideologies and utopias are so interwoven

It is easy to concentrate only on ideologies and to forget utopias, which in Mannheim's view were as important as ideologies, although equally distorted. It is the interplay of ideologies and utopias that is so interesting, on both individual and societal levels. The difference between the two is not always clear, since ideologies and utopias are so intertwined. In the course of my research for this book, it was much easier to identify collective utopias, which were often manifested in declarations or public speeches, than individual utopias. Once utopias are communicated to others and shared, it becomes more difficult to separate them from ideologies. They do not always go together, and the ruptures between the two levels can only be seen when both micro and macro levels are studied. Understanding an ideology as permanent and unchangeable is not helpful, and adding the concept of a utopia to my analysis certainly calls into question such permanence.

When conducting archival research it is more difficult to trace utopias than ideologies. In my view, utopias are not always even shared with others but remain individuals' own. Utopias are more dreamlike than ideologies: it is difficult to dream about communism and capitalism as ideologies, but one can dream of love, as Lasswell did in one of his poems: 'If I must fly, behind the sky when I die I think I might hold a light – a satellite – high above my love.'[4] Nonetheless, I found the concepts of ideology and utopia helpful when analysing the comparative communications undertaken by members of the forefront generation. Coleman writes that Raymond Williams' (1921–1988) concept of a structure of feeling 'emphasise[s] a distinction from more formal concepts of "world-view" or "ideology"' and proposes an approach 'concerned with meanings and values as they are actively lived and felt' (Coleman 2018, p.606; Williams 1977, p.132). I have always liked Williams' concept because it captures three things: (1) the structural aspect of ideology (institutions play a key role), (2) the temporal aspect of ideology (dominant, residual and emergent) (Williams 1977), and (3) the emotional aspect of ideology, which Mannheim perhaps associated more with utopias. Like Williams (1977, pp.133–34), I also acknowledge how difficult it is to capture the structure of feeling of a certain period because this always disappears along with its bearers and we can only rely on the written documents that remain.

I borrow here Williams' concepts of dominance, residuality and emergence (Williams 1977, pp.120–24) and apply these to utopias. The interplay of ideologies and utopias at individual and collective levels, and defined by their temporality, makes the task of analysis more challenging but also more interesting. A dominant ideology and a utopia, for example internationalism, might come from both macro (institutions) and micro levels (individuals), which supported each other. But there are other instances where this did not happen, for example when institutions supported McCarthyism but researchers stuck to their internationalism. Or when an organisation (the AP) supported the 'entente cordiale' with long-standing partners but an individual (Cooper) presented a new utopia that went against a previously dominant ideology. Since so many members of the forefront generation, both academics and men of practice, worked on policy science, their ideologies and utopias were often institutional ones, existing at a macro level, because of their close relationship with the institutions that supported them financially and otherwise.

Mannheim reminds us about the struggle between different ideologies. He writes that,

> if we are speaking of the 'spirit of an epoch', for example, we must realize, as in the case of other factors, too, that this *Zeitgeist*, the mentality of a period, *does not pervade the whole society at a given time*. The mentality which is commonly attributed to an epoch has its proper seat in one (*homogeneous or heterogeneous*) social group which acquires special significance at a particular time and is thus able to put *its own intellectual stamp* on all the other groups without either destroying or absorbing them. (Mannheim 1936/2000, p.313)

Krause (2019, p.1) defines the notion of the Zeitgeist, the spirit of the time, as 'a hypothesis for a pattern in meaningful practices that is specific to a particular historical time-period, links different realms of social life and social groups, and extends across geographical contexts'. Krause is critical of Mannheim, who in her view did not go far enough in suggesting that just two opposing Zeitgeists define a period. According to Krause (2019, p.4), Zeitgeists are not necessarily shared by all and each epoch may have different conflicting Zeitgeists. She proposes the following properties as defining a Zeitgeist: (1) duration, (2) scope, (3) course, and (4) media and carriers (p.6). Krause (2019, p.8) concludes that 'more research is needed to examine how particular Zeitgeists extend across time, across geographical and across social space, and how they are made possible across a geographically dispersed setting'. Analysing their carriers, as I have in this book, offers an opportunity to analyse how Zeitgeists are formed, maintained and contested. Krause's useful critique notwithstanding, however, for me Mannheim's two concepts of utopia and ideology capture the battle for hearts and minds better than those of a structure of feeling or a Zeitgeist.

The interplay between ideology and utopia is clearly seen during the period covered by this study. At the same time, both are difficult and elusive to track, for the reasons I have tried to show, and I did consider using the concepts of a structure of feeling or a Zeitgeist instead. However, neither of these concepts fully emphasises the struggle between different structures of feeling, the battle of wills between them, as well as do the concepts of ideology and utopia. Again, I would emphasise how important it is to study the life histories of individuals who are actors in and carriers of different ideologies and utopias.

7.2 The concept of a generation

I started this book by describing certain actors as the 'forefront generation', which was deeply affected by the events of two world wars. Mannheim suggested a new concept of a generation, in order not only to understand how ideologies change but to move away from an analysis of ideology solely based on structures. Mannheim's concept of a generation also distantiates him from many Marxist scholars who had argued that an ideology was something practised by the ruling class on the working class, both of which they understood as homogenous entities with little internal diversity. Much of Mannheim's work concerns intellectuals, even when he wrote about generations. Intellectuals are in his view not a class per se. He sees them as having more autonomy than the working class and also as having some agency in terms of societal change. In my introduction to this book, when I introduced his concept of a generation, I emphasised three views adopted from Mannheim. These were: (1) that generations are socially constructed, either by their own members or by other generations; (2) that generations are both national and transnational, and (3) that belonging to the same generation does not always result in a shared ideology or utopia but may also include intra- and intergenerational conflicts.

(1) Social construction of generations

What is different in the experiences of the forefront generation is that, although all its members were marked by the two world wars, they all also grew up in different circumstances and had experiences they did not share, most evidently in the disparity between the experience of the émigrés (sometimes like Mannheim and Leites even doubly exiled) and those who were born and lived in the US. Equally important, if not more important, especially when studying past generations, is the 'story told by a generation' and the 'story about a generation' (Ben-Ze'ev and Lomsky-Feder 2009, p.1048). The discursive constructs (Timonen and Conlon 2015, p.2) that arise from these stories become the only route to understanding generations that are long gone, like the one that features in this book.

Generations tell their own stories in order to justify their actions vis-à-vis previous generations. A good example of this is that of Kecskemeti's and

Mannheim's generation, who saw themselves as radically different from their parents' generation. As a contemporary wrote of his and Kecskemeti's generation as compared with that of their fathers, remembering lines from a short story by Dezső Kosztolányi (1885–1936):[5]

> We have been romantics – they have been pragmatics. No two generations ever differed as much as ours and theirs. When we were twenty, our fathers made careful calculations about the prospects of their career we might follow, about the annuities and pensions we might get when we retire after a lifetime of diligent work. With this security in the background we could easily afford to reject the routine of an ordered life … For them, this 'very ordinary life' was adventure itself, for around them the disorder was the rule. We chain-smoked, ruined ourselves, never ceased to be born in bright or sordid loves. They do not smoke, they do their gymnastics, they marry young. We wanted to die five or six times a day. They would prefer to live: if possible.

The life that Kecskemeti's generation imagined for themselves as young intellectuals in Budapest turned out to be very different from that they were compelled to live, a catastrophe beyond imagination. While the forefront generation was influenced mainly by the traumas of the two wars (although only Goldsen, Lerner, Peterson and Stoddard served in either of them), they also experienced other, less collective, generational conflicts with their own parents (Gluck 1985, pp.76–77). Lasswell's rebellion against his religious and teetotal parents is a known example of such a personal generational conflict, as is the refusal of Speier's father to pay for his son's higher education (Bessner 2018, p.288). Cooper also fought his own generational conflicts inside and outside his organisation and made of that a generational story.

Many of the European émigré scholars personally experienced the rise of Nazism in Europe and had to flee for their lives. Those members of the forefront generation who were born in the US never had that experience and could never, sympathetic as they may have been, fully understand the traumas experienced by those who had to leave their home countries because they were persecuted. Clearly, wartime research at the Library of Congress bound together a group of people with different backgrounds and experiences. However, the ideology that the forefront generation shared was also shared by others not participating in that project, such as Cooper or the Illinois Three. Mannheim writes that 'whether youth will be conservative, reactionary, or progressive, depends (if not entirely, at least primarily) on whether or not the existing social structure and the position they occupy in it provide opportunities for the promotion of their own social and intellectual ends' (Mannheim 1936/2000, p.297), thus emphasising the clear influence of social structure on those involved in comparative communications in the US.

Mannheim (1936/2000, p.296) also argues that members of any single generation can only participate in a temporally limited section of the historical process. The forefront generation, as depicted in this book, and especially some of its members, were active for many decades. One of Lasswell's first articles, for example, was published in 1925 (Lasswell 1925) and one of his last in 1979 (Lasswell and Fox 1979), a year after his death. One could argue that his influence gradually increased, but also towards the end of his life began to decrease. He was actively publishing, but increasingly only with old friends with whom he had connections, such as Schramm and Lerner (Eulau and Zlomke 1999). When Lasswell died in 1978 his friends and colleagues promoted his work, but he was no longer in the forefront. He was still being quoted seven years after the end of his academic career, but Eulau and Zlomke found that 'most references to Lasswell are superficial (perfunctory, suggestive, deferential), although a few are more substantial (critical, extending)'. They concluded that Lasswell's legacy was 'undervalued and underused, to the discipline's detriment' (Eulau and Zlomke 1999, p.75). Lasswell, like everybody else, could not choose how he would be remembered and probably thought that content analysis, which was collectively designed and developed, was not his greatest achievement. Naming him as the 'father of content analysis', while failing to understand his attempts to save democratic societies from totalitarianism (in his case mainly from communism), results in a failure to give a full picture of his lifelong intellectual struggles with a world in turmoil. But this is how collective memory works: so much of what an individual's contemporaries value as important disappears with that individual's death, until something is rediscovered decades or centuries later.

Just as Mannheim predicted, we see here the continuous emergence of new groups and the continuous withdrawal of previous participants, and a new generation of academics with new theories and methodologies appears in the period under study. According to Mannheim, this 'serves the necessary social purpose of enabling us to forget. If society is to continue, social remembering is just as important as forgetting and action starting from scratch' (Mannheim 1936/2000, p.294). Succeeding generations, when evaluating comparative communications, have certainly remembered the early work of some while forgetting that of others. As discussed in Chapter 6, one of the works that is remembered is Siebert, Peterson and Schramm's *Four Theories of the Press* (1956), which had a very slow start but then became the 'bible' of comparative communications studies. Many scholars of different generations in media and communications studies became highly critical of the book, although most of them owe to these authors the concept of a system. Its reputation was dormant for many decades before the book was woken from its sleep by these critics. It became famous because it was criticised – to the extent that it began to feel as if no book in international communication or political communication could start without first criticising *Four Theories*. Still, no matter that the attention was negative, what mattered was that it became a landmark to which everybody had to refer. *Four Theories* has far outlived its generational lifetime.

Figure 7.1: How *Four Theories of the Press* was cited between the 1970s and the 2020s

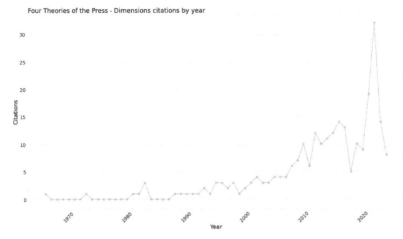

Four Theories of the Press - Dimensions citations by year

Source: Figure created by Paul Flannery using data obtained on 16 October 2023, from Digital Science's Dimensions platform. https://app.dimensions.ai. See also Vartanova (2018, p.6) for Google Scholar data on citations.
Note: Data prior to 2000 is incomplete.

Its influence on subsequent generations has extended beyond the 30 years that Mannheim estimated to be the active span of a generation (Mannheim 1936/2000, p.278).

In this book, I have divided the forefront generation in terms of their experience and of their utopias, but also of how their careers developed and how they were remembered in the stories told by others. Professional success is conventionally often measured by promotions, money and fame (not necessarily in that order). In these terms, we could say that some members of the forefront generation were more successful than others. For example, Cooper, Lasswell and Schramm certainly achieved fame through their writings, combined with their positions, and many led a financially comfortable life, especially when compared with their peers in post-war Europe. But many also valued the freedom they enjoyed in their professions. Cooper achieved 'fame and fortune', nonetheless noting how little he earned compared with competitors who worked for the United Press Associations, while emphasising how he valued the principles of AP more than anything. Lasswell became a professor of law at Yale, had a house in New York and was paid handsomely by RAND Corporation. Schramm died watching television in Honolulu, where he worked at the East-West Center's Communication Institute (Rogers 1994, p.470). The émigré scholars Leites (who died in Paris) and Kecskemeti lived, probably comfortably, in California and were probably well paid by RAND Corporation. They could consider themselves lucky since from 1935 onwards graduate faculties in the US received over 5,000 requests every year for positions (Bessner 2012, p.115) and American men coming home from the front were competing for those same positions. It is likely that RAND Corporation offered them a better life than academia.

(2) Generations are both national and transnational

A generation has most often been defined in the context of a single nation, especially when writing about the history of an academic discipline. In this context it has become, almost without exception, a part of a national – for example, of US or German – history of communication research. There is something about writing a history of a discipline that almost automatically nationalises it, to the extent that foreign academics are not seen as Insiders but rather as visitors or even Outsiders. Since I am not writing a history of a field or a discipline but about early comparative communications before it became 'disciplined', it has been easier for me to see its transnational connections. These transnational connections had already been recognised by the writers of early histories of communication studies as a field, and of its so-called four 'founding fathers' (Berelson 1959; Rogers 1994; Schramm 1980; Schramm, Chaffee and Rogers 1997), although this has since been contested many times (see, for example, Pooley 2017), with the inclusion of two émigrés in the history of communication studies in the US. Lazarsfeld and Lewin were émigré scholars, while the third 'founding father', Harold Lasswell, spent long periods in Europe after World War I. This leaves only Carl Hovland as a thoroughly 'US-born-and-bred' academic. Even so, in this book, I try to show that the role of other émigré scholars in comparative research has not been adequately acknowledged and Mannheim, Kecskemeti and Leites have been written out from intellectual histories of media and communications studies by the 1960s and 1970s generations.

In making the argument that generations are both transnational and national it is not enough to look only at the nationalities of a generation's members, which often change during their lifetimes. There are other important factors, including the academic and intellectual traditions they come from, their knowledge of languages, their intellectual upbringing, the theories, concepts and methodologies they use, the objects of their study, and who they collaborate with. Cooper's work could be used an example here. Although an American by birth, education and experience, his business ventures and professional conflicts were also international by their very nature. Or take Lasswell, with his early European experiences and collaboration with émigré scholars. But the overall narrative becomes almost without exception a national story, a history of US communication studies or of news agencies in the US, where the early pioneers may have been from somewhere else but eventually the 'national' takes over. This happened with Schramm, who not only decided in the books he edited who was 'in' or 'out' but also, having visited Korea, made himself an expert on Soviet Communist theories without having ever visited the USSR or being able to speak

Russian. One can nonetheless say that he made an attempt to see the world outside the US, if only through US eyes.

Does comparative communications cosmopolitanise the research process, making it more than two separate fields of the national and the international? Blumler, McLeod and Rosengren (1992, p.3) famously wrote that comparative research opens up an existing field, goes beyond existing boundaries and thus cosmopolitanises the field. According to them, 'comparative inquiry cosmopolitanizes, opening our eyes to communication patterns and problems unnoticeable in our spatial and temporal milieux' (p.3). This is not entirely different from what Tillich was writing as early as in 1937 of émigré academics:

> They seek the foreign not for the sake of the foreign but in the hope that through the foreign they will find a higher realisation of what is their own. And, conversely, the factor that makes people receive those who are migrating is the belief that in the foreign humanity their own humanity is enclosed and that both may be increased by a creative synthesis. Humanity, existing beyond the cleavage between our own and the foreign, gives meaning to migration and justifies separation from soil and tribe, condemns tyrannic seclusion, gives hope to the creative mind, which is the permanent émigré in the world. (Tillich 1937, p.305)

However, this does not always happen, especially when academics need to choose sides, as in times of a conflict or a war. As this book has shown, nationalism always seems to win out over cosmopolitanism when a new academic field is being established. The process of mutual reliance becomes a key issue here at both individual and organisational level. Merton (1972, p.10) writes:

> Michael Polanyi (1958, 1959, 1964, 1967) noted, more perceptively than anyone else I know, how the growth of knowledge depends upon *complex sets of social relations* based on a largely *institutionalized reciprocity of trust* among scholars and scientists. In one of his many passages on this theme, he observes that in an ideal free society each person would have perfect access to the truth: to the truth in science, in art, religion, and justice, both in public and private life. But this is not practicable; each person can know directly very little of truth and must trust others for the rest. Indeed, to assure *this process of mutual reliance* is one of the main functions of society. It follows that such freedom of the mind as can be possessed by *men is due to the services of social institutions, which set narrow limits to man's freedom and tend to threaten it even within those limits.* (my emphasis)

One needs to ask the critical question of whether comparative communications cosmopolitanises those who work within it, or those who fund it, or those who make use of its results. Comparative communications did open up new opportunities for researchers from outside the US but after their arrival they were asked to commit themselves to the goals set by the US government and US universities, organisations and funders. From the chapters featured in this book we can see how émigré scholars were trusted when they were needed to work on policy science. Not all of them undertook this, but those who did became policy researchers serving US military goals. In the Cold War atmosphere, their research may have strengthened rather than broken boundaries (Blumler, McLeod and Rosengren 1992, p.2).

Thus, comparative research does not automatically have a cosmopolitanising effect. It is potentially cosmopolitanising, but this potentiality is dependent on several issues outlined by Merton and mentioned above. There is always an expectation that the émigré scholars will be the ones to change, not the nationals, as I know from my personal experience as a Finnish migrant to the UK. Beck (2009, p.17) writes of cosmopolitan moments:

> when Kuhn's (1962) concept of a paradigm shift, first renders the novelty of social facts describable and knowable. For uncovering the empirical facts of the world risk society not only presupposes the availability of a corresponding theory but also *practical* changes in the social and methodological organization of the social sciences.

His concept of a cosmopolitan moment can be combined with Blyth's (2006) concept of a punctuation that potentially transforms our conceptions of what research is about. World War II provided a moment, a punctation, when research could potentially be done differently both content-wise and organisationally. To an extent it did so, but the difference between the national and the international would again become evident with the new subfield of international communication.

(3) Not always a shared ideology or utopia

The concept of a generation was helpful to me in analysing the forefront generation in this book. Despite the differences in their biological ages, it shared traumatic experiences of two world wars. Still, like ideologies and utopias, a generational experience is never universal. If we think, for example, of émigré scholars and of how their experience divided them into the members of the Frankfurt School (see, for example, Jay 1973/1996) and the RAND Corporation scholars, we can see how the same experiences can result in espousal of contradictory ideologies and utopias.

As pointed out in Chapter 1, the making of unfounded generalisations is a potential pitfall of analysing both 'a story told by' and 'a story about' generations as supposedly homogenous units that share the same ideologies and utopias. In particular, intergenerational conflicts are made visible by the telling of a story about a generation, be this by the generation itself or by those who followed it. This is why Kecskemeti and Speier, for example, were so disheartened by Jay's (1973/1996) book, which, in their view, told a story only of some members of their generation. The use of the concept of a generation, when labelling earlier generations as 'the first generation' and then justifying writers' own approach by labelling themselves as the next generation, is something that is present in many books about media and communications studies (see, for example, Nordenstreng and Schiller 1979, p.4). The labelling of a previous generation as homogenous gives an opportunity to criticise its research and to present one's own work as representing a whole generation.

Analysis of intragenerational conflicts often presents these as paradigmatic conflicts inside and between generations. Intragenerational conflicts inside the forefront generation, as evidenced in the archival materials I studied, concerned mainly methodologies (qualitative versus qualitative) but were also between different approaches (psychoanalytical versus behaviouralism, history versus 'modern communication studies'). In their own time, however, these were not paradigmatic in the sense that they took place inside an established discipline. Cooper's intragenerational conflict was made very public by him for political reasons. In this way, we can see both hidden and public intra- and intergenerational conflicts, but awareness of these depends on who is telling the story. This, again, emphasises how important it is to study the intellectual histories of the Insiders and Outsiders of a particular generation in order to understand what is neglected when we concentrate only on a few Insiders without highlighting the role of Outsiders, whose voice was not heard.

7.3 Insiders and Outsiders

Merton (1972, pp.11–12) further complicates the idea of a unified concept of a generation by introducing the concepts of Insider and Outsider, and the question of whether members of the intelligentsia can be Insiders or Outsiders in relation to society. The concepts of Insiders/Outsiders have also helped me to explore the *power relationships* of individuals and research groups not only vis-à-vis society but also between themselves. Merton (1972, pp.11–12) argues that 'particular groups of Insiders, at every moment of history, have enjoyed monopolistic and/or privileged access to particular kinds of knowledge, while Outsiders have been excluded from these'. Applying this to the early development of comparative communications lets me now address the question of who became an Insider or an Outsider, and whether an individual's position could change during their lifetime.

Being or *becoming* an Insider or an Outsider depends very much on who establishes the criteria for this and is also much influenced by dominant ideologies concerning what is valued in a particular society. There are two aspects to consider here. The first is how Insiders and Outsiders see themselves in these roles, and the second is how others see them. When émigré scholars arrived in the US, they lost their status as Insiders within European academia. Shils (1995, p.226), for example, observes that many German émigré scholars suffered from sensitivities of rank in the relatively loosely stratified structure of Anglo-American universities. The fame of Mannheim's *Ideology and Utopia*, which inspired many members of the forefront generation, did not travel well to Anglo-American academia. Shils observes that, in the US,

> in the mid-1930s, with the possible exception of [Robert] Merton and a handful of German refugees in the social sciences – I was the only person who had read Mannheim's sociological writing. (Shils 1995, p.228)

Mannheim himself was at LSE in London, and not happy there. Here is the testimony of one contemporary:

> Upon arriving in London, I began attending his [Mannheim's] lectures and one of his seminars [at LSE], but these were a faint echo of those given in Frankfurt. There were few students, the teacher still struggled with the language, and the intellectual curiosity that had once united teacher and student was totally absent. Mannheim's seminars for advanced students were attended mostly by Americans, and they too displayed little of the alertness of Mannheim's previous students ... Mannheim did not hide his distress, but neither did he complain. (Kettler and Meja 2012, p.236)

It is important to analyse both what it means to become an Insider and what it means to lose that position. Many European intellectual émigrés lost their position and never felt that they had regained it. There is also the question of feeling an *emotional* Outsider, which never leaves a person, no matter how successful they are. Merton (1972, p.29) writes of 'Outsiders who have been systematically frustrated by the social system: The disinherited, deprived, disenfranchised, dominated, and exploited Outsiders'. However, it is revealing how little sympathy émigrés received, even from someone such as Lasswell, probably one of the more sympathetic ones, who wrote in 1937:

> In retrospect, intellectual exiles have played important parts in the diffusion of skill and attitude, notably in the spread of skills of political analysis, and of attitudes of political importance. When they deteriorate their skill or devalue the intellectual life (despite favorable opportunities in their second country), they express in themselves the lack of self-respect and self-containedness of the intellectual life of their time and place. (Lasswell 1937, pp.315–16)

The issue of becoming an Insider was a difficult one for émigré scholars. Many had left behind successful and established careers in Europe and now needed to restart those careers, as did Mannheim as a lecturer at LSE (Shils 1995, p.226). The 'Silent Decade' (Horowitz 1996, p.357) of the McCarthy era further silenced people and made them denounce or hide their pasts. According to Horowitz (1996, p.358), there is no question that McCarthyism's greatest successes were within academic institutions and the cultural media. However, many émigré scholars such as Leites and Kecskemeti made their early careers in the US through having access to wartime and post-war classified materials that very few academics had access to, and thus became Insiders. And they survived, protected by the force of RAND Corporation, less vulnerable to the forces that marginalised those like Stoddard who were at universities. And, of course, each of them was, from experience, hostile to Soviet Communism, which had been responsible for the diasporic uprootings each had suffered. As Merton (1972, p.37) observed, the boundaries between Insiders and Outsiders can be very permeable, especially in such exceptional circumstances.

Becoming an In- or Outsider is also associated with the prestige, or lack of prestige, of different academic fields. Communication studies did not exist as a field of its own, and many academics who became interested in communication stayed in their own fields. Those who became early communication scholars took a risk but also had an opportunity to define the field, as Schramm did. Cooper's example shows that one could have a successful career even without an academic degree and achieve a post at the top of a powerful organisation, but in his case only by first climbing slowly through its ranks and then going against dominant thinking inside and outside his organisation.

Merton remarked that the most stringent version of the distinction between Insiders and Outsiders maintains that they must arrive at different and presumably incompatible findings and interpretations even when they examine the same problems. The less vehement version, according to Merton, argues only that they will not deal with the same questions and so will simply talk past one another (Merton 1972, p.16). The forefront generation, as depicted in this book, all dealt with the same questions and did talk to one another, mainly because they shared the same experience of the two world wars that brought the world to chaos. This made them members of the same generation despite their differences of age, personal history, nationality and location. One could also raise the question of whether Outsiders in fact have more freedom than Insiders. Of course, they lack recognition, material or symbolic, but at the same time they enjoy a freedom that Insiders do not always have to choose topics that do not attract Insiders' attention.

Certain groups, such as émigré scholars, can seldom become full Insiders. The only hope of such Outsiders is that generations to come will find their work, after the work of Insiders has perhaps been forgotten. The relationship between Insiders and Outsiders is not fixed across time. There is always movement between the two, and Insiders can never be sure of their position or how long their influence will last, even if during their lifetime they may be financially and academically rewarded with many accolades. In contrast, Outsiders tend to have a high degree of psychological robustness, not needing to worry about their changing status. Insiders need Outsiders to appreciate their work, as much as they need other Insiders to 'scratch their backs' in the hope of favours returned. Outsiders can also become known for being critical of Insiders' work and thereby themselves become Insiders. The boundaries between Insiders and Outsiders thus need to be porous, but they cannot be too porous. The elite position of Insiders can only be maintained if access is limited and if the group remains relatively small. By definition, not everybody can be an Insider.

In order to evaluate the usefulness and relevance of knowledge about a particular period, one always needs to take into account evaluations of who was then an Insider and who was an Outsider. The sociology of knowledge must include critical historical analysis in order to avoid the very fallacies of the period under study. If it concentrates only on the Insiders of a particular period, it often thereby misses the critical voices of that same period and is thus unable to renew itself. It closes the door to any collaborative or incremental development of understanding. Merton's Insider/Outsider concept also gives us an opportunity to review the issues of equality, diversity and inclusion within these two categories, and to apply these to knowledge production.

7.4 Merton's four criteria for evaluating comparative communications – plus one new one

Finally, we need to ask how Merton's four criteria can be used to help us understand how comparative communications was born. When Merton (1949/1968, p.494) compares sociology of knowledge with mass communication research, he uses the following criteria: (1) their characteristic subject matter and definitions; (2) their concepts of data; (3) their utilisation of research techniques, and (4) the social organisation of their research activities. I can also suggest a fifth criterion, that of funding. Let us now try to evaluate these criteria while analysing how comparative communications started in the US. It is important to remember that comparative communications was not founded only by academics but was brought into being under exceptional circumstances of war and Cold War by both academics and men of practice, who developed comparative approaches to communications as a practical, policy-science-oriented and war-fighting exercise.

(1) Characteristic subject matter and definitions

The word propaganda was used in early comparative communications, especially during World War II, just to study war propaganda. Propaganda as a concept was defined, even academically, as something deceitful, something hidden in the message. Lasswell's work especially tried to reveal hidden, underlying messages within messages. For Cooper, no definitions were needed: propaganda was something issued by others, not by the United States. Likewise, for research teams during World War II, the propaganda they studied was foreign propaganda and no further definitions were needed. For Schramm, Peterson and Siebert, propaganda was not a key concept, but at the same time the difference between press systems was also reflected in the content of messages, in whose interests were being served. In short, what was later called international communication studies was born out of propaganda studies. It has a heritage of defining 'us' against 'them', by nationality and by values, just as press systems were also defined in national and value terms. Theoretically, international communication has mainly followed the theorisation in international politics, taking nation states and their media systems and international organisations as naturalised starting points (Rantanen 2010).

Political science probably had more influence than any other field on early comparative communications, and we can see its long-standing influence not only in international communication but also in political communication, which brings together communication scholars and political scientists. The forefront generation established the ways in which research would be carried out, including its key concepts, methods and data, and continues to do so today. Theoretical and conceptual thinking was largely absent, or at least weak, in early comparative communications, since one of its main emphases was on the development of new methodologies. Some concepts originating from that early research are still dominant, such as the concept of a flow as used by Cooper. Lasswell's work was probably the most theoretical, especially his attempts to define propaganda and to combine psychoanalysis with propaganda studies. Like comparative politics, the international communication research that came after comparative communications has often been criticised for its weak theorisation (Lee 2015, p.4).

Comparative communications was open from its very beginning to outside influences because most of its funding came from outside academia. The forefront generation was aware of its policy science orientation and promoted it, along with an oppositional relationship with the Frankfurt School. Adorno (1945/1996, pp.229–30) refers to 'exploitive administrative research' and 'benevolent administrative research'. Several authors have since pointed out that the division into administrative and critical schools does not do justice to the research carried out in both 'schools' (see, for example, Katz and Katz 2016; Lang 1979). The division is, however, helpful, since it shows us how researchers at the time themselves reflected on their own work and wrote their own generational story. It also shows how powerful the critical school has been in its story of a generation, since this debate has lasted for several decades (see 'Introduction to the Special Issue' 2016). The division, although admittedly unjustified, nonetheless helps us to discuss policy science and its legacy in international communication. Policy science, in my view, is a much better term than administrative research because the former actually reveals something about its outcomes. As Lasswell (1951a, p.4) writes, 'policy science is the term often used when researchers are providing policy-makers with pragmatic, problem-solving recommendations'.

One of the reasons for weak theorisation, apart from the practical orientation of early comparative communications research, is the utopianism embedded in this and also in international communication. There have been periods, such as that following World War II, when research tended to overemphasise the role of communication, and especially of news, in promoting world peace. When this becomes a doctrine, as it did in the UN Charter, research becomes more policy-oriented, with more theory-oriented research possibly prevented because the results are needed for political decision-making. This was again seen when research was needed to support the New World Information and Communication Order (NWICO) in the 1970s and 1980s (Carlsson 2003). In the early 1950s, Merton and Lerner (1951, p.282) wrote of policy scientists:

> How does the man of knowledge influence the society in which he operates? Here we need to consider the functions which the man of knowledge typically performs in any society: scientist, teacher and advisor. As scientist, he advances knowledge beyond the limits within which he found it. As teacher, he diffuses knowledge among his contemporaries and their progeny. As adviser, he applies knowledge through policy guidance to great men and small, to men of affairs, to princes and presidents.

In their view, this combination was possible in the democratic society in which they thought they lived. What they could not see was the influence of policy science on comparative communications that exceeded national boundaries. The fields of political science and communication studies shared several academics whose work contributed to both fields. Blyth (2006, p.493) argues that political science's inability to predict any of the great events of the 1930s had proved a serious embarrassment and paved the way for those who followed in the 1940s, the behaviouralists, and their attempt to rebuild political science along explicitly predictive lines. Because comparative communications was established during a period when communication research did not exist as an independent field, it naturally attracted both scholars and men of practice from different fields including political science, psychology and sociology. International communication indeed became a popular topic and, according to Hanson, by the mid-1950s the bibliography of *International Communication and Political Opinion* (Smith and Smith 1956) contained almost 2,600 entries on relevant research since 1945. The categories included political persuasion and propaganda activities, channels of international communication, audience characteristics, and methods of research and intelligence (Hanson 2020).

(2) Concepts of data and (3) utilisation of research techniques

What was defined as data greatly influenced the key theoretical conceptualisations of propaganda. Researchers needed to go where propaganda was to be found, and it was primarily to be found in what came to be called the mass media, including newspapers, notably elite newspapers and broadcast news. Lasswell's first article (1925) studied propaganda in Prussian school books, while the main interest of the research covered in this book was the news media of that period. Propaganda research gave birth to media and communication studies in general and to comparative communications in particular. If we look at later studies carried out in the 1950s, we see that these often concentrate on elite newspapers and news (International Press Institute 1953; Schramm 1959a). Another aspect of the concept of data relates to access to the data. The propaganda researchers active during World War II set a precedent for close collaboration between academic and policy science when academics needed policymakers to secure access to data. This close collaboration continues until today, when academics voluntarily collaborate with policymakers.

Perhaps one of the most influential areas where those conducting early comparative communications played a key role was the development and utilisation of research techniques. One technique stands out: that of content analysis. It was not Lasswell alone who invented and developed this but the whole research team at the Library of Congress, who worked on it collectively. It was, again, practically oriented, geared to winning the war. The success of content analysis, in both communication studies and comparative communications, has lasted until this day, with many students using it in their theses. It would probably be fair to say that content analysis has become the most used research technique in communication(s) studies around the world.

Eventually, largely because of the behaviouralism that became popular in the 1950s, content analysis became primarily quantitative. When it was later used in international communication, especially in news flow studies, it was adopted almost without any questioning of its premises (International Press Institute 1953; Sreberny-Mohammadi et al. 1985) and would continue to be used for decades. As Chang (2015, p.60) argues, international communication research has produced a body of knowledge through empirical studies that have mostly followed the same school of thought. For example, Hur (1984, p.374) found that 90 per cent of international news flow studies used content analysis. This trend continues today: quantitative content analysis is by far the most popular method in comparative journalism studies (Hanusch and Vos 2020).

(4) Social organisation of research activities

Comparative communications started when there was no such discipline of communication studies, not even a field. It started when individual researchers and men of practice in existing fields became interested in it and men of practice promoted it for organisational and political purposes. Its beginnings could perhaps be fairly described as informal, taking place partly outside academia. It was spontaneous, sometimes short-term, and deeply influenced by the needs of organisations and governments. Much of the work was done by foreigners, and it was collective work.

International communication is still a field where academics and non-academics work together. It is often funded by organisations outside academia. Because international communication never became a fully institutionalised subfield of communication studies, there has always been a heavy reliance on outside funding. Many major research projects in international communication have been funded by organisations such as UNESCO or the International Press Institute, with a different but not necessarily less normative agenda of research from the US foundations (see, for example, International Press Institute 1953; Kayser 1953; Sreberny-Mohammadi et al. 1985). Mowlana's (1973) study covering the 1950s and 1960s in international communication research shows a heavy concentration of research on Western European countries. According to Chang (2015, p.55), his research revealed that almost all publications in the field were in English, with the remainder in only three other languages: Spanish, French and German. Hanusch and Vos (2020) show in their study of published articles in comparative journalism research that authors from non-Western countries are still on the margins.

Unlike comparative politics, comparative communications failed to institutionalise itself in university departments. In political science there are countless departments around the world that teach comparative or international politics or international relations. There are also numerous academic journals devoted to these fields. In communication and media studies international communication is a subfield with a recognised status, but there are very few departments dedicated to it. Unlike in political science, where comparative politics is accepted as a field of its own, in media and communication studies there is no distinctive subfield called comparative communications: comparative research is carried out separately but as part of international communication, political communication, and global media and communications studies. As a result, as Chang (2015, p.61) argues,

> in international communication, comparative research has generated more heat than light. Part of the reason is that, over the past four decades, the field as a whole has engaged in research activities that are stuck in an outdated mode of replaying past experience without any serious intellectual attempt to go beyond the conceptual boundaries of existing frameworks in knowledge production.

Perhaps all this can help us to understand why comparative work did not institutionalise itself – in the same way as the sociology of knowledge never became established as a productive part of sociology (Shils 1974, p.86) – as a field or even as a subfield, although it was given the name of international communication. It did, however, become generally accepted within communication studies, where comparative research has been and is done, but this is not labelled 'international communication studies' or 'comparative research'. At the same time, this shows how comparative communications, because of its informal start, was never a closed field and even accepted foreign academics as long as they were willing to take positions that were not permanent and were outside academia. It was also open enough to accept non-academic work, such as Cooper's, when mutual interests met.

(5) Funding

It is important to remember that comparative communications was not alone in its policy science orientation. In the 1930s and 1940s, comparative research in politics was mainly policy-oriented – what Cox (1986, p.208) calls, in international politics/international relations, the ethos of 'problem-solving' (Griffiths and O'Callaghan 2001, pp.190–91). The problem-solving ethos also characterised early comparative communications and the field of international communication as a whole, mainly due to its funding. It was funded by foundations and government for very practical reasons: to win the psychological war (Simpson 1994). The Rockefeller Foundation (see, for example, Buxton 2003) and the Ford Foundation were even considered the 'best and the most plausible kind of funding cover for [the] CIA' (Saunders 2000, p.135). As Saunders (2000, p.139) writes about the Ford Foundation,

> the architects of the foundation's cultural policy in the aftermath of the Second World War were perfectly attuned to the political imperatives which supported America's looming presence on the world stage. At times, it seemed as if the Ford Foundation was simply an extension of the government in the area of cultural propaganda.

However, even the foundations came under suspicion. Funding was a factor that Merton (1949/1968) did not take into account in his evaluation of early communication studies, although it contributed to the overall ideology of the time.

The importance of funding ran throughout the archival materials I studied. Comparative communications research was born outside academia, although many academics worked on it together with men of practice. It would not have been possible without funding from foundations, governments or international organisations. That funding meant that researchers were not completely free to choose their topics or methods, and the funders were not in general very interested in developing theory at the expense of practical applied results. Many researchers lived from one project to the next, before ending up in research institutes like RAND Corporation rather than being given chairs in universities. This may have affected the prestige of communication research in general and thus prevented it from developing the status needed for further development as an academic field of study.

7.5 Why does this all matter?

In this book I have examined comparative communications in order to understand how knowledge was produced. I have studied, using Mannheim's and Merton's concepts, the life histories of those who produced it. But we need to ask: why does this matter now? It matters, to quote Merton (1972, p.9), because, 'as the society becomes polarised, so do the contending claims to truth'. We are now again living through a period of extreme polarisation, both internationally and nationally, and again we see contending claims to 'truth'. When the times are polarised, to again quote Merton (1972, p.19), 'groups in conflict want to make their interpretation the prevailing one of how things were and are and will be'. However, there are times when the struggle over 'the truth' becomes more intense, such as in war or conflict.

I have explored periods of polarisation in the US when internationalism was briefly favoured after World War I, and again during World War II, when there was a shared enemy (Nazi Germany), which was followed again by a brief period of internationalism, and then by the new shared enemy of communism during the Cold War. In all these periods, many academics and men of practice followed the government-promoted ideology, even though in principle they had academic and institutional freedom to do otherwise. This shows how powerful ideologies are, even in a country where freedom and liberty are demonstrably part of the national ethos.

Comparative communications was vulnerable because it needed financial support from outside academia, but at the same time its importance was at least acknowledged outside academia. It was not as successful as comparative politics, for example, in being legitimised, as was Almond and Verba's (1963) study, by academic funders. This had long-term consequences for future research in the field, which remained dependent on external funders including international organisations, governments and private funders. It did not achieve its full potential because of this lack of institutional and financial support. Nonetheless, many academics and men of practice share a utopian view that international communication plays a major role in promoting peace and understanding among nations. This utopia divides as much as unifies them because it is difficult to reach an understanding on how to achieve these. This is probably the longest surviving legacy of early comparative communications. Being or becoming an Insider depends very much on access to data, on working together with organisations or institutions, but at the same time it potentially reduces the freedom of individual researchers who may choose the status of an Outsider.

International communication still exists as a field of battle between ideologies and utopias, often mixed together. This takes us back to the importance of *Wissenssoziologie* and sociology of knowledge, and especially to its historical approach. In my view, it is almost impossible to critically review the value of knowledge while members – and especially Insiders – of a generation are still alive. One can only attempt impartially to evaluate knowledge after a generation is gone, and probably not even then if the intellectual span of a generation is longer than its biological span. Thus, the concept of a generation and its division into Insiders and Outsiders has been paramount, both for *Wissenssoziologie* and for the sociology of knowledge, when trying to understand utopias and ideologies in comparative communications, a field yet to be institutionally born. One can only hope that new generations will in time discover the research neglected by the Insiders of previous generations and that nobody will be treated in the way that Károly Mannheim was.

Notes

[1] P. Kecskemeti to H. Speier on 20 March 1979. Hans Speier Papers 1922–1989. Autobiographical writings. Correspondence A–K, Box 3, Series No 2–3. German and Jewish Intellectual émigré Collection. M.E. Grenander Department of Special Collections and Archives, University Libraries, University at Albany, State University of New York.

[2] D. Lerner. Itinerary, no date. Harold Dwight Lasswell Papers, General Files 1043, Series I, Box 58, Folder 795. Manuscripts and Archives, Yale University Library.

[3] H. Speier to P. Kecskemeti on 5 June 1977. Hans Speier Papers 1922–1989. Autobiographical writings, Correspondence A–K, Box 3, Series No 2–3. German and Jewish Intellectual émigré Collection. M.E. Grenander Department of Special Collections and Archives, University Libraries, University at Albany, State University of New York.

[4] Poem, no date. Harold Dwight Lasswell Papers. Bibliographical/Memorabilia Files 1043, Series V, Box 5, Folder 3. Manuscripts and Archives, Yale University Library.

[5] Litvan, G. In memoriam of Paul Kecskemeti on 25 October 1980. Hans Speier Papers 1922–1989. Autobiographical writings. Correspondence A–K, Box 3, Series No 2–3, German and Jewish Intellectual émigré Collection. M.E. Grenander Department of Special Collections and Archives, University Libraries, University at Albany, State University of New York.

References

Adorno, Theodor (1945/1996) 'A Social Critique of Radio Music', *The Kenyon Review*, vol. 18, no. 3/4, pp.229–35. https://www.jstor.org/stable/4337446

Almond, Gabriel A. and Verba, Sidney (1963) *The Civic Culture: Political Attitudes and Democracy in Five Nations*, USA: Princeton University Press.

Beck, Ulrich (2009) 'Critical Theory of World Risk Society: A Cosmopolitan Vision', *Constellations*, vol. 16, no. 1, pp.3–22. https://doi.org/10.1111/j.1467-8675.2009.00534.x

Ben-Ze'ev, Efrat and Lomsky-Feder, Edna (2009) 'The Canonical Generation: Trapped between Personal and National Memories', *Sociology*, vol. 43, no. 6, pp.1047–65. https://doi.org/10.1177/0038038509345698

Berelson, Bernard (1959) 'The State of Communication Research', *Public Opinion Quarterly*, vol. 23, no. 1, pp.14–17. https://doi.org/10.1086/266840

Bessner, Daniel (2012) '"Rather More than One-Third Had No Jewish Blood": American Progressivism and German-Jewish Cosmopolitanism at the New School for Social Research, 1933–1939', *Religions*, vol. 3, no. 1, pp.99–129. https://doi.org/10.3390/rel3010099

Bessner, Daniel (2018) *Democracy in Exile: Hans Speier and the Rise of the Defense Intellectual*, USA: Cornell University Press.

Blumler, Jay G.; McLeod, Jack M.; and Rosengren, Karl E. (1992) 'An Introduction to Comparative Communication Research', in Blumler, Jay G.; McLeod, Jack M.; and Rosengren, Karl E. (eds) *Comparatively Speaking: Communication and Culture Across Space and Time*, USA: Sage, pp.3–18.

Blyth, Mark (2006) 'Great Punctuations: Prediction, Randomness, and the Evolution of Comparative Political Science', *The American Political Science Review*, vol. 100, no. 4, pp.493–98. https://doi.org/10.1017/S0003055406062344

Breiner, Peter (2013) 'Karl Mannheim and Political Ideology', in Freedman, Michael; Sargent, Lyman T.; and Stear, Marc (eds) *The Oxford Handbook of Political Ideologies*, UK: Oxford University Press, pp.38–55.

Buxton, William J. (2003) 'John Marshall and the Humanities in Europe: Shifting Patterns of Rockefeller Foundation Support'. *Minerva*, vol. 41, no. 2, pp.133–53. https://doi.org/10.1023/A:1023606814200

Carlsson, Ulla (2003) 'The Rise and Fall of NWICO: From a Vision of International Regulation to a Reality of Multilevel Governance', *Nordicom Review*, vol. 24, no. 2, pp.31–67. https://doi.org/10.1515/nor-2017-0306

Caute, David (1978) *The Great Fear: The Anti-Communist Purge under Truman and Eisenhower*, USA: Simon and Schuster.

Chang, Tsan-Kuo (2015) 'Beyond Lazarsfeld: International Communication Research and Its Production of Knowledge', in Lee, Chin-Chuan (ed.) *Internationalizing 'International Communication'*, USA: University of Michigan Press, pp.41–65.

Coleman, Rebecca (2018) 'Theorizing the Present: Digital Media, Pre-emergence and Infra-structures of Feeling'. *Cultural Studies*, vol. 32, no. 4, pp.600–22. https://doi.org/10.1080/09502386.2017.1413121

Cox, Robert W. (1986) 'Social Forces, States and World Orders: Beyond International Relations Theory', in Keohane, Robert O. (ed.) *Neorealism and Its Critics*, USA: Columbia University Press, pp.204–05.

Eulau, Heinz and Zlomke, Susan (1999) 'Harold D. Lasswell's Legacy to Mainstream Political Science: A Neglected Agenda', *Annual Review of*

Political Science, vol. 2, pp.75–89.
https://doi.org/10.1146/annurev.polisci.2.1.75

Federal Bureau of Investigation (FBI) Dallas Walker Smythe File. https://
www.documentcloud.org/documents/20613406-ef2f230d15919ac9d
2c090f509126b3e98bfe75cb_q102985_r364624_d2648342

Gitlin, Todd (1978) 'Media Sociology: The Dominant Paradigm', *Theory and
Society*, vol. 6, no. 2, pp.205–53. https://doi.org/10.1007/BF01681751

Glander, Timothy (1996) 'Wilbur Schramm and the Founding of Communication Studies', *Educational Theory*, vol. 46, no. 3, pp.373–91.
https://doi.org/10.1111/j.1741-5446.1996.00373.x

Gluck, Mary (1985) *Georg Lukács and His Generation, 1900–1918*, USA:
Harvard University Press.

Griffiths, Martin and O'Callaghan, Terry (2001) *International Relations: The
Key Concepts*, UK: Routledge.

Hanson, Elizabeth C. (2020) 'A History of International Communication
Studies', in *Oxford Research Encyclopedia of International Studies*.
https://doi.org/10.1093/acrefore/9780190846626.013.63

Hanusch, Folker and Vos, Tim P. (2020) 'Charting the Development of a
Field: A Systematic Review of Comparative Studies of Journalism', *International Communication Gazette*, vol. 82, no. 4, pp.319–41.
https://doi.org/10.1177/1748048518822606

Horowitz, Irving L. (1996) 'Culture, Politics and McCarthyism: A Retrospective from the Trenches', *The Independent Review*, vol. 1, no. 1, pp.101–10.
https://www.independent.org/pdf/tir/tir_01_1_07_horowitz.pdf

Hur, Kyoon K. (1984) 'A Critical Analysis of International News Flow
Research', *Critical Studies in Mass Communication*, vol. 1, no. 4,
pp.365–78. https://doi.org/10.1080/15295038409360047

International Press Institute (1953) *The Flow of News: A Study by the International Press Institute*, Switzerland: International Press Institute.

'Introduction to the Special Issue: Critical versus Administrative Policy
Studies—Celebrating 75 Years since Paul Lazarsfeld's "Remarks on
Administrative and Critical Communication Research"' (2016) *Journal
of Information Policy*, vol. 6, pp.1–3.
https://doi.org/10.5325/jinfopoli.6.2016.0001

Jay, Martin (1973/1996) *The Dialectical Imagination: A History of the
Frankfurt School and the Institute of Social Research, 1923–1950*, USA:
University of California Press.

Katz, Elihu and Katz, Ruth (2016) 'Revisiting the Origin of the Administrative versus Critical Research Debate', *Journal of Information Policy*, vol. 6,
pp.4–12. https://doi.org/10.5325/jinfopoli.6.2016.0004

Kayser, Jacques (1953) *One Week's News: Comparative Study of 17 Major Dailies for a Seven-Day Period*, France: UNESCO. https://unesdoc.unesco.org/ark:/48223/pf0000062870

Kecskemeti, Paul (1952/1997) 'Introduction', in Kecskemeti, Paul (ed.) *Essays on the Sociology of Knowledge* by Mannheim, Karl, UK: Routledge and Kegan Paul, pp.1–32.

Kettler, David and Meja, Volker (2012) 'Karl Mannheim's Jewish Question', *Religions*, vol. 3, no. 2, pp.228–50. https://doi.org/10.3390/rel3020228

Krause, Monika (2019) 'What Is Zeitgeist? Examining Period-Specific Cultural Patterns', *Poetics*, vol. 76, pp.18–30. https://doi.org/10.1016/j.poetic.2019.02.003

Lang, Kurt (1979) 'The Critical Functions of Empirical Communication Research: Observations on German-American Influences', *Media, Culture & Society*, vol. 1, no. 1, pp.83–96. https://doi.org/10.1177/016344377900010010

Lasswell, Harold D. (1925) 'Prussian Schoolbooks and International Amity', *Journal of Social Forces*, vol. 3, no. 4, pp.718–22. https://doi.org/10.2307/3005082

Lasswell, Harold D. (1937) 'The Influence of the Intellectual Exile', *Social Research*, vol. 4, no. 3, pp.305–16. https://doi.org/10.1353/sor.2015.0002

Lasswell, Harold D. (1951a) 'The Policy Orientation', in Lerner, Daniel and Lasswell, Harold D. (eds) *The Policy Sciences: Recent Developments in Scope and Method*, USA: Stanford University Press, pp.3–15.

Lasswell, Harold D. and Fox, Merritt B. (1979) *The Signature of Power: Buildings, Communications, and Policy*, USA: Transaction.

Lee, Chin-Chuan (2015) 'International Communication Research: Critical Reflections and a New Point of Departure', in Lee, Chin-Chuan (ed.) *Internationalizing 'International Communication'*, USA: University of Michigan Press, pp.1–28.

Malherek, Joseph (2022) *Free-Market Socialists: European Émigrés Who Made Capitalist Culture in America, 1918–1968*, Hungary: Central European University Press.

Mannheim, Karl (1936/2000) *Essays on the Sociology of Knowledge. Collected Works, Vol. 5.* Edited by Paul Kecskemeti, UK: Routledge.

Mannheim, Karl (1932/1993) 'The Sociology of Intellectuals'. *Theory, Culture & Society*, vol. 10, no. 3, pp.69–80. https://doi.org/10.1177/026327693010003004

Merton, Robert K. (1949/1968) *Social Theory and Social Structure* (1968 enlarged ed.), USA: Free Press.

Merton, Robert K. (1972) 'Insiders and Outsiders: A Chapter in the Sociology of Knowledge', *American Journal of Sociology*, vol. 78, no. 1, pp.9–47. https://doi.org/10.1086/225294

Merton, Robert K. and Lerner, Daniel (1951) 'Social Scientists and Research Policy', in Lerner, David; Lasswell, Harold D.; Fischer, Harold H.; Holdgard, Ernest R.; Padover, Saul K.; De Sola Pool, Ithiel; and Rothwell, C. Easton (eds) *The Policy Sciences. Recent Developments in Scope and Method*, USA: Stanford University Press, pp.282–310.

Mowlana, Hamid (1973) 'Trends in Research on International Communication in the United States', *International Communication Gazette*, vol. 19, no. 2, pp.79–90. https://doi.org/10.1177/001654927301900202

Nordenstreng, Kaarle and Schiller, Herbert I. (1979) 'Introduction', in Nordenstreng, Kaarle and Schiller, Herbert I. (eds) *National Sovereignty and International Communication*, USA: Ablex, pp.3–8.

Peters, John D. (2006) 'The Part Played by Gentiles in the Flow of Mass Communications: On the Ethnic Utopia of Personal Influence', *The Annals of the American Academy of Political and Social Science*, vol. 608, no. 1, pp.97–114. https://doi.org/10.1177/0002716206292425

Polanyi, Michael (1958) *Personal Knowledge*, UK: Routledge & Kegan Paul.

Polanyi, Michael (1959) *The Study of Man*, UK: Routledge & Kegan Paul.

Polanyi, Michael (1964) *Science, Faith and Society*, USA: University of Chicago Press.

Polanyi, Michael (1967) *The Tacit Dimension*, USA: Routledge & Kegan Paul.

Pooley, Jefferson (2017) 'Wilbur Schramm and the "Four Founders" History of U.S. Communication Research', *Коммуникации. Медиа. Дизайн*, vol. 2, no. 4, pp.5–16. http://dx.doi.org/10.17613/M6Q859

Rantanen, Terhi (2010) 'Methodological Inter-nationalism in Comparative Media Research: Flow Studies in International Communication', in Roosvall, Anna and Salovaara-Moring, Inka (eds) *Communicating the Nation: National Topografies of Global Media Landscapes*, Sweden: Nordicom Publications, pp.25–39. https://www.nordicom.gu.se/sv/publications/communicating-nation

Rogers, Everett (1994) *A History of Communication Study: A Biographical Approach*, USA: Free Press.

Saunders, Frances (2000) *Who Paid the Piper? The CIA and the Cultural Cold War*, UK: Granta.

Schramm, Wilbur (1959) *One Day in the World's Press: Fourteen Great Newspapers on a Day of Crisis*, USA: Stanford University Press.

Schramm, Wilbur (1974) *Men, Messages, and Media: A Look at Human Communication*, USA: Harper & Row.

Schramm, Wilbur (1980) 'The Beginnings of Communication Study in the United States', *Annals of the International Communication Association*, vol. 4, no. 1, pp.73–82. https://doi.org/10.1080/23808985.1980.11923795

Schramm, Wilbur; Chaffee, Steven H.; and Rogers, Everett M. (1997) *The Beginnings of Communication Study in America: A Personal Memoir*, USA: Sage.

Shils, Edward (1974) '"Ideology and Utopia" by Karl Mannheim', *Daedalus*, vol. 103, no. 1, pp.83–89.

Shils, Edward (1995) 'Karl Mannheim', *The American Scholar*, vol. 64, no. 2, pp.221–35. https://www.jstor.org/stable/41212318

Siebert, Fred S.; Peterson, Theodore; and Schramm, Wilbur (1956) *Four Theories of the Press: The Authoritarian, Libertarian, Social Responsibility, and Soviet Communist Concepts of What the Press Should Be and Do*, USA: University of Illinois Press.

Simpson, Christopher (1994) *Science of Coercion: Communication Research and Psychological Warfare, 1945–1960*, USA: Oxford University Press.

Smith, Bruce L. and Smith, Chitra M. (1956) *International Communication and Political Opinion: A Guide to the Literature*, USA: Princeton University Press.

Sreberny-Mohammadi, Annabelle; Nordenstreng, Kaarle; Stevenson, Robert; and Ugboajah, Frank O. (1985) *Foreign News in the Media: International Reporting in 29 Countries*, No 93, France: UNESCO. https://unesdoc.unesco.org/ark:/48223/pf0000065257

Stoddard, George W. (1981) *The Pursuit of Education: An Autobiography*, USA: Vantage Press.

Tillich, Paul (1937) 'Mind and Migration', *Social Research*, vol. 4, no. 3, pp.295–305. https://www.jstor.org/stable/40981563

Timonen, Virpi and Conlon, Catherine (2015) 'Beyond Mannheim: Conceptualising How People "Talk" and "Do" Generations in Contemporary Society', *Advances in Life Course Research*, vol. 24, June, pp.1–9. http://x.doi.org/10.1016/j.alcr.2015.03.001

Vartanova, Elena L. (2018) 'From the Theories of Press to the Models of Mass Media: Considering the History of the Genesis of Comparative Studies on Media Systems', *Kommunikatsii. Media, Design*, vol. 3, no. 2, pp.5–16. https://cmd-journal.hse.ru/article/view/7917/8675

Williams, Raymond (1977) *Marxism and Literature*, UK: Oxford University Press.

Acknowledgements

This is one of those books that has taken a long time to write. It goes back several decades to the Department of Communication, directed by Osmo A. Wiio (1928–2013) at the University of Helsinki, where I was a student and teacher, but also to the University of Illinois at Urbana-Champaign, where I spent six months as an Asla-Fulbright scholar in 1991. When I joined Media@ LSE in 2000, directed by Roger Silverstone (1945–2006), my annual visits to the University of Southern California as director of LSE's double MSc programme in Global Media and Communications with the USC Annenberg School for Communication and Journalism significantly advanced my interest to do research on comparative communications, as did my participation in various comparative research projects.

However, this book could not have been written without past and present LSE colleagues, especially Richard Collins, Heather Dawson and Jean Morris. Richard suggested Mannheim's *Ideology and Utopia* when I was seeking a theoretical framework for this book. He also let me use his extensive home library, full of 'classics', and remained interested and unfailingly helpful in making wise commentary until the very end. Heather and her colleagues in the LSE Library, in my view the best social science library in the world, filled my most peculiar loan requests from far and near in record time with their professionalism and collegial generosity. Jean, with her most attentive and educated ear in multiple languages, revised several versions of the manuscript to help me find my voice in a language that is not my own. Patrick Dunleavy, Lucy Lambe and Alice Park from LSE Press believed in my manuscript when nobody else did and provided many insightful comments to improve it as did Sarah Worthington at the final stage. Chenhao Ye, supported financially by my department, helped me with my bibliography, and Paul Flannery created Figure 7.1.

Archival research also goes back many years and my thanks do not necessarily reach those who helped me in the beginning. Most recently, I especially would like to thank Francesca Pitaro and Valerie Komor (AP Corporate Archives), Karin Scaria-Braunstein (Archiv für die Geschichte der Soziologie in Österreich), Chloe Gerson (Robert D. Farber University Archives & Special Collections), László Vikárius (Budapest Bartók Archives), Cheryl Fox (Library of Congress Archives), Daniel Payne (LSE Library and Special Collections), Mária Németh and Dobó Gábor (Petőfi Irodalmi Múzeum), Erik Newman and Cara McCormick (RAND Corporation Archives), Rory Carruthers (Reuters Archives), Randy Sowell (Harry S. Truman Library) and Joanne Kaczmarek and Sammi Merritt (University of Illinois Archives at Urbana-Champaign) for their generous help.

I am also grateful to several individuals in different countries for their help, which varied from getting access to materials to comments (always useful) or to more general support. They are: Stefanie Averbeck-Lietz, Péter Bajomi-Lázár, Erkki Berndtson, Ilana Burgess, David Cooper, James Curran, Szilvia Elek, Zsuzsa Ferge, Myria Georgiou, Larry Gross, Tom Hollihan, Margaret Hung, Laura Killick, Ullamaija Kivikuru, Ritva Levo-Henriksson, Bingchun Meng, Hannu Nieminen, Tuija Parikka, Jeff Pooley, Reviewers 2 and 3, Patti Riley, Hannele Seeck, Marsha Siefert, Ivan Szekely, Wendy Willems, the members of the History of Media Studies Working Group and all individuals and organisations who have been kind enough to reply to my many queries. I received a small research grant from the British Academy to use for some of my archival research.

Finally, I thank *sydämeni pohjasta* the members (this time in reverse alphabetical order) of my transnational family in five geographic locations: Sampo, Richard, Nyrki, Matt, Luke, Laura, Henna, Guy and Alex in trying to teach me what really matters in life outside academia.

About the author

Terhi Rantanen (MSc; LicSc; DocSc; Docent, Helsinki University) is Professor in Global Media and Communications at the London School of Economics and Political Science (LSE). She is the founder of two double MSc programmes, with the University of Southern California (USC), which she directed from 2000 to date, and with Fudan University, Shanghai, which she directed for its first three years. Since the beginning of her career, she has been conducting research on globalisation and the media, and especially on news organisations but also on the history of knowledge production.

Archival sources and bibliography

Archival sources

American Council for Émigrés in the Professions Records, 1930-1974. M.E. Grenander Department of Special Collections and Archives, University Libraries, University at Albany, State University of New York, Albany, NY, United States.

Annual Reports, 1954–55. Office of the University President. University of Illinois Archives, Champaign, IL, United States.

Archiv für die Geschichte der Soziologie in Österreich (AGSÖ), Graz, Austria.

Association for Education in Journalism and Mass Communication Papers (A.E.J.) Michigan State University, School of Journalism (MCHC70-65) Wisconsin Historical Society, Madison, WI, United States.

The Associated Press (AP) Corporate Archives. New York, NY, United States and the AP Collections Online.

The Athenaeum Club Archive. London, United Kingdom.

Charles E. Merriam Papers. Hanna Holborn Gray Special Collections Research Center, University of Chicago Library, Chicago, IL, United States.

Commission on Freedom of the Press Records. Hanna Holborn Gray Special Collections Research Center, University of Chicago Library, Chicago, IL, United States.

Cooper, K.W. mss (1946–1959) Lilly Library, Indiana University, Bloomington, IN, United States.

Ernő (Ernest) Manheim Papers. Archiv für die Geschichte der Soziologie in Österreich (AGSÖ), Graz, Austria.

Frederick S. Siebert Papers. Dean's Office (1932-1948, 1979, 1982). University of Illinois Archives, Champaign, IL, United States.

George D. Stoddard Papers, 1915–2001. University of Illinois Archives, Champaign, IL, United States.

Hans Speier Papers. German and Jewish Intellectual émigré Collection. M.E. Grenander Department of Special Collections and Archives, University Libraries, University at Albany, State University of New York, Albany, NY, United States.

Harold Dwight Lasswell Papers. Manuscripts and Archives, Yale University Library, New Haven, CT, United States.

Institute of Communications Research. Dean's Office, 1921–1972, 1987–1988. University of Illinois Archives, Champaign, IL, United States.

Institute of Communications Research Subject File, 1947–1983, University of Illinois Archives, Champaign, IL, United States.

Ithiel de Sola Pool File. Federal Bureau of Investigation (FBI), Washington, DC, United States.

Ithiel de Sola Pool Papers. Hanna Holborn Gray Special Collections Research Center, University of Chicago Library, Chicago, IL, United States.

Karl Mannheim File. The London School of Economics and Political Science (LSE) Papers. LSE Archives, London, UK.

Louis Wirth Papers. Hanna Holborn Gray Special Collections Research Center, University of Chicago Library, Chicago, IL, United States.

Melville E. Stone Papers. The Newberry Library, Chicago, IL, United States.

The MIT History Collection. Image Collection Online. Massachusetts Institute of Technology, Cambridge, MA, United States.

Nathan Leites Papers. Hanna Holborn Gray Special Collections Research Center, University of Chicago Library, Chicago, IL, United States.

New School Faculty Vertical Files. The New School Archives and Special Collections, New York, NY, United States.

Paul Kecskemeti Papers. The Robert D. Farber University Archives & Special Collections Department at Brandeis University, Waltham, MA, United States.

Petőfi Literary Museum, Budapest, Hungary.

Philleo Nash Psychological Strategy Board Files. Harry S. Truman Library, Independence, MO, United States.

Photographic Subject File, 1868–. Image Collection Online. University of Illinois Archives, Champaign, IL, United States.

President Lloyd Morey. Annual Reports, 1954–55. University of Illinois Archives, Chicago, IL, United States.

RAND Corporation Archives. RAND Corporation. Santa Monica, CA, United States.

Records of General Manager Kent Cooper. The Associated Press (AP) Corporate Archives. New York, NY, United States.

Records of the Board & Annual Meetings. The Associated Press (AP) Corporate Archives. New York, NY, United States.

Reuters Archives. London, United Kingdom.

Robert K. Merton Papers. Rare Book & Manuscript Library, Columbia University, New York, NY, United States.

Roy Winston Howard Papers. The Collections of the Manuscript Division. Library of Congress, Washington, DC, United States.

Roy W. Howard Papers. The Media School Archive, Indiana University, Bloomington, IN, United States.

Roy W. Howard Photograph Collection. Image Collection Online. The Media School Archive, Indiana University, Bloomington, IN, United States.

Sir Roderick Jones Papers. Reuters Archives, London, United Kingdom.

Social Science Research Council (SSRC) Records. Rockefeller Archive Center. Sleepy Hollow, NY, United States.

Staff Appointments File, 1905–2001. University of Illinois Archives, Champaign, IL, United States.

Theodore B. Peterson Papers, 1933–2001. University of Illinois Archives, Champaign, IL, United States.

The University of Chicago Photographic Archive. Online. University of Chicago Library, Chicago, IL, United States.

Wilbur Schramm File. Federal Bureau of Investigation (FBI), Washington, DC, United States.

Bibliography

Abercrombie, Nicholas; Hill, Stephen; and Turner, Bryan S. (1980) *The Dominant Ideology Thesis*. UK: Allen & Unwin.

Adair-Toteff, Christopher (2019) 'Mannheim, Shils, and Aron and the "End of Ideology" Debate', *Politics, Religion & Ideology*, vol. 20, no. 1, pp.1–20. https://www.doi.org/10.1080/21567689.2018.1554481

Adorno, Theodor (1945/1996) 'A Social Critique of Radio Music', *The Kenyon Review*, vol. 18, no. 3/4, pp.229–35. https://www.jstor.org/stable/4337446

Adorno, Theodor W. (1955) 'Das Bewußtsein der Wissenssoziologie', in Ders, Prismen (ed.) *Kulturkritik und Gesellschaft*, Germany: Suhrkamp, pp.32–50.

Adorno, Theodor W.; Frenkel-Brunswik, Else; Levinson, Daniel J.; and Sanford, R. Nevitt (1950) *The Authoritarian Personality*, USA: Harper & Brothers.

Albrow, Martin (1989) 'Sociology in the United Kingdom after the Second World War', in Genov, Nikolaï (ed.) *National Traditions in Sociology*, UK: Sage, pp.194–219.

'Alexander and Juliette George' (no date). http://plunkettlakepress.com/ajg.html

Almond, Gabriel A. (1956) 'Comparative Political Systems', *The Journal of Politics*, vol. 18, no. 3, pp.391–409. https://doi.org/10.2307/2127255

Almond, Gabriel A. (1987) *Harold Dwight Lasswell, 1902–1978: A Biographical Memoir*, USA: National Academy of Sciences. http://www.nasonline.org/publications/biographical-memoirs/memoir-pdfs/lasswell-harold.pdf

Almond, Gabriel A. (1998) *Plutocracy and Politics in New York City*, USA: Westview Press.

Almond, Gabriel A. and Coleman, James S. (1960) *The Politics of The Developing Areas*, USA: Princeton University Press.

Almond, Gabriel A. and Powell, G. Bingham (1966) *Comparative Politics: A Developmental Approach*, USA: Little, Brown and Company.

Almond, Gabriel A. and Verba, Sidney (1963) *The Civic Culture: Political Attitudes and Democracy in Five Nations*, USA: Princeton University Press.

Altschull, Herbert J. (1995) *Agents of Power: The Media and Public Policy*, USA: Longman.

Anderson, Perry (1980) *Arguments within English Marxism*, UK: NLB.

Angell, Robert C. (1950/1953) 'International Communication and World Society', in Berelson, Bernard and Janowitz, Morris (eds) *Reader in Public Opinion and Communication*, USA: Free Press of Glencoe, pp.369–80.

'A.P. Called Greatest Cooperative Effort. News Service Formed to "Keep Pure the Channels of Public Information," Cooper Tells Insurance Presidents Group—Says It Has Contributed to Brotherhood of American Citizenship' (1926) *Editor & Publisher*, vol. 59, no. 29, 11 December. https://archive.org/details/sim_editor-publisher_1926-12-11_59_29/page/6/mode/2up

'AP Enjoined from Observing Membership Provision By-laws' (1944) *Editor & Publisher*, vol. 77, no. 3, 15 January. https://archive.org/details/sim_editor-publisher_1944-01-15_77_3

'Ármin Kecskeméti' (2008) https://www.jewishvirtuallibrary.org/kecskem-x00e9-ti-x00c1-rmin

Arrow, Kenneth J. (1955) 'Review of *Meaning, Communication, and Value*, by P. Kecskemeti', *Econometrica*, vol. 23, no. 1, pp.103–04. https://doi.org/10.2307/1905585

Ascher, William and Hirschfelder-Ascher, Barbara (2003) *Revitalizing Political Psychology. The Legacy of Harold D. Lasswell*, USA: Lawrence Erlbaum.

Ashcraft, Karen L. and Simonson, Peter (2016) 'Gender, Work, and the History of Communication Research: Figures, Formations, and Flows', in Simonson, Peter and Park, David W. (eds) *The International History of Communication Study*, USA: Routledge, pp.47–68.

Associated Press v. United States (1943) 52 F. Sup 362. USA: US District Court for the Southern District of New York.

Associated Press v. United States (1945) 326 U.S. 1, 65 S. Ct 1416 (145). USA: U.S. Supreme Court.

Averbeck, Stefanie (1999) *Kommunikation als Prozeß. Soziologische Perspektiven in der Zeitungswissenschaft 1927–1934*, Germany: LIT Verlag.

Averbeck, Stefanie (2001) 'The Post-1933 Emigration of Communication Researchers from Germany: The Lost Works of the Weimar Generation', *European Journal of Communication*, vol. 16, no. 4, pp.451–475. https://doi.org/10.1177/0267323101016004002

Barboza, Amalia (2020) *Karl Mannheim*, Germany: Herbert von Halem Verlag.

Bates, Stephen (2018) 'Media Censures: The Hutchins Commission on the Press, the New York Intellectuals on Mass Culture', *International Journal of Communication*, vol. 12, pp.4784–801. https://ijoc.org/index.php/ijoc/article/view/8223

Bateson, Gregory (1966) *From Versailles to Cybernetics*. https://archive.org/details/css_000051

Bauman, Zygmunt (2017) *Retrotopia*, UK: Polity Press.

Beck, Ulrich (2009) 'Critical Theory of World Risk Society: A Cosmopolitan Vision', *Constellations*, vol. 16, no. 1, pp.3–22. https://doi.org/10.1111/j.1467-8675.2009.00534.x

Beck, Ulrich (2011) 'Cosmopolitanism as Imagined Communities of Global Risk', *American Behavioral Scientist*, vol. 55, no. 10, pp.1346–61. https://ww.doi.org/10.1177/0002764211409739

Bell, Laird (1949) 'Are We Afraid of Freedom?' *Bulletin of the American Association of University Professors (1915–1955)*, vol. 35, no. 2, pp.301–12. https://doi.org/10.2307/40220354

Beniger, James R. (1992) 'Comparison, Yes, but—The Case of Technological and Cultural Change', in Blumler, Jay G.; McLeod, Jack M.; and Rosengren, Karl E. (eds) *Comparatively Speaking: Communication and Culture Across Space and Time*, USA: Sage, pp.35–52.

Bennett, Andrew (2008) 'Building Communities, Bridging Gaps: Alexander George's Contributions to Research Methods', *Political Psychology*, vol. 29, no. 4, pp.489–507. http://www.jstor.org/stable/20447141

Ben-Ze'ev, Efrat and Lomsky-Feder, Edna (2009) 'The Canonical Generation: Trapped between Personal and National Memories', *Sociology*, vol. 43, no. 6, pp.1047–65. https://doi.org/10.1177/0038038509345698

Berelson, Bernard (1952) *Content Analysis in Communication Research*, USA: Hafner.

Berelson, Bernard (1959) 'The State of Communication Research', *Public Opinion Quarterly*, vol. 23, no. 1, pp.14–17. https://doi.org/10.1086/266840

Berelson, Bernard and de Grazia, Sebastian (1947) 'Detecting Collaboration in Propaganda', *Public Opinion Quarterly*, vol. 11, no. 2, pp.244–53. https://doi.org/10.1093/poq/11.2.244

Berelson, Bernard and Janowitz, Morris (1950) *Reader in Public Opinion and Communication*, USA: Free Press.

Berelson, Bernard and Lazarsfeld, Paul F. (1948) *The Analysis of Communication Content*, Norway: Universitetets studentkontor.

Berlin, Isaiah (2013) *The Crooked Timber of Humanity: Chapters in the History of Ideas* (2nd ed.), USA: Princeton University Press.

Berndtson, Erkki (1987) 'The Rise and Fall of American Political Science: Personalities, Quotations, Speculations', *International Political Science Review/Revue Internationale de Science Politique*, vol. 8, no. 1, pp.85–100. http://www.jstor.org/stable/1600723

Berndtson, Erkki (1997) 'Behavioralism: Origins of the Concept'. Prepared for Presentation at the XVIIth World Congress of the International Political Science Association 17–21 August, Seoul, South Korea. https://web.archive.org/web/20090514010256/http:/www.valt.helsinki.fi/vol/tutkimus/julkaisut/verkko/behavior.htm

Bessner, Daniel (2012) '"Rather More than One-Third Had No Jewish Blood": American Progressivism and German-Jewish Cosmopolitanism at the New School for Social Research, 1933–1939', *Religions*, vol. 3, no. 1, pp.99–129. https://doi.org/10.3390/rel3010099

Bessner, Daniel (2018) *Democracy in Exile: Hans Speier and the Rise of the Defense Intellectual*, USA: Cornell University Press.

Blanchard, Margaret A. (1977) 'The Hutchins Commission, the Press and the Responsibility Concept', *Journalism Monographs*, vol. 49, May, pp.1–59. http://www.aejmc.org/home/wp-content/uploads/2012/09/Margaret-A.-Blanchard.The-Hutchins-Commission.May-1977.pdf

Blanchard, Margaret A. (1987) 'The Associated Press Antitrust Suit: A Philosophical Clash over Ownership of First Amendment Rights', *The Business History Review*, vol. 61, no. 1, pp.43–85. https://doi.org/10.2307/3115774

Bleyer, Wollard G. (1926) 'The Press and Public Opinion in International Relations', *Journalism Quarterly*, vol. 3, no. 2, pp.7–20. https://doi.org/10.1177/107769902600300203

Bloch, Ernst (1959/1986) *The Principle of Hope*, UK: Basil Blackwell.

Blum, John M. (1976) *V Was for Victory: Politics and American Culture during World War II*, USA: Harcourt Brace.

Blumler, Jay G. (1981) 'Mass Communication Research in Europe: Some Origins and Prospects', in Burgoon, Judee K. (ed.) *Communication Yearbook 5*, USA: Transaction Books, pp.145–56.

Blumler, Jay G. and Gurevitch, Michael G. (1995) 'Towards a Comparative Framework for Political Communication Research', in Chaffee, Steven H. (ed.) *The Crisis of Public Communication*, UK: Sage, pp.165–93.

Blumler, Jay G.; McLeod, Jack M.; and Rosengren, Karl E. (1992) 'An Introduction to Comparative Communication Research', in Blumler, Jay G.; McLeod, Jack M.; and Rosengren, Karl E. (eds) *Comparatively Speaking: Communication and Culture Across Space and Time*, USA: Sage, pp.3–18.

Blyth, Mark (2006) 'Great Punctuations: Prediction, Randomness, and the Evolution of Comparative Political Science', *The American Political Science Review*, vol. 100, no. 4, pp.493–98. https://doi.org/10.1017/S0003055406062344

Borgos, Anna (2021) *Women in the Budapest School of Psychoanalysis: Girls of Tomorrow*, UK: Routledge.

Bourdieu, Pierre (1979/1984) *Distinction: A Social Critique of the Judgement of Taste*, UK: Routledge.

Bourdieu, Pierre (1986) 'The Forms of Capital', in Richardson, John G. (ed.) *Handbook of Theory and Research for the Sociology of Education*, USA: Greenwood, pp.241–58.

Bourdieu, Pierre (1988) *Homo Academicus*, USA: Stanford University Press.

Bourdieu, Pierre (1993) *The Field of Cultural Production*, USA: Columbia University Press.

Breiner, Peter (2004) 'Translating Max Weber: Exile Attempts to Forge a New Political Science', *European Journal of Political Theory*, vol. 3, no. 2, pp.133–49. https://doi.org/10.1177/1474885104041043

Breiner, Peter (2013) 'Karl Mannheim and Political Ideology', in Freedman, Michael; Sargent, Lyman T.; and Stear, Marc (eds) *The Oxford Handbook of Political Ideologies*, UK: Oxford University Press, pp.38–55.

Brown, Chris (2001) 'Fog in the Channel: Continental International Relations Theory Isolated (or an Essay on the Paradoxes of Diversity and Parochialism in IR Theory)', in Crawford, Robert and Jarvis, Darryl S. (eds) *International Relations: Still an American Social Science?* USA: State University of New York Press, pp.203–20.

Bulmer, Martin (1985) 'The Development of Sociology and of Empirical Social Research in Britain', in Bulmer, Martin (ed.) *Essays on the History of British Sociological Research*, UK: Cambridge University Press, pp.3–38.

Bulmer, Martin (1996) 'Edward Shils as a Sociologist', *Minerva*, vol. 34, no. 1, pp.7–21. https://www.jstor.org/stable/41821007

Bush, Michael (2021) 'Robert K. Merton'. *Oxford Bibliographies in Criminology*. https://www.doi.org/10.1093/OBO/9780195396607-0299

Buxton, William J. (2003) 'John Marshall and the Humanities in Europe: Shifting Patterns of Rockefeller Foundation Support', *Minerva*, vol. 41, no. 2, pp.133–53. https://www.jstor.org/stable/41821239#metadata_info_tab_contents

'C.R. Walgreen takes Niece From College; Drug Chain Head Attacks 'Red Teaching' at the University of Chicago' (1935) *The New York Times*, 12 April. https://www.nytimes.com/1935/04/12/archives/cr-walgreen-takes-niece-from-college-drug-chain-head-attacks-red.html

Caldwell, Mary E. (1979) 'Statement Made at or Prepared for Memorial Service in New Haven, at the Yale Law School Auditorium, on April 7, 1979', in *Harold Dwight Lasswell, 1902–1978: Ford Foundation Professor Emeritus of Law and the Social Sciences, Yale University: In Commemoration and Continuing Commitment*, USA: Yale Law School, Policy Sciences Center, Ogden Foundation, pp.44–49.

Calhoun, Craig (2003) *Robert Merton Remembered. Footnotes*, vol. 31, no. 3, pp.3–8. https://www.asanet.org/wp-content/uploads/fn_2003_03_march.pdf

Calhoun, Craig (2010) 'Introduction: On Merton's Legacy and Contemporary Sociology', in Calhoun, Craig (ed.) *Robert K. Merton: Sociology of Science and Sociology as Science*, USA: Columbia University Press, pp.1–31.

Carey, James W. (1989) *Communication as Culture: Essays on Media and Society*, USA: Unwin Hyman.

Carlsson, Ulla (2003) 'The Rise and Fall of NWICO: From a Vision of International Regulation to a Reality of Multilevel Governance', *Nordicom Review*, vol. 24, no. 2, pp.31–67. https://doi.org/10.1515/nor-2017-0306

Cartier, Jacqueline M. (1988) *Wilbur Schramm and the Beginnings of American Communication Theory: A History of Ideas*. PhD thesis, USA: University of Iowa.

Casebier, Allan and Copi, Irving (1994) 'Abraham Kaplan 1918–1993', *Proceedings and Addresses of the American Philosophical Association*, vol. 67, issue. 4, pp.137–40. http://www.jstor.org/stable/3130752

Caute, David (1978) *The Great Fear: The Anti-Communist Purge under Truman and Eisenhower*, USA: Simon & Schuster.

Chaffee, Steven H. (1974) 'The Pathways of Proteus', in Westley, Bruce H. (ed.) *Contributions of Wilbur Schramm to Mass Communication Research. Journalism Monograph, No.36*, USA: Association for Education in Journalism, pp.1–8. https://files.eric.ed.gov/fulltext/ED099879.pdf

Chaffee, Steven H. and Rogers, Everett M. (1997) 'Institutionalization of Advanced Communication Study in American Universities', in Schramm, Wilbur *The Beginnings of Communication Study in America: A Personal Memoir*, USA: Sage, pp.155–80.

Chang, Tsan-Kuo (2015) 'Beyond Lazarsfeld: International Communication Research and Its Production of Knowledge', in Lee, Chin-Chuan (ed.) *Internationalizing 'International Communication'*, USA: University of Michigan Press, pp.41–65.

Chauncey, George; Duberman, Martin B.; and Vicinus, Martha (1991) 'Introduction', in Duberman, Martin; Vicinus, Martha; Chauncey, George (eds) *Hidden From History: Reclaiming the Gay and Lesbian Past*, UK: Penguin, pp.1–13.

Christians, Clifford G.; Glasser, Theodore L.; McQuail, Denis; Norden-streng, Kaarle; and White, Robert A. (2009) *Normative Theories of the Media: Journalism in Democratic Societies*, USA: University of Illinois Press.

Clark, Jon; Modgil, Celia; and Modgil, Sohan. (1990) *Robert K. Merton: Consensus and Controversy*, UK: Falmer.

Cmiel, Kenneth (1996) 'On Cynicism, Evil, and the Discovery of Communication in the 1940s', *Journal of Communication*, vol. 46, no. 3, pp.88–107. https://doi.org/10.1111/j.1460-2466.1996.tb01491.x

Coggeshall, Reginald (1942) 'Peace Conference Publicity: Lessons of 1919', *Journalism Quarterly*, vol. 19, no. 1, pp.1–11.

Coleman, Rebecca (2018) 'Theorizing the Present: Digital Media, Pre-emergence and Infra-structures of Feeling'. *Cultural Studies*, vol. 32, no. 4, pp.600–22. https://doi.org/10.1080/09502386.2017.1413121

Commission on Freedom of the Press (1947) *A Free and Responsible Press. A General Report on Mass Communication: Newspapers, Radio, Motion Pictures, Magazines, and Books*, USA: University of Chicago Press.

Committee on International Communications Research (1952) 'Proceedings of the Committee on International Communications Research', *Public Opinion Quarterly*, vol. 16, no. 4, pp.705–08. https://doi.org/10.1086/266434

Congdon, Lee (1991) *Exile and Social Thought: Hungarian Intellectuals in Germany and Austria, 1919–1933*, USA: Princeton University Press.

Connolly, John (2019) 'Generational Conflict and the Sociology of Generations: Mannheim and Elias Reconsidered', *Theory, Culture & Society*, vol. 36, no. 7–8, pp.153–72. https://doi.org/10.1177/0263276419827085

Cooper, Kent (1942) *Barriers Down: The Story of the News Agency Epoch*, USA: Farrar & Rinehart.

Cooper, Kent (1945a) 'Crusade for Truth. Kent Cooper Heads a Unique American Campaign for Worldwide Freedom of the Press, Meaning What?' *Fortune*, April, 31, 146–49.

Cooper, Kent (1945b) 'AP Put Under Court Control by Demand of FDR–Cooper', *Editor & Publisher*, vol. 78, no. 43, 20 October, p.11. https://rchive.org/details/sim_editor-publisher_1945-10-20_78_43

Cooper, Kent (1946) *Anna Zenger, Mother of Freedom*, USA: Farrar, Straus and Company.

Cooper, Kent (1947) 'Cooper Criticizes "Voice of America"; It Is Impotent, He Says at Medill School Jubilee, Speaking Not as AP Chief', *The New York Times*, 27 May. https://www.nytimes.com/1947/05/27/archives/cooper-criticizes-voice-of-america-it-is-impotent-he-says-at-medill.html

Cooper, Kent (1956) *The Right to Know: An Exposition of the Evils of News Suppression and Propaganda*, USA: Farrar, Straus and Cudahy.

Cooper, Kent (1959) *Kent Cooper and the Associated Press: An Autobiography*, USA: Random House.

Coser, Lewis A (1984) *Refugee Scholars in America. Their Impact and Their Experiences*, USA: Yale University Press.

Cox, Michael (2021) '"His Finest Hour": William Beveridge and the Academic Assistance Council'. https://blogs.lse.ac.uk/lsehistory/2021/04/28/his-finest-hour-william-beveridge-and-academic-assistance-council

Cox, Robert W. (1986) 'Social Forces, States and World Orders: Beyond International Relations Theory', in Keohane, Robert O. (ed.) *Neorealism and Its Critics*, USA: Columbia University Press, pp.204–05.

Creel, George (1920) *How We Advertised America: The First Telling of the Amazing Story of the Committee on Public Information that Carried the Gospel of Americanism to Every Corner of the Globe*, USA: Harper & Brothers.

Cross, Harold and American Society of Newspaper Editors (1953) *The people's right to know; legal access to public records and proceedings*, USA: Columbia University Press.

Curran, James (2011) *Media and Democracy*, UK: Routledge.

Cuthbert, Marlene (1980) 'Reaction to International News Agencies: 1930s and 1970s Compared', *Gazette*, vol. 26, no. 2, pp.99–110.

Dale, Henry (1936) *The Protection of Science and Learning*, UK: Society for Protection of Science and Learning.

'Daniel Lerner Appointed Professor of International Communication December 10' (1957) MIT Press release. https://cdn.libraries.mit.edu/dissemination/diponline/AC0069_NewReleases/NewsRelease_1950/AC0069_1957/AC0069_195712_007.pdf

Davis, Elmer (1951) 'War Information', in Lerner, Daniel (ed.) *Propaganda in War and Crisis: Material for American Policy*, USA: George W. Stewart, pp.274–313.

Davison, W. Phillips (2006) *A Personal History of World War II: How a Pacifist Draftee Accidentally Became a Military Government Official in Postwar Germany*, USA: iUniverse.

Davison, W. Phillips and George, Alexander L. (1952) 'An Outline for the Study of International Political Communications', *Public Opinion Quarterly*, vol. 16, no. 4, pp.501–11. https://doi.org/10.1086/266413

Dayé, Christian (2020) *Experts, Social Scientists, and Techniques of Prognosis in Cold War America*, Austria: Palgrave Macmillan.

de Sola Pool, Ithiel (1952) *The 'Prestige Papers': A Survey of Their Editorials*, USA: Stanford University Press.

de Sola Pool, Ithiel (1954) *Research in International Communication*, USA: Massachusetts Institute of Technology. Center for International Studies.

de Sola Pool, Ithiel (1955) *Progress of the International Communications Program*, USA: Massachusetts Institute of Technology. Center for International Studies.

de Sola Pool, Ithiel (1969) 'Content Analysis and the Intelligence Function', in Rogow, Arnold A. (ed.) *Politics, Personality, and Social Science in the Twentieth Century: Essays in Honor of Harold D. Lasswell*, USA: University of Chicago Press, pp.197–224.

de Sola Pool, Ithiel (ed.) (1959) *Trends in Content Analysis*, USA: University of Illinois Press.

Deflem, Mathieu (2018) 'Merton, Robert K', in Turner, Bryan S. (ed.) *The Wiley Blackwell Encyclopaedia of Social Theory*, USA: Wiley-Blackwell, pp.1–3. https://drive.google.com/file/d/1ccnjy6CpqGsQfML2XUr1o j61DJ7QFIWi/view?pli=1

Delia, Jesse (1987) 'Communication Research: A History', in Berger, Charles R. and Chaffee, Steven H. (eds) *Handbook of Communication Science*, USA: Sage, pp.20–98.

Dennis, Everette E. and Wartella, Ellen (1996) *American Communication Research. The Remembered History*, USA: Lawrence Erlbaum Associates.

Desmond, Robert W. (1937) *The Press and World Affairs*, USA: D. Appleton -Century.

'Directors and Members of the AP Join In Honoring Melville E. Stone' (1918) *Editor & Publisher*, vol 50, no. 46, 27 April, p.1. https://archive .org/details/sim_editor-publisher_1918-04-27_50_46/page/4/mode /2up

Doob, Leonard W. (1947) 'The Utilization of Social Scientists in the Overseas Branch of the Office of War Information', *American Political Science Review*, vol. 41, no. 4, pp.649–67. https://doi.org/10.2307/1950646

Dorzweiler, Nick (2015) 'Frankfurt Meets Chicago: Collaborations between the Institute for Social Research and Harold Lasswell, 1933–1941', *Polity*, vol. 47, no. 3, pp.352–75. https://doi.org/10.1057/pol.2015.10

Douglass, Paul F. and Bomer, Karl (1932) 'The International Combination of News Agencies', *Annals of the American Academy of Political and Social Science*, vol. 162, pp.265–68.
https://journals.sagepub.com/doi/pdf/10.1177/000271623216200138

'Draft Convention of the Gathering and International Transmission of News' (1948) United Nations Conference on Freedom of Information.
https://igitallibrary.un.org/record/212470

Dunn, William N. (2019) *Pragmatism and the Origins of the Policy Sciences Rediscovering Lasswell and the Chicago School*, UK: Cambridge University Press.

Eagleton, Terry (2007) *Ideology: An Introduction*, UK: Verso.

Easton, David (1950) 'Harold Lasswell; Policy Scientist for a Democratic Society', *The Journal of Politics*, vol. 12, no. 3, pp.450–77.
https://doi.org/10.2307/2126297

Easton, David (1953) *The Political System: An Inquiry into the State of Political Science*, USA: Alfred A. Knopf.

Edmunds, June and Turner, Bryan S. (2005) 'Global Generations: Social Change in the Twentieth Century', *The British Journal of Sociology*, vol. 56, no. 4, pp.559–77.
https://doi.org/10.1111/j.1468-4446.2005.00083.x

Eisenstadt, Shmuel N. (1968) 'Social Institutions: Comparative Study', in Sills, David L. (ed.) *International Encyclopedia of the Social Sciences, Vol. 14*, USA: Macmillan & Free Press, pp.421–28.

Eisenstadt, Shmuel N. (1987) 'The Classical Sociology of Knowledge and Beyond', *Minerva*, vol. 25, no. 1/2, pp.77–91.
https://doi.org/10.1007/BF01096857

'Eleanor Blum Papers, 1962–1991' (no date) University of Illinois Archives.
https://archon.library.illinois.edu/archives/index.php?p=collections/controlcard&id=4635

Emerson, Thomas I. and Helfeld, David M. (1948) 'Loyalty among Government Employees', *The Yale Law Journal*, vol. 58, no. 1, pp.1–143.
https://doi.org/10.2307/793350

Emery, John R. (2021) 'Moral Choices without Moral Language: 1950s Political-Military Wargaming at the RAND Corporation', *Texas National Security Review*, vol. 4, no. 4, pp.12–31. http://dx.doi.org/10.26153/tsw/17528

Ennis, Thomas W. (1978) 'Harold D. Lasswell Dead at 76; Was Top US Political Scientist', *The New York Times*, 20 December. https://www.nytimes .com/1978/12/20/archives/harold-d-lasswell-dead-at-76-was-top-us -political-scientist.html

Entwisle, John (no date) 'Sir Roderick Jones's Finest Hour', *The Baron*. https://www.thebaron.info/archives/sir-roderick-joness-finest-hour

Epstein, Joseph (1996) 'My Friend Edward', *Minerva*, vol. 34, no. 1, pp.103–23. https://www.jstor.org/stable/41821015

Eulau, Heinz (1966) *Political Behavior in America: New Directions*, USA: Random House.

Eulau, Heinz (1968) 'The Behavioral Movement in Political Science: A Personal Document', *Social Research*, vol. 35, no. 1, pp.1–29. https://www.jstor.org/stable/40969896

Eulau, Heinz (1977) 'The Hoover Elite Studies Revisited', *Social Science History*, vol. 1, no. 3, pp.392–400. https://doi.org/10.1017/S0145553200022136

Eulau, Heinz (1979) 'Statement Made at Service in New York City, at the New York Academy of Sciences, on December 21, 1978 and Other Memorial Items', in *Harold Dwight Lasswell, 1902–1978: Ford Foundation Professor Emeritus of Law and the Social Sciences, Yale University: In Commemoration and Continuing Commitment*, USA: Yale Law School, Policy Sciences Center, Ogden Foundation, pp.87–97.

Eulau, Heinz and Zlomke, Susan (1999) 'Harold D. Lasswell's Legacy to Mainstream Political Science: A Neglected Agenda', *Annual Review of Political Science*, vol. 2, pp.75–89. https://doi.org/10.1146/annurev.polisci.2.1.75

Eulau, Heinz and Zlomke, Susan (1999) 'Harold D. Lasswell's Legacy to Mainstream Political Science: A Neglected Agenda', *Annual Review of Political Science*, vol. 2, pp.75–89. https://doi.org/10.1146/annurev.polisci.2.1.75

Farr, James; Hacker, Jacob S.; and Kazee, Nicole (2006) 'The Policy Scientist of Democracy: The Discipline of Harold D. Lasswell'. *American Political Science Review*, vol. 100, no. 4, pp.579–87. https://doi.org/10.1017/S0003055406062459

Farr, James; Hacker, Jacob S.; and Kazee, Nicole (2008) 'Revisiting Lasswell', *Policy Sciences*, vol. 41, no. 1, pp.21–32. https://doi.org/10.1007/s11077-007-9052-9

Federal Bureau of Investigation (FBI) Dallas Walker Smythe File. https:// www.documentcloud.org/documents/20613406-ef2f230d15919ac9d 2c090f509126b3e98bfe75cb_q102985_r364624_d2648342

'Ferment in the Field. Introduction' (1983) *Journal of Communication*, Vol. 33, no 3, pp.4–5. https://doi.org/10.1111/j.1460-2466.1983.tb02400.x

Fischer, Ariane (2009) 'Settling Accounts with the Sociology of Knowledge: The Frankfurt School, Mannheim, and the Marxian Critique of Ideology Qua Mental Labor', *The South Atlantic Quarterly*, vol. 108, no. 2, pp.331–63. https://doi.org/10.1215/003828762008036

Forrest, Wilbur (1945) 'Letter to Stettinius Outlines Mission', *Editor & Publisher*, vol. 78, no. 25, 18 June, p.4. https://archive.org/details/sim_editor-publisher_1945-06-16_78_25/page/n79/mode/2up

Frederick, Howard H. (1981) *The Life Work of Ithiel De Sola Pool: An Assessment and Bibliography*. Colloquium in International Communication, USA: The American University. https://www.academia.edu/30119424/The_Life_and_Work_of_Ithiel_de_Sola_

Freedman, Lawrence Z. (1981) 'Harold Dwight Lasswell (1902–1978): In Memoriam', *Political Communication*, vol. 1, no. 2, pp.103–06. https://doi.org/10.1080/10584609.1981.9962720

Freud, Sigmund and Strachey, James (1899/1954) *The Interpretation of Dreams* (new ed.), UK: Allen and Unwin.

Fuller, Steve (2006) *The Philosophy of Science and Technology Studies*, UK: Routledge.

Gabel, Joseph (1976) 'Utopian Consciousness and False Consciousness', *Telos*, vol. 29, Fall, pp.181–86. https://doi.org/10.3817/0976029181

Gabel, Joseph (1991) *Mannheim and Hungarian Marxism*, USA: Transaction.

Gábor, Éva (1996) *Mannheim Károly levelezése* 1911–1946, Hungary: Argumentum Kiadó M T A Lukács Archívum. http://real-eod.mtak.hu/650/1/ArchivumiFuzetek_1996_12.pdf

Galtung, Johan and Ruge, Mari Holmboe (1965) 'The Structure of Foreign News', *Journal of Peace Research*, vol. 2, no. 1, pp.64–91. https://doi.org/10.1177/002234336500200104

Gary, Brett J. (1992) *American Liberalism and the Problem of Propaganda: Scholars, Lawyers, and the War on Words, 1919-1945*, USA: University of Pennsylvania.

Gary, Brett J. (1996) 'Communication Research, the Rockefeller Foundation, and Mobilization for the War on Words, 1938–1944', *Journal of Communication*, vol. 46, no. 3, pp.124–48. https://doi.org/10.1111/j.1460-2466.1996.tb01493.x

Gary, Brett J. (1999) *The Nervous Liberals: Propaganda Anxieties from World War I to the Cold War*, USA: Columbia University Press.

Geertz, Clifford (1973) *The Interpretation of Cultures*, USA: Harper and Row.

Geoghegan, Vincent (2004) 'Ideology and Utopia', *Journal of Political Ideologies*, vol. 9, no. 2, pp.123–38. https://doi.org/10.1080/1356931041000169172

George, Alexander L. (1956) 'Prediction of Political Action by Means of Propaganda Analysis', *Public Opinion Quarterly*, vol. 20, no. 1, pp.334–45. https://doi.org/10.1086/266623

George, Alexander L. (1959) *Propaganda Analysis: A Study of Inferences Made from Nazi Propaganda in World War II*, USA: Row, Peterson & Co.

George, Alexander L. (2019) 'Prediction of Political Action by Means of Propaganda Analysis', in Caldwell, Dan (ed.) *A Pioneer in Political and Social Sciences*, USA: Springer, pp.75–87.

George, Juliette (2008) 'Recollections of Alex George', *Political Psychology*, vol. 29, no. 4, pp.475–87. https://doi.org/10.1111/j.1467-9221.2008.00645.x

'George Stoddard Dies at the Age of 84 in 1981. Educator Led 4 Universities' (1981) *The New York Times*, 29 December. https://www.nytimes.com /1981/12/29/obituaries/george-stoddard-dies-at-84-educator-led-4 -universities.html

Gilman, Nils (2003) *Mandarins of the Future: Modernization Theory in Cold War America*, USA: Johns Hopkins University Press.

Gitlin, Todd (1978) 'Media Sociology: The Dominant Paradigm', *Theory and Society*, vol. 6, no. 2, pp.205–53. https://doi.org/10.1007/BF01681751

Glander, Timothy (1996) 'Wilbur Schramm and the Founding of Communication Studies', *Educational Theory*, vol. 46, no. 3, pp.373–91. https://doi.org/10.1111/j.1741-5446.1996.00373.x

Glander, Timothy (2000) *Origins of Mass Communications Research during the American Cold War: Educational Effects and Contemporary Implications*, UK: Routledge.

Gluck, Mary (1985) *Georg Lukács and His Generation, 1900–1918*, USA: Harvard University Press.

Goldsen, Joseph (1959) (ed.) *Outer Space in World Politics*, USA: Frederick A. Praeger.

Goldstein, Jacob (1943) 'An Exploratory Analysis of Opinion Trends with Special Reference to Conscription in the United States', *Sociometry*, vol. 6, no. 2, pp.156–81. https://doi.org/10.2307/2785355

Gouldner, Alwin W. (1979) *The Future of Intellectuals and the Rise of the New Class: A Frame of Reference, Theses, Conjectures, Arguments, and an Historical Perspective on the Role of Intellectuals and Intelligentsia in the International Class Contest of the Modern Era*, UK: Macmillan.

Gramling, Oliver (1940/1969) *AP (Associated Press): The Story of News*, USA: Kennikat Press.

Griffiths, Martin and O'Callaghan, Terry (2001a) *International Relations: The Key Concepts*, UK: Routledge.

Griffiths, Martin and O'Callaghan, Terry (2001b) 'The End of International Relations?' in Griffiths, Martin and O'Callaghan, Terry (eds) *International Relations—Still an American Social Science? Toward Diversity in International Thought*, USA: State University of New York Press, pp.187–202.

Grimley, Matthew (2007) Moot (Act. 1938–1947). *Oxford Dictionary of National Biography*. https://www.oxforddnb.com/view/10.1093/ref:odnb/9780198614128.001.0001/odnb-9780198614128-e-67745

Gross, Larry P. (1993) *Contested Closets: The Politics and Ethics of Outing*, USA: University of Minnesota.

Guback, Thomas H. (1969) *The International Film Industry: Western Europe and America Since 1945*, USA: Indiana University Press.

Guback, Thomas H. (1995) 'Marxism', in Nerone, John (ed.) *Last Rights: Revisiting Four Theories of the Press*, USA: University of Illinois Press, pp.125–52.

'Guide to the Ithiel de Sola Pool Papers 1935–1948' (2011) *Biographical Note*. University of Chicago Library. https://www.lib.uchicago.edu/e/scrc/findingaids/view.php?eadid=ICU.SPCL.POOLI

'Guide to the Louis Wirth papers, 1918–1952' (2008) University of Chicago Library. https://www.lib.uchicago.edu/e/scrc/findingaids/view.php?eadid=ICU.SPCL.WIRTH

'Guide to the Morris Janowitz Collection 1940–1989' (2009) University of Chicago Library. https://www.lib.uchicago.edu/e/scrc/findingaids/view.php?eadid=ICU.SPCL.JANOWITZM

Gunaratne, Shelton A. (2005) *The Dao of the Press: A Humanocentric Theory*, USA: Hampton Press.

Gurukkal, Rajan (2019) *History and Theory of Knowledge Production: An Introductory Outline*, UK: Oxford University Press. https://doi.org/10.1093/oso/9780199490363.001.0001

'György Kecskeméti' (2008) https://www.jewishvirtuallibrary.org/kecskem-x00e9-ti-gy-x0151-rgy

Hachten, William A. and Hachten, Harva (1992) *The World News Prism: Changing Media of International Communication*, USA: Iowa State University Press.

Halliday, Fred (1985) 'Book Reviews: A "Crisis" of International Relations?' *International Relations*, vol. 8, no. 4, pp.407–12. https://doi.org/10.1177/004711788500800

Hallin, Daniel C. and Mancini, Paolo (2004) *Comparing Media Systems: Three Models of Media and Politics*, USA: Cambridge University Press.

Hallin, Daniel C. and Mancini, Paolo (2012) *Comparing Media Systems Beyond the Western World*, USA: Cambridge University Press.

Hammersley Martyn (2021) 'Planning versus the Market: The Dispute between Hayek and Mannheim and Its Contemporary Relevance', *British Journal of Sociology*, vol. 72, no. 5, pp.1464–78. https://doi.org/10.1111/1468-4446.12893

Hammersley, Martyn (2022) 'Karl Mannheim's Ideology and Utopia and the Public Role of Sociology', *Journal of Classical Sociology*, vol. 22, no. 2, pp.176–98. https://doi.org/10.1177/1468795X20986382

Hanitzsch, Thomas (2008) 'Comparing Media Systems Reconsidered: Recent Development and Directions for Future Research', *Journal of Global Mass Communication*, vol. 1, no. 3/4, pp.111–17.

Hannerz, Ulf (1992) *Cultural Complexity: Studies in the Social Organization of Meaning*, USA: Columbia University Press.

'Hans Speier Papers, 1922–1989' (no date) M.E. Grenander Department of Special Collections and Archives, University Libraries, University at Albany, State University of New York. https://archives.albany.edu/description/catalog/ger084

Hanson, Elizabeth C. (2020) 'A History of International Communication Studies', in *Oxford Research Encyclopedia of International Studies*. https://doi.org/10.1093/acrefore/9780190846626.013.63

Hanusch, Folker and Vos, Tim P. (2020) 'Charting the Development of a Field: A Systematic Review of Comparative Studies of Journalism', *International Communication Gazette*, vol. 82, no. 4, pp.319–41. https://doi.org/10.1177/1748048518822606

Hardt, Hanno (1979) *Social Theories of the Press: Early German and American Perspectives*, USA: Sage Publications.

Hardt, Hanno (1988) 'Comparative Media Research: The World According to America', *Critical Studies in Mass Communication*, vol. 5, no. 2, pp.129–46. https://doi.org/10.1080/15295038809366693

Hardt, Hanno (1992) *Critical Communication Studies: Communication, History, and Theory in America*, UK: Routledge.

Hayek, Friedrich A. von (1944) *The Road to Serfdom*, UK: Routledge and Kegan Paul.

Heaney, Michael T. and Hansen, John M. (2006) 'Building the Chicago School', *American Political Science Review*, vol. 100, no. 4, pp.589–96. https://doi.org/10.1017/S0003055406062460

Heeren, John (1971) 'Karl Mannheim and the Intellectual Elite', *The British Journal of Sociology*, vol. 22, no. 1, pp.1–15. https://doi.org/10.2307/588721

Herman, Ellen (1995) *The Romance of American Psychology: Political Culture in the Age of Experts*, USA: University of California Press.

Hester, Al (1971) 'An Analysis of News Flow from Developed and Developing Nations', *Gazette*, vol. 17, no. 1–2, pp.29–43. https://doi.org/10.1177/0016549271017001

Hewitt, Nelson E. (1935) *How Red Is the University of Chicago?* USA: Advisory Associates.

Horowitz, Irving L. (1996) 'Culture, Politics and McCarthyism: A Retrospective from the Trenches', *The Independent Review*, vol. 1, no. 1, pp.101–10. https://www.independent.org/pdf/tir/tir_01_1_07_horowitz.pdf

Hounshell, David (1997) 'The Cold War, RAND, and the Generation of Knowledge, 1946–1962', *Historical Studies in the Physical and Biological Sciences*, vol. 27, no. 2, pp.237–67. https://doi.org/10.2307/27757779

Howie, Marguerite R. (1961) 'Karl Mannheim and the Sociology of Knowledge', *The Journal of Education*, vol. 143, no. 4, pp.55–71. https://doi.org/10.1177/002205746114300040

Huang, Chenju (2003) 'Transitional Media vs. Normative Theories: Schramm, Altschull, and China', *Journal of Communication*, vol. 53, no. 3, pp.444–59. https://doi.org/10.1111/j.1460-2466.2003.tb02601.x

Hur, Kyoon K. (1984) 'A Critical Analysis of International News Flow Research', *Critical Studies in Mass Communication*, vol. 1, no. 4, pp.365–78. https://doi.org/10.1080/15295038409360047

Hvidsten, Andreas H. (2019) 'Karl Mannheim and the Liberal Telos of Realism', *International Relations*, vol. 33, no. 3, pp.475–93. https://doi.org/10.1177/0047117819846544

Iacobelli, Teresa (2021) *The Rockefeller Foundation's Refugee Scholar Program*. https://resource.rockarch.org/story/the-rockefeller-foundations-refugee-scholar-program-world-war-ii-nazi-europe

'In Remembrance of Jacques Kayser' (1963) *Gazette*, vol. 9, no. 4, pp.1–3. https://doi.org/10.1177/001654926300900407

Institut für Sozialforschung (1936) *Studien über Autorität und Familie: Forschungsberichte aus dem Institut für Sozialforschung*, Bd. 5, France: F. Alcan.

'International Congress Will Consider Plans for World-Wide News Service' (1919) *Editor & Publisher*, vol. 72, no. 7, 17 July, p.9. https://archive.org/details/sim_editor-publisher_1919-07-17_52_7

International Press Institute (1953) *The Flow of News: A Study by the International Press Institute*, Switzerland: International Press Institute.

Inter-Ocean Publishing Co. v. Associated Press (1900) 184 Ill. 438, USA: Illinois Supreme Court.

'Introduction to the Special Issue: Critical versus Administrative Policy Studies—Celebrating 75 Years since Paul Lazarsfeld's 'Remarks on Administrative and Critical Communication Research' (2016) *Journal of Information Policy*, vol. 6, pp.1–3. https://doi.org/10.5325/jinfopoli.6.2016.0001

Isaac, Joel (2007) 'The Human Sciences in Cold War America', *The Historical Journal*, vol. 50, no. 3, pp.725–46.
https://doi.org/10.1017/S0018246X07006334

'Ithiel de Sola Pool' (1997) https://web.mit.edu/m-i-t/profiles/profile_ithiel.html

Iwanaga, Shinkichi (1980) *Story of Japanese News Agencies: A Historic Account From Meiji Restoration (1868) to the End of World War II (1945)*, Japan: Institute of News Service Research.

Izzo, Alberto (1998) 'Conditioning or Conditionings? Revisiting an Old Criticism on Mannheim by Merton', in Merton, Robert K.; Mongardini, Carlo; and Tabboni, Simonetta (eds) *Robert K. Merton and Contemporary Sociology*, USA: Transaction, pp.213–20.

Janis, Irving L. (1943) 'Meaning and the Study of Symbolic Behavior', *Psychiatry*, vol. 6, no. 4, pp.425–39. https://doi.org/10.1080/00332747.1943.11022475

Janis, Irving L. and Fadner, Raymond H. (1943a) 'A Coefficient Imbalance for Content Analysis'. Library of Congress, Experimental Division for the Study of War-Time Communication, Document No 31.

Janis, Irving L. and Fadner, Raymond H. (1943b) 'A Coefficient of Imbalance for Content Analysis', *Psychometrika*, vol. 8, no. 2, pp.105–19.
https://doi.org/10.1007/BF02288695

Janis, Irving L.; Fadner Raymond H.; and Janowitz, Morris (1942a) 'Content Analysis Technique'. Library of Congress, Experimental Division for the Study of War-Time Communication, Document No 33.

Janis, Irving L.; Fadner, Raymond H.; and Janowitz, Morris (1942b) 'The Reliability of a Content Analysis Technique'. Experimental Division for the Study of War-Time Communication, Document No 32.

Janis, Irving L.; Fadner, Raymond H.; and Janowitz, Morris (1943) 'The Reliability of a Content Analysis Technique', *The Public Opinion Quarterly*, vol. 7, no. 2, pp.293–96.
https://www.jstor.org/stable/2745657#metadata_info_tab_contents

Janowitz, Morris (1968) 'Harold D. Lasswell's Contribution to Content Analysis'. *The Public Opinion Quarterly*, vol. 32, no. 4, pp.646–53.
https://doi.org/10.1086/267652

Janowitz, Morris (1969) 'Content Analysis and the Study of the "Symbolic Environment"', in Rogow, Arnold A. (ed.) *Politics, Personality, and Social*

Science in the Twentieth Century: Essays in Honor of Harold D. Lasswell, USA: University of Chicago Press, pp.155–70.

Jay, Martin (1973/1996) *The Dialectical Imagination: A History of the Frankfurt School and the Institute of Social Research, 1923–1950*, USA: University of California Press.

Jay, Martin (1974/1994) 'The Frankfurt School's Critique of Karl Mannheim and the Sociology of Knowledge', in Bernstein, Jay M. (ed.) *The Frankfurt School: Critical Assessments*, UK: Routledge, pp.175–90.

Jehlen, Myra (1986) 'Introduction: Beyond Transcendence', in Bercovitch, Sacvan and Jehlen, Myra (eds) *Ideology and Classic American Literature*, UK: Cambridge University Press, pp.1–20.

John, Richard R. (2020) 'When Techno-diplomacy Failed: Walter S. Rogers, the Universal Electrical Communications Union, and the Limitations of the International Telegraph Union as a Global Actor in the 1920s', in Fickers, Andreas and Balbi, Gabriele (eds) *History of the International Telecommunication Union (ITU): Transnational Techno-diplomacy from the Telegraph to the Internet*, Germany: De Gruyter Oldenbourg, pp.55–76.

Johnson, David K. (2004) *The Lavender Scare: The Cold War Persecution of Gays and Lesbians in the Federal Government*, USA: University of Chicago Press.

Jones, J. (no date) *The Meaning of Symbols in Psychoanalysis*. http://www.freudfile.org/psychoanalysis/symbols.html

Jones, Paul K. and Pusey, Michael (2010) 'Political Communication and "Media System": The Australian Canary', *Media, Culture & Society*, vol. 32, no. 3, pp.451–71. https://doi.org/10.1177/016344370936117

Jones, Roderick S. (1951) *A Life in Reuters*, UK: Hodder & Stoughton.

Julia Mannheim (née Láng) (1893–1995) *Psychoanalytikerinnen. Biografisches Lexikon*. https://www.psychoanalytikerinnen.de/greatbritain _biographies.html#Mannheim

Kadarkay, Arpad (1991) *Georg Lukacs: Life, Thought and Politics*, UK: Basil Blackwell.

Kaiser, David (1998) 'A Mannheim for All Seasons: Bloor, Merton, and the Roots of the Sociology of Scientific Knowledge', *Science in Context*, vol. 11, no. 1, pp.51–87. https://doi.org/10.1017/S026988970000291X

'Kaplan (Abraham) Papers' (no date). https://oac.cdlib.org/findaid/ark:/13030/c86q1z11

Kaplan, Abraham (1943) 'Content Analysis and the Theory of Signs', *Philosophy of Science*, vol. 10, no. 4, pp.230–47.

Karácsony, András (2008) 'Soul–Life–Knowledge: The Young Mannheim's Way to Sociology', *Studies in East European Thought*, vol. 60, no. 1/2, pp.97–111. https://doi.org/10.1007/s11212-008-9040-4

Karádi, Éva (1985) 'Einleitung', in Karádi, Éva and Vezér, Erzsébet (eds) *Georg Lukács, Karl Mannheim und der Sonntagskreis*, Germany: Sendler, pp.7–27.

Karl, Barry D. (1974) *Charles E. Merriam and The Study of Politics*, USA: University of Chicago Press.

Katz, Elihu (1977) *Social Research on Broadcasting, Proposals for Further Development: A Report to the British Broadcasting Corporation*, UK: British Broadcasting Corporation.

Katz, Elihu and Katz, Ruth (2016) 'Revisiting the Origin of the Administrative versus Critical Research Debate', *Journal of Information Policy*, vol. 6, pp.4–12. https://doi.org/10.5325/jinfopoli.6.2016.0004

Katz, Elihu; Peters, John Durham; Liebes, Tamar; and Orloff, Avril (2002) (eds) *Canonic Texts in Media Research: Are There Any? Should There Be? How About These?* UK: Polity.

Kayser, Jacques (1953) *One Week's News: Comparative Study of 17 Major Dailies for a Seven-Day Period*, France: UNESCO. https://unesdoc.unesco.org/ark:/48223/pf0000062870

Kecskeméti, Pál (1926) 'A szociológia történetfilozófiai megalapozása: Mannheim Károly', *Századunk*, vol. 1, pp.447–57.

Kecskemeti, Paul (1931) 'Communists Demand Hitler's Arrest'. https://www.upi.com/Archives/1931/10/12/Communists-demand-Hitlers-arrest/7781144211301

Kecskemeti, Paul (1950) 'Totalitarian Communications as a Means of Control', *Public Opinion Quarterly*, vol. 14, no. 2, pp.224–34. https://doi.org/10.1086/266181

Kecskemeti, Paul (1952a) 'Introduction', in Mannheim, Karl *Essays on the Sociology of Knowledge*, UK: Routledge and Kegan Paul, pp.1–32.

Kecskemeti, Paul (1952b) *Meaning, Communication, and Value*, USA: University of Chicago Press.

Kecskemeti, Paul (1953a) *Totalitarianism and the Future*, USA: RAND Corporation.

Kecskemeti, Paul (1953b) *Sociological Aspects of the Information Process*, USA: RAND Corporation.

Kecskemeti, Paul (1956) 'The Soviet Approach to International Political Communication', *Public Opinion Quarterly*, vol. 20, no. 1, pp.299–308. https://doi.org/10.1086/266618

Kecskemeti, Paul (1958a) 'Limits and Problems of Decompression: The Case of Hungary', *The Annals of the American Academy of Political and Social Science*, vol. 317, pp.97–106. https://www.jstor.org/stable/1031082

Kecskemeti, Paul (1958b) *Strategic Surrender: The Politics of Victory and Defeat*, USA: Stanford University Press.

Kecskemeti, Paul and Leites, Nathan (1947) 'Some Psychological Hypotheses on Nazi Germany: I', *The Journal of Social Psychology*, vol. 26(2), pp.141–83. https://doi.org/10.1080/00224545.1947.9921742

Kecskemeti, Paul and Leites, Nathan (1948a) 'Some Psychological Hypotheses on Nazi Germany: II', *The Journal of Social Psychology*, vol. 27, no. 1, pp.91–117. https://doi.org/10.1080/00224545.1948.9918914

Kecskemeti, Paul and Leites, Nathan (1948b) 'Some Psychological Hypotheses on Nazi Germany: III', *The Journal of Social Psychology*, vol. 27, no. 2, pp.241–70. https://doi.org/10.1080/00224545.1948.9918929

Kecskemeti, Paul and Leites, Nathan (1948c) 'Some Psychological Hypotheses on Nazi Germany: IV', *The Journal of Social Psychology*, vol. 28, no. 1, pp.141–64.

Kettler, David (2002) *Contested Legacies: The German-Speaking Intellectual and Cultural Emigration to the US and UK, 1933–1945*, Germany: Galda & Wilch.

Kettler, David (2012) *The Liquidation of Exile: Studies in the Intellectual Emigration of the 1930s*, UK: Cambridge University Press.

Kettler, David and Loader, Colin (2013) 'Weimar Sociology', in Gordon, Peter E. and McCormick, John P. (eds) *Weimar Thought: A Contested Legacy*, USA: Princeton University Press, pp.15–34.

Kettler, David and Meja, Volker (1993) 'Their "Own Peculiar Way": Karl Mannheim and the Rise of Women', *International Sociology*, vol. 8, no. 1, pp.5–55. https://doi.org/10.1177/026858093008001001

Kettler, David and Meja, Volker (1995) *Karl Mannheim and the Crisis of Liberalism: The Secret of These New Times*, USA: Routledge.

Kettler, David and Meja, Volker (2012) 'Karl Mannheim's Jewish Question', *Religions*, vol. 3, no. 2, pp.228–50. https://doi.org/10.3390/rel3020228

Kettler, David; Meja, Volker; and Stehr, Nico (1984) *Karl Mannheim*, UK: Tavistock.

Kilminster, Richard (1993) 'Norbert Elias and Karl Mannheim: Closeness and Distance', *Theory, Culture & Society*, vol. 10, no. 3, pp.81–114. https://doi.org/10.1177/026327693010003005

Kirchick, James (2022) *Secret City: The Hidden History of Gay Washington*, USA: Henry Holt and Company.

Klapper, Joseph T. (1960) *The Effects of Mass Communication.* USA: Free Press of Glencoe.

Klaus, Elisabeth and Seethaler, Josef (2016) *What Do We Really Know about Herta Herzog? Exploring the Life and Work of a Pioneer of Communication Research*, USA: Peter Lang.

Knights, Peter R. (1967) 'The Press Association War of 1866–1867', *Journalism and Communication Monographs*, December, no. 6.

Knobloch-Westerwick, Silvia and Glynn, Carroll J. (2011) 'The Matilda Effect—Role Congruity Effects on Scholarly Communication: A Citation Analysis of Communication Research and Journal of Communication Articles', *Communication Research*, vol. 40, no. 1, pp.3–26. https://doi.org/10.1177/0093650211418339

Kögler, Hans H. (1997) 'Alienation as Epistemological Source: Reflexivity and Social Background after Mannheim and Bourdieu', *Social Epistemology*, vol. 11, no. 2, pp.141–64.

Komor, Valerie S. (2021) *AP at 175: A Photographic History.* https://apimagesblog.com/historical/2021/1/30/ap-at-175-a-photographic-history

Kracauer, Siegfried (1952) 'The Challenge of Qualitative Content Analysis', *The Public Opinion Quarterly*, vol. 16, no. 4, pp.631–42. https://doi.org/10.1086/266427

Krause, Monika (2019) 'What Is Zeitgeist? Examining Period-Specific Cultural Patterns', *Poetics*, vol. 76, pp.18–30. https://doi.org/10.1016/j.poetic.2019.02.003

Krippendorff, Klaus (1980/2004) *Content Analysis: An Introduction to Its Methodology*, UK: Sage.

Kris, Ernst and Leites, Nathan C. (1947) 'Trends in the 20th Century Propaganda', in Roheim, Geza (ed.) *Psychoanalysis and Social Sciences – An Annual, Vol. 1*, UK: Imago, pp.393–41.

Kris, Ernst and Speier, Hans (1944) *German Radio Propaganda: Report on Home Broadcasts during the War*, USA: Oxford University Press.

Krohn, Claus-Dieter (1996/2013) *Intellectuals in Exile: Refugee Scholars and the New School for Social Research*, USA: University of Massachusetts Press.

Kuckhoff, Greta (1972) *Vom Rosenkraz zur Roten Kapelle*, Germany: Verlag Neues Leben.

'Kuckhoff, Greta' (no date) 'Biographische Angaben aus dem Handbuch "Wer war wer in der DDR?"' https://www.bundesstiftung-aufarbeitung.de/de/recherche/kataloge-datenbanken/biographische-datenbanken/greta-kuckhoff

Kuhn, Thomas (1962) *The Structure of Scientific Revolutions*, USA: University of Chicago Press.

Kumata, Hideya; Schramm Wilbur; University of Illinois at Urbana-Champaign Institute of Communications Research; and United States Information Agency (1955) *Four Working Papers on Propaganda Theory*, USA: University of Illinois Press.

Kurzweil, Edith (1996) 'Psychoanalytic Science: From Oedipus to Culture', in Ash, Mitchell G. and Söllner, Alfons (eds) *Forced Migration and Scientific Change: Émigré German-Speaking Scientists and Scholars After 1933*, UK: Cambridge University Press, pp.139–55.

Lamberti, Marjorie (2006) 'The Reception of Refugee Scholars from Nazi Germany in America: Philanthropy and Social Change in Higher Education', *Jewish Social Studies*, vol. 12, no. 3, pp.157–92. https://www.jstor.org/stable/pdf/4467750.pdf

Lang, Kurt (1979) 'The Critical Functions of Empirical Communication Research: Observations on German-American Influences', *Media, Culture & Society*, vol. 1, no. 1, pp.83–96. https://doi.org/10.1177/016344377900100107

Lässig, Simone (2017) 'Strategies and Mechanisms of Scholar Rescue: The Intellectual Migration of the 1930s Reconsidered', *Social Research: An International Quarterly*, vol. 84, no. 4, pp.769–807. https://doi.org/10.1353/sor.2017.005

Lassman, Peter (1992) 'Responses to Fascism in Britain, 1930–1945. The Emergence of the Concept of Totalitarianism', in Turner, Stephen P. and Käsler, Dirk (eds) *Sociology Responds to Fascism*, UK: Routledge, pp.214–40.

Lasswell, Harold D. (1925a) 'Prussian Schoolbooks and International Amity', *Journal of Social Forces*, vol. 3, no. 4, pp.718–22. https://doi.org/10.2307/3005082

Lasswell, Harold D. (1925b) 'The Status of Research on International Propaganda and Opinion', *Papers and Proceedings of the American Sociological Society*, vol. 20, pp.198–209.

Lasswell, Harold D. (1927) *Propaganda Technique in the World War*, USA: A.A. Knopf.

Lasswell, Harold D. (1927) *Propaganda Technique in the World War*, USA: A.A. Knopf.

Lasswell, Harold D. (1930) *Psychopathology and Politics*, USA: University of Chicago Press.

Lasswell, Harold D. (1931) 'The Measurement of Public Opinion', *American Political Science Review*, vol. 25, no. 2, pp.311–26. https://doi.org/10.2307/1947659

Lasswell, Harold D. (1933) 'The Psychology of Hitlerism', *Political Quarterly*, vol. 4, no. 3, pp.373–84. https://doi.org/10.1111/j.1467-923X.1933.tb02291.x

Lasswell, Harold D. (1935a) 'Collective Autism as a Consequence of Culture Contact: Notes on Religious Training and the Peyote Cult at Taos', *Zeitschrift für Sozialforschung*, vol. 4, no. 2, pp.232–47. https://doi.org/10.5840/zfs19354260

Lasswell, Harold D. (1935b) 'The Person: Subject and Object of Propaganda', *The Annals of the American Academy of Political and Social Science*, vol. 179, no. 1, pp.187–93. https://doi.org/10.1177/000271623517900124

Lasswell, Harold D. (1935c) *World Politics and Personal Insecurity*, USA: McGraw-Hill.

Lasswell, Harold D. (1937) 'The Influence of the Intellectual Exile', *Social Research*, vol. 4, no. 3, pp.305–16. https://doi.org/10.1353/sor.2015.0002

Lasswell, Harold D. (1938a) 'A Provisional Classification of Symbol Data', *Psychiatry*, vol. 1, no. 2, pp.197–204. https://doi.org/10.1080/00332747.1938.11022172

Lasswell, Harold D. (1938b) 'What Psychiatrists and Political Scientists Can Learn from One Another', *Psychiatry*, vol. 1, no. 1, pp.33–39. https://doi.org/10.1080/00332747.1938.11022172

Lasswell, Harold D. (1941) 'The World Attention Survey: An Exploration of the Possibilities of Studying Attention Being Given to the United States by Newspapers Abroad', *Public Opinion Quarterly*, vol. 5, no. 3, pp.456–62. https://doi.org/10.1086/265515

Lasswell, Harold D. (1942) 'Analyzing the Content of Mass Communication. Brief Introduction'. Library of Congress, Experimental Division for the Study of War-Time Communication, Document No 11.

Lasswell, Harold D. (1943/2003) 'On the Policy Sciences in 1943', *Policy Sciences*, vol. 36, no. 1, pp.71–98. https://doi.org/10.1023/A:1022999931810

Lasswell, Harold D. (1948) 'The Structure and Function of Communication in Society', in Bryson, Lyman (ed.) *The Communication of Ideas*, USA: Institute for Religious and Social Studies, pp.37–51.

Lasswell, Harold D. (1949) 'Why Be Quantitative?' in Lasswell, Harold D. and Leites, Nathan (eds) *Language of Politics: Studies in Quantitative Semantics*, USA: G.W. Stewart, pp.40–52.

Lasswell, Harold D. (1951a) 'The Immediate Future of Research Policy and Method in Political Science', *American Political Science Review*, vol. 45, no. 1, pp.133–42. https://doi.org/10.2307/1950887

Lasswell, Harold D. (1951b) 'The Policy Orientation', in Lasswell, Harold D. and Lerner, Daniel (eds) *The Policy Sciences: Recent Developments in Scope and Method*, USA: Stanford University Press, pp.3–15.

Lasswell, Harold D. (1963) *The Future of Political Science*, USA: Atherton Press.

Lasswell, Harold D. (1968) 'The Future of the Comparative Method', *Comparative Politics*, vol. 1, no. 1, pp.3–18. https://www.jstor.org/stable/421372#metadata_info_tab_contents

Lasswell, Harold D. and Associates (1942) 'The Politically Significant Content of the Press: Coding Procedures', *Journalism Quarterly*, vol. 19, no. 1, pp.12–23. https://doi.org/10.1177/107769904201900102

Lasswell, Harold D. and Blumenstock, Dorothy (1938) 'The Technique of Slogans in Communist Propaganda', *Psychiatry*, vol. 1, no. 4, pp.505–20. https://doi.org/10.1080/00332747.1938.11022212

Lasswell, Harold D. and Blumenstock, Dorothy (1939a) 'The Volume of Communist Propaganda in Chicago', *The Public Opinion Quarterly*, vol. 3, no. 1, pp.63–78. https://doi.org/10.1086/265260

Lasswell, Harold D. and Blumenstock, Dorothy (1939b) *World Revolutionary Propaganda: A Chicago Study*, USA: Alfred A. Knopf.

Lasswell, Harold D. and Fox, Merritt B. (1979) *The Signature of Power: Buildings, Communications, and Policy*, USA: Transaction.

Lasswell, Harold D. and Goldsen, Joseph M. (1947) 'Public Attention, Opinion, and Action', *International Journal of Opinion and Attitude Research*, vol. 1, no. 1, pp.3–11.

Lasswell, Harold D. and Lerner, Daniel (1965) *World Revolutionary Elites: Studies in Coercive Ideological Movements*, USA: Massachusetts Institute of Technology Press.

Lasswell, Harold D.; Leites, Nathan; and Associates (1949) *Language of Politics: Studies in Quantitative Semantics*, USA: George W. Stewart.

Lasswell, Harold D.; Lerner, Daniel; and de Sola Pool, Ithiel (1952a) *The Comparative Study of Symbols: An Introduction*, USA: Stanford University Press.

Lasswell, Harold D.; Lerner, Daniel; and de Sola Pool, Ithiel (1952b) 'Scope and Methods of the RADIR Project', in Lasswell, Harold D.; Lerner, Daniel; and De Sola Pool, Ithiel (eds) *Comparative Study of Symbols: An Introduction*, USA: Stanford University Press, pp.26–28.

Lasswell, Harold D.; Smith, Bruce Lannes; and Casey, Ralph D. (1946) *Propaganda, Communication, and Public Opinion: A Comprehensive Reference Guide*, USA: Princeton University Press.

Lazarsfeld, Paul F. (1941) 'Remarks on Administrative and Critical Communications Research', *Studies in Philosophy and Social Science*, vol. 9, no. 1, pp.2–16. https://doi.org/10.5840/zfs1941912

Lazarsfeld, Paul F. (1952) 'The Prognosis for International Communications Research', *Public Opinion Quarterly*, vol. 16, no. 4, pp.481–90. https://doi.org/10.1086/266411

Lazarsfeld, Paul F. (1969) 'An Episode in the History of Social Research. Memoirs', in Fleming, Donald and Bailyn, Bernard (eds) *The Intellectual Migration. Europe and America, 1930–1960*, USA: Harvard University Press, pp.270–227.

Lazarsfeld, Paul F. and Merton, Robert K. (1943) 'Studies in Radio and Film Propaganda', *Transactions of the New York Academy of Sciences*, vol. 6, no. 2, pp.58–74. https://doi.org/10.1111/j.2164-0947.1943.tb00897.x

Lazarsfeld, Paul F. and Merton, Robert K. (1948/1964) 'Mass Communication, Popular Taste and Organized Social Action', in Bryson, Lyman (ed.) *The Communication of Ideas*, USA: Institute for Religious and Social Studies, pp.95–118.

Lazarsfeld, Paul F.; Berelson, Bernard; and Gaudet, Hazel (1944) *The People's Choice: How the Voter Makes Up His Mind in a Presidential Campaign*, USA: Duell, Sloan and Pearce.

Lazarsfeld, Paul F. and Thielens, Wagner Jr (1958) *The Academic Mind: Social Scientists In a Time of Crisis*, USA: Free Press.

Lee, Chin-Chuan (2015) 'International Communication Research: Critical Reflections and a New Point of Departure', in Lee, Chin-Chuan (ed.) *Internationalizing 'International Communication'*, USA: University of Michigan Press, pp.1–28.

Leff, Laurel (2019) *Well Worth Saving: American Universities' Life-And-Death Decisions on Refugees from Nazi Europe*, USA: Yale University Press.

Leites, Nathan C. (1951a) *The Operational Code of the Politburo*, USA: McGraw Hill.

Leites, Nathan C. (1951b) *A Study of Bolshevism*, USA: Free Press.

Leites, Nathan C. (1959) *On the Game of Politics in France*, USA: Stanford University Press.

Leites, Nathan C. and Bernaut, Elsa (1954) *Ritual of Liquidation: The Case of the Moscow Trials*, USA: Free Press.

Leites, Nathan C.; Bernaut, Elsa; and Garthoff, Raymond L. (1951) 'Politburo Images of Stalin', *World Politics*, vol. 3, no. 3, pp.317–39. https://doi.org/10.2307/2009118

Lemberg, Diana (2019) *Barriers Down: How American Power and Free-flow Policies Shaped Global Media*, USA: Columbia University Press.

Lerner, Daniel (1949) *Sykewar: Psychological Warfare Against Germany, D-Day to VE-Day*, USA: G.W. Stewart.

Lerner, Daniel (1968) 'Lasswell, Harold D.', in Sills, David L. (ed.) *International Encyclopaedia of the Social Sciences*, USA: Free Press, pp.405–10.

Lerner, Daniel; de Sola Pool, Ithiel; and Lasswell, Harold D. (1951) 'Comparative Analysis of Political Ideologies: A Preliminary Statement', *Public Opinion Quarterly*, vol. 15, no. 4, pp.715–33. https://doi.org/10.1086/266356

Lerner, Daniel; de Sola Pool, Ithiel; and Schueller, George K. (1951) *The Nazi Elite*, USA: Stanford University Press.

Levitas, Ruth (1979) 'Sociology and Utopia', *Sociology*, vol. 13, no. 1, pp.19–33. https://doi.org/10.1177/003803857901300102

Levitas, Ruth (2000) 'For Utopia: The (Limits of the) Utopian Function in Late Capitalist Society', *Critical Review of International Social and Political Philosophy*, vol. 3, no. 2–3, pp.25–43. https://doi.org/10.1080/13698230008403311

Levitas, Ruth (2013) *Utopia as Method: The Imaginary Reconstitution of Society*, UK: Palgrave.

Levyatan, Yaniv (2009) 'Harold D. Lasswell's Analysis of Hitler's Speeches', *Media History*, vol. 15, no. 1, pp.55–69. https://doi.org/10.1080/13688800802583299

Library of Congress (no date) *Annual Report of the Librarian of Congress 1941 /1942–1943/1944*, USA: Library of Congress. https://babel.hathitrust.org /cgi/pt?id=mdp.39015036841743&seq=53&q1=wartime+communications

Lijphart, Arendt (1971) 'Comparative Politics and the Comparative Method', *The American Political Science Review*, vol. 65, no. 3, pp.682–93. https://doi.org/10.2307/1955513

Lippmann, Walter (1922) *Public Opinion*, USA: Harcourt, Brace and Company.

Lippmann, Walter (1925) *The Phantom Public*, USA: Harcourt, Brace and Company.

Littlejohn, Stephen W. (1978) *Theories of Human Communication*, USA: Merrill.

Loader, Colin (1997) 'Free Floating: The Intelligentsia in the Work of Alfred Weber and Karl Mannheim', *German Studies Review*, vol. 20, no. 2, pp.217–34. https://doi.org/10.2307/1431946

Löblich, Maria and Scheu, Andreas M. (2011) 'Writing the History of Communication Studies: A Sociology of Science Approach', *Communication Theory*, vol. 21, no. 1, pp.1–22. https://doi.org/10.1111/j.1468-2885.2010.01373.x

Loewenberg, Gerhard (2006) 'The Influence of European Emigré Scholars on Comparative Politics, 1925–1965', *The American Political Science Review*, vol. 100, no. 4, pp.597–604. https://doi.org/10.1017/S0003055406062472

Loewenstein, Karl (1944) 'Report on the Research Panel on Comparative Government', *The American Political Science Review*, vol. 38, no. 3, pp.540–48. https://doi.org/10.2307/1948903

Lowenstein, Ralph L. and Merrill, John C. (1990) *Macromedia: Mission, Message and Morality*, USA: Longman.

Lowenthal, Leo (1952) 'Introduction', *The Public Opinion Quarterly*, vol. 16, no. 4, pp.v–x. https://doi.org/10.1093/poq/16.4.481-a

Lucas, Jennifer C. and Sisco, Tauna S. (2012) 'Generations and Gender in the 2008 US Democratic Primaries', in Steele, Brent J. and Acuff, Jonathan M. (eds) *Theory and Application of the 'Generation' in International Relations and Politics*, USA: Palgrave Macmillan, pp.147–76.

Lyon, E. Stina (2011) 'Karl Mannheim and Viola Klein: Refugee Sociologists in Search of Social Democratic Practice', in Marks, Shula; Weindling, Paul; and Wintour, Laura (eds) *In Defence of Learning: The Plight, Persecution, and Placement of Academic Refugees, 1933–1980s*. Proceedings of the British Academy. British Academy Scholarship Online, pp.177–90. https://doi.org/10.5871/bacad/9780197264812.003.0012

MacBride, Sean (1980) *Many Voices, One World: Communication and Society Today and Tomorrow: Towards a New More Just and More Efficient World Information and Communication Order*, UK: Kogan Page.

Magyar Néprajzi Lexikon (Hungarian Encyclopaedia of Ethnography) (no date). http://mek.niif.hu/02100/02115/html/

Malherek, Joseph (2022) *Free-Market Socialists: European Émigrés Who Made Capitalist Culture in America, 1918–1968*, Hungary: Central European University Press.

Manheim, Ernest (1947) 'Karl Mannheim, 1893–1947', *American Journal of Sociology*, vol. 52, no. 6, pp.471–74. https://doi.org/10.1086/220067

Mannheim, Karl (1922) *Die Strukturanalyse der Erkenntnistheorie.* Kant-Studien/Ergänzungshefte (no. 57), Germany: Reuther & Reichard.

Mannheim, Karl (1927) 'Das Problem der Generationen', *Kölner Zeitschrift für Soziologie und Sozialpsychologie*, vol. 7, no. 2, pp.157–85.

Mannheim, Karl (1928) 'Das Problem der Generationen', *Kölner Zeitschrift für Soziologie und Sozialpsychologie*, vol. 8, no. 3, pp.309–30.

Mannheim, Karl (1929) *Ideologie und Utopie*, Germany: F. Cohen.

Mannheim, Karl (1932/1993) 'The Sociology of Intellectuals', *Theory, Culture & Society*, vol. 10, no. 3, pp.69–80. https://doi.org/10.1177/026327693010003004

Mannheim, Karl (1934) 'The Crisis of Culture in the Era of Mass-Democracies and Autarchies', *The Sociological Review*, vol. 26, no. 2, pp.105–29. https://doi.org/10.1111/j.1467-954X.1934.tb01902.x

Mannheim, Karl (1935) 'Utopia', in Seligman, Edwin R.A. (ed.) *Encyclopaedia of the Social Sciences*, USA: Macmillan, pp.200–03.

Mannheim, Karl (1936) *Ideology and Utopia: An Introduction to the Sociology of Knowledge*. Translated by Louis Wirth and Edward Shils. UK: Routledge & Kegan Paul, Trench, Trubner & Co; USA: Harcourt, Brace & Co.

Mannheim, Karl (1936/2000) *Essays on the Sociology of Knowledge. Collected Works, Vol. 5*. Edited by Paul Kecskemeti, UK: Routledge.

Mannheim, Karl (1953) *Essays on Sociology and Social Psychology*. Edited by Paul Kecskemeti, UK: Routledge & Kegan Paul.

Mannheim, Karl (1960) *Ideology and Utopia. An Introduction to the Sociology of Knowledge*. Translated by Louis Wirth and Edward Shils. UK: Routledge & Kegan Paul.

Mannheim, Karl (1980) 'Eine soziologische Theorie der Kultur und ihrer Erkennbarkeit (Konjuktives und kommunikatives Denken)', in Kettler, David; Meja, Volker; and Stehr, Nico (eds) *Karl Mannheim. Strukturen des Denkens*, Germany: Suhrkamp Verlag, pp.155–322.

Mannheim, Karl (2000) 'The Problem of Generations', in Paul Kecskemeti (ed.) *Essays on the Sociology of Knowledge. Collected Works* (Vol. 5), UK: Routledge, pp.276–322.

Mannheim, Karl and Gábor, Éva (2003) *Selected Correspondence (1911–1946) of Karl Mannheim, Scientist, Philosopher, and Sociologist*, USA: Edwin Mellen Press.

Marcuse, Herbert (1970) *Five Lectures: Psychoanalysis, Politics, and Utopia*, UK: Allen Lane.

Marcuse, Herbert and Sherover-Marcuse, Erica (1979) *The Aesthetic Dimension: Toward a Critique of Marxist Aesthetics*, USA: Beacon Press.

Markham, James W. (1956) 'Journalism School Courses in International Communications', *Journalism Quarterly*, vol. 33, no. 2, pp.201–06. https://doi.org/10.1177/107769905603300207

Marler, Charles (1990) 'Fredrick Siebert and the Legal Method', in Sloan, David Wm (ed.) *Makers of the Media Mind Journalism Educators and their Ideas*, USA: Lawrence Erlbaum, pp.187–94.

Martin, L. John and Chaudhary, Anju G. (1983) *Comparative Mass Media Systems*, USA: Longman.

Marwick, Arthur (1988) *Total War and Social Change*, UK: Palgrave Macmillan.

Mattelart, Armand (1979) *Multinational Corporations and the Control of Culture: The Ideological Apparatuses of Imperialism*, UK: Harvester Press.

McIntyre, Jerilyn S. (1987) 'Repositioning a Landmark: The Hutchins Commission and Freedom of the Press', *Critical Studies in Media Communication*, vol. 4, no. 2, pp.136–60. https://doi.org/10.1080/15295038709360122

McKenzie, Robert (2006) *Comparing Media from around the World*, USA: Pearson.

McQuail, Denis (1994) *Mass Communication Theory: An Introduction*, UK: Sage.

Mede, Niels G.; Schäfer, Mike S.; Metag, Julia; and Klinger, Kira (2022) 'Who Supports Science-Related Populism? A Nationally Representative Survey on the Prevalence and Explanatory Factors of Populist Attitudes toward Science in Switzerland.' *PloS One*, vol. 17, no. 8, pp.1–20. https://doi.org/10.1371/journal.pone.0271204.t002

Meja, Volker and Kettler, David (1993) 'Cultural Politics in Karl Mannheim's Sociology: Introduction to the Transaction Edition', in Wolff, Kurt H. (ed.) *From Karl Mannheim*, USA: Routledge, pp.vii–xxxvi.

Meja, Volker and Stehr, Nico (1990) *Knowledge and Politics: The Sociology of Knowledge Dispute*, UK: Routledge.

Meng, Bingchun and Rantanen, Terhi (2015) 'A Change of Lens: A Call to Compare the Media in China and Russia', *Critical Studies in Media Communication*, vol. 32, no. 1, pp.1–15. https://doi.org/10.1080/15295036.204.997831

Merriam, Charles E. (1919) 'American Publicity in Italy', *The American Political Science Review*, vol. 13, no. 4, pp.541–55. https://doi.org/10.2307/1944209

Merriam, Charles E. and Lasswell, Harold D. (1924) 'Current Public Opinion and the Public Service Commissions', in Cooke, Morris Llewellyn (ed.) *Public Utility Regulation*, USA: Ronald Press, pp.276–95.

Merrill, John C. (1974) *The Imperative of Freedom: A Philosophy of Journalistic Autonomy*, USA: Hastings House.

Merrill, John C. (2002) 'The Four Theories of the Press Four and a Half Decades Later: A Retrospective', *Journalism Studies*, vol. 3, no. 1, pp.133–36. https://doi.org/10.1080/14616700120107374

Merrill, John C. and Lowenstein, Ralph L. (1979) *Media, Messages, and Men: New Perspectives in Communication*, USA: Longman.

Merton, Robert K. (1937) 'The Sociology of Knowledge', *Isis*, vol. 27, no. 3, pp.493–503. http://dx.doi.org/10.1086/347276

Merton, Robert K. (1938) 'Science, Technology and Society in Seventeenth Century England', in Sarton, George (ed.) *Osiris: Studies on the History and Philosophy of Science, and on the History of Learning and Culture*, Belgium: St. Catherine Press, pp.362–632.

Merton, Robert K. (1941) 'Karl Mannheim and the Sociology of Knowledge', *Journal of Liberal Religion*, vol. 2, pp.125–47.

Merton, Robert K. (1949) *Social Theory and Social Structure*, USA: Free Press.

Merton, Robert K. (1949/1968) *Social Theory and Social Structure* (1968 enlarged ed.), USA: Free Press.

Merton, Robert K. (1957) 'Karl Mannheim and the Sociology of Knowledge', in Merton, Robert K. (ed.) *Social Theory and Social Structure*, USA: Free Press, pp.489–508.

Merton, Robert K. (1972) 'Insiders and Outsiders: A Chapter in the Sociology of Knowledge', *American Journal of Sociology*, vol. 78, no. 1, pp.9–47. https://doi.org/10.1086/225294

Merton, Robert K. (1973) *The Sociology of Science: Theoretical and Empirical Investigations*, USA: University of Chicago Press.

Merton, Robert K. (1994) *A Life of Learning (1994 Charles Homer Haskins Lecture)* USA: American Council of Learned Societies.

Merton, Robert K. and Lazarsfeld, Paul F. (1950) *Continuities in Social Research: Studies in the Scope and Method of 'The American Soldier'*, USA: Free Press.

Merton, Robert K. and Lerner, Daniel (1951) 'Social Scientists and Research Policy', in Lerner, David; Lasswell, Harold D.; Fischer, Harold H.; Holdgard, Ernest R.; Padover, Saul K.; De Sola Pool, Ithiel; and Rothwell, C. Easton (eds) *The Policy Sciences. Recent Developments in Scope and Method*, USA: Stanford University Press, pp.282–310.

Merton, Robert K.; Fiske, Marjorie; and Curtis, Alberta (1946) *Mass Persuasion; The Social Psychology of a War Bond Drive*, USA: Harper & Brothers.

Meyen, Michael (2015) *Fachgeschichte als Generationsgeschichte.* http://blexkom.halemverlag.de/fachgeschichte-als-generationsgeschichte

Meyen, Michael (2016) 'Biografie und Generation in der Kommunikationswissenschaft', in Averbeck-Lietz, Stephanie and Meyen, Michael (eds) *Handbuch nicht standardisierte Methoden in der Kommunikationswissenschaft*, Germany: Springer VS, pp.385–98.

'MIT Professor Lucian W. Pye, Leading China Scholar, Dies at 86' (2008) MIT News. https://news.mit.edu/2008/obit-pye-0908

Mock, James R. and Larson, Cedric (1939) *Words that Won the War: The Story of the Committee on Public Information, 1917–1919*, USA: Princeton University Press.

Morrison, David (1988) 'The Transference of Experience and the Impact of Ideas: Paul Lazarsfeld and Mass Communication Research', *Encyclopaedia of Communication*, vol. 10, pp.185–209.

Morrison, David (2022) 'Lazarsfeld's Legacy| Paul Lazarsfeld: Living in Circles and Talking Around Tables', *International Journal of Communication*, vol. 16, pp.616–25. https://ijoc.org/index.php/ijoc/article/view/18891/3664

Morrison, David E. (2008) 'Opportunity Structures and the Creation of Knowledge: Paul Lazarsfeld and the Politics of Research', in Park, David W. and Pooley, Jefferson (eds) *The History of Media and Communication Research. Contested Memories*, USA: Peter Lang, pp.179–204.

Mowlana, Hamid (1973) 'Trends in Research on International Communication in the United States', *International Communication Gazette*, vol. 19, no. 2, pp.79–90. https://doi.org/10.1177/001654927301900202

Mowlana, Hamid (1985) *International Flow of Information: A Global Report and Analysis*, France: UNESCO.

Mowlana, Hamid (1986/1997) *Global Information and World Communication: New Frontiers in International Relations*, USA: Longman.

Mowlana, Hamid (2004) 'International Communication. The Journey of a Caravan', *The Journal of International Communication*, vol. 10, no. 2, pp.7–32. https://doi.org.uk/10.1080/13216597.2004.9751972

Munck, Gerardo L. (2006) *The Past and Present of Comparative Politics*, USA: Helen Kellogg Institute for International Studies. https://kellogg.nd.edu/sites/default/files/old_files/documents/330_0.pdf

Mundt, Whitney R. (1991) 'Global Media Philosophies', in Merrill, John C. (ed.) *Global Journalism: Survey of International Communication*, USA: Longman, pp.11–27.

Muth, Rodney (1990) 'Harold Dwight Lasswell: A Biographical Profile', in Muth, Rodney; Finley, Mary M; and Muth, Marcia F. (eds) *Harold D. Lasswell: An Annotated Bibliography*, USA: New Haven Press, pp.1–48.

'Nachlass Greta Kuckhoff' (no date). http://www.argus.bstu.bundesarchiv.de/N2506-35612/index.htm

Nardi, Peter M. (1999) *Gay Men's Friendships: Invincible Communities*, USA: University of Chicago Press.

Némedi, Dénes (1992) '"Sociologists", Sociographers, and "Liberals": Hungarian Intellectuals Respond to Fascism', in Turner, Stephen P. and Käsler, Dirk (eds) *Sociology Responds to Fascism*, UK: Routledge, pp.151–67.

Nerone, John (1995) *Last Rights: Revisiting Four Theories of the Press*, USA: University of Illinois Press.

Nerone, John (2004) 'Four Theories of the Press in Hindsight: Reflections on a Popular Model', in Semat, Mehdi (ed.) *New Fronters in International Communication Theory*, USA: Rowman and Littlefield, pp.21–32.

Neumann, Franz L. (1953a) *The Cultural Migration: The European Scholar in America*, USA: University of Pennsylvania Press.

Neumann, Franz L. (1953b) 'The Social Sciences', in Neumann, Franz L.; Peyre, Henri; Panofsky, Erwin; Köhler, Wolfgang; and Tillich, Paul (eds) *The Cultural Migration: The European Scholar in America*, USA: University of Pennsylvania Press, pp.4–26.

Neun, Oliver; Kunze, Jan-Peter; and Mannheim, Karl (2018) *Karl Mannheim Schriften Zur Soziologie*, Germany: Springer Fachmedien Wiesbaden, pp.15–32. https://doi.org/10.1007/978-3-658-22120-1

'New York to Be the News-Clearing House of the World' (1916) *Editor & Publisher*, vol. 49, no. 22, 11 November, p.1. https://archive.org/details /sim_editor-publisher_1916-11-11_49_22/page/n3/mode/2up

Nietzel, Benno (2016) 'Propaganda, Psychological Warfare and Communication Research in the USA and the Soviet Union during the Cold War', *History of the Human Sciences*, vol. 29, no. 4–5, pp.59–76. https://doi.org/10.1177/0952695116667881

Nordenstreng, Kaarle and Schiller, Herbert I. (1979) 'Introduction', in Nordenstreng, Kaarle and Schiller, Herbert I. (eds) *National Sovereignty and International Communication*, USA: Ablex, pp.3–8.

Norris, Pippa and Inglehart, Ronald (2019) *Cultural Backlash: Trump, Brexit, and Authoritarian Populism*, UK: Cambridge University Press.

Oldfield, Sybil (2022) *The Black Book: The Britons on the Nazi Hit List*, UK: Profile Books.

Oren, Ido (2003) *Our Enemies and US: America's Rivalries and the Making of Political Science*, USA: Cornell University Press.

Palmer, Barbara (2006) 'Alexander George, "Giant" in International Relations, Dead at 86', *Stanford News*, https://news.stanford.edu/news/2006/august23/obitgeorge-082306.html

Park, David W. and Pooley, Jefferson (2008) *The History of Media and Communications Research: Contested Memories*, USA: Peter Lang.

Parsons, Talcott (1951) *The Social System*, UK: Routledge and Kegan Paul.

Perivolaropoulou, Nia (1992) 'Karl Mannheim et sa génération'. *Mil neuf cent. Revue d'histoire intellectuelle (Cahiers Georges Sorel)*, vol. 10, no. 1, pp.165–86.

Perry, Helen S. (1982) *Psychiatrist of America: The Life of Harry Stack Sullivan*, USA: Belknap Press of Harvard University Press.

Peters, John D. (1986a) 'Institutional Sources of Intellectual Poverty in Communication Research', *Communication Research*, vol. 13, no. 4, pp.527–59. https://doi.org/10.1177/009365086013004002

Peters, John D. (1986b) *Reconstructing Mass Communication Theory*, USA: Stanford University.

Peters, John D. (2006) 'The Part Played by Gentiles in the Flow of Mass Communications: On the Ethnic Utopia of Personal Influence', *The Annals of the American Academy of Political and Social Science*, vol. 608, no. 1, pp.97–114. https://doi.org/10.1177/0002716206292425

Peterson, Ted (1945) 'British Crime Pamphleteers: Forgotten Journalists'. *Journalism & Mass Communication Quarterly*, vol. 22, no. 4, pp.305–16. https://doi.org/10.1177/107769904502200401

Peterson, Ted (1948) 'The Fight of William Hone for British Press Freedom', *Journalism Quarterly*, vol. 22, no. 2, pp.132–38. https://journals.sagepub.com/doi/10.1177/107769904802500203

Philips, Susan U. (2001) 'Gender Ideology: Cross-cultural Aspects', in Smelser, Neil J. and Baltes, Paul B. (eds.) *International Encyclopedia of the Social & Behavioral Sciences*, UK: Pergamon, pp. 6016–20. https://doi.org/10.1016/B0-08-043076-7/03962-0

Picard, Robert (1985) *The Press and the Decline of Democracy: The Democratic Socialist Response in Public Policy*, UK: Greenwood Press.

Pickard, Victor (2014) *America's Battle for Media Democracy: The Triumph of Corporate Libertarianism and the Future of Media Reform*, USA: Cambridge University Press. https://doi.org/10.1017/CBO9781139814799

Pilcher, Jane (1994) 'Mannheim's Sociology of Generations: An Undervalued Legacy', *The British Journal of Sociology*, vol. 45, no. 3, pp.481–95.

Planning Committee of the Center for International Studies at the Massachusetts Institute of Technology (1954) 'A Plan of Research in International Communication: A Report', *World Politics*, vol. 6, no. 3, pp.358–77. https://doi.org/10.2307/2009069

Polanyi, Michael (1958) *Personal Knowledge*, UK: Routledge & Kegan Paul.

Polanyi, Michael (1959) *The Study of Man*, UK: Routledge & Kegan Paul.

Polanyi, Michael (1964) *Science, Faith and Society*, USA: University of Chicago Press.

Polanyi, Michael (1967) *The Tacit Dimension*, USA: Routledge & Kegan Paul.

Pooley, Jefferson (2007) 'Edward Shils' Turn against Karl Mannheim: The Central European Connection', *The American Sociologist*, vol. 38, no. 4, pp.364–82. https://doi.org/10.1007/s12108-007-9027-5

Pooley, Jefferson (2011) 'From Psychological Warfare to Social Justice: Shifts in Foundation Support for Communication Research', in Jansen, Sue C.; Pooley, Jefferson; and Taub-Pervizpour, Lora (eds) *Media and Social Justice*, USA: Palgrave Macmillan, pp.211–40.

Pooley, Jefferson (2017) 'Wilbur Schramm and the "Four Founders" History of U.S. Communication Research', *Коммуникации. Медиа. Дизайн*, vol. 2, no. 4, pp.5–16. http://dx.doi.org/10.17613/M6Q859

Pooley, Jefferson (2019) *The Remobilization of the Propaganda and Morale Network, 1947–1953*. https://doi.org/10.33767/osf.io/g9rp4

Pooley, Jefferson and Katz, Elihu (2008) 'Further Notes on Why American Sociology Abandoned Mass Communication Research', *Journal of Communication*, vol. 58, no. 4, pp.767–86. https://doi.org/10.1111/j.1460-2466.2008.00413.x

Popper, Karl (1957/2002) *The Poverty of Historicism* (2nd ed.), UK: Taylor & Francis Group.

Preston William (1989) 'The History of U.S.-UNESCO Relations', in Preston, William; Herman, Edward S.; and Schiller, Herbert I. (eds) *Hope and Folly: The United States and UNESCO 1945–1985*, USA: Minnesota University Press, pp.3–188.

'Proceedings of the Committee on International Communications Research' (1952) *Public Opinion Quarterly*, vol. 16, no. 4, pp.705–08. https://doi.org/10.1086/266434

Purhonen, Semi (2016) 'Generations on Paper: Bourdieu and the Critique of "Generationalism"', *Social Science Information*, vol. 55, no. 1, pp.94–114. https://doi.org/10.1177/0539018415608967

Pye Family China Album (no date). https://www.virginiapye.com/album

Pye, Lucian W. (1963) *Communications and Political Development*, USA: Princeton University Press.

Rajagopal, Arvind (2020) Communicationism: Cold War Humanism. *Critical Inquiry*, vol. 46, no. 2, pp.353–80. https://doi.org/10.1086/706683

Rakow, Lana F. (2008) 'Feminist Historiography and the Field: Writing New Histories', in Park, David W. and Pooley, Jefferson (eds) *The History of Media and Communication Research: Contested Memories*, USA: Peter Lang, pp.113–39.

Rantanen, Terhi (1990) 'Foreign News in Imperial Russia: The Relationship between International and Russian News Agencies, 1856–1914', *Annales Academiae Scientiarum Fennicae, Dissertationes humanarum litterarum*, Finland: Suomalainen tiedeakatemia. http://acadsci.fi/julkaisut/AASF_HumDiss_58_Rantanen.pdf

Rantanen, Terhi (1992) 'Mr. Howard Goes to South America. The United Press Associations and Foreign Expansion', Roy W. Howard Monographs in Journalism and Mass Communication Research, no. 2, USA: Indiana University. http://fedora.dlib.indiana.edu/fedora/get/iudl:2530612/OVERVIEW

Rantanen, Terhi (1994) 'Howard Interviews Stalin: How the AP, UP and TASS Smashed the International News Cartel', Roy W. Howard Monographs in Journalism and Mass Communication Research, no. 3, USA: Indiana University.
http://fedora.dlib.indiana.edu/fedora/get/iudl:2530632/OVERVIEW

Rantanen, Terhi (1998) 'After Five O'clock Friends: Kent Cooper and Roy W. Howard', USA: Indiana University. Roy W. Howard Monographs in Journalism and Mass Communication Research, no. 4.
http://fedora.dlib.indiana.edu/fedora/get/iudl:2530662/OVERVIEW

Rantanen, Terhi (2004) *The Media and Globalisation*, UK: Sage.

Rantanen, Terhi (2006) 'Foreign Dependence and Domestic Monopoly: The European News Cartel and US Associated Presses, 1861–1932', *Media History*, vol. 12, no. 1, pp.19–35. https://doi.org/10.1080/13688800600597145

Rantanen, Terhi (2010) 'Methodological Inter-nationalism in Comparative Media Research: Flow Studies in International Communication', in Roosvall, Anna and Salovaara-Moring, Inka (eds) *Communicating the Nation: National Topographies of Global Media Landscapes*, Sweden: Nordicom Publications, pp.25–40.
https://www.nordicom.gu.se/sv/publications/communicating-nation

Rantanen, Terhi (2012) 'Quickening Urgency: The Telegraph and Wire Services in 1846–1893', in Valdivia, Anharad N. (ed.) *The International Encyclopedia of Media Studies, vol. 1: Media History and the Foundations of Media Studies*, USA: Wiley-Blackwell.
https://doi.org/10.1002/9781444361506.wbiems015

Rantanen, Terhi (2017) 'A "Crisscrossing" Historical Analysis of Four Theories of the Press', *International Journal of Communication*, vol. 11, pp.3454–75. https://ijoc.org/index.php/ijoc/article/view/6253

Rantanen, Terhi (2019) 'News Agencies from Telegraph Bureaus to Cyberfactories', in *Communication. Oxford Research Encyclopedias*, UK: Oxford University Press. https://oxfordre.com/communication/view/10.1093/acrefore/9780190228613.001.0001/acrefore-9780190228613-e-843

Rantanen, Terhi (2020) 'An American in London – Harold D Lasswell at LSE in 1923'. https://blogs.lse.ac.uk/lsehistory/2020/01/14/an-american-in-london-harold-d-lasswell-at-lse-in-1923/

Read, Donald (1990) 'Sir Roderick Jones and Reuters: Rise and Fall of a News Emperor', in Fraser, Derek (ed.) *Cities, Class and Communications: Essays in Honour of Asa Briggs*, UK: Harvester Wheatsheaf, pp.175–99.

Read, Donald (1999) *The Power of News: The History of Reuters* (2nd ed.), UK: Oxford University Press.

Read, William H. (1976) *America's Mass Media Merchants*, USA: Johns Hopkins University Press.

Remmling, Gunter W. (1961) 'Karl Mannheim: Revision of an Intellectual Portrait', *Social Forces*, vol. 40, no. 1, pp.23–30. https://doi.org/10.2307/2573467

Renaud, Jean-Luc (1985) 'US Government Assistance to AP's World-Wide Expansion', *Journalism Quarterly*, vol. 62, no. 1, pp.10–36. https://doi.org/10.1177/107769908506200102

Ricoeur, Paul (1986) *Lectures on Ideology and Utopia*, USA: Columbia University Press.

Rogers, Everett M. (1981) 'The Empirical and the Critical Schools of Communication Research', *Annals of the International Communication Association*, vol. 5, no. 1, pp.125–44. https://doi.org/10.1080/23808985.181.11923842

Rogers, Everett M. (1994) *A History of Communication Study: A Biographical Approach*, USA: Free Press.

Rogow, Arnold A. (ed.) (1969) *Politics, Personality, and Social Science in the Twentieth Century: Essays in Honor of Harold D. Lasswell*, USA: University of Chicago Press.

Rosewater, Victor (1930) *History of Cooperative News-Gathering in the United States*, USA: D. Appleton.

Roskin, Michael (1974) 'From Pearl Harbor to Vietnam: Shifting Generational Paradigms and Foreign Policy'. *Political Science Quarterly*, vol. 89, no. 3, pp.563–88. https://doi.org/10.2307/2148454

Rosten, Leo (1971) *People I Have Loved, Known or Admired*, UK: W.H. Allen.

Rosten, Leo (1991) 'Harold D. Lasswell', in Shils, Edward (ed.) *Remembering the University of Chicago. Teachers, Scientists, and Scholars*, USA: University of Chicago Press, pp.276–86.

Rotheit, Rudolf (1919) *Die Friedensbedingungen der deutschen Presse — Los von Reuter und Havas!* Germany: Puttkammer & Mühlbrecht.

Rowland, Allison L. and Simonson, Peter (2013) 'The Founding Mothers of Communication Research: Towards History of a Gendered Assemblage', *Critical Studies in Mass Communication*, vol. 31, no. 1, pp.3–26. https://doi.org/10.1080/15295036.2013.849355

Rutkoff, Peter M. and Scott, William B. (1986) *New School: A History of the New School for Social Research*, USA: Free Press.

Sagarin, Edward and Kelly, Robert J. (1969) 'Karl Mannheim and the Sociology of Knowledge', *Salmagundi*, no. 10/11, pp.292–302.

Salerno, Roger A. (1987) *Louis Wirth: A Bio-bibliography*, USA: Greenwood.

Sargent, Lyman T. (2008) 'Ideology and Utopia: Karl Mannheim and Paul Ricoeur', *Journal of Political Ideologies*, vol. 13, no. 3, pp.263–73. https://doi.org/10.1080/13569310802374479

Saunders, Frances (2000) *Who Paid the Piper? The CIA and the Cultural Cold War*, UK: Granta.

Sayner, Joanne (2013) *Reframing Antifascism: Memory, Genre and the Life Writings of Greta Kuckhoff*, UK: Palgrave Macmillan.

Scharnberg, Harriet (2016) 'The A and P of Propaganda: Associated Press and Nazi Photojournalism', *Zeithistorische Forschungen / Studies in Contemporary History*, vol. 13. https://doi.org/10.14765/zzf.dok-1414

Schiller, Herbert I. (1969) *Mass Communications and American Empire*, USA: Beacon Press.

Schiller, Herbert I. (1975) 'Genesis of the Free Flow of Information Principles: The Imposition of Communications Domination', *Instant Research on Peace and Violence*, vol. 5, no. 2, pp.75–86. http://www.jstor.org/stable/40724768

Schiller, Herbert I. (1976) *Communication and Cultural Domination*, USA: M.E. Sharpe.

Schmidt, Péter (1933a) 'A harmadik birodalomból', *Századunk*, vol. 8, pp.229–33.

Schmidt, Péter (1933b) 'Az ellenforradalom gyözelme Németországban', *Századunk*, vol. 9, pp.97–105.

Schmidt, Péter (1935) 'Hitler három éve', *Századunk*, vol. 10, pp.74–82.

Schramm, Wilbur (1948) *Communications in Modern Society: Fifteen Studies of the Mass Media Prepared for the University of Illinois Institute of Communications Research*, USA: University of Illinois Press.

Schramm, Wilbur (1949) *Mass Communications: A Book of Readings Selected and Edited for the Institute of Communications Research in the University of Illinois*, USA: University of Illinois Press.

Schramm, Wilbur (1954) *The Process and Effects of Mass Communication*, USA: University of Illinois Press.

Schramm, Wilbur (1957a) *Responsibility in Mass Communication*, USA: Harper & Brothers.

Schramm, Wilbur (1957b) 'Twenty Years of Journalism Research', *Public Opinion Quarterly*, vol. 21, no. 1, pp.91–107. https://doi.org/10.1086/266689

Schramm, Wilbur (1959a) 'Comments on "The State of Communication Research"', *The Public Opinion Quarterly*, vol. 23, no. 1, pp.6–9. https://doi.org/10.1086/266841

Schramm, Wilbur (1959b) *One Day in the World's Press: Fourteen Great Newspapers on a Day of Crisis*, USA: Stanford University Press.

Schramm, Wilbur (1963) 'Communication Research in the United States', in Schramm, Wilbur (ed.) *The Science of Human Communication*, USA: Basic Books, pp.1–16.

Schramm, Wilbur (1967) 'Communication and Change', in Lerner, Daniel and Schramm, Wilbur (eds) *Communication and Change in the Developing Countries*, USA: University of Hawaii Press, pp.5–32.

Schramm, Wilbur (1974) *Men, Messages, and Media: A Look at Human Communication*, USA: Harper & Row.

Schramm, Wilbur (1980) 'The Beginnings of Communication Study in the United States', *Annals of the International Communication Association*, vol. 4, no. 1, pp.73–82. https://doi.org/10.1080/23808985.1980.11923795

Schramm, Wilbur (1985) 'The Beginnings of Communication Study in the United States', in Rogers, Everett M. and Balle, Francis (eds) *The Media Revolution in America and in Western Europe*, UK: Ablex Publishing, pp.200–11.

Schramm, Wilbur; Chaffee, Steven H.; and Rogers, Everett M. (1997) *The Beginnings of Communication Study in America: A Personal Memoir*, USA: Sage.

Schramm, Wilbur and Riley, John W. (1951a) 'Communication in the Sovietized State, as Demonstrated in Korea', *American Sociological Review*, vol. 16, no. 6, pp.757–66. https://doi.org/10.2307/2087502

Schramm, Wilbur and Riley, John W. (1951b) *The Reds Take a City: The Communist Occupation of Seoul, with Eye-Witness Accounts*, USA: Rutgers University Press.

Schudson, Michael (2008) 'The "Lippmann-Dewey Debate" and the Invention of Walter Lippmann as an Anti-Democrat 1985–1996', *International Journal of Communication*, vol. 2, pp.1031–42.

Schudson, Michael (2015) *The Rise of the Right to Know: Politics and the Culture of Transparency 1945–1975*, USA: Belknap Press.

Schuman, Howard and Scott, Jacqueline (1989) 'Generations and Collective Memories', *American Sociological Review*, vol. 54, no. 3, pp.359–81. https://doi.org/10.2307/2095611

Schwarzlose, Richard A. (1978) 'A Conversation with Fredrick S. Siebert', *Journalism History*, vol. 5, no. 4, pp.106–23. https://doi.org/10.1080/0094679.1978.12066894

Schwarzlose, Richard A. (1989a) *Kent Cooper*, USA: Greenwood Press.

Schwarzlose, Richard A. (1989b) *The Nation's Newsbrokers, Vol. 1: The Formative Years From Pretelegraph to 1865*, USA: Northwestern University Press.

Schwarzlose, Richard A. (1989c) *The Nation's Newsbrokers, Vol. 2: The Rush to Institution From 1865 to 1920*, USA: Northwestern University Press.

Seidelman, Raymond and Harpham, Edward J. (1985) *Disenchanted Realists: Political Science and the American Crisis*, USA: State University of New York Press.

Servaes, Jan (2015) 'Beyond Modernization and the Four Theories of the Press', in Lee, Chin-Chuan (ed.) *Internationalizing 'International Communication'*, USA: University of Michigan Press, pp.66–89.

Shah, Hemant (2011) *The Production of Modernization: Daniel Lerner, Mass Media, and the Passing of Traditional Society*, USA: Temple University Press.

Sherburne, Edward G. (1953) 'International Communications Research', *Public Opinion Quarterly*, vol. 16, no. 1, pp.481–701. https://doi.org/10.1007/BF02713258

Shils, Edward (1974) '"Ideology and Utopia" by Karl Mannheim', *Daedalus*, vol. 103, no. 1, pp.83–89. http://www.jstor.org/stable/20024190

Shils, Edward (1975) *Center and Periphery: Essays in Macrosociology*, USA: University of Chicago Press.

Shils, Edward (1985) 'On the Eve: A Prospect in Retrospect', in Bulmer, Martin (ed.) *Essays on the History of British Sociological Research*, UK: Cambridge University Press, pp.165–78.

Shils, Edward (1995) 'Karl Mannheim', *The American Scholar*, vol. 64, no. 2, pp.221–35. http://www.jstor.org/stable/41212318

Sica, Alan (2010) 'Merton, Mannheim, and the Sociology of Knowledge', in Calhoun, Craig (ed.) *Robert K. Merton: Sociology of Science and Sociology as Science*, USA: Columbia University Press, pp.164–80.

Siebert, Fred S. (1948) 'Communications and Government', in Schramm, Wilbur (ed.) *Mass Communications* (2nd ed.), USA: University of Illinois Press, pp.219–26.

Siebert, Fred S. (1952) *Freedom of the Press in England, 1476–1776: The Rise and Decline of Government Control*, USA: University of Illinois Press.

Siebert, Fred S. (1956) *The Mass Media in a Free Society*, USA: New York University School of Commerce Accounts and Finance Department of Journalism.

Siebert, Fred S.; Peterson, Theodore; and Schramm, Wilbur (1956) *Four Theories of the Press: The Authoritarian, Libertarian, Social Responsibility, and Soviet Communist Concepts of What the Press Should Be and Do*, USA: University of Illinois Press.

Silberstein-Loeb, Jonathan (2014) *The International Distribution of News: The Associated Press, Press Association, and Reuters, 1848–1947*, UK: Cambridge University Press.

Sills, David L. (1980) 'In Memoriam: Bernard Berelson, 1912–1979', *The Public Opinion Quarterly*, vol. 44, no. 2, pp.274–75. http://www.jstor.org/stable/2748438

Sills, David L. (1987) *Paul Lazarsfeld 1901–1976. A Biographical Memoir. National Academy of Sciences*. http://www.nasonline.org/publications /biographical-memoirs/memoir-pdfs/lazarsfeld-paul-f.pdf

Simonson, Peter (2010) *Refiguring Mass Communication: A History*, USA: University of Illinois Press.

Simonson, Peter (2016) 'Herta Herzog and the Founding Mothers of Mass Communication Research', in Klaus, Elizabeth and Seethaler, Josef (eds) *What Do We Really Know about Herta Herzog?* Germany: Peter Lang, pp.61–84.

Simonson, Peter; Morooka, Junya; Xiong, Bingjuan; and Bedsole, Nathan (2019) 'The Beginnings of Mass Communication: A Transnational History', *Journal of Communication*, vol. 69, no. 5, pp.513–38. https://doi.org/10.1093/joc/jqz027

Simonson, Peter and Park, David W. (2016) *The International History of Communication Study*, USA: Routledge.

Simonson, Peter; Peck, Janice.; Craig, Robert T.; and Jackson, John (2012) (eds) *The Handbook of Communication History*, UK: Taylor & Francis Group.

Simonson, Peter and Weimann, Gabriel (2003) 'Critical Research at Columbia', in Katz, Elihu; Peters, John Durham; Liebes, Tamar; and Orloff, Avril (eds) *Canonic Texts in Media Research*, UK: Polity, pp.12–38.

Simpson, Christopher (1993) 'U.S. Mass Communication Research, Counterinsurgery, and Scientific "Reality"', in Solomon, William S. and McChesney, Robert W. (eds.) *Ruthless Criticism: New Perspectives in U.S. Communication History*, USA: University of Minnesota Press, pp.313–48.

Simpson, Christopher (1994) *Science of Coercion: Communication Research and Psychological Warfare, 1945–1960*, USA: Oxford University Press.

Smith, Bruce L. (1943) 'Scientific and Semi-scientific Literature on War Information and Censorship', *Journalism Quarterly*, vol. 20, no. 1, pp.1–20. https://doi.org/10.1177/107769904302000101

Smith, Bruce L. (1956) 'Trends in Research on International Communication and Public Opinion, 1945–1955', *Public Opinion Quarterly*, vol. 20, no. 1, pp.182–95. https://doi.org/10.1086/266607

Smith, Bruce L. (1969) 'The Mystifying Intellectual History of Harold D. Lasswell', in Rogow, Arnold A. (ed.) *Politics, Personality, and Social Science in the Twentieth Century: Essays in Honor of Harold D. Lasswell*, USA: University of Chicago Press, pp.41–106.

Smith, Bruce L. and Smith, Chitra M. (1956) *International Communication and Political Opinion: A Guide to the Literature*, USA: Princeton University Press.

Smith, Dennis (1988) *The Chicago School: A Liberal Critique of Capitalism*, UK: Macmillan Education.

Sobel Robert (1976) *The Manipulators. America in the Middle Age*, USA: Anchor Press/Doubleday.

'Social Science Research Council records' (no date). https://dimes.rockarch .org/collections/iNo7dbyWw2GwSwKsC3nDj3?category=&limit =40&query=The%20Social%20Science%20Research%20Council%20

Solberg, Winton U. and Tomilson, Robert W. (1997) 'Academic McCarthyism and Keynesian Economics: The Bowen Controversy at the University of Illinois', *History of Political Economy*, vol. 29, no. 1, pp.55–81. https://doi.org/10.1215/00182702-29-1-55

'Solve Red Angle in Crash Death; Papers Traced' (1938) *Chicago Daily Tribune*, 24 October.

Solzhenitsyn, Alexandr (1973) *The Gulag Archipelago*, USA: Harper & Row.

Sparks, Colin and Reading, Anna (1998) *Communism, Capitalism, and the Mass Media*, UK: Sage.

Speier, Hans (1976) '"The Dialectical Imagination: A History of the Frankfurt School and the Institute of Social Research, 1923–1950. By Martin Jay". (Boston, Mass.: Little, Brown & Co., 1973. Pp. 382. $3.95, paper.)', *American Political Science Review*, vol. 70, no. 4, pp.1276–78. https://doi.org/10.2307/1959402

Speier, Hans (1989) *The Truth in Hell and Other Essays on Politics and Culture, 1935–1987*, USA: Oxford University Press.

Sproule, J. Michael (1997) *Propaganda and Democracy: The American Experience of Media and Mass Persuasion*, UK: Cambridge University Press.

Sproule, J. Michael (2008) '"Communication": From Concept to Field to Discipline', in Park, David W. and Pooley, Jefferson (eds) *The History of Media and Communication Research: Contested Memories*, USA: Peter Lang, pp.163–78.

Sreberny-Mohammadi, Annabelle; Nordenstreng, Kaarle; Stevenson, Robert; and Ugboajah, Frank O. (1985) *Foreign News in the Media: International Reporting in 29 Countries*, No 93, France: UNESCO. https://unesdoc.unesco.org/ark:/48223/pf0000065257

Stanton, Frank N. and Lazarsfeld, Paul F. (1949) *Communications Research: 1948–1949*, USA: Harper & Brothers.

Steele, Brent J. (2012) 'Never Trust Anyone Who Remembers Jerry Rubin: The Promise of Generational Conflict', in Steele, Brent J. and Acuff, Jonathan M. (eds) *Theory and Application of the 'Generation' in International Relations and Politics*, USA: Palgrave Macmillan, pp.25–46.

Steele, Brent J. and Acuff, Jonathan M. (2012) *Theory and Application of the 'Generation' in International Relations and Politics*, USA: Palgrave Macmillan.

Stevenson, Robert L. (1992) 'Defining International Communication as a Field', *Journalism Quarterly*, vol. 69, no. 3, pp.543–53. https://doi.org/10.1177/107769909206900302

Stoddard, George W. (1981) *The Pursuit of Education: An Autobiography*, USA: Vantage Press.

Stone, Melville E. (1921) *Fifty Years a Journalist: Line Cuts by Paul Brown*, USA: Doubleday, Page & Company.

Storey, Graham (1951) *Reuters' Century, 1851–1951*, UK: Parrish.

Stowe, Leland (1927) 'Tainted News in Peace', *New Republic*, 10 August.

'Summary: The Macy Conferences' (no date) *American Society for Cybernetics*. http://www.asc-cybernetics.org/foundations/history/MacySummary.htm

'Supreme Court Rules against AP, 5-3. Special Meeting of Board Is Called' (1945) *Editor & Publisher*, vol. 78, no. 26, 23 June, p.5. https://archive.org/details/sim_editor-publisher_1945-06-23_78_26

Tankard, James W. (1988) 'Wilbur Schramm: Definer of a Field', *The Journalism Educator*, vol. 43, no. 3, pp.11–16. https://doi.org/10.1177/107769588804300303

'Text of Federal Court's Decision in the Government's Suit against the Associated Press' (1943) *The New York Times*, 7 October. https://www.nytimes.com/1943/10/07/archives/text-of-federal-courts-decision-in-the-governments-suit-against-the.html

'The Press: Young Man with a Mission' (1946) *Time*, 11 February. https://content.time.com/time/subscriber/article/0,33009,854150-1,00.html

'The Rise and Fall of President George D. Stoddard' (2022) Illinois Library. https://guides.library.illinois.edu/c.php?g=348250&p=2350903

'The United States and the Founding of the United Nations, August 1941–October 1945' (2005) US Department of State Archive. https://2001-2009.state.gov/r/pa/ho/pubs/fs/55407.htm

Thomass, Barbara (2007) 'Comparing Media Systems: The Development of Analytical Tools and Theoretical Concepts Over the Last 50 years'. Paper presented at the IAMCR Conference, France: Paris.

Thompson, John B. (1991) *Ideology and Modern Culture: Critical Social Theory in the Era of Mass Communication*, Polity Press.

Tiede, Hans-Joerg (2022) 'Lazarsfeld's Legacy. Paul Lazarsfeld and the Limited Effect of McCarthyism on the Academic Mind', *International Journal of Communication*, vol. 16, pp.646–54. https://ijoc.org/index.php/ijoc/article/view/18661

Tillich, Paul (1937) 'Mind and Migration', *Social Research*, vol. 4, no. 3, pp.295–305. https://www.jstor.org/stable/40981563

Timonen, Virpi and Conlon, Catherine (2015) 'Beyond Mannheim: Conceptualising How People "Talk" and "Do" Generations in Contemporary Society', *Advances in Life Course Research*, vol. 24, June, pp.1–9.

Toepfl, Florian (2016) 'Beyond the Four Theories: Toward a Discourse Approach to the Comparative Study of Media and Politics', *International Journal of Communication*, vol. 10, pp.1530–47. https://ijoc.org/index.php/ijoc/article/view/4669

Tomlinson, John (1999) *Globalization and Culture*, USA: University of Chicago Press.

Torgerson, Douglas (2019a) 'Lasswell in the Looking Glass: A "Mirror" for Critical Policy Studies', *Critical Policy Studies*, vol. 13, no. 1, pp.122–30. https://doi.org/10.1080/19460171.2018.1512877

Torgerson, Douglas (2019b) 'Lasswell in the Looking Glass: Another Look', *Critical Policy Studies*, vol. 13, no. 2, pp.230–35. https://doi.org/10.1080/1460171.2019.1618355

Tunstall, Jeremy (1977) *The Media Are American: Anglo-American Media in the World*, UK: Constable.

Tunstall, Jeremy (2008) *The Media Were American: U.S. Mass Media in Decline*, USA: Oxford University Press.

Tworek, Heidi (2019) *News from Germany. The Competition to Control World Communications, 1900–1945*, USA: Harvard University Press.

UNESCO (1953) *News Agencies: Their Structure and Operation*, France: UNESCO. https://unesdoc.unesco.org/ark:/48223/pf0000073446

United Nations Charter: Preamble (no date). https://www.un.org/en/about-us/un-charter/preamble

United Nations Economic and Social Council (1948) *United Nations Conference on Freedom of Information*, Switzerland: United Nations. https://igitallibrary.un.org/record/212470

United Nations General Assembly (1948) *The Universal Declaration of Human Rights*, France: United Nations. https://www.un.org/en/about-us/universal-declaration-of-human-rights#:~:text=Article%2019,media%20and%20regardless%20of%20frontiers

Vaca-Baqueiro, Maira T. (2017) *Four Theories of the Press: 60 Years and Counting*, USA: Routledge.

Varão, Rafiza (2021) 'A First Glance at the Work of Dorothy Blumenstock Jones', *Revista Mediterránea de Comunicación/Mediterranean Journal of Communication*, vol. 12, no. 2, pp.17–34. https://www.doi.org/10.14198/MEDCOM.19325

Vartanova, Elena (2009) *Mass Media Theory: Current Issues*, Russia: MediaMir.

Vartanova, Elena L. (2018) 'From the Theories of Press to the Models of Mass Media: Considering the History of the Genesis of Comparative Studies on Media Systems', *Kommunikatsii. Media, Design*, vol. 3, no. 2, pp.5–16. https://cmd-journal.hse.ru/article/view/7917/8675

Verba, Sidney; Pye, Lucian; and Eulau, Hans (2005) *Gabriel A. Almond January 12, 1911–December 25, 2002. Biographical Memoirs*, Vol. 87, USA: National Academies Press. http://www.nasonline.org/publications/biographicalmemoirs/memoir-pdfs/almond-gabriel-a.pdf

Vogel, Ezra F. (2008) 'Lucian Pye, 1921–2008'. *The China Quarterly*, vol. 196, December, pp.912–18. http://www.jstor.org/stable/20192274

Vogt, Kristoffer C. (2016) 'The Post-industrial Society: From Utopia to Ideology', *Work, Employment & Society*, vol. 30, no. 2, pp.366–76. https://www.jstor.org/stable/26655576

Wahl-Jorgensen, Karin (2004) 'How Not to Found a Field: New Evidence on the Origins of Mass Communication Research', *Journal of Communication*, vol. 54, no. 3, pp.547–64. https://doi.org/10.1111/j.1460-2466.2004.tb02644.x

Wake, Naoko (2008) 'On Our Memory of Gay Sullivan: A Hidden Trajectory', *Journal of Homosexuality*, vol. 55, no. 1, pp.150–65. https://www.tandfonline.com/doi/abs/10.1080/00918360802129444

Wallerstein, Immanuel (1986) 'Marxisms as Utopias: Evolving Ideologies', *American Journal of Sociology*, vol. 91, no. 6, pp.1295–308. https://doi.org/10.1086/228422

'Walter Phillips Davison '39' (2013) *Princeton Alumni Weekly*. https://paw.princeton.edu/memorial/walter-phillips-davison-'39

Weidlinger, Tom (2019) *The Restless Hungarian: Modernism, Madness, and The American Dream*, USA: SparksPress.

White, Llewellyn and Leigh, Robert D. (1946) *Peoples Speaking to Peoples: A Report on International Mass Communication from the Commission on Freedom of the Press*, USA: University of Chicago Press.

Whitty, Geoff (2004) 'Mannheim, Karl [Károly] (1893–1947)'. *Oxford Dictionary of National Biography*. https://doi.org/10.1093/ref:odnb/53147

Wiener, Norbert (1948) *Cybernetics : or control and communication in the animal and the machine*. France: Hermann & Co.

'Will Seek Laws to Guard News Property' (1926) *Editor & Publisher*, vol. 59, no. 14, 4 September, p.9. https://archive.org/details/sim_editor-publisher_1926-09-04_59_15

Willens, Doris (1951) 'Reuters Celebrates Its 100th Anniversary, London, July 11. World Press Leaders to Attend with Kent Cooper Honoured', *Editor & Publisher*, vol. 84, no. 24, 9 June, p.9. https://archive.org/details/sim_editor-publisher_1951-06-09_84_24

Williams, Raymond (1977) *Marxism and Literature*, UK: Oxford University Press.

Wirth Marvick, Elizabeth (1979) *Psychopolitical Analysis. Selected Writings of Nathan Leites*, USA: SAGE.

Wirth, Louis (1936) 'Preface', in Mannheim, Karl *Ideology and Utopia. An Introduction to the Sociology of Knowledge*. Translated by Louis Wirth and Edward Shils, UK: Routledge & Kegan Paul, pp.xi–xii.

Woldring, Henk E.S. (1986) *Karl Mannheim. The development of his thought: Philosophy, sociology and social ethics, With a detailed biography*, New York: St Martin's Press.

Wolfenstein, Martha and Leites, Nathan C. (1947) 'An Analysis of Themes and Plots', *The Annals of the American Academy of Political and Social Science*, vol. 254, no. 1, pp.41–48. https://doi.org/10.1177/000271624725400108

Wolfenstein, Martha and Leites, Nathan (1950) *Movies: A Psychological Study*, USA: Free Press.

Wolff, Kurt H. (1971/1993) *From Karl Mannheim*, USA: Transaction.

'World Wire Services Meet at Geneva. Commission Called by League Preparing Agenda for 1927 Press Conference – Howard, Named Executive Committee Head, Wins Plea for Public Sessions and Moves Keynote Resolution' (1926) *Editor & Publisher*, vol. 59, no. 13, 21 August, p.5. https://rchive.org/details/sim_editor-publisher_1926-08-21_59_13

Xu, Bin (2019) 'Intragenerational Variations in Autobiographical Memory: China's "Sent-Down Youth" Generation', *Social Psychology Quarterly*,

vol. 82, no. 2, pp.134–57.
https://doi.org/10.1177/0190272519840641

Ylä-Anttila, Tuukka (2018) 'Populist Knowledge: "Post-truth" Repertoires of Contesting Epistemic Authorities', European Journal of Cultural and Political Sociology, vol. 5, no. 4, pp.356–88.
https://doi.org/10.1080/2325823.2017.1414620

Zittoun, Philippe (2019) 'The Two Lasswells: Implications for Critical Policy Studies', *Critical Policy Studies*, vol. 13, no. 2, pp.211–15.
https://doi.org/10.1080/19460171.2019.1620622

Index

Milton Keynes UK
Ingram Content Group UK Ltd.
UKHW020632300424
441981UK00008B/81